Literature Now

D1567781

# Literature Now
## Key Terms and Methods for Literary History

Edited by Sascha Bru, Ben De Bruyn and Michel Delville

EDINBURGH
University Press

© editorial matter and organisation Sascha Bru, Ben De Bruyn and Michel Delville, 2016
© the chapters their several authors, 2016

Edinburgh University Press Ltd
The Tun—Holyrood Road,
12(2f) Jackson's Entry,
Edinburgh EH8 8PJ

www.euppublishing.com

Typeset in 10/12 Goudy Old Style
by Iolaire Typesetting, Newtonmore, and
Printed and bound in the United States of America

A CIP record for this book is available from the British Library

ISBN 978 1 4744 0990 2 (hardback)
ISBN 978 1 4744 0991 9 (webready PDF)
ISBN 978 0 7486 9925 4 (paperback)
ISBN 978 0 7486 9926 1 (epub)

# Contents

# Notes on Contributors

**David Ayers** teaches Critical Theory at the University of Kent, Canterbury. He is the author of *Wyndham Lewis and Western Man* (Macmillan, 1992), *English Literature of the 1920s* (Edinburgh University Press, 1999), *Modernism: A Short Introduction* (Blackwell, 2004) and *Literary Theory: A Reintroduction* (Blackwell, 2008). His forthcoming book is entitled *Modernism, Internationalism and the Russian Revolution*.

**Thomas O. Beebee** is a practising translator and Distinguished Professor of Comparative Literature and German at the Pennsylvania State University where he has been a faculty member since 1986. His books include *Clarissa on the Continent* (Penn State Press, 1991), *The Ideology Of Genre* (Penn State Press, 1994), *Epistolary Fiction in Europe* (Cambridge University Press, 1999), *Millennial Literatures of the Americas, 1492–2002* (Oxford University Press, 2008), *Nation and Region in Modern European and American Fiction* (Purdue University Press, 2008) and *Transmesis: Inside Translation's Black Box* (Palgrave, 2012).

**Sascha Bru** teaches Literary Theory at Leuven University. He has a wide interest in modern writing and (media) aesthetics but is particularly interested in issues related to European modernism and the classical avant-gardes. He is the author of *Democracy, Law and the Modernist Avant-Gardes: Writing in the State of Exception* (Edinburgh University Press, 2009) and (co-)editor of various books, including *The Oxford Critical and Cultural History of Modernist Magazines, Vol. III: Europe 1890–1940* (Oxford University Press, 2013).

**Ben De Bruyn** is an Associate Professor of Comparative Literature at Maastricht University, the Netherlands. Mainly interested in twentieth and twenty-first century fiction, he has published on three sets of topics, namely theories and histories of reading practices, the representation of space, place and planet, and the literary imagination of commodities and various lifestyle practices. He is the author of *Wolfgang Iser: A Companion* (De Gruyter, 2012).

**Ortwin de Graef** teaches English Literature at Leuven University. He has written extensively on Romanticism, Victorian literature and other nineteenth-century post-Romantic writing. In recent years his work has focused on forms of aesthetic ideology and on imaginaries of the state. He is the author of many books, including *Serenity in Crisis: A Preface to Paul De Man, 1939–1960* (University of Nebraska Press, 1993) and *Titanic Light: Paul De Man's Post-Romanticism, 1960–1969* (University of Nebraska Press, 1995).

**Michel Delville** teaches American and Comparative Literature at the University of Liège. He is co-director of the international research network OLITH and has published widely on modern poetry and its representation of the senses. His books include *The American Prose Poem* (University of Florida Press, 1998), *Sound as Sense: US Poetry &/In Music* (Lang, 2003), *Crossroads Poetics: Text, Image, Music, Film & Beyond* (Litteraria Pragensia, 2013) and *Eating the Avant-Garde* (Routledge, 2008). He is currently writing a new book on cultural representations of hunger.

**Ed Folsom** teaches at the University of Iowa. His research has focused on nine-teenth- and twentieth-century American poetry and culture. He has published widely on Walt Whitman and has also written about a great variety of twentieth-century American poets. In recent years he has become involved with electronic scholarship, co-editing a CD-ROM archive of Whitman's work and co-directing an online Whitman archive. His forthcoming book, with University of California Press, is called *Walt Whitman's* Leaves of Grass: *The Biography of a Book*.

**David Glover** teaches at the University of Southampton. He has published on a variety of topics including popular literature, cultural studies, gender studies, Victorian and Edwardian writing, early modernism, Gothic writing and crime fiction. He is the co-editor, with Scott McCracken, of *The Cambridge Companion to Popular Fiction* (Cambridge University Press, 2012) and his most recent book is entitled *Literature, Immigration, and Diaspora in Fin-de-Siècle England: A Cultural History of the 1905 Aliens Act* (Cambridge University Press, 2012).

**Julian Hanna** teaches English Literature at the University of Lisbon. Previously he worked at Columbia University and the University of Glasgow. His research deals with the manifesto in English art and literature since 1870. Apart from several essays on modern manifestos and modernist authors like D. H. Lawrence, Wyndham Lewis and John Dos Passos, he is the author of *Key Concepts in Modernist Literature* (Palgrave, 2009).

**Scott McCracken** teaches English at Keele University. His main research interests are literature and culture 1880–1920, modernism, gender, critical theory and popular fiction. His authored books include *Masculinities, Modernist Fiction and the Urban Public Sphere* (Manchester University Press, 2007) and *Walter Benjamin's Arcades Project: An Unguided Tour* (Manchester University Press, 2008). With David Glover he also co-edited the *Cambridge Companion to Popular Fiction* (Cambridge University Press, 2012).

**Tyrus Miller** teaches at the University of California Santa Cruz. He is a specialist in modernist literature and has published widely on avant-garde aesthetics, philosophy and social theory and the interrelations of the arts in the twentieth century. He is the author of *Late Modernism: Politics, Fiction and the Arts between the World Wars* (University of California Press, 1999), *Time Images: Alternative Temporalities in Twentieth-Century Theory, Literature and Art* (Cambridge Scholars Publishing, 2009) and *Singular Examples: Artistic Politics and the Neo-Avant-Garde* (Northwestern University Press, 2009).

**Jonathan Monroe** teaches Comparative Literature as well as Writing and Rhetoric at Cornell University. He is the author of articles on modern poetry and poetics and of *A Poverty of Objects: The Prose Poem and the Politics of Genre* (Cornell University Press, 1987) and *Local Knowledges, Local Practices* (Pittsburgh University Press, 2006). His current research includes two book-length projects on contemporary poetry and postcolonial poetries.

**Timothy Morton** teaches English at Rice University. His research interests include ecology, philosophy, literature and the environment, ecotheory, biology, physical sciences, literary theory, food studies, sound and music, materialism, poetics, Romanticism, Buddhism, and literatures in English, 1700–1900. He is the author of ten books, including *Cultures of Taste/Theories of Appetite* (Palgrave, 2004), *Ecology Without Nature* (Harvard University Press, 2007), *The Ecological Thought* (Harvard University Press, 2010) and *Realist Magic: Objects, Ontology, Causality* (Open Humanities Press, 2013).

**Julian Murphet** teaches English and Film Studies at the University of New South Wales. His research concentrates on the interface between literature and other media, on the history of US literature, and on the ethical dimension of cinema. His publications include *Multimedia Modernism: Literature and the Anglo-American Avant-Garde* (Cambridge University Press, 2009), *Narrative and Media*, co-ed. with Helen Fulton, Rosemary Huisman and Anne Dunn (Cambridge University Press, 2005) and *Literature and Visual Technologies*, co-ed. with Lydia Rainford (Palgrave, 2003).

**Thomas G. Pavel** is Gordon J. Laing Distinguished Service Professor in Romance Languages and Literature at the University of Chicago. His work covers a wide range of issues in (French) literature, culture and philosophy and has a strong focus on the genre and history of the novel. His publications include *La Pensée du roman* (Gallimard, 2003, English version forthcoming), *The Spell of Language: Post-Structuralism and Speculation* (University of Chicago Press, 2001) and *Fictional Worlds* (Harvard University Press, 1986).

**Sarah Posman** is a postdoctoral researcher (FWO) at Ghent University. Her research centres on American experimental poetry. She has co-edited *The Aesthetics of Matter: Modernism, the Avant-Garde and Material Exchange* (De Gruyter 2013) and

*Gertrude Stein in Europe: Talking, Listening, Refiguring* (forthcoming). She is working on a monograph that deals with Gertrude Stein and vitalism.

**Jed Rasula** is Helen S. Lanier Distinguished Professor of English at the University of Georgia. Rasula has a wide interest in modern and premodern writing but his research has particularly focused on the roles of tradition, innovation and inspiration in modern literature. His many publications include *Imagining Language* with Steve McCaffery (MIT 1998, paperback edition 2001), *Syncopations: Contemporary American Poetry and the Stress of Innovation* (University of Alabama Press, 2004) and *Modernism and Poetic Inspiration: The Shadow Mouth* (Palgrave, 2009).

**Carrie Rohman** teaches English Literature at Lafayette College. She is the author of *Stalking the Subject: Modernism and the Animal* (Columbia University Press, 2009). Her work has appeared in such journals as *Hypatia, American Literature, Mosaic, Criticism* and *Deleuze Studies*, and in a number of edited volumes. She is currently writing about animality and aesthetics in twentieth-century literature, dance and performance art.

**Sydney J. Shep** teaches Print Culture at the Victoria University of Wellington. A trained letterpress printer and bookbinder, she uses this practical experience in her research in the interdisciplinary domain of book history. Apart from facilitating a large number of collective digital humanities projects, she has published widely on post-national or transnational book history as well as on archival research.

# Introduction[1]

Sascha Bru, Ben De Bruyn, Michel Delville

The study of literature has always been haunted by methodological questions. In the course of the twentieth century, the complex set of intersecting discourses and meta-discourses called literary theory became the privileged site for such reflection. Literary history was often dismissed as an ancillary discipline solely concerned with the biographies of authors, the chronicle of literary schools and movements, and the faithful reconstruction and preservation of texts. Yet in recent decades, literary history has achieved a new if perhaps implicit prominence, becoming one of the primary sites for theoretical reflection in an age which is supposed to have left theory behind. If the theorists of earlier decades often defined themselves in opposition to historical research, in other words, the literary historians of today may very well be the theorists of the present. Looking at recent historical scholarship, we encounter a remarkable level of theoretical sophistication, with fascinating uses of a variety of approaches that includes book history, media studies, postcolonial criticism, cognitive theory, memory studies, affect theory, sensory studies, queer theory, ecocriticism, literary Darwinism, 'distant reading' and digital humanities. More than ever, the history of literature is the place where new methods originate, are tested and find their ultimate application. A good illustration of history's ubiquity is the recent attempt to delineate the condition of literature after postmodernism and to determine what is contemporary about contemporary literature. Even scholars of literature now, apparently, cannot avoid thinking in historical terms. Today, we are all literary historians.

This book, far from aiming to be exhaustive, intends to mark this exciting and seemingly ubiquitous turn to history in literary studies and to guide scholars and students in coming to terms with that turn. The book explores how literary history and its terminological and conceptual structures are affected by these many new theories and contexts, and it seeks to highlight how our very understanding of literature, like literature itself, is now in the process of fundamentally changing.

After deconstruction, New Historicism and the newer approaches of the last two decades, even such core terms as 'history' and 'context' can no longer be taken for granted. In a way, we could say that Fredric Jameson's famous call, expressed in

*The Political Unconscious* (1981), to 'always historicize' literature and the methods and concepts we use in understanding literary texts is itself in the process of being reinterpreted, re-examined in the light of its own historicity. In the 1980s and 1990s, literary critics interpreted his injunction to mean rubbing texts up against their most immediate 'contexts' – understood in ideological, social, or cultural terms. In recent years, new approaches have called this procedure into question: digital humanities question our most fundamental assumptions about books and reading; cognitive approaches highlight the human brain instead of particular historical contexts; advocates of 'surface reading' and amateur uses have taken issue with the suspicious and specialised protocols of politicised interpretations; animal-, emotion- and object-centric methods have displaced the human subject from its formerly privileged position of self-authored rationality; postcolonial and transnational approaches continue to unsettle categories such as national culture and world literature; and ecological approaches increasingly view literary history as a mere blip on the screen of planetary history, or 'deep time'.

A close look at these newer historicisms reveals that they share a number of concerns. At the turn of the twenty-first century, many forms of literary scholarship are characterised by a heightened focus on materiality (via books, objects, the human mind), on reading (its uses, its technologies, its histories), on scalar variability (because of the use of text-mining protocols and the confrontation with the slow processes of human evolution and climate change) and on collaborative models of teaching and research (these big questions require newly ambitious, cross-national, cross-medial and cross-temporal mindsets and research programmes). These shifts demonstrate that history – like literature – is no longer what or where it used to be. They also imply that we should take stock, and reconsider their implications for our shared instruments: the key terms of literary history.

Like our methods, our key terms have undergone important transformations in recent decades – even if their established meanings remain important for students and scholars alike. Raymond Williams's classic *Keywords: A Vocabulary of Culture and Society* (1976) already stressed the need to attend to the historical and contingent nature of keywords instead of considering them as stable and neutral categories divorced from the social and political conditions in which they emerged and developed. Williams's historical semantics attempted to chronicle the complexities and variations of the moral and political meaning of keywords, poised as they are between change and continuity, description and evaluation. Likewise the chapters contained in this volume actively return to the history of these terms and their original contexts so as to acquire a more nuanced understanding of their new uses and connotations, creating new descriptive possibilities for literature now and then.

Key terms are inevitably complex, not just because they combine old and new methods and meanings, but also because they figure in ordinary speech as well and crop up in different disciplinary contexts. Earlier scholars have noted as much – just consider Hans Blumenberg's take on *Begriffsgeschichte*, with its anti-Cartesian insistence on the resistance of figurative speech to conceptualisation,[2] or Mieke Bal's plea for the systematic study of 'travelling concepts' like subject, image, intention and tradition.[3] Blumenberg is right in saying that we cannot reduce everything to univocal concepts and Bal correctly adds that such conceptual ambiguity proves productive rather than confusing as long as this mix of connotations, disciplines and historical contexts is acknowledged and taken into account. But this presupposes a thorough introduction to these terms and their histories, one that is not afraid to take a position in contemporary debates. One of this book's main purposes is thus to offer, not a dictionary with unambiguous and transhistorical definitions, but an open-ended toolbox of vital concepts and transversal methodologies that may guide critical thinking more effectively by exploring the complex meanings and histories of these terms. To that end, every chapter briefly rehearses previous research before going on to highlight the term's present and future relevance, paying special attention to problems of applicability and possibilities for productive interdisciplinarity. Instead of a lexicon, this yields a verbal laboratory.

*Literature Now* provides readers with an overview of some of the most important terms used in the past and the present to understand forms of literature both old and new. Obviously, no book can claim to comprehend such a vast and protean field as literary history – which is why we have made a selection that, though limited, is based on a number of principles. While our agenda is transhistorical in the sense that we accentuate those issues that are vital to grasping the mechanics of literary change in any period, first of all, special attention is given to issues that are indispensable for analysing modern (roughly, post-1800) literatures. Additionally, we have chosen terms that are particularly relevant for contemporary literary studies and that reveal most clearly how literary history now functions in analogous ways to theory. 'Medium' might be more relevant in this sense than 'discourse', 'book' more urgent than 'text', 'popular' a better choice than 'classic'. The terms in this book are also situated at a certain level of abstraction: 'genre' rather than 'lyric' or 'novel', 'subject' rather than 'class', 'race' or 'gender', 'period' rather than 'medieval', 'modern' or 'contemporary'. Even so, we could have included many more terms, obviously, and everyone will find his or her most unfortunate omission. It should be noted, however, that many of these missing terms probably crop up in chapters which appear to focus on a different topic – concepts are often related, after all, and it is difficult and potentially counterproductive to disentangle them fully. At least in some cases, moreover, an argument can be made that these missing terms are less central to our project. We chose not to include separate chapters on 'narrative' and 'memory', for example, because we feel that they have already been discussed extensively in separate volumes that are better able to do justice to their non-literary dimensions. 'Space' and 'place' receive little explicit attention, though they are crucial to the section on channels, because our argument leads us to emphasise a temporal turn that has been much less visible than the spatial turns which have been treated before by several publications. There are no chapters on 'reader' and 'author' either, not because these terms aren't being used any more or because students shouldn't know about intentional fallacies, dead authors and author-functions (or implied readers, interpretive communities and poaching fans), but because we felt that some of the most exciting developments in these fields might be represented more accurately if these topics were routed through terms like 'book' (think of Leah Price's analysis of 'nonreading', the ways in which people use books when they're not reading) or debates on 'invention' (as in Kenneth

Goldsmith's argument on behalf of 'uncreative writing'). But this is not to say that these topics are absent; narrative is discussed in the chapter on time, for example, space in the chapters on book and translation, among others, and the chapters on subjects and objects often mention authors, readers and characters – as do, inevitably if perhaps obliquely, most of the other pages in this book.

To help the reader navigate the book, its overview of key terms is organised into four broader sections – channels, subjects/objects, temporalities and aesthetics – which together offer a composite picture of literature, this remarkable set of channels where diverse subjects and objects mingle in distinct aesthetic forms and overlapping temporalities. These sections and chapters, which we briefly summarise below, offer timely theoretical reflections, canonical examples and lists of recommended reading, creating a resource for all students and scholars interested in literary studies today and in how we think about those other key terms, 'literature' and 'history' 'now', not to celebrate novelty for novelty's sake or to jettison older insights which might still prove relevant but to rethink the role of literature in history and of history in literary studies.

## CHANNELS

Literature is always in the process of changing and today this is no different. Most sociologists of literature, including Pierre Bourdieu and Niklas Luhmann, agree that the material and institutional infrastructure of what people from Western countries call 'modern' literature, emerges, roughly, from 1800 onwards, as the result of a long process of professionalisation. As libraries and book stores, publishing houses, the press and magazines, academies and prizes as well as schools and universities increasingly came to focus on literature in printed form, and subsequently on different genres and types of literature, its production, distribution, consumption and critical reception gained a relative institutional autonomy in society which literature had not enjoyed in premodern times – even though many scholars of premodern literature, too, tend to project a sense of autonomy onto the types of literary writing they study. The process of professionalisation and functional differentiation, whereby agents or actors and institutions within the realm of literature come to take on different roles and specific tasks, formed part of a larger trend in modern society that imposed upon literature as well the model of the free market. Technological innovations around 1900, such as the invention of cheaper types of paper, the rotary press, and the gradual democratisation of education with the resultant rise of literacy rates, not only added to the institutional autonomisation of literature, they also turned literature into a mass phenomenon.

A considerable number of literary historians today focus on the institutional aspects of writing just highlighted. The rise of periodical studies and the many publications focusing on bookshops or publishing houses need but be mentioned here. This materialist approach highlights how literature never happens in a vacuum. No one simply stumbles onto a literary experience; as readers, spectators and listeners, we need to be primed for such experiences, the supporting words adequately framed, enduringly preserved and recorded in languages and material supports of various types. To function properly, in other words, literature does not just require authors, readers and texts, but also books and other media, translations that enable its passage across space and archives that preserve its documents across time, as well as schools and other institutions that train readers and writers alike. Instead of a spontaneous spiritual dialogue among individuals, a closer look at literary history reveals a deeply material and highly mutable network of such overlapping, crisscrossing and occasionally competing channels.

Literary historians turning to the institutional framing of literature now almost as a rule observe how literature is once again going through fundamental changes. Several decades ago, when the Internet was still young, Bourdieu claimed that the modern process of professionalisation had given rise to two distinct fields of literature: one of so-called 'high' literature, marked by restricted production, low financial profit yet substantial cultural and symbolic value or 'capital'; the other a subfield of large-scale cultural production or 'popular' literature, where economic profit by far outweighs anything else. According to Jim Collins,[4] among others, such a distinction no longer seems valid in an age like ours, where the institution of academic criticism appears to have lost its authority to the many platforms of lay and para-academic criticism that can now be found on the Internet, promoting personalised and eclectic reading tastes. As such self-cultivating tastes today go hand in glove with a market penchant for 'high' literary novels turned Hollywood box office successes, and with 'high' literary authors transformed into popular icons, literary culture needs to be situated in what may well be a new field altogether, one that mingles the large- and the small-scale at once. Even the notion of individual authorship and the author's unique oeuvre, according to Mark McGurl,[5] is in the process of being transformed by the vast institutional spread of academic writing programmes that increasingly equip the writers of today with the same skills and tastes.

As literature now is clearly evolving from a materialist point of view, so do the terms and methods of literary history. The first section in the book explores four institutional channels of key importance in the historical study of literature, namely archive, book, medium and translation. Paying attention to these channels and to the institutional dimensions of literature more generally not only raises our awareness of literature's material conditions of production, distribution and reception, but also forces us to consider the role of space and place in more detail. Literary history may be inherently preoccupied with temporality (a notion discussed at length elsewhere in this volume), but that does not mean spatial issues are irrelevant, far from it in fact. Archives are located in particular places, even if they are increasingly available online as well. And books, media and translations all underline, in various ways, that literature is an inherently mobile phenomenon, which refuses to sit still, by circulating in various editions, being remediated in new forms and being translated for other markets and audiences, modes of travel that require specialised agents and protocols – in a word, institutions – which help to steer this traffic in the right (or, indeed, wrong) direction. Reviewing these different institutions further highlights the important role of new digital media. As every contribution in this section indicates, the channels of literature are undergoing significant alterations in the age of digital reproduction.

In his chapter on 'Archive', Ed Folsom examines the role of this seemingly innoc-uous channel in three related steps. He begins by returning to the classic insights of Michel Foucault and Jacques Derrida, who underlined the theoretical complexity of the archival impulse and, as with the related notion of the canon, the political implications of its inclusions and exclusions – issues which are not just relevant for literary scholars, obviously. In contrast to these theoretical and expansive reflections on the archive, Folsom continues, Carolyn Steedman has argued for a more pragmatic approach, which highlights the ordinary, everyday character of archives and the fact that they do not just exercise power over us but that we also have power over them by turning their artefacts into broader narratives. As Derrida already anticipated, furthermore, several dimensions of the archival impulse need to be rethought when the means of communication change – as has happened in the past decades with the advent of databases and the systematic shift from material to virtual archives. The issue of control changes when specialised 'archivists' handling specific items are replaced with a vaguer category of 'archivers' manipulating code in ways that are not always transparent. Digital textuality further implies that archives no longer contain single objects but also easily accessible and reproducible texts. Interestingly, this development simultaneously creates a heightened desire for the actual material items behind these digital texts, and their physical properties. Turning to his own fascinating work for the Walt Whitman Archive, Folsom does not just discuss the challenges involved in archiving these canonical writings but also the ways in which Whitman himself anticipated these challenges in his writings; eerily familiar in this sense, his manuscripts already register a condition of data overload, in which linear, ordered narratives are overwhelmed by messy data, leading to ever-new if inevitably unsuccessful attempts to stem the tide, retake control and archive everything.

Sydney Shep's chapter on 'Book' reminds us that we should provide as much attention to the carrier of a literary text as to its content, a lesson which is central to book history but has acquired further weight from the recent work of scholars working in postcolonial and material culture studies. Whatever a text may want to say, this message (complex enough in itself) always interacts with its particular mate-rial form, with the existing traces of its production, distribution and reception and with the new context in which it currently operates. This lesson remains important, even though the advent of digital culture has fundamentally altered our existing definitions of book, print and literacy, not to mention reading and publishing, transforming the traditional study of books into the analysis of what we might call 'textual platforms'. In this new context, Shep draws attention to three topics: the material book, the material text and digital materiality. As far as the material book is concerned, there have been other physical carriers for text throughout the ages, but the modern codex has nevertheless endured for a long time, which explains why this incarnation of the book has acquired such a quasi-magical function in modern culture, and why it has shaped our protocols of reading, writing and researching so decisively. To investigate the role of the material book, Robert Darnton has intro-duced the idea of the communications circuit, which includes not just authors and readers, but also publishers, printers, book smugglers and paper merchants, paving the way for 'object biographies' that trace the circulation of books by studying their material properties quasi-forensically. Further demonstrating the importance of space and material agency to this discussion, Shep's own work on situated knowledges highlights the complex interplay between people, places and publications. Text may appear to be format-blind, she continues, but we should not overlook its materiality either. What does typography tell us, for instance, as readers and researchers? Should we look *through* type or *at* it? Nor should we forget about the materiality of digital texts, as Matthew Kirschenbaum and Johanna Drucker, among others, have argued. These seemingly disembodied artefacts have a material dimension as well, which is layered and performative, and once again provides vital clues about their production, transmission and reception. Bearing this digital materiality in mind is important, because new 'distant reading' techniques that base their findings on large sets of texts may lead us to overlook the fact that these corpuses only include certain editions of texts and that digital copies of these editions are actually new versions of these texts, which add an additional layer of features (with potential distortions and unexpected connotations). Now more than ever, in other words, the versatile topic of the book requires versatile students and researchers, eager to investigate the material properties of books, texts and new digital artefacts.

Although books and archives are media too, Julian Murphet's contribution on 'Medium' focuses more on so-called new media and the complex relation between literary history and the changing media ecology. In general terms, he observes, a medium occupies the middle position between two other things, which implies that it can both enable and impede communication across this divide. Differently put, media can extend communication across time and space, creating the possibility of transnational and transhistorical dialogue, but they do so through technical interventions that necessarily disrupt the intimacy of face-to-face interactions. In historical terms, Murphet continues, writing functioned as the primary medium for a remarkably long period of time, as it enjoyed a monopoly on the storage and dissemination of cultural knowledge. Because of this primacy, people lost sight of the fact that writing was a medium at all, ignoring its material dimensions, overlooking its social exclusions (via literacy and illiteracy) and shrugging off the representational challenges posed by other media, encouraging overly spiritual conceptions of writing and its highest achievements in literary works. Towards the end of the nineteenth century and throughout the twentieth century, however, the introduction of new mass media like film, gramophone, typewriter, radio, television and computer challenged the hegemony of writing, puncturing these spiritual illusions and creating the conditions for ever-new struggles between the evolving species of the modern media ecology. To make sense of these struggles as literary historians, Murphet argues, we need to bear four topics in mind: remediation, transposition, the senses and the marketplace. Remediation refers to the fact that media continually refashion each other or, to put a finer point on it, that media products always contain other media, an observation which implies that the search for medium specificity, a popular strategy when media were newly confronted with each other's materiality at the beginning of the twentieth century, was doomed from the start. The plots of classic novels were quickly adapted by the movie industry, for instance, and the typical settings, characters and intrigues associated with that industry, conversely, found their way into new novels.

A second strategy is transposition, the process whereby a medium like writing assimilates the formal and technical procedures of other media, for instance the montage techniques of cinema, often developing these strategies into new, potentially more genuine and radical directions. Even more fundamentally, the rise and widespread use of these new mass media (like writing before it) transform and reorganise the human senses by first stressing their autonomy (sight is not hearing, for example) and then overstimulating them (with 3D film, for instance) – a process that has left its traces throughout literary history. Finally, Murphet concludes, these new media also retroactively demonstrated the ways in which art and culture had always been material, commercial affairs and anticipated the current cultural climate, in which authors are often reduced to just one more type of 'content creator', no different from and ultimately less interesting from a commercial standpoint than film producers or video game programmers.

Thomas Beebee discusses yet another aspect of literary practice that highlights space as well as the impact of new digital technologies, namely 'Translation'. For a long time, Beebee begins, this activity has been relegated to the sidelines if not simply ignored altogether. In many cases, after all, literary history focuses on individual authors and national traditions, not on the systematic role of translation within changing literary practices. In such a framework, world literature is simply the sum of distinct, compartmentalised national traditions, not the result of complex, entangled relations between people, texts and things that are constantly being regrouped into different traditions. Even when translation is discussed, moreover, its history is often atomised into a set of sub-topics rather than studied as a coherent problem in its own right. To describe the systematic function of translation in detail, Beebee continues, we should attend to the lessons of book history, polysystems theory and postcolonial studies. Book history is interesting for translation studies because it corrects intellectual history's one-sided focus on disembodied ideas by tracking the concrete methods and infrastructure that enable the circulation of texts. Such an analysis reveals that the focus on individual authors is problematic, as it ignores the fact that the author is often part of a broader team of text producers that in many cases includes translators. Polysystems theory is interesting as well, as it integrates the concrete findings of book history into a more general model of the relations between different cultures and literatures. According to theorists like Itamar Even-Zohar, Gideon Toury and Susan Basnett, translation is a literary subsystem that functions according to relatively autonomous rules. In most cases, polysystems theory argues, translation occupies a peripheral position, but this changes when the overall literary system is 'weak' for whatever reason (the literature in question is young, peripheral, undergoing change). This systematic approach enables researchers to study the role of translations in fascist regimes, for instance, and leaves room for a phenomenon like pseudo-translations; uninteresting according to critics purely interested in an accounting of similarities and differences between source and target texts, their structural position is nevertheless remarkably similar to that of real translations. Supplementing both the contextualised framing of book history and the abstract models of polysystems theory, postcolonial approaches make explicit the political dynamic of translation and cultural transfer, which often involves a struggle over cultural power, and decisively unsettles the idea of a self-enclosed national literature. These three approaches, Beebee concludes, may be fruitfully complemented by work on world literature and digital humanities. World literature sketches the contours of a cosmopolitan cultural ethic, but it also presupposes big data sets, requiring us to consider new tools such as data visualisations of various kinds as well as forms of topic modelling. These appear promising, Beebee claims, but we should be careful that they do not reinforce the existing lack of attention for the important literary channel that is translation.

## SUBJECTS AND OBJECTS

Throughout its history, literature has raised important questions about what it means to be (and to represent) a subject and an object, gradually expanding the range of topics and perspectives that could be included in writing. Literary works obviously deal with human subjects, first of all, registering and complicating differences between and within races, classes and genders, and assigning as well as withdrawing agency and autonomy to these seemingly self-authored subjects who turn out, in many cases, to be *subjected* to outside forces. This section further complicates the notion of the autonomous subject by enriching it with recent work on the body and the senses, on the productive tension between humans and other animals and on the ways in which inanimate objects of various scales and complexities highlight the limitations of our frequently anthropocentric presuppositions. After exploring these diverse modes of subjectivity (and their associated ideologies) and the ways in which they inform and shape authors, characters and readers alike, the section finally considers the political dimension of literary history's understanding of alterity and community. Often unconcerned with the actual process of elections, parliamentary debate and the like, literary scholars systematically draw on a broader notion of politics that requires further scrutiny.

In the first chapter, on 'Subjects', Ortwin de Graef examines gender, class and race as the three pillars of subject-formation and self-fashioning. De Graef traces the makings of the modern subject to Kant and Descartes, and shows how it is inextricably intertwined with a notion of freedom that develops in the seventeenth and eighteenth centuries and that insists on the independence of the subject and his (yes, always his) potential for self-determination. For the great majority of thinkers, the advent of the 'modern' subject in the seventeenth and eighteenth centuries begins with Cartesian philosophy and has been widely acknowledged (and criticised) as the birth of an autonomous agent, in other words a concept which comes close to our modern notion of the self-determined 'self' or 'individual' caught in a movement towards self-knowledge and empowerment theorised in Descartes' *cogito*: a self-present, transparent 'I' which was also to inform Kantian and Husserlian transcendental philosophies.

Unsurprisingly, the polysemy and the transversality of the term 'subject' – which can denote such antipodal conditions as political subjection and subjective autonomy and freedom – has generated a fair amount of controversy among Western philosophers. The paradigm of the logocentric, self-contained 'bourgeois' subject was targeted by Michel Foucault and other representatives of 'anti-humanist' social theory and anthropology who stressed the essentially constructed nature of the subject and exposed its conscious or unconscious submission to state-administered mechanisms of surveillance, discipline and punishment deployed by diverse discursive formations and societal institutions (prison, school, family, ...).

Meanwhile, discussions about the subject in literature became increasingly dominated by theories about the writing and reading subject as a text and/or as a network of subjective representations and performances. The Lacanian and Derridean notions of a decentred subject constituted in and by language, for example, have been widely applied to the study of literature to account for the dialectical exchange between reader and text during the act of reading. Reading the self textually also implies that the textuality of the subject is inseparable from the construction of literary texts as they are unwoven into different, often contradictory meanings (a typical case in point is the history of the successive interpretations of Edgar Allan Poe's 'The Purloined Letter' by Lacan, Derrida, Barbara Johnson, Slavoj Žižek and others).

Another important turn in the definition of the subject within literary history was signalled by the increasing dominance of identity politics in both feminist and postcolonial studies which, in different but related ways, grounded their approach to subjectivity in an examination of the impact of patriarchal and colonial value systems on subject formation and the establishment of strategies to deal with the experience of oppression. Theoreticians of the posthuman such as Katherine Hayles started to reconsider (dis-)embodiment in terms of the increasingly complex relationships between bodies and machines while further problematising the idea of autonomous subjectivity, as also happened in the field of cyberpunk and post-cyberpunk fiction. All these examples show how the flexibility of the term 'subject' has generated multiple sites of invention and intervention in literary history, critical theory and philosophy.

Descartes' cogito argument elevated thinking to the only possible path to (self-)consciousness, relegating the life of the senses to the margins of philosophy. Integrating the senses into a discussion of subject/object relationships necessarily complicates the task of the (post-)modern and contemporary subject confronted with the necessity to achieve subjecthood and overcome subjection. The new technologies of storage and dissemination of literary material (discussed in the opening section of this book) have prompted a reconsideration of how the senses relate to the way in which we produce and consume texts and how they are transformed under the pressure of mechanical and electronic mediation (Julian Murphet's chapter on 'Media' reminds us of Marx's pronouncement that the entire history of technology and, indeed, mankind is geared towards the cultivation and expansion of the human sensorium). What is more, recent scholarship has challenged the visio- and verbo-centric hierarchy of the senses in the history of Western philosophy by re-evaluating the supposedly 'lesser' or 'lower' senses of taste and smell in the context of, for instance, food studies, affect theory and, more generally, the 'cultures of taste'. It is only by drawing attention to historical variations in the representation of the human senses that literary history can account for how we move from a disordered jumble of sense impressions to a sense of self as some 'thing' separable, to some extent, from the flow of things in which readers and characters alike are inevitably enmeshed.

Michel Delville's chapter on 'Senses' briefly investigates the impact of post-Freudian, post-Bakhtinian and post-Deleuzian theories about corporeality on literary history before turning to how each of the five senses has enriched and complicated human perception, using examples ranging from J. K. Huysmans to F. T. Marinetti, Jean-Paul Sartre, Aldous Huxley, Patrick Süskind and Helen Keller. After considering theories of the grotesque body as both the receptor and the producer of social meaning, Delville's essay argues for a polysensory approach to subject/object relationships that challenges the traditional hierarchies between the senses and combats traditional idealistic notions of selfhood while challenging the dominant paradigms of the closed body, bourgeois or otherwise. The chapter ends with a brief consideration of how affect theory applied to literary studies might constitute a valuable avenue of research in subject/object relationships, one which was already delineated by, for example, Huysmans's aesthetic of boredom, Kafka's hunger stories or Sartre's analysis of disgust elicitors in *La nausée*.

De Graef's analysis of the modern subject also reminds us that the modern notion of the (self-present) subject presupposes the use of a symbolic or material technology which alienates humans from their natural condition as animals by throwing them into an existence made of unforeseeable, unrealised futures. The implications of this in the context of literary studies are manifold. Consider, for example, Lisa Zunshine's application of 'Theory of Mind' research to the field of literary studies, which shows what literary studies can learn from developmental and evolutionary psychology, especially as regards readers' desire to exercise their mind-reading capacities. Over the last two centuries in particular, literature has not ceased to produce new models for reading the mind of fictional characters, from the Victorian dramatic monologue to the modernist stream of consciousness and on to William Gibson's explorations of cyberconsciousness. In approaching the condition of the subject in literary texts, it is necessary to attend to the movements of consciousness itself and its centrality in the perception, representation and, some will argue, construction of reality. In examining how literature represents consciousness, as we have seen, we should not neglect the role of the body and the senses, including the lower senses which constantly confront us with our own status as seeing, listening, touching, tasting and smelling animals.

Developing such insights, Carrie Rohman's chapter considers the ways in which human-like animals and animal-like humans unsettle hard-and-fast distinctions between both terms. By considering the animal kingdom as the ground upon which the human seeks to define itself, Rohman's chapter goes beyond an indictment of how non-human animals have been either ignored by literary scholars or considered as ancillary elements to support textual analysis. Even though literary studies initially seemed to lag behind other disciplines (both within and outside the humanities) in addressing the need for an accounting of animality, recent years have seen the emergence of alternative ways of accounting for animals in literary history, such as Colleen Glenney Boggs's biopolitical theory – which applies a general investigation of plural subjectivities to the study of animals and animality in American literature

– or Cary Wolfe's posthuman take on Wallace Stevens's fascination with the ahuman otherness of birds, an approach which urges us to reconceptualise accepted normative perceptual and conceptual modes against the background of the entire sensorium of animal life.

As boundaries between the animal and the human, the organic and the non-organic are often blurred in literature, recent literary historical research further considers non-human and non-sentient entities. Both Rohman's chapter on animals and Timothy Morton's object-oriented theory suggest ways to think the subject outside the frame of the human, with the aim of forcing us to contemplate and interrogate subject/object boundaries as well as the limits of human perspective and our desire for (self-)knowledge. In similar ways, animal- and object-oriented studies return us to essential issues surrounding subject formation such as the preconditions and circumstances necessary for the 'elevation' of an individual to subjectivity (where do we/can we draw the line between subject and object? when does a human body become a subject? are subject and subjectivity cognate or correlative notions?, etc.).

In addressing the consequences of throwing all non-human creatures into a single group, (critical) animal studies scholars question an attitude which consolidates the autonomy and singularity of the human at the same time as it fails to discriminate between the complexities displayed by other creatures. Timothy Morton's 'object'-oriented theory extends this notion to speechless things, arguing that any vision of self as subject in relation to its 'natural' environment necessarily depends on a recognition of the status of 'Nature' as an artificial construct. Sharpening our views of non-sentient entities, which withdraw from humans in ways that can nevertheless be investigated, is of vital importance in redefining literary history by emphasising, for example, the connections between cultural time and 'deep' geological time. By placing literary history in such a vast evolutionary perspective, Morton's post-ecological model embarks on an exploration of 'nature' and its representations that culminates in a reflection on non-sentient objects and their peculiar forms of agency which cannot be reduced to our perception of objects or their use-value. More generally, Morton's brand of 'object-oriented ontology' engages with the issue of whether being is dependent on consciousness of being while simultaneously questioning models of identity based on binary dichotomies between inside and outside, essence and appearance, as evidenced in his assessment of the shifting temporalities and complicated causalities which govern P. B. Shelley's poetry and poetics.

David Ayers's chapter on 'Politics' rounds off this exploration of how literary practices have gradually included the most diverse subjectivities by reflecting on the conception of community, identity and politics behind many literary histories. When literary scholars use the term 'politics', he points out, they often presuppose, first, that the term does not refer to the day-to-day administration of a nation, say, but to the ensemble of human relations within a society, and second, that human consciousness will gradually become more capacious and enlightened as history unfolds, enabling us to extend subjectivity from the rich to the poor, for instance, or the human to the animal, or the subject to the object. These valuable ideas are ultimately indebted to the philosophy of Hegel, Ayers continues, which nevertheless has a bad reputation because it pays insufficient attention to cultural differences and suggests that there is an underlying rationality at work in history which ensures a positive outcome. In thinking about subjects, objects and the communities imagined in literary history, we should therefore try to think the productive components of Hegel's work in a way that avoids its dubious presuppositions. That these presuppositions may lead to destructive effects is shown by the Russian revolution, in which Hegel's optimistic reading of communal experience is undermined by a historical reality in which everyday life was subjected to ever-greater political control. As Adorno and Horkheimer later observed, the outcome of history is often far from rational, discrediting Hegel's argument that historical change is unidirectional and will ultimately lead to beneficial results. The belief in progress and liberty for all receives a further blow, Ayers notes, in recent work on biopolitics, which convincingly demonstrates that not just our minds but our bodies too have become the object of a totalising administration that leaves little room for individual variation and spontaneous change. Subjects and objects are not becoming ever-more free, but ever-more subjected. So much for the grand narratives of historical progress and the unquestioned acceptance of deliberate state intervention for the benefit of all. The horrors described by Adorno, Foucault and Agamben are not imaginary, to be clear, but Ayers nevertheless argues that we should look for alternatives to their pessimistic accounts of modern politics. Jean-Luc Nancy's anti-Hegelian embrace of alterity is one option, though Ayers rightly observes that the celebration of difference in literary studies often silently reinstates a notion of communal identity for local and pragmatic purposes. Jacques Rancière's work sketches another model, in which politics refers to the repeated attempt to redistribute the sensible and to include ever-more subjects and identities in a democratic community to come – a process in which art and literature can play crucial roles. In thinking about subjects and objects, in other words, the challenge for future literary histories is not just to include formerly neglected perspectives, like those of formerly ignored minorities, of the 'lower' senses, of non-human animals and inanimate things, but also to rethink the ways in which these perspectives may meet and form new communities – a precarious process, to be sure, but not a direct descent into unreason either.

## TEMPORALITIES

If time refers to the chronologically measured flow of years, decades and centuries, temporality designates the lived experience of this temporal flow, the ways in which humans feel about this accumulation of existential moments. Did the year pass quickly, do we feel part of this decade, are we even able to experience a century? Temporality also refers to how humans think about the flow of time, with some scholars arguing for narratives of progress (where b decisively improves on an obsolete a) and others highlighting decay (where b stands for a watered-down version of a glorious a). Is history moving towards a certain goal, as teleological accounts maintain, does it proceed according to cycles, with rises towards a certain peak followed by inevitable falls, or is there no clear direction or regular pattern to be discerned at all? How can we avoid talking about such questions, moreover, seeing that poems, plays, novels and films inevitably unfold in the lived time of the recipient, that every literary movement eagerly identifies precursors and future objectives, and that literary writing, since antiquity, is compared to the writings of historians? These are important questions, which acquire even more importance in a book devoted, precisely, to the concepts we use to track the movement of literature across time, this cultural practice that refuses to sit still and traverses spatial and temporal boundaries with remarkable ease – provided the necessary channels are intact. At a moment when history has acquired a new centrality in literary studies especially, we should think carefully about the time and temporality of literature, its history and historicity.

To address these issues, the section on temporalities focuses on five important terms: 'Time', 'Invention', 'Event', 'Generation' and 'Period'. In a first and wide-ranging contribution that demonstrates the extent to which time and literature interpenetrate, Tyrus Miller discusses 'Time' in its relation to interpretation, narrative and historiography. He begins by outlining the fundamental preliminaries provided by figures like Lessing, Kant, Heidegger and Dilthey, which argued for the essential link between time on the one hand and writing, imagination, existence and reading on the other. Turning to interpretation, Miller discusses the contributions of Erich Auerbach, Hayden White and Hans-Georg Gadamer, who described how the hermeneutic process, with its roots in biblical scholarship, creates an open-ended relation between past and present in which certain aspects of the past continue to resonate. As far as narrative is concerned, critics have highlighted that the implied time of the represented event often fails to coincide with the textual time of its literary representation, drawing attention to mismatches in terms of order, duration and frequency. If such descriptions limit themselves at times to an exclusive consideration of form, notions like Mikhail Bakhtin's 'chronotope' reintroduce context and demonstrate that time and space, narrative and history constitutively interpenetrate. Critics like Benjamin, De Man and Deleuze, finally, downplay the importance of chronological periodisation in favour of the existential, nonlinear time of reading – an experience which, at least potentially, hints at alternative forms of historiography. As these reflections demonstrate, the ties between time and literature are deep and manifold.

If Miller's contribution effectively frames the entire section, the next two terms are related. Both 'Invention' and 'Event' deal with the process through which novelty emerges in literary history and further highlight that radical originality is difficult to conceptualise. There are also differences between these two terms, however, as the latter is more closely linked to history and revolution and the former to rhetoric and convention. Jed Rasula's contribution examines the roots of invention in classical rhetoric before considering the ways in which invention-via-imitation was gradually replaced by invention-via-originality, a modern break that opened fascinating new avenues for art even as it created a heavy burden for artists. Starting from scratch is difficult, and the ancient idea of inspiration remarkably tenacious. By exploring the material means of writing in more detail, writers ultimately arrived at the idea of open works, forms of writing which formed genres unto themselves. These original works function as dissident voices in increasingly standardised societies, allegedly, even though these societies simultaneously enshrine the notion of novelty and put pressure on the idea of dissidence via originality. Focusing more strongly on literature's relation to social and political turning points, Scott McCracken's chapter begins by outlining Paul Ricoeur's definition of the event, which indicates that, unlike general laws, singular events only happen once, could have happened differently and, inevitably, fail to match their representations. Developing the latter claim, the chapter goes on to investigate the tension between events and their narrative representation, which enables readers to make sense of the event even as it also contains and distorts its singularity. If this is true of narratives in general, what about the formally challenging narratives of literary works? Do they enable us to experience socially and politically unprecedented 'events' in a more direct, individualised fashion, which opens up rather than closes down the future? To answer that question, the chapter considers Virginia Woolf's *Jacob's Room* and Chinua Achebe's *Things Fall Apart*, two canonical works that are not just linked to certain political events but also demonstrate the ways in which literary narratives refuse to lock down historical events into clear causal sequences. This is a vital dimension of literature, the chapter concludes, even if we should be wary of quasi-mystical claims that end up sacralising events, putting these moments of revolutionary energy and untapped potential effectively beyond rationalisation.

The next two chapters are related as well, and ask what the right scale of literary history is; if we want to capture literary change, should we focus primarily on the relatively short-term unit of the 'Generation' or on broader 'Periods' like the nineteenth century or even longer processes such as modernity or the Anthropocene? Returning to the pioneering work of sociologist Karl Mannheim and to a set of related figures like José Ortega y Gasset, Julian Hanna reflects on attempts to describe historical developments in terms of particular (literary) generations, paying special attention to the moment when Mannheim was working and the analysis of 'generation' first acquired prominence, namely the modernist period. Importantly, generation in the technical sense does not simply refer to the members of a particular age cohort who share certain historical experiences (often wars and other traumatic experiences, unfortunately, like the Great War, the Vietnam War, or 9/11). Only certain generations become true or full 'generations' in the sense that they actively participate in developing a distinct way of seeing the world and in leaving their mark on social (or literary) reality. Being a generation is not just a matter of biology but also of style. The succession of generations is what keeps history fresh, but it inevitably also leads to tension: struggles between major and minor generations, between on the one hand established authorities and on the other emerging voices or belated figures characterised by what Harold Bloom famously called 'the anxiety of influence'. Examining a number of literary movements, Hanna demonstrates that these ideas are still relevant, but he rightly notes that, contra Mannheim's suggestion, it is perhaps wrong to say that, as a rule, the same generation should share the same location. Generations are not only united by certain historical experiences, after all, but also by specific media technologies, which increasingly erode this former importance of location.

If event and generation explore relatively small-scale units of up to about thirty years, Ben De Bruyn's chapter on period examines larger slices of time. He begins by outlining the many critiques levelled at period concepts like middle ages, sixteenth century and romanticism; these concepts are confusingly ambiguous, ignore differences between individual authors and readings, exclude certain minorities from the historical process and turn literary history into a linear sequence of box-like periods. That is why several contemporary critics have argued for an alternative approach, which stresses nonlinear, anachronistic experiences and, inspired by the work of Bruno Latour, replaces periodising boxes with more open-ended networks. Returning to the Wellek-Lovejoy debate, the chapter goes on to show that it is not that easy to let go of period concepts, however, as they help to establish the disciplinary identity and autonomy of literary studies, and may be used, at least in some cases, to make sense of literary history. After discussing the pros and cons of traditional forms of periodisation, the final section examines the recent turn to big or slow history and to drastically longer periods. Inspired by not-so-recent developments such as climate change, these long periods reveal the unexpected relevance of older and less established genres and simultaneously encourage us to revise our notions of history, humanity and causality.

## AESTHETICS

In the final section of this book we survey a series of terms that allow us to gauge how the aesthetic evaluation of texts in literary history takes place: 'Beauty', 'Mimesis', 'Style', 'Popular', and 'Genre'. If the terms in the preceding clusters may arguably be applied to any (modern) literary work, this final cluster considers terms and methods that seek to map and distinguish between different and differently evaluated forms of literature. In a way the chapters and terms collected here can be said to zoom in on the discourse(s) that circulate(s) in the modern literary field as described above. What classes of texts, what genres and specific subsets of works have been said to circulate within literary institutions? What can we learn from texts' characteristics and their reception histories about aesthetic value judgements and how do these judgements change over time? How have recent and earlier methods made sense of the dialectics of high and vernacular cultures, as well as of the aesthetic and the an- or inaesthetic?

In the first chapter on 'Beauty', Sascha Bru notes how in response to the many new historicising approaches developed in recent decades, a considerable number of critics, among them the New Formalists and New Aestheticists, have argued for a return to the surface of the text, away from the depths of historical interpretation. Representatives of these movements often do not oppose literary historical research per se, but they all agree that literary studies of recent decades has paid so much attention to the context – however understood – of writing that the object of study itself, the literary text, has ended up being buried under too many layers of interpretation. Some here argue, therefore, that to salvage that text and its true value, we need to return to the close reading of form. This is the real value of literature, it is said: its beauty, a beauty whose textual form belongs to literature alone and which can, as such, be experienced independently from all external concerns. Bru's chapter then goes on to argue that while aesthetic theories – through the categories they put forward (beauty, the sublime, the interesting or the ugly) – always strive for metahistorical knowledge, they also always bear the stamp of the historical and cultural moment in which they arose. What we think of or experience as beautiful, in literature and elsewhere, is always filtered and shaped by the material culture in which such thoughts or experiences are articulated. Why then, Bru asks, do many critics today, including Elaine Scarry and Dave Hickey, adamantly stress the importance of beauty? The answer, Bru suggests by tracing the role of beauty from romanticism into the present, may well reside in the fact that today the aesthetic category of beauty no longer applies to matters of art and literature alone. Beauty, of course, has always been attached to other domains than art as well – to nature or to people, for example – but with the quasi-ubiquity of design today nearly all commodities produced in our culture are somehow made beautiful or at least aestheticised. While not denying that the experience of literature has an aesthetic dimension, Bru concludes that the literary historians of the future would do well to follow the example of scholars like Sianne Ngai, for whom aesthetic experience is one experience among others, and for whom all-encompassing aesthetic categories such as beauty no longer appear productive. A whole set of other, perhaps 'weaker' aesthetic categories is in circulation today, such as the cute and the zany, which prove far more insightful when we wish to come to grips with the way in which people voice their experience of literature now and with the history in which it figures.

Ever since antiquity the notion of beauty has been related to two aspects: on the one hand, beauty was long regarded as the expression of the divine or transcendent, on the other hand, art and literature, forming the domain of the beautiful par excellence, have always been related to the idea of imitation. While the Enlightenment and secularisation made it increasingly hard to cling to the first aspect, the second one stubbornly persists to this day, as Thomas Pavel shows in his chapter on 'Mimesis'. Covering over two thousand years of reflection on this notion, from Plato to Kendall Walton, Pavel distinguishes two basic facets of mimesis: artistic imitation (representation, re-enactment) and behavioural imitation. If many have followed Aristotle in warning against conflating the quasi-emotions and quasi-beliefs made possible by literature with actual beliefs and emotions, Pavel argues that we can only gain from relating them to one another. Modern readers do not normally mix up fiction and reality, but they do not simply identify with the represented actors in texts, but also with their norms and ideals. In fact, Pavel notes, many texts present us with characters that act highly implausibly, but the values and maxims they stand for nonetheless give them mimetic quality. When we recognise the force of this dimension of mimesis, the term becomes a highly rich one, a search-light that continues to make visible formerly overlooked aspects of canonised as well as forgotten popular forms of writing.

That form and style are essential components of aesthetic value judgements goes without saying. But how do we study style's history? In her chapter on 'Style', Sarah Posman draws the card of literary aesthetics, canvassing the treatment of style in modern literature, from Gustave Flaubert, aestheticism and modernism into the present. Her survey unmasks an ever failing yet always productive search for, on the one hand, a pure style, for literary language as such, and a highly individual or personalised style on the other. Today, Posman suggests, this double search seems to have reached an end with the types of writing Marjorie Perloff isolates in her *Unoriginal Genius* (2012), works that often consist entirely of found, public language 'uncreatively' transcribed, or of languages not or barely mastered by its poets. In our digital age there seems to be too much language available already. To organise this mass of language and literary styles within it, literary historians would do well, according to Posman, to practise a stylistics that seeks to reunite itself with linguistics, as Gilles Philippe and Julien Piat, among others, have recently done in their history of French literary language. Cognitive stylistics, she continues, could prove helpful as well to determine if literary language is experienced differently than other types of language. For we know well what writers and literati have had to say about the specifics of literary language. The scandal, as Rita Felski and several others have argued in recent years, is that we know little if nothing about the act of uncritical reading, about the way in which lay or less trained readers approach that thing we study and incessantly historicise.

What if anything is the difference between so-called 'high' and 'popular' literature? This is the question David Glover tackles in his chapter. Like all other contributions in this section, Glover's first considers the history of the term and its manifestations, before isolating the exemplary case of novelist J. G. Ballard, a writer whose work seems to resist being classified as either 'high' or 'popular'. If Ballard is neither or both, Glover asserts, it is not because he is singular, but because when we test our received ideas about popular fiction against actual practices, we come to see that it is very hard to isolate what moves popular taste. Attempts to do so have thus far fallen prey to the mistake of generic oversimplification. Singling out Franco Moretti's practice of distant reading in *Graphs, Maps, Trees: Abstract Models for a Literary History* (2005), in which the author follows the fate of forty-four prose genres over two centuries, Glover shows how Moretti comes up with strange generic labels, especially for the more popular genres, in this time-span. Mentioning *fin de siècle* genres such as the 'imperial romance' and 'imperial Gothic', Moretti can be shown to project assumptions of 1970s postcolonial cultural criticism onto his corpus. As to why certain popular genres appear, disappear and reappear, and why some last remarkably long and others whither quickly, Moretti leaves readers wondering. What we today still call genre fiction, therefore – romance, detective, science fiction, … – historically proves a rather impalpable phenomenon, unless we recognise, Glover concludes, that the success or failure of a popular literary phenomenon depends on an always situated and ever complex dynamic that involves narrative flexibility as well as fluid reader affiliations.

For the literary historian writing at a time when generic instability has simply become the norm, in short, the taxonomic logic often associated with 'Genre' theory appears to be caught in the throes of its former existence as a stable and prescriptive discourse, unencumbered by considerations of politics, aesthetic quality and canon formation. The retrieval and revaluation of forgotten, minor, neglected or marginal genres and modes (the sensationalist novel, the fairy tale, the prose poem, the list, the detective story, nonfiction prose, the grotesque, the picturesque, …), the proliferation of hybrid, cross-cultural and cross-discursive forms and the preoccupation with inter-genericity and pastiche all testify to a network of complications, contradictions and paradoxes which have long exceeded the hierarchies and paradigms of traditional genre theories, whether of the prescriptive or descriptive variety.

The implications of this in the field of literary history are manifold: they range from the influence of reader-response approaches suggesting that readers ascribe genres to texts, to Jonathan Monroe's suggestion that a given text's generic orientation lies less in its formal features than in the different use-values it has been assigned over time. The question thus becomes not only whether writers are actually practising a genre 'from within' or 'from without' but also whether a genre should be approached as a theoretical and/or a pragmatic category. The pragmatic approach to genre, which has become dominant in recent genre theory, does not seek to dismiss genre as a category of classification – rather, it subordinates the desire for formal categorisation to a process of negative differentiation which insists that genre is only identifiable as both a system of classification and a discursive, interpretive and historically determined framework.

While some have challenged the tendency to read genre as a genderless or classless set of formal conventions, others have questioned attempts to draw a firm line between established (sub-)genres and modes such as prose and poetry (highlighting the advent of free verse and the prose poem, for instance) or to classify fiction and nonfiction as two separate entities: what to think, for example, of the many species of literary or 'creative' nonfiction as they manifest themselves in such diverse genres and sub-genres of nonfiction as memoirs, biographies, letters, speeches or essays? The history of modern and contemporary poetics thus has provided important new perspectives on issues related to the historicity of genre. As attested by Jonathan Monroe's take on the prose poem's literary and historical significance and his subsequent analysis of the 'second Baudelairean revolution', generic labels necessarily postulate socially and politically conditioned assumptions which lay the institutional and ideological foundations of any reader's 'generic competence'.

Monroe's plea that the history of genres should be considered not merely as a literary feature but rather as an epistemological category once again points to a fundamental methodological principle underlying the making of this book, namely that literary texts are embedded into their historical background as much as into their transhistorical critical and theoretical contexts. Literary history can thus be understood as the history of the imaginary resolutions of real contradictions not only within literature but also in the relationship between literature and society at large. Literary history is not just about biographies, chronicles or editions, it is also an ever-changing laboratory – for literature and for its students. Closing *Literature Now* with considerations of the mutability of genre and markers of genericity further underlines that this book does not aim to circumscribe or regulate the language of literary scholars but to illustrate that literary history continues to matter, and may even matter now more than ever, in its attempt to think through the rich interplay between old and new, book and medium, subject and object, event and epoch, canonical and popular forms, new historicisms and new aestheticisms.

# PART I

# Channels

## CHAPTER I

# Archive

## Ed Folsom

Several decades ago – indeed, even in the early 1990s – 'archive' was a fairly benign term in literary criticism, something taken for granted but seldom questioned. But that all changed with the publication in 1995 of Jacques Derrida's highly influential and aptly named *Archive Fever*, which initiated a feverish interest in the concept of the archive, an interest that has spawned countless books and essays in the past twenty years that have complicated, expanded, and interrogated the nature and meaning of the archive. Before Derrida, *archive* indicated a fairly static and staid physical place, a place to which historians and literary scholars and others travelled to access the dusty records of the past – the 'official' past of governmental records, for example, or the literary past of an author's manuscripts and letters. After Derrida, however, *archive* quickly came to indicate something more theoretical and abstract, something much more vast having to do with the very nature of the 'past', with 'origins' and 'memory', with how (or if) the past ever can be accessed, with who controls the collecting and organising of the materials out of which we gather and create the stories of the past, with what materials are repressed or otherwise kept out of the archives. When we read Derrida on the archive, questions proliferate: how much of what we could think of as archives in fact exists outside of official archives and resides instead in garbage heaps or even in lost voices still travelling somewhere on sound waves? How much exists in the endless writings stored on tapes or records or disks or other outmoded technologies that are difficult if not impossible to access? How much of an archive is stored in the deep and inaccessible parts of any single human brain?

*Archive*, then, seems to have broken into two competing definitional directions: one points towards a theoretical vastness of a largely inaccessible past, a place that preserves the impressions of the past (pressed onto paper) that are themselves the very record of the loss of the present moment in which a living body made the impression, a place that beckons (and perhaps repels) us with the shimmering but always fading prospect of discovering the mystery of our origins, a giant realm of all the fragments of the human past; the other points towards the relative sparsity of the human record, the relative handful of fragments and bits and pieces of the past contained in and on physical objects stored in enclosures named 'archives'. The debate has bled from history and literary criticism and philosophy into politics, sociology, anthropology, geography, medicine, the hard sciences. Any area of knowledge has its own archive and its own ongoing struggle with what is and isn't (should be and shouldn't be) contained there; anything with a past has an archive (and an accompanying set of questions about that archive). 'There is no political power without control of the archive, if not memory', wrote Derrida; 'Effective democratization can always be measured by this essential criterion: the participation in and the access to the archive, its constitution, and its interpretation.'[1] What had seemed for so long the rather innocuous place of storing fragments of the past quickly came to seem portentous, mysterious, incomprehensible, wondrous, enmeshed in the very definition of power (to control the archive is to control the past and, in some sense, to control what can be made of it).

Derrida jump-started the ongoing debate over *archive*, but its theoretical complexity had already been indicated by Michel Foucault in the 1960s, particularly in his *Archaeology of Knowledge* in 1969. For Foucault, the archive (in the sense of vast state-controlled repositories of records of its citizens and its past) was largely a development of the eighteenth and nineteenth centuries, when vast museums and libraries and records offices were built to contain the traces of the past that authorities of various sorts determined were worth preserving. In 1967, Foucault put it this way:

> The idea of accumulating everything, of establishing a sort of general archive,
> the will to enclose in one place all times, all epochs, all forms, all tastes,
> the idea of constituting a place of all times that is itself outside of time and
> inaccessible to its ravages, the project of organizing in this way a sort of
> perpetual and indefinite accumulation of time in an immobile place, this
> whole idea belongs to our modernity.[2]

And for Foucault, these vast new archives themselves were a source of power, the ultimate arbiters of what could be said: 'the archive is the first law of what can be said; the system that governs the appearance of statements as unique events'.[3] The archive, writ large, is for Foucault a kind of generator and controller of social meaning: what is in the archive sets the rules for what statements we can make – our archives in fact circumscribe and control what we can make of ourselves.

The historian Carolyn Steedman has offered some fascinating rebuttals to the Foucauldian/Derridean theoretical inflation of the archive and its power – what she calls 'the archive as a way of seeing, or a way of knowing; the archive as a symbol or form of power'[4] – and she instead points to 'the *ordinariness*, the unremarkable nature of archive, and the everyday disappointments that historians know they will find there'.[5] While Derrida defined archive fever as 'the desire to recover moments of inception: to find and possess all sorts of beginnings',[6] Steedman argues that real archives are 'far less portentous, difficult and meaningful than Derrida's archive would seem to promise'.[7] In fact, she says, 'in actual Archives, though the bundles may be mountainous, there isn't in fact, very much there'.[8] What the researcher in real archives finds is not abundance but lack, 'selected and consciously chosen documentation from the past' mixed with 'mad fragmentations that no one intended to preserve and that just ended up there'[9] – this is the 'dust' that Steedman points to as the proper metaphor of the archive, 'a prosaic place where the written and fragmentary traces of the past are put in boxes and folders, bound up, stored, catalogued',[10] 'just sit[ting] there until [they are] read, and used, and narrativised'.[11] This narrativisation is the key for Steedman – the power not that the archive has over us but that *we have* over it, the power to weave a story *out of* the dust, to narrate a story that the fragments support (though others might fabricate a different narrative out of the same chaotic heap of fragments). 'The Archive', then, 'is also a place of dreams', she says, the originary site of interpretation.[12]

Before Foucault began to tease out the ways that archives were in fact discourse and were the tools of power, then, archives (as Steedman reminds us) had for a couple of centuries seemed a neutral repository of the artefacts that traced and stored a culture's memory. After Foucault, however, no archive could seem isolated or insulated from power, and the etymological roots of the word (as Derrida reminds us) – back through the Greek *arkhon*, with the suggestions of 'rule' and 'command' and 'beginning', and the Greek *arkheia* ('public records'), *arkheion* ('town hall'), and *arkhe* ('government') – are a mixture of 'origin' and 'governing', of origins and control. There is, we're all aware now after Foucault and Derrida, a tension at the very heart of the concept of 'archive', between a desire to accumulate records of the past, of origins, and a desire to control what records of the past get preserved and what get excluded (or destroyed). It is that constructive/destructive tension that Derrida taps into in *Archive Fever*, in which thanatos and eros are equally at play in any desire to return to origins, in any desire to destroy archives, in any desire to pass on the past through the present to the future.

We sometimes think of archives as preserving the story of our past, but archives, of course, are incapable of telling stories; as Steedman argues, those who enter archives are the ones who emerge with stories, who construct narratives, and those narratives themselves become the archives of archival research. Who controls the stories that archives seem to tell is every bit as important as who controls what the archive collects (for the telling of stories embedded in archives is also, increasingly, the telling of stories of what the archive has silenced). This endless interaction between the person who enters the archives and the archives themselves – an interaction between the figure who wants to gather fragments in order to piece together a narrative and the stubborn 'dust' of the fragments themselves, which in and of themselves have no story to tell – has become even more complex in the emerging era of vast database archives.

## ONLINE ARCHIVES: DATABASE, ARCHIVER, TEXT

The two competing claims for the archive, then – one theoretical and expansive, the other pragmatic and reductive – have in the past twenty years been challenged by a whole new notion of the archive, one brought about by the development of the

Internet and widely accessible databases that have once again essentially altered our ideas of what the *archive* can mean. When Derrida argued that the archive is a place inscribed and circumscribed by power, and when he and Foucault pointed out that we can say what we say about the past not only because certain authorities have determined what remnants of the past are preserved but also because of what technologies of recording the past were available to archivists in any particular historical period, they had early glimmers of how archival remnants themselves are continually subject to shifting modes of technology. *Archive Fever* is a kind of theoretical interrogation of the Freudian archives of psychoanalysis, and at one point Derrida wonders what those archives would be like if the electronic revolution had occurred earlier and Freud's correspondence had been conducted via, say, email instead of recorded in letters:

> One can dream or speculate about the geo-techno-logical shocks which would have made the landscape of the psychoanalytic archive unrecognizable for the past century if [...] Freud, his contemporaries, collaborators and immediate disciples, instead of writing thousands of letters by hand, had had access to MCI or AT&T telephonic credit cards, portable tape recorders, computers, printers, faxes, televisions, teleconferences, and above all E-mail.[13]

Derrida recognises that 'the technical structure of the *archiving* archive [...] determines the structure of the *archivable* content even in its very coming into existence and in its relationship to the future'.[14] The past, in other words, would have been a different past if the means of communicating had been different, for an entirely different archive would have formed, and quite different artefacts would have been preserved: 'This means that, *in the past*, psychoanalysis would not have been what it was [...] if E-mail, for example, had existed.'[15] Derrida is writing in the mid-1990s, of course, at the very beginnings of the Internet revolution, when online archives were just beginning to form and just beginning to learn how to identify and define themselves. But even then, he could feel 'the unlimited upheaval under way in archival technology'.[16]

Quite quickly, the expansive and theoretical sense of the archive began to hold sway as the digital revolution heated up. Now an entire generation of scholars has grown up with the perception that archives are accessible via computers. Steedman's actual 'dust' has increasingly given way to what Paula Amad has named 'digital dust', the vaster and cleaner but ultimately every bit as messy (if not messier) electronic collections that we call up on our screens.[17] Archives have come to be, then, not only the physical place of dusty documents but more and more the virtual places of multiple media – film archives, television archives, recording archives, musical archives, performance archives. Entire new areas of investigation in fields like media archaeology and new media archives have formed, and media theorists like Wolfgang Ernst have begun questioning just what Archive has (or can) come to mean in the digital age, questioning whether the archive has become simply 'metaphorical in multi-media space'.[18] Building on Foucault, Ernst says that his particular brand of 'media archeology is an archaeology of the technical conditions of the sayable and thinkable in culture, an excavation of how techniques direct human or nonhuman utterances'.[19] The term 'media archive', then, can mean archives of media (like a film archive) or archives of the technical aspects of a particular medium (an archive of computer codes, an archive of discarded and abandoned media tools). Digital humanist Alan Liu sees the term *archive* quickly coming to be a metaphor for 'what we are not yet able to grasp about the nature of digital collections'.[20] There is now a growing sense of *archive* as all of those endless digital pieces and fragments of information that hover in virtual space waiting to be searched and funnelled, bit by bit, to the small rectangle of the computer screen.

Information theorist Lev Manovich identifies what he sees as a 'battle' between two broad and metaphorical approaches to storing and accessing information. He writes:

> As a cultural form, the database represents the world as a list of items, and it refuses to order this list. In contrast, a narrative creates a cause-and-effect trajectory of seemingly unordered items (events). Therefore, database and narrative are natural enemies. Competing for the same territory of human culture, each claims an exclusive right to make meaning out of the world.[21]

*Database*, I've argued elsewhere, is the emerging genre of the twenty-first century, a technological voracity for accumulating information, for building archives.[22] In the ancient but recently accelerating ongoing tension between archive-database and narrative, digital archives are playing a key role in facilitating the development of a new kind of archival narrative – a narrative that is much more conscious of, attached to, and interactive with the mass of fragments out of which it comes and into which it dissolves. (We can imagine database biographies, for example, that would tell the narrative of someone's life but would link sentence by sentence to scans of the documents that support each claim, would link to biographies of the figures who seem peripheral in the telling of this person's life but who actually have equally rich lives of their own, would link to other biographies of the same person so that we could see how any particular incident has been narrated and contextualised by previous biographers.)

So recent examinations of the concept of the archive have emphasised and expanded on Derrida's notion that an archive is defined by what it excludes and silences, by what lies *outside* it, because without an outside, there is no 'inside', no 'house' to preserve the past that has been determined (by whoever makes such determinations) to deserve preservation. David Greetham, for example, has examined the 'poetics of archival exclusion', with its challenge to exceed archive's boundaries and seek in the refuse and garbage of both what is left in the archive and what is left outside it a new disorderly view of what *archive* could be.[23] Paul Voss and Marta Werner have defined 'a poetics of the archive' – 'an imaginative site – a conceptual space whose boundaries are forever changing'.[24] Steedman has written of 'real archive fever', fed by 'the great, brown, slow-moving strandless river of Everything', in contradistinction to 'its tiny flotsam that has ended up in the record office you are working in [...y]our craft is to conjure a social system from a nutmeg grater'.[25] In recent years, then, the archive debate has questioned just who the *archon* of the archive really is – the controlling power that makes it and controls it or the user who narrates its fragments and omissions – and who, in the age of the digital archive/database, the *archon* is coming to be (the builders of databases? archiving programs? sophisticated searchers of databases?).

This is an inauspicious time, then, to be trying to pin down the resonance of the term *archive* in criticism and theory, because it is a term undergoing remarkable transformation in this historical moment, moving (as Derrida's play on 'the *archiving* archive' suggests) from the largely nominative to the predicative, from cool to hot, from isolated physical place to which researchers travel, to a virtual place travelling at unimaginable speed to researchers' computer screens. *Archiving* is the rage now, the fever, even as the *archive* itself as the familiar/mysterious physical repository seems to be evaporating into a luminous, ever-receding (or ever-expanding) invisibility, buried deep in the digital encoding of massive databases. Archiv*ists* have given way to archiv*ers*: those who were previously defined as 'occupied with' the archive as much as 'doing' archival work – the *archivists* whose '-ist' carried the associations of 'expert in', 'believing in' – have now yielded to those who *do* archiving, who buy and use archiving software, who build archives by building databases that contain encoded entries, as our access to the remnants of the past slips from the material to the electronic – a virtual past that paradoxically seems more populated and accessible the further it slips from materials into code. Today archiving is often done by or with software (the now familiar refrain that 'we are all digital humanists now'[26] – because we all navigate digital realms in carrying out our scholarly work – could be updated to 'we are all archivers now', since we all routinely build archives of electronic materials downloaded from online databases), and the once careful and intimate relationship that the archivist had to the material of the collection he or she oversaw and catalogued and described has given way to a more distanced relationship as archiving tools process and store and categorise vast amounts of electronic documents that exceed anyone's capacity to know, precisely, what even is in the archive (and, given the infinite linking on the Web, where any particular archive ends and others begin). *Archivers* work at increasing speeds to store increasing amounts of data, as *archivists* come to occupy a nostalgic niche among the materials that are being turned (or have long since been turned) electronic via scans and transcriptions. Google's Ngram, itself a kind of mysterious archive of vast amounts of material that can only vaguely be identified ('millions of books'), reveals that 'archivist' as a term began to decline in usage in the early 2000s, just as 'archiver' began to flourish.

*Archive* at this moment, then, vacillates between its fading denotation (as a physical repository of the documents that constitute the remnants of a particular past, a place that one seeking that past had to travel *to*) and its fast emerging connotation (as a massively expanding virtual repository of what we might call archive's *text*, the material gathered from multiple archival sources and re-mediated to electronic scans and transcriptions, that via the Internet travels *to* the seeker). Endless thousands of archives are now being created with archiving software out of materials that were never material, born-digital archives that maintain and retain remnant data from particular pasts. Historians Francis X. Blouin, Jr., and William Rosenberg, in their influential *Processing the Past: Contesting Authority in History and the Archives*,[27] explore the implications of this shift. In an interview, Blouin is asked a question about whether, once an archive becomes 'one big mass of textual data subject to keyword searching', it really matters 'how it is organized in terms of the structure and data'. He answers: 'I think the jury's out on that. I think the question is – how confident can we be that in going through a collection of thousands or millions of digital documents, technology will get us to the specific document we want and set that document in a meaningful context?' And Rosenberg adds:

> What historians don't realize is that if you take a category that has not been regarded as an essential category in the way the documentation has been assembled and preserved, you're going to get so many hits in response to your inquiry that the material's going to be unmanageable. If you put in 'gender' or you put in 'women' or you put in a name, without the mediations that archivists have traditionally provided to historians to help sort through this material, mediations that are reflected in finding aids and how those materials are organized, it will be extremely difficult for historians to use these vast vaults of material in any efficient way. Millions and millions of electronic documents cannot be usefully mediated by archivists as traditional paper materials have been, structuring and ordering them in ways that suggested their possible historical value.[28]

This shift – from entering a physical archive overseen by an archivist to accessing an electronic one overseen by an archiver – is a key part of the evolution of what we are coming to mean by the terms *archive* and *archival research*.

A simple statement like 'Her work is primarily archival research' connotatively and denotatively means something very different today than it did a couple of decades ago. Some of the most accomplished archival work in scholarship today is being executed entirely at a computer screen in a scholar's own room, as new sets of archival skills emerge. As Blouin and Rosenberg indicate, knowing how to construct effective keyword searches and how to outfox unreliable OCR transcriptions of scanned materials become requisite skills that can make all the difference between a successful and unsuccessful search. But keyword searches are only a rudimentary form of searching that is quickly giving way to much more sophisticated computer searching methods that allow for literary research to be accomplished across previously unimaginable numbers of texts, as programs search for particular syntactical patterns or plot elements or uses of chapter epigraphs. 'Distant reading' is the term that literary scholar Franco Moretti uses to describe the work he is doing at the Stanford Literary Lab, a kind of database reading that allows scholars to analyse literature across a vast range of texts, analysing patterns across thousands of novels instead of doing a close reading of a few novels.[29] Stephanie Blalock, for example, has recently discovered over three hundred previously unknown reprintings of Walt Whitman's early fiction in nineteenth-century American and international newspapers, using various databases; her work has completely re-made our conception of the impact of Whitman's fiction and is leading to a reassessment of his renown as a fiction writer in the years before he published *Leaves of Grass*.[30] Her work, as is the case with most database research, would have been unthinkable in material archives.

*Text* has become another hot critical term during the same decades that *archive* has heated up. *Text* was Roland Barthes' focus, and the pleasures of the text for him had to do with separating the text from the biographical and psychobiographical tyranny of the author, to sever the text from its author in order to liberate its interpretive possibilities.[31] But in terms of archives, the key importance of *text* is that, until the digital era, 'text' (as opposed to the printed books or manuscripts that contained that text in material form) was a kind of theoretical concept: a sequence of words that could travel from one instantiation to another or could float in some space outside of materiality. In theory, text could be separated from the books or manuscripts that held it just as it could be separated from the author who wrote it. To give a text an author, for Barthes, was to impose limits on that text; to give a text a material book is to set another kind of limit (the physical book, after all, as we've all learned in an era of material studies, can very much affect our interpretation of the text). The death of the author thus anticipates the death of the book: as text was liberated from its material origins, it could exist, so we imagined, in some nonmaterial realm. And, with digital textuality, that is exactly what happened: suddenly Walt Whitman's 'Song of Myself' could be transferred from device to device with the click of a button, its distinctive sequence of words infinitely and instantly malleable, transferable, virtual, presentable in endless typefaces and colours and sizes, its distinctive diction displayable in word clouds. Text began now, and not just in theory, to seem wildly disembodied, liberated from materials, no longer contained in a book or on paper that had been dedicated only to *a single* text but rather occupying temporarily the same screen that displayed … well, anything.

So, soon, archives themselves came to seem equally disembodied. I have experienced this as I've edited (with Kenneth M. Price) the online *Walt Whitman Archive*[32] over the past fifteen years. Whitman's manuscripts, in high-quality scans and in encoded transcriptions, now travel through the same electronic circuits and ride the same radio waves that all texts do. And so electronic archives have come to be material archives' *text*, having the same relation to the physical archive that the electronic text of *Leaves of Grass* has to the physical books. Any device can now display documents that only a few years ago (or a few weeks ago, or earlier today) could only be accessed physically and materially in housed collections. Just as text embodied in manuscript on a leaf of paper is material and singular, so is an archive, then, the repository of material and singular things, objects in the most physical sense. But *text* is language loosed from print and ink and paper, released from its material container, fluid and interchangeable across various formats or typefaces or platforms, appearing as endlessly accessible *virtual* objects. We physically visit an archive to examine physical objects, but we digitally visit databases to examine virtual objects. Digital archives, then, are *texted* archives, where materiality is released into endless repetitions and re-mediations.

We have only gradually come to realise the implications of the fact that we are not actually accessing the manuscripts or books that we retrieve on our screens: we are instead accessing the *texts* of those materials. Those scans are as ephemeral as disembodied text: the images and the texts all travel in an immaterial realm, and all are composed on our computer screens of the same very finite array of pixels. And thus we have begun to experience a largely unexpected consequence of things going digital – a deep and palpable yearning for the materials which were the bases for the electronic scans and transcriptions that now travel the endless circuits of the virtual world. Just as Derrida and others have so effectively described archival desire – the burning need to touch origins, precisely because so little of the material impress of origins exists after whatever event or period is being archived – the re-mediation of archives into databases has created a new kind of archive fever: a renewed and often intense desire for the physical object itself whose text (again, it *is* text, no matter how fine the scan) we have accessed electronically. This is part of the reason that 'book studies' has developed as a field in precise concurrence with the movement of text from books and manuscripts to electronic code. As *archive* has shifted in usage from the physical to the immaterial collection, a new nostalgia for the physical archive has emerged: we desire the *origin* of those virtual images and transcriptions, their material embodiments, because those embodiments offer us a sense of *palpable* closeness to the past. In addition, as programs to alter photographic scans get more sophisticated, there is a growing concern with authenticity: as with any text that has been lifted from its material embodiment, errors and alterations (accidental or intentional) can be made. An intensified new sense of the 'aura' around the original object, as Walter Benjamin described, is emerging from the computer world's endless capacity to reproduce physical archives' texts in an infinite array of electronic reproductions.[33] (When we began the *Whitman Archive*, we thought that the easy availability of scans of Whitman's manuscripts would significantly lessen the demand to handle the fragile material papers in physical archives, but, in fact, the availability of the scans has increased the desire to touch the original documents, because the massive access to the scans has introduced thousands of more researchers to the material mysteries of those documents – each scan indicating pinholes and paper types and erasures and tears that demand to be examined physically, because the digital text of the manuscript can only suggest important physical properties that pure textual transcriptions would have rendered entirely invisible.)

## WHITMAN'S DATABASE

When Price and I began the online *Whitman Archive*, we realised that we were choosing to archive a writer who was himself fascinated with what in his time was a relatively new concept of the archive – the then-fresh attempts to gather massive amounts of information about the past into monitored places that could be searched. Whitman built a poetry out of this intriguing new idea of archiving; he in fact created a poetics of the archive, and I want to conclude by suggesting how we can discover in Whitman's writings an emerging sense of what the archive is coming to mean in our own time. Whitman was experiencing an environment exploding with data, as free lending libraries and massive museums were opening in the growing urban environment around him and were offering access to previously unimagined realms of knowledge. Even New York City itself – with its huge influx of immigrants, creating an environment rich in multiple languages, clashing customs, divergent dress – offered

Whitman on his daily walks encounters with wild juxtapositions of luxury and poverty, with a kind of chaotic fullness of experience that seemed to defy all previous forms of literature to contain it. One of Whitman's archived manuscripts records his intense struggle with how a poet could possibly deal with the new onslaught of data that he was experiencing in the mid-nineteenth-century world that Foucault identified as the time of the emergence of the archival impulse; it is one of the earliest documents to capture this modern anxiety of trying to tell a narrative that was continually threatened by the suddenly overwhelming amount of data available:

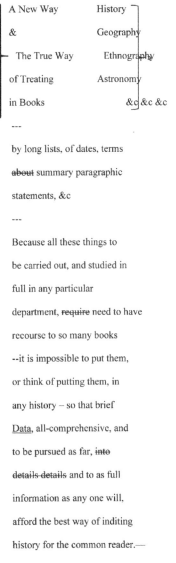

Figure 1.1    *Walt Whitman, Ms. Leaf recto (A New Way & The True Way …)*[34]

Here Whitman begins to theorise what would become his distinctive cataloguing technique: a poetic form that could deal with 'Data, all-comprehensive', could pursue a subject in its 'details' and 'full information' in order to write a history in a 'New Way' and, for the first time, a 'True Way'. Near the surface of these notes we can feel the tension Manovich identifies between narrative and database, and we can trace it in Whitman's own compositional techniques, something that we can see for the first time now that we have gathered all the poetry manuscripts for the online archive, allowing us to discern how Whitman conceived of the things he would come to call poems. For him, the world was a kind of pre-electronic database, and his notebooks and notes are full of lists of particulars – sights and sounds and names and activities – that he dutifully enters into the record. In some manuscripts, we find drafts of poems that sound much like the published poems but contain the same lines arranged in a very different order.

One manuscript of 'Song of Myself', for example, has lines that are dispersed throughout the printed poem: two lines appear on page 20 of the 1855 edition, another on page 24, one in the preface, one on page 42, one on page 16, one on page 34; another line appears in a different poem in *Leaves*, and yet another is part of his pre-1855 manuscript poem 'Pictures'. Whitman formed entire lines as they would eventually appear in print, but then he treated each line like a separate data entry, a unit available to him for endless re-ordering, as if his lines of poetry were portable and interchangeable, could be shuffled and almost randomly scattered to create different but remarkably similar poems. Just as Whitman shuffled the order of his poems up to the last minute before publication – and he would continue shuffling and conflating and combining and separating them for the rest of his career as he moved from one edition of *Leaves* to the next – so also he seems to have shuffled the very *lines* of his poems, in sometimes quite dramatic ways, right up to their being set in type. He was an early practitioner, in other words, of what we might call the database genre. Anyone who has read one of Whitman's cascading catalogues knows this: those catalogues always indicate an endless database, suggest a process that could continue for a lifetime, hint at the massiveness of the database that comprises our sights and hearings and touches, each of which could be entered as a separate line of the poem, forming an archive of his experience. Throughout 'Song of Myself', we can always feel the unruly rhythms of this never-ending sensory catalogue, incorporating the details of the world as they flow nonstop into the poet's (and our) open and receptive senses. Many of his early critics complained of the way his poetry sounded like an unsorted list; what those critics record is a deep unease with the emerging experience of the world as messy data rather than ordered narrative.

The battle between database and narrative that Manovich posits, then, explains something about the way Whitman's poems work, as they keep shifting from moments of narration to moments of what we might call data ingestion. In 'Song of Myself', we encounter pages of data entries that pause while a narrative frame takes over again, never containing and taming the unruly catalogues and always carrying us to the next exercise in incorporating detail. We might recall Emerson's formulation of Whitman's work as a 'mixture of the Bhagvat Gita and the *New York Herald*'. The universal and the particular create the tension that Whitman had to negotiate: the only way to represent the universal was through the suggestion of database, all the particulars with none left out. This is one reason that Whitman loved photography: it captured these particulars and was the first technology that suggested Database, as it recorded all the messy detail that presented itself to the camera's lens, which had its own kind of beauty for Whitman – a democratic beauty of fullness, not exclusion, requiring an eye for completeness, not a discriminating eye that pre-selected what we saw. As we have been archiving Whitman online, then, we have been discovering just how thoroughly Whitman himself was inventing something we might call an archiving poetry.

When we think of Whitman's writing as a kind of proto-Database approach, we find that he is making a disarming claim: his text cannot, and will not, hide the conditions of its composing. He built a democratic literary style out of the fragmentation of indiscriminate experience, and the result is what he calls the 'convulsiveness' of his text, as he described his Civil War book, *Memoranda During the War*:

> As I have look'd over the proof-sheets of the preceding Memoranda, I have once or twice fear'd that my little tract would prove, at best, but a batch of convulsively written reminiscences. Well, be it so. They are but items, parts of the actual distraction, heat, smoke and excitement of those times – of the qualities that then and there took shape. The War itself with the temper of society preceding it, can indeed be best described by that very word, Convulsiveness.[35]

I want to draw attention here to Whitman's uses of two words – 'tract' and 'distraction' – that in an essential way define his archiving impulses. The word 'tract' that Whitman employs here, oddly, to describe his Civil War memoranda, derives from the Middle Latin *tractio*: the act of drawing or pulling. On leaving an archive, we draw or pull something from it. We can extract, abstract, detract, distract. An archive, the larger it is, can seem *intractable* – hard to shape or work with; unmanageable; stubborn. We are *attracted* to it (that's archive fever), in part by its intractability. In the archive, we can easily become distracted, and, in despair, extract or abstract, which always involves detracting. We usually think of a *tract*, when we apply the term to writing, as a pamphlet, a brief treatise, for general distribution, on a religious or political topic; but Whitman uses it in its more general sense to suggest an expanse or area, a region; a stretch, a system of related parts or organs (like the digestive tract); a period of time (from the Latin *tractus* – again, a drawing out, as in *protracted*). Archives are in fact tracts, and we are seeing this more clearly the vaster they come to seem in their database forms: they are regions, expanses, systems of related parts. And every part of an archive is a 'tract', in the sense of a drawing out: a particular piece of correspondence or jotted note draws out an expression of events or emotions or opinions, just as a religious or political tract does; a photograph draws out or extracts an image in time ('portrait' means, etymologically, a drawing out, an extracting from). And, for Whitman, writing embodies *distraction*, getting off the track, losing the narrative in the convulsive chaos of the database.

The *Whitman Archive*, then, brings its reader *closer* to creative distractions already implicit in Whitman's writing. Those distractions are always potentially lost in book publication, where conventions of completion seek to clean up the writer's archive of work, necessarily abstracting it from its origins. If Whitman is proto-hypertextual in his writing, it is because he favours such textual distractions and resists the conventions and abstractions of completion. The *Whitman Archive* – the digital archive of Whitman's work – thus more faithfully reiterates a complicated and 'convulsive' textual archive of the poet's writings and experiences.

N. Katherine Hayles has argued that narrative is 'an essential technology for humans',[36] and, of course, it is, but database is the equally essential counter-technology, the innate desire to pile up and absorb experiences and ideas and material things that don't sort themselves immediately into narrative – items we can access later as pieces of a narrative if and when they fit the story, history, or syntax of meaning we are at any point seeking to construct. Keeping a commonplace book edges towards Database; keeping a journal towards Narrative. Whitman's poetry and much of his prose edges towards Database, leaving many readers who seek narrative frustrated. Whitman's work, then, very much invested in the poetics of the archive, becomes one of the early suggestions of how the archival impulse – translated into database – would begin to essentially alter our ways of thinking and constructing representations of the world.

## FURTHER READING

Blouin, Jr., Francis X. and William G. Rosenberg. *Processing the Past: Contesting Authority in History and the Archives*. New York: Oxford University Press, 2011.

Derrida, Jacques. *Archive Fever: A Freudian Impression*, trans. Eric Prenowitz. Chicago: University of Chicago Press, 1996.

Ernst, Wolfgang. 'Does the Archive Become Metaphorical in Multi-Media Space?'. In *New Media, Old Media: A History and Theory Reader*, ed. Wendy Hui Kyong Chun and Thomas Keenan. New York: Routledge, 2005, pp. 105–23.

Ernst, Wolfgang. *Digital Memory and the Archive*. Minneapolis: University of Minnesota Press, 2013.

Foucault, Michel. *The Archaeology of Knowledge*, trans. A. M. Sheridan Smith. New York: Pantheon, 1972.

Manoff, Marlene. 'Theories of the Archive from Across the Disciplines'. *portal: Libraries and the Academy* 4: 1 (2004), 9–25.

Merewether, Charles, ed. *The Archive*. Cambridge, MA: MIT Press, 2006.

Robertson, Craig, ed. *Media History and the Archive*. London: Routledge, 2011.

Steedman, Carolyn. *Dust*. Manchester: Manchester University Press, 2001.

Voss, Paul J. and Marta L. Werner, eds. *Studies in the Literary Imagination* 32, no. 1 (Spring 1999). Special Issue: 'Toward a Poetics of the Archive'.

## CHAPTER 2

# Book

Sydney J. Shep

To date, the codex as a vessel, carrier or vehicle for content has been the predominant focus of Western literary critical engagement. Unless a scholar has been trained in the principles and practices of descriptive bibliography, content remains king; furthermore, promiscuous remediation or repurposing into other media forms often results in an erasure of local contexts. However, new directions in book history, the impact of postcolonial and material culture studies, the rise of digital humanities, and the development of new communication technologies have all led to a re-examination and contextualisation of older media forms and their social and cultural impacts. In his 1983 address to the Bibliographic Society, D. F. McKenzie noted that 'what we much too readily call "the book" is a friskier and therefore more elusive animal than the words "physical object" will allow'.[1] Today, the term 'book' is opening out to embrace a wide range of memory archives including print ephemera, landscapes, visual and aural media, inscriptional spaces, maps, buildings and performative sites. Similarly, the definition of 'print' has expanded to include all inscriptional forms from the performativity of oral cultures to the scribal gestures of cave painters, monastic scribes and graffiti artists, to the world of electronic coding and pixelated display. New digital imperatives are pressuring us to pause and reflect on the historical continuum and interpenetration of communication forms, how those forms represent and structure our knowledge practices, and how new modes of 'literacy' are shaping contemporary societies and cultures. For literary historians, understanding these developments in the context of the material book, material texts, and digital materiality is key to new scholarly practices and insights.

## THE MATERIAL BOOK

'Book' is often used as a convenient form of shorthand to encompass many different material manifestations of text. Writing systems certainly predated the codex form of the book and can be found on many surfaces and in a wide array of formats: clay tablets, stone stele, metal plates and stamps, ceramic and bone shards, bamboo sticks, palm leaves, silk. The term 'book' – like its synonym 'codex' from the Latin *caudex* – is derived from its earliest material substrate: wood. Whether created from blocks carved from a beech tree or leaves split from the trunk of a tree, in the history of communication technologies, the codex solved a number of design challenges. It enabled information to become portable, shifting messages off the cave wall and into a more human-scale form that could move easily across space and through time. Unlike the wax tablet which recorded ephemeral information that could be melted, erased and rewritten, the codex was made of more durable materials: parchment, vellum, or paper bound into wooden and leather-covered boards, studded with bosses and jewels, often held firmly closed by clasps and locks, and chained to reading desks in monastic libraries. The codex also resolved several issues of pointing and referencing by shifting from the continuous, sequential scroll or *volumen* that required unrolling to be read to the affordances of the segmented stack of bound leaves written or printed on both sides; the double-page spread became the unit of engagement until a page was turned, thus revealing another opening. The addition of paratextual features such as half and full title pages, page numbers and folio marks, running heads and footers, tables of contents and indices, and footnotes or endnotes furnished a repertoire of navigational strategies to aid the reader and guide the researcher.

The book has endured as the pre-eminent reading machine for some seventeen centuries. Its resonance is such that the term has entered the contemporary lexicon as a powerful cultural metaphor to describe everything from legal processes ('bring to book') to new technological interfaces (PowerBook). Furthermore, the iconic value and talismanic role of books permeate religion, politics and popular culture: swearing on a book, whether a Bible, a Torah, or a Qur'an, is a marker of truth and reaffirms one's commitment to sacred objects, spaces and rituals; dropping, tearing, burning or otherwise destroying a book exposes the fragility of the medium and disrupts the customary link between the body of the book and the human condition. Until recently, the book has also shaped our systems and methods of information organisation and are enshrined in our library cataloguing conventions as well as the architecture of buildings, bookshelves, reading furniture, and lighting. Structured information access and retrieval, whether of printed or digital texts, is still called 'bibliography'. Historically, bibliography or the study of books was divided into five subspecies: enumerative (or the listing of books); annotated (critically evaluating the content of books in structured, thematic lists); descriptive (understanding the physical features of books); analytical (reconstructing the ideal or perfect production process); historical (documenting the historical contexts of books and their transmission). Today, the study of books as cultural objects focuses on their production, distribution, reception and survival, but the field also increasingly embraces media history and media archaeology, software studies, critical code studies and platform studies. Its multidisciplinarity makes it as frisky as its objects of inquiry, but also enriches the field and makes it receptive to the future landscape of knowledge production in all its many forms. To put it another way, as Matthew Kirschenbaum and Sarah Werner point out, 'if book history is the study of how platforms shape and deliver texts, then today's platforms of pixels and plastic are as much a part of those studies as paper and papyrus'.[2]

Extending the forensic tradition of Anglo-American descriptive and analytic bibliography, Jerome McGann called for an investigation of those often invisible linguistic and bibliographic codes that reveal how meaning is made through the intersections of historically specific physical and aesthetic features such as paper, type, layout, printing, illustration and binding with the historically situated reader. In this early concept of the 'social text',[3] McGann echoed McKenzie's notion of the 'sociology of texts' which evolved in response to his own attempts to wrestle with what he called the 'broken phial', or the fundamental indeterminacy of texts. In McKenzie's 1969 article entitled 'Printers of the Mind',[4] he chastised early twentieth-century bibliographers' blindness to the historical evidence of printing house archives that recorded actual textual production practices rather than those imagined or reconstructed based solely on a close, self-contained examination of the artefact. By trying to define both book and text, McKenzie proposed that texts register the 'indeterminate relation between indexical sign and symbolic meaning' and concluded that 'what constitutes a text is not the presence of linguistic elements but the act of construction'.[5] Once bibliography added this kind of Herbert Spencer-inspired sociology to the study of material forensics, Anglo-American textual scholarship moved from an insistence upon composing the 'ideal' text to 'the qualities of mediation as a social process'.[6] McGann subsequently talked about the 'socialisation of texts'[7] to position acts of reading and interpretation within a network of influences extending beyond the author to embrace the publisher, bookseller and librarian as well as the various social, cultural, political and economic conjunctures informing manufacture and reception.

## BOOK HISTORY FOR LITERARY HISTORIANS

In the field of book history, these networks have been graphically represented as a life-cycle or communication circuit,[8] firstly by historian Robert Darnton who foregrounded historical actors and agents responsible for the flow of intellectual property during the eighteenth-century Enlightenment and French revolution, then by bibliographers Thomas R. Adams and Nicolas Barker who emphasised the various processes from creation to consumption and preservation of what they termed 'bibliographic records'. Repositioning Darnton in light of Pierre Bourdieu's theories of cultural production, Peter D. McDonald has argued that the task of the literary historian is to reconstruct the 'predicament' of the book, thus enabling the writing of a new kind of object biography to complement literary critical interpretations. Since textual records like books travel through time and space, such a biography or 'it-narrative'[9] also documents various acts of transmission that leave their paratextual traces on the material form, whether as marginalia and marks of ownership, or as a 'cultural tracer' whose residue or 'literary replication'[10] reappears as café gossip and popular songs, lectures and theatrical performances, spurious reviews and learned rebuttals. Provenance research and an understanding of the history of reading all contribute to a new understanding of books as witnesses to cultural formation in action.

Literary historians working on contemporary books and publishing can turn to reconceptualisations of the communication circuit that more accurately reflect the current structure of the industry and its players. The traditional publishing value chain is a linear rendering of the core book production functions, from concept to consumer, with each agent in the process adding significant value. South African scholar Elizabeth Le Roux has incorporated models from political sociology in order to understand the role of university presses under the apartheid regime.[11] By introducing a six-point spectrum from resistance to complicity, she has inserted Bourdieu's fields of cultural production directly into the value chain and conceptualised the politicisation of the publishing industry as a continuum, thereby nuancing our understanding of the complexities of the industry. With paradigms shifting in the digital domain and contemporary publishers increasingly bypassing retailers in favour of targeting readers directly, the value chain is currently being reconfigured as a value network, a model more suited to the world of open access and e-publishing. Claire Squires and Padmini Ray Murray, for example, have developed the digital publishing communications circuit that accounts for the disruptions and disintermediations of the unbound book in the late twentieth century.[12] They have also mapped the rise of self-publishing and foregrounded the changing role of readers who now embrace the multivariate functions of consumer, borrower, reviewer, content generator, crowd-funder and subscriber, amongst others. The ability of publishers to control the flow of information is giving way to acts of autonomous production: the Espresso Book Machine that prints and binds a 300-page book of your choice in three minutes; reading devices that enable you to customise the font and layout of your favourite novel, turning readers into writers, designers and remix artists.

Two new models framing the study of books and print culture have recently been developed. In her exposé of nineteenth-century international book publishing, marketing and bookselling in the Anglo world, book historian Alison Rukavina has built on the philosophical work of Gilles Deleuze and Félix Guattari. She reconceives the ubiquity and resilience of the book trades as the product of fluid and flexible social networks with rhizomatic nodes and links that are at once malleable, responsive and ever-changing. Unlike much literary criticism that privileges the imperial centres of a London or an Edinburgh, Rukavina demonstrates that agents in the colonial periphery exerted pressure on the metropole to modify if not change publishing practices and channels for distribution.[13]

The rise of transnationalism, translocality and theories of *histoire croisée* or entangled histories along with network analysis and material culture studies inform Sydney J. Shep's model of situated knowledges that links the material record (bibliography) to people (prosopography) and places (placeography).[14] Various nodes of intersection between adjacent elements suggest rich veins of contextual research: the life geographies of individual actors; the object biographies of individual books and texts; the politics of the archival spaces in which material records are deposited, described and discovered. The three primary elements converge in a zone of investigation termed the event horizon. Adapted from general relativity and quantum mechanics, this multi-dimensional contact zone situates the research process as one of constant, energetic interplay between people, places and things. For literary as well as book historians, this model reflects the spatial turn in history as well as the agency of material forms, and represents a vibrant, holistic approach to the production, dissemination, consumption and preservation of texts. It also addresses the legacy of national book histories that shaped early scholarship in the field, and opens the way for a more globalised understanding that reflects the inherent mobility and mutability of the book.

## THE MATERIAL TEXT

If 'book' refers to an increasing array of physical and digital artefacts, 'text' has likewise morphed from a synonym for the noun 'book' to a verb describing the act of instant messaging: 'txting'. The computer-enabled linking of one text to another through hypertext is now embedded into everyday practice. The ubiquitous repurposing of text into different editions, formats and genres implies that text can be and often is format blind. Reading the content in an ebook version of a modern edition of a nineteenth-century novel on a Kindle is presumed to be the same as reading a digitised copy of the original accessed in snippet view through a digital library, or a signed first edition in a prestigious archive surrounded by the author's personal papers and the publisher's reader's reports. The four-fold hierarchical system FRBR [Functional Requirements for Bibliographic Records] is a conceptual entity-relationship model of the bibliographical universe based on the user's perspective that informs much library cataloguing practice today.[15] It uncouples text from carrier, and assumes that the 'work' is the intellectual creation, which is then 'expressed' through a chosen medium, then 'manifested' in a particular physical form, and finally rendered concrete in a single, specific 'item'. Text as an act of construction rather than a stand-alone linguistic entity is not yet addressed in the web data interchange model of RDF (Resource Description Framework) nor in the open-linked data cataloguing system of RDA (Resource Description and Access).[16] The harmonised CIDOC-CRM (Conceptual Reference Model) and FRBRoo (FRBR object-oriented) community does not appear to have addressed the indeterminacy of texts, even though many digital humanities projects have seen the benefits of aligning their ontologies within such a conceptual framework that enables semantic interoperability across document structures.[17] Finally, the continuum model developed by the Australian archives and records management community is more concerned with capturing recordkeeping practices than understanding the malleability of those records.[18] And yet, these architects of information, like bibliographers and book historians, should be those best equipped to take on the challenge of new media forms and the resultant new definitions of text. As N. Katherine Hayles reiterates, such forms of 'embodied textuality' expose 'materiality as an emergent property' and emphasise the irreducible and dynamic intercrossings of social, cultural and technological processes that bring objects, including texts, into being.[19]

Can text exist apart from its vehicle of instantiation? What is gained or what is lost in ignoring or erasing the carriers of information? As book and media historians Roger Chartier and Guglielmo Cavallo note, 'authors do not write books; they write texts that become material objects'. Moreover, material instantiation is also an act of engagement: 'reading is not a solely abstract intellectual operation; it involves the body, is inscribed within a space, and implies a relationship to oneself or to others'.[20] Even across media forms, as Paul Eggert suggests, 'whether the textual carrier be the physical page, a computational capacity, or the sound waves that transmit orally declaimed verse, there is always a material condition for the existence of text'.[21] Scholars of media archaeology and proponents of new materialism such as Wolfgang Ernst and Jussi Parikka also highlight the centrality of the material in their study of the hardware and software of culture.

## READING MATERIAL FORMS

Given this awareness of materiality as central to the social shaping of knowledge, literary historians are now obliged to include in their intellectual toolkits an analysis of the visual, tactile, sonic, olfactory, even gustatory evidence of a book's legacy of production, distribution, reception and survival. An investigation of the physical features of material objects provides important evidence for how texts are consumed as well as insights into the cultural embeddedness of specific acts of consumption and spatiotemporal arenas of transmission. Take, for instance, the physical substrate. It is easy to assess the production values, market placement and cost of a book based simply on a forensic analysis of the selection of paper and its contemporary condition. A sixteenth-century folio lectern Bible printed on handmade linen rag paper and bound in heavy, blind stamped leather boards is of a size, quality and permanence quite different from a late nineteenth-century sextodecimo Bible printed on thin, yellowing, woodpulp paper with a machine quarter-bound soft cover and a cheap, vegetable-tanned spine piece now suffering from irreversible red rot. And what if we consider the text itself? In the 1930s, the English typographer and book designer Beatrice Warde used the metaphor of a crystal goblet to describe the role of type in the pursuit of legibility and intelligibility. Just as we can savour the colour, bouquet and taste of a fine wine better in a crystal vessel than one made of wood, metal or stone, so too should well-crafted fonts be the invisible gateway to the appreciation and understanding of texts. If Warde advocated looking *through* type to text, by contrast, Leipzig-born Jan Tschichold, exponent of the Bauhaus modernist movement and later chief designer for Penguin Books, emphasised looking *at* types. Expressive typography foregrounded the instrumental role of type in making meaning, and the typographer was responsible for selecting and rendering fonts fit for purpose, designing a work to specifically expose a particular interpretation. The concrete poets of the early twentieth century took typography into their own hands to design exuberant performative page displays that fused the visual with the verbal. Contemporary book artists and graphic novelists continue to foreground if not explode the assumed boundaries of form and function as they explore the poetics and politics of cultural engagement.

Like paper and type, each physical feature of a book shapes the reading experience and constitutes a kind of material thinking that impacts the processing of information. Hayles terms this co-evolution of the human and the technological often revealed in the interpenetration of analogue-digital hybrid forms 'technogenesis'.[22] And, whenever the reader makes material interventions whether they be underlining, annotations, the addition of marginalia, turning down the corner of a page, or spilling a cup of coffee over the artefact – as well as their digital equivalents – these traces reflect a history of use that becomes, in turn, forensic evidence for the next generation of readers and researchers.

The shift from the manuscript book to the printed book as the dominant Western communication form has often been construed as a shift from the creation of unique craft objects to industrialised, editioned works that serve up repeatable, stable texts and thus fix meaning. However, manuscripts were often products of proto-industrialised scribal workshops that existed long after the invention of printing, particularly in non-European and Asian contexts where romanised scripts, type-casting in metal, and handsetting types could not accommodate or supplant local calligraphic traditions. By contrast, each item in a printed edition could be different, if only because of it being produced at a different moment in time. Replacing worn types, discovering and correcting missed compositional errors, uneven inking, misregistration or misaligned backing-up, misfeeding causing paper creases, and other vagaries of human and machinic endeavour meant change was a constant in the print shop. Using signature and folio marks, finished pages were collated, then temporarily bound before being sold to a buyer whose first testament to ownership was the commissioning of a unique, bespoke binding. As Owen Gingerich has eloquently demonstrated, every single extant copy of the early editions of Copernicus' printed treatise *De revolutionibus* carries with it a set of unique cultural traces such as provenance marks by individuals and institutions or annotations and other forms of marginalia that, once analysed, document knowledge in transit of an, albeit contested, heliocentric universe.

## DIGITAL MATERIALITY

If materiality is a constituent property of physical books, it is also now recognised as central to the study of digital objects and an important focus for literary historians who deal with ebooks, born digital texts, and various transmedia, hybrid genres. Kirschenbaum distinguishes between two types of digital materiality: forensic and formal.[23] Forensic materiality consists of the physical evidence of production, distribution, reception and preservation which can be detected through the identification and analysis of various traces, residues, marks and inscriptions visible to human sight or accessible through instrumentation. On the one hand, chips, touch screens, terminals, cables, keyboards and mice are all capable of recording human and machine interactions. On the other hand, nanotechnology's magnetic force microscopy can reveal the bit pattern cut into a computer disk and expose recoverable areas of corruption whether through chemical degradation of the physical substrate or multiple overwritings. Digital forensics is analogous to the activities of book historians and bibliographers working in the domain of manuscript and print artefacts who analyse, amongst other material manifestations, the physical characteristics of paper composition and manufacture, handwriting styles and inks, printmaking, illustration, and bookbinding techniques. Both embrace a kind of 'crime scene investigation' process using extant material evidence and inductive reasoning to argue for patterns of textual transmission, licit or illicit interventions, or artefactual legacies of the publishing process.

Formal materiality engages with the architecture of digital media and their symbolic forms, whether the structure of individual software programs, embedded data standards and metadata encoding, or operating system configurations. Like forensic materiality, there is always a physical manifestation, but whereas the forensic is focused on attributes, formal materiality concentrates on the digital environment which Kirschenbaum defines as 'an abstract projection supported and sustained by its capacity to propagate the illusion (or call it a working model) of *immaterial* behavior: identification without ambiguity, transmission without loss, repetition without originality'.[24] Despite this illusion, existing (if hidden) content can be formally exposed using built-in functionality such as 'reveal source', and 'show header' or by deploying encryption keys; the existence of errors discloses the Achilles heel of an imperfect system in motion.

Johanna Drucker has recently proposed that two forms of materiality be added to the lexicon of forensic and formal: distributed and performative. Each of them usefully complements and extends Kirschenbaum's distinction and draws on a wide range of philosophies and approaches. Distributed materiality, based on the work of informatics and encryption specialist Jean-François Blanchette, relates to 'the complex of interdependencies on which any digital artifact depends for its basic existence'; that is, the 'co-dependent, layered contingencies on which the functions of drive, storage, software, hardware, systems, and networks depend'.[25] Performative materiality, drawn from studies in cognition, perception, reader-response, textual hermeneutics and interface design, further emphasises the functional dimension of materiality, its existence defined by and interdependent upon use, interactivity, process; that is, 'what something *is* has to be understood in terms of what it *does*, how it works within machinic, systemic, and cultural domains'.[26] Like Chartier and Cavallo, many scholars, Drucker included, argue that materiality only exists in acts of perception, in performance, in use, and in practice.

## NEW SCHOLARLY PRACTICES FOR LITERARY HISTORIANS

The emergence of data mining, distant reading, data visualisation, advanced image processing and geographic information systems-inflected spatial analysis as scholarly practices undertaken by digital humanists calls into question historic definitions of books and texts as well as traditional interpretive practices such as close reading. Computationally enabled textual analysis requires relatively large data sets that are mined for patterns in language, structure, emotion and meaning. Students in the Stanford Literature Lab, for example, 'read' 1,200 novels in a single course; the *Mapping the Republic of Letters* project uses spatial analysis to visualise the networks and relationships recorded in over 63,000 documents between over 8,000 seventeenth- and eighteenth-century Enlightenment correspondents. The justification for these new, machine-based methods is that past assumptions based on close reading can now be tested with a far larger corpus of material, more often than not available in digitised formats and in quantities no scholar could manually process during a single lifetime. In addition, new questions are being asked for which new tools and methods are required, as well as new modes of teaching and scholarly communication. As Drucker points out, however, humanists need to be aware of the context-bound nature of data and recognise that it is not a 'given' or a set of objective facts. Instead, she has adopted the Latin term *capta*, meaning 'taken', to emphasise the situated, contingent and often incomplete nature of humanities data.[27] Similarly, we need to recognise that the mass digitisation efforts of Google Books, the Internet Archive, the Hathi Trust and others, are based on the selection of the most convenient or easily accessible instance of one title that then stands in for the complete edition(s) of the work. This form of surrogacy belies the fact that a digitised object is a new artefact exhibiting the characteristics of its own production processes – if we know how to read the electronic evidence – as it elides the distinguishing features of its parent. Smarter ways of presenting electronic information with higher resolution capture and presentation, image-processing software that can expose watermarks occluded by text, and infrared spectrography that exposes palimpsests or post-production interventions are now being deployed to aid the researcher in analysing the materiality of digital culture.

Literary historians are increasingly using tools and techniques from the digital humanities to explore, for example, sentiment in the eighteenth-century novel, or the textual transmission of a single title across time and space. They are participating in large-scale crowdsourcing collaborations, whether transcribing the works of Bentham, deciphering the palaeography of early manuscripts, or releasing machine-readable text from the digitised images in the Early English Books Online project. In this space of what might be termed 'digital incunabula', Stephen Ramsay has coined the phrase 'algorithmic criticism' to describe the shift in humanities research from 'criticism to creation, from writing to coding, from book to tool'.[28] In *Reading Machines*, Ramsay observes,

> 'Algorithmic criticism' sounds for all the world like a set of methods
> for exploiting the sudden abundance of digital material related to the
> humanities. If not a method, then perhaps a *methodology* for coping with it,
> handling it, comprehending it. But in the end, it is simply an attitude toward
> the relationship between mechanism and meaning that is expansive enough
> to imagine building as a form of thinking.[29]

It appears to be no coincidence, then, that McKenzie's 'acts of construction' which constitute a 'text' sit comfortably beside Ramsay's 'algorithmic criticism' which builds 'txt' one embodied byte at a time. If literary and book historians want access to digital tools that enable and enhance their existing and future scholarly practices but do not want to reinvent themselves as computer programmers, they need to be in at the ground floor of the collaborative development process. As Kirschenbaum and Doug Reside have recently observed, 'new textual forms require new work habits, new training, new tools, new practices, and new instincts. Details regarding file formats and media types are no more or less exotic from the purview of textual studies than the minute particulars of letterpress, paper making and bookbinding.'[30] Since books are frisky, malleable and promiscuous, literary historians both today and tomorrow must also be nimble, agile and deft.


## FURTHER READING

Gaskell, Philip. *New Introduction to Bibliography*. New Castle, DE: Oak Knoll, 1995.

Hayles, N. Katherine. *How We Think: Digital Media and Contemporary Technogenesis*. Chicago: University of Chicago Press, 2012.

Howsam, Leslie. *Old Books and New Histories: An Orientation to Studies in Book and Print Culture*. Toronto: University of Toronto Press, 2006.

Jackson, Heather J. *Marginalia: Readers Writing in Books*. New Haven: Yale University Press, 2001.

Johns, Adrian. *The Nature of the Book: Print and Knowledge in the Making*. Chicago: University of Chicago Press, 1998.

Kirschenbaum, Matthew. *Mechanisms: New Media and the Forensic Imagination*. Cambridge, MA: MIT Press, 2007.

McKenzie, D. F. *Bibliography and the Sociology of Texts*. Cambridge: Cambridge University Press, 1999.

Pearson, David. *Books as History: The Importance of Books Beyond Their Texts*. New Castle, DE: Oak Knoll, 2008.

Ramsay, Stephen. *Reading Machines: Toward an Algorithmic Criticism*. Chicago: University of Illinois Press, 2011.

van der Weel, Adriaan. *Changing our Textual Minds: Towards a Digital Order of Knowledge*. Manchester: Manchester University Press, 2012.

## CHAPTER 3

# Medium

## Julian Murphet

A medium is defined principally as a 'middle state', or that which falls 'between two degrees [...] or classes',[1] a fact that has allowed for the term's development into a word meaning any 'intermediate agency, instrument, or channel',[2] which gives it a communicational currency. Obviously, what comes between two positions can either impede or enable the passage of sensory material from one to the other: a brick wall blocks out all visual information on its far side, while a transparent pane of glass allows for an almost perfect view of it. A medium typically works as a compromise between these two extreme alternatives; it makes perceptible or intelligible on the basis of a physical impedance or blockage. Our ambivalent use of the word 'screen' demonstrates this paradox: as a word for the physical occlusion of a given datum ('screened out'), it also names the dominant two-dimensional information platform of the last hundred years. A medium is what, by interposing, prevents *direct* communication between two points, but in doing so extends communicability itself – either outward in spatial reach, or inward in temporal durability.

## WRITING AND ITS OTHERS

The status of literature, or even language, as a medium is a vexed philosophical and linguistic issue, dating at least as far back as Plato's ambiguous consideration of linguistic 'naturalism' in the *Cratylus*, and his critique of writing in the *Phaedrus*. In John Durham Peters's summation, what is at stake in Plato's disdain for the medium of written words is a 'fierce longing for contact with an untouchable other', an almost erotic desire for one-to-one spiritual communion that has both driven the history of mediation and periodically lashed out at it.[3] Our millennial drive towards ever-greater degrees and intensities of connectivity has taken place through (and spurred the invention of) technologies which, because they are not human, evidently compromise and distort the human qualities of our contact with others. Writing was historically the first of these technologies. By transferring the singular act of oral utterance to a durable platform requiring a complex new set of skills (literacy), it irreparably soured the dream of an intimate transmission of knowledge. In writing, the spatially distant become close-to-hand, the dead continue to teach, and the anonymous masses tune in to a signal possibly meant for an elite few. The prosthetics of mediation can be seen to wean the human being away from a hypothetical 'immediacy' of amatory intercourse between souls, and hook it up instead to artificial and lifeless techniques that substitute for the spiritual communion of knowledge. But this lifeless travesty of spoken intercourse nevertheless allows for the reliable transmission of cultural information from one generation to the next, makes available the general intellect itself, and guarantees the continuity of two overlapping practices that have not ceased intertwining since Plato – literature and philosophy – as well as the very conception of history itself.

Writing was never alone as a medium. In 1605 Francis Bacon declared that it was not necessary 'that cogitations be expressed by the medium of words. For whatsoever is capable of sufficient differences, and those perceptible by the sense, is in nature competent to express cogitations'.[4] The human senses could just as well discriminate among systematic differences articulated through *other* media to arrive at ideas. So, for instance, the use of iconography throughout the mostly illiterate middle ages served to shore up the authority of the Church through 'sufficient differences' of tone, line and figure – be it in paint, coloured glass or dyed fabrics – to 'express' Biblical stories; or again, the 'sufficient differences' specific to mummery and music enabled unlettered plebeians to identify the various liturgical 'cogitations' so expressed.

As a technical requirement, literacy set a determinate limit to literature's social reach, even as it required an exhaustive pedagogy in order to master it: in spelling, handwriting, style, rhetoric, logic and a host of other modal and formal niceties. As a medium, 'printed letters' (the literal meaning of literature) clearly abetted a structural division of labour that restricted *the means of literary production* to a small and privileged propertied class, while the social majority was by and large reduced to the role of consumers, if not excluded outright from the republic of letters. There was something inherently divisive and inequitable about literature as the pre-eminent medium of information storage and exchange during the age of Enlightenment.

Beginning with the stabilisation of photographic technology in the 1830s, and progressing with breathtaking rapidity over several decades after 1880, industrial capitalist societies spawned a sequence of unprecedented technological platforms for the delivery and storage of information: wired telegraphy, telephony, typewriting, phonography, wireless telegraphy, broadcast radio, motion pictures in nickelodeon and cinematic format, electric sound recording and so on. Alongside these defined media of inscription and dissemination, bourgeois society also devised means to facilitate the movement of bodies and goods at speeds and in volumes that vastly outstripped the capacities of earlier phases of the capitalist mode of production: by steam train, steam ship, electric streetcar, the combustion engine, airplanes and the entire physical and temporal infrastructure of a social organisation that could no longer continue to grow on the basis of animal power – paved roads, railways, timetables, airports and synchronised clocks.

If we take 'media' to refer to this congeries of related technological and infrastructural developments, enabling the efficient transmission between far-flung places of

the vast amounts of information, persons and commodities that made modern capitalist accumulation possible, then we can see how it is that language might have lost
its claim to being a privileged medium. While printed text remained indispensable
to the bureaucratisation of what Lisa Gitelman has called 'paper knowledge'[5] – at
the level of Parliamentary record, police archives and official company reporting,
for example – it had nevertheless lost out to the telegraph and telephone as a means
of instant social communication, and to the new mass-broadcast media (radio and
cinema above all) as an instrument of ideological saturation and influence.

For the roughly three hundred years that sustained the privileged relationship
between humanism and the book (which lasted from the Renaissance, through
the Enlightenment, down to the final crisis at the turn of the twentieth century),
literature had been progressively abstracted out of the status of a medium by virtue
of its very monopoly. That is to say, literature, because it had no serious competitor
medium over the spread and preservation of cultural knowledge/power, tended to
fall out of sight as a medium at all, and to assume a well-nigh 'spiritual' status as the
intellectual lynchpin of an entire order of things. Just as the money form crystallised
as the exceptional medium among media that allowed for the exorbitant growth of a
market economy, modernity relied on literature as the mediatic 'first among equals'
that stabilised the cultural coordinates of Western civilisation and empire. If money
ceases to be seen as a means, and is misprisioned as an end of economic activity, so
literature stops being recognised as a mere means and is elevated to the mystic status
of learning's end and origin both – *alpha* and *omega* of the alphabet, with poetry as
the 'general equivalent' of the imagination.

This has encouraged at least one media theorist to speculate that it was precisely
the invention and success of such media as the phonograph, typewriter and film, that
finally exposed writing as a medium – a lowly material channel – after all. Friedrich
Kittler has been paraphrased as arguing that '[i]n the modernist landscape of medial
specialization, writing is one medium among others, with its own limitations and
possibilities, and the writer a media specialist, a professional of the letter'.[6] This
self-conscious humbling signifies a dramatic reversal of fortunes for a means of
communication that had, not long before, enjoyed such command over the domain
of knowledge that it had conjured away its very materiality in myths of phonocen-
tricity and romantic dreams of genius, organic form and the creative imagination
– none of which gave much thought to the materiality of the letter.

What we habitually refer to as literature proper (that subset of printed matter
whose purpose is not to record veridical statements, but to reflect freely on its own
technical means – in fictive, poetic and other forms) occupied a special place within
what Kittler called the 'discourse network' of the Enlightenment and its romantic
aftermath. In these exceptional forms, writers could test the inner and outer limits
of writing as a means of communication without necessarily being held to the epistemological and methodological standards that governed the discursive regimes of
science, philosophy and history – without, indeed, being supposed to 'communicate'
anything at all beyond the pleasures specific to language. For as long as the printed
word enjoyed a culturally hegemonic position at the hub of a network of interrelated
sign systems, 'imaginative' literature effectively stabilised an entire economy of

signification, by supplying it with the stories and personae that gave it identity over time.

For Jacques Rancière, it was literature in its heyday that underwrote the innumerable inferences between 'realistic' painting and the imaginary worlds to which it gestured. Literature sutured representational painting to the figures it was supposed to express and which endowed its flat canvases with illusory depth. 'The bond between painting and the third dimension is a bond between painting and the poetic power of words and fables.'[7] In the discourse network of the Enlightenment, we recognise a system-wide deference of all signifying practices to the literary master signifier, in a manner that upheld social inequality. This mimetic order (where the sign systems of all other media refer back to the literary sign system) is a 'system of relations that subordinate the resemblance of images to the ordering of actions, the visibility of painting to the quasi-visibility of the words of poems, and the poem itself to a hierarchy of subjects and actions'.[8] Once again, literature's privileged place at the medial centre of an entire order of things was simultaneously a means of preserving the privileges that attached to it, both social and aesthetic.

With the shake-up of that monopoly by the newer media technologies of the late nineteenth century, however, literature's place shifted dramatically. Where once it had held all of culture together in a web of analogical relations certified by tradition and embedded in multiple institutions, it 'lost this special status circa 1900 in the interest of thorough equality among materials. Literature became word art put together by word producers.'[9] Resigned to this sudden decline in status as the consequence of a successful competitor's victory over the ecology of media (the ascent of what Benjamin called 'mechanical reproducibility'), so-called 'high' literature responded by 'cut[ting] out everything available to the other media'. It occupied only 'the margin left to it by the other media'.[10] Popular literature, on the other hand, a novel literary category made possible by new technologies of photomechanical mass printing, magazine formats, mass literacy, cheaper types of paper, and the very collapse of the written word into mere 'culture', pursued an alternative path: adapting itself to the rhythms and appetites of a new cultural economy, and explicitly transforming itself into a servo-mechanism for the newer industries of cinema and radio.

Or so the story usually goes. In what remains of this chapter, I will explore some of the paradoxes and contradictions presented by the extraordinarily rapid success of the mechanical and electric mass media for the practices of literary history and analysis. There seem to be four ways of approaching the matter: (1) the return of literature to the status of 'one medium among many' recalls to mind the initial definition of a medium as what *comes between*, and raises the question of what happens when literature situates itself 'between' the new mass media and its own dwindling readership, or conversely finds that the other media have interpolated themselves between it and its former consumers; it then becomes imperative to attend to (2) the various ways in which literature adapted to its new situation by 'borrowing' technical and formal features from its media adversaries, or pretended to refuse any accommodation with them; on the other hand, there could scarcely be any question that (3) the very matter with which literature had historically come to concern itself – everyday life, sensory experience, social reproduction, the field of social action, types of persons and so forth – had been transformed beyond recall by the new media themselves, requiring the older institution to track these modifications to its raw material on its own terms; while (4) the longitudinal picture nevertheless portended grim futures for that very institution at an economic level, where the market for printed material could be expected to undergo an absolute decline in relation to those for recorded sound, motion pictures and newer kinds of signifying systems on unheralded material platforms (television and computation). Although we can only scratch the surface here, this methodological division into the topics of (1) *remediation*, (2) *transposition*, (3) *the history of the senses*, and (4) *the means of cultural production*, at least provides future work in literary history with workable coordinates for an informed approach to the actuality of literature's evolving place within the media systems that surround it.

## REMEDIATION

If after 1900 all media confronted one another as formal equals before the bar of public opinion, and each was thus thrown back upon its own peculiar materiality to fight competitively for a place in the transitional media ecology, *media specificity* logically emerged as a concept to explain the aesthetic results – otherwise known as modernism. Clement Greenberg famously codified one of the core principles of the ideology of modernism; though he wrote of 'arts' instead of media, the point is the same:

> Each art, it turned out, had to effect this demonstration on its own account. What had to be exhibited and made explicit was that which was unique and irreducible not only in art in general, but also to each particular art. Each art had to determine, through the operations peculiar to itself, the effects peculiar and exclusive to itself.[11]

Media, however, whilst demonstrably different in materiality and application, cannot be 'peculiar and exclusive' to themselves, since it is their very nature to *come between* practices and forms of sensible appearance. As Rancière puts it,

> a medium is not a 'proper' means or material. It is a surface of conversion: a surface of equivalence between the different arts' ways of making; a conceptual space of articulation between these ways of making and forms of visibility and intelligibility determining the way in which they can be viewed and conceived.[12]

No medium is an island unto itself; there is only a complex archipelago that facilitates communication among its primary nodes by way of the various migratory paths that crisscross it. Kittler puts it this way: 'the untranslatablity of media is essential to the possibility of their coupling and transposition',[13] which is as much to say that Greenberg's mistake was to have misunderstood that what is 'unique and irreducible' to any given medium is just what makes it available to monstrous 'couplings' and incorporations.

Media theory takes the point a crucial step further. For Marshall McLuhan, a medium not only is never alone in an ecological sense; the inevitable sociality among media is ceaselessly internalised within each one. In his influential formulation, 'the "content" of any medium is always another medium'.[14] 'The content of a movie is a novel or a play or an opera', for instance, and this opportunistic exploitation of extrinsic media materials is precisely what makes the movie 'strong and intense' – 'just because it is given another medium as "content"'.[15] What McLuhan frames as an invariable law of media cannibalism has been elaborated into a more flexible theoretical proposition by Jay David Bolter and Richard Grusin. Their notion of 'remediation' explains why it is that a medium can never simply pursue 'the effects peculiar and exclusive to itself', since, in a context of 'equality among materials', it must continually 'refashion its predecessors and other contemporary media' in order to be accepted as a medium at all.[16] Failure to do so is tantamount to lapsing from the domain of communication altogether, since it is only the sum total of media practices at any given moment that determines what does, and what does not, count as a message in the first place. So, to 'remediate' another medium in the process of implementing its own techniques is to ensure the host medium's viability within the wider network of information exchange. 'Our culture conceives of each medium or constellation of media as it responds to, redeploys, competes with, and reforms other media'[17] – to be a medium is to be amongst media the way any species is amongst others in an ecosystem whose sustainability depends upon their incessant mutual interaction: adaptive, exploitative and parasitic.

What did this entail for literature? On the one hand, literature experienced a series of historical shocks contingent upon its remediation by new media. The nascent film industry, for instance, once it realised that the key to economic success with the middle class resided in its ability to tell recognisable stories in a legible format, turned to the existing literary corpus of novels, poems, stories and plays as its logical raw material. The stabilisation of narrative cinema depended upon a wholesale remediation of the literary archive; a situation not lost on Virginia Woolf, who wrote that

> All the famous novels of the world, with their well-known characters and
> their famous scenes, only asked, it seemed, to be put on the films. What could
> be easier and simpler? The cinema fell upon its prey with immense rapacity,
> and to the moment largely subsists upon the body of its unfortunate victim.
> But the results are disastrous to both. The alliance is unnatural. Eye and brain
> are torn asunder ruthlessly.[18]

For Woolf, this systemic remediation resulted in aesthetic deformations of both media. For Scott Fitzgerald, the tone was more melancholy than outraged:

> I saw that the novel, which at my maturity was the strongest and supplest
> medium for conveying thought and emotion from one human being to

another, was becoming subordinated to a mechanical and communal art
that [...] was capable of reflecting only the tritest thought, the most obvious
emotion.[19]

His terms are exact: one medium subordinated to another, in a remediation that
apparently worked only one-way. But the facts were more complex.

Literature, too, fighting for survival against this ransacking of its archive, proved
adept in its own 'remediations' of cinematic – not to mention telephonic, telegraphic,
phonographic and radiophonic – materials. So *The Waste Land* features a key scene
with a gramophone, Proust's masterpiece meditates on the vocal dissociations of the
telephone, Henry James's 'In the Cage' is set in a London telegraphist's office, and
Joyce's *Ulysses* turns in part on the activities of an Irish newspaper: and none of this
incidental, but of the essence of these texts' modernity.

> Going to the cinema, listening to the wireless, reading newspapers, were [...]
> taken for granted as stock activities of fictional characters. Newspaper reports,
> newspaper tycoons and film moguls, radio announcers and film stars became
> obligatory to the up-to-the-minute novel or drama. Nor, if they wanted to be
> alert and socially observant, must poems miss out on such phenomena.[20]

Able to position itself to advantage by incorporating the enemy on its own
formal terms, literature could then either satirise its foreign media 'contents', or
perform more subtle judgements, as when Winifred Holtby's narrator in *South Riding*
describes the heroine's thought processes at the cinema: 'Lovely she thought it. It
filled her with vague longings. She looked at the languishing lady on the screen and
saw sinuous movements, hips slim as a whiting's, wet dark lips and lashes luxuriant as
goose-grass in a hedge bottom. She thought: I'm a back number. Nobody wants me.'[21]
George Orwell could afford more venom: 'He hated the pictures, of course, seldom
went there even when he could afford it. Why encourage the art that is destined to
replace literature? But still, there is a kind of soggy attraction about it. [... I]t's the
kind of drug we need. The right drug for friendless people.'[22] While Evelyn Waugh's
bleak prognosis for civilisation after the demise of literature, in *Vile Bodies*, leaves
the reader with a bitter aftertaste indelibly associated with the airplanes, zeppelins,
gossip columns, racing cars, film sets and telephonic exchanges that characterise his
satiric tale. Modern literature is positively full of such material; that fullness, with
other media, *is* its modernity – the necessary alteration of its formal physiognomy
under heated competitive pressure.

## TRANSPOSITION

'Art is modern', wrote Theodor Adorno, 'when, by its mode of experience and as the
expression of the crisis of experience, it absorbs what industrialisation has developed
under the given relations of production.'[23] And the most relevant development of
the industrial capitalist mode of production for literature was of course the mass

media themselves. If literature was not simply going to fall helplessly behind in the struggle for mediatic survival, it would have to do more than remediate cinema and radio as so much 'content'; it would have to assimilate the technical advances represented by those media, and 'absorb' them into its own formal protocols. As Adorno saw it, the formal potentials lurking in the newer media were all too often 'thwarted' by their mode of production, since the profit motive dictated an overuse of the most familiar and repetitive of devices in film and radio. In a situation where these newer mechanical and electric media were systematically remediating literature, stymieing their own aesthetic development, literature could return the favour at a deeper level to promote its own interests and so 'safeguard' the real aesthetic potential of the new means of cultural production.[24] This was how it was, as André Bazin would put it, that so many 'so-called "film techniques" [...] are actually never used in the cinema', and why 'film-makers continue to deprive themselves of [...] technique[s] that could be so useful to them':[25]

> It would seem as if the cinema was fifty years behind the novel. If we
> maintain that the cinema influences the novel then we must suppose that
> it is a question of a potential image ... We would then be talking about
> the influence of a nonexistent cinema, an ideal cinema, a cinema that the
> novelist would produce if he were a filmmaker; of an imaginary art that we are
> still awaiting.[26]

If literature became the primary venue in which the true 'potential' of cinema, radio and phonograph could be developed, that was because its relative freedom from the highly rationalised industrial division of labour allowed for a genuine exploration of aesthetic possibilities raised by the new media, but denied expression in them.

We have learned to discern a logic of 'transposition', whereby technical features left dormant or latent in the host medium are fastened onto and 'developed' in another, generally older one. It is thanks to this opportunistic logic that literature, rather than merely succumbing to the irresistible march of audio-visual media, managed for so long to secure its ideological position at the summit of the media pecking order, at least in intellectual circles. As Fredric Jameson puts it, while film 'entertained a merely fitful relationship to the modern', literature, by 'intelligently and opportunistically absorbing the techniques of film back into its own substance, remained throughout the modern period the ideologically dominant paradigm of the aesthetic and continued to hold open a space in which the richest varieties of innovation were pursued'.[27]

So when McLuhan wrote to Ezra Pound during his incarceration at St Elizabeth's in 1948 that 'Your Cantos I now judge to be the first and only serious use of the great technical possibilities of the cinematograph', he was not insulting the great poet, but delivering the highest praise.[28] What Ron Bush calls 'Pound's new emphasis on juxtaposing whole blocks of material'[29] in the Cantos had already inspired Pound's disciple, Louis Zukofsky, to write to his mentor: 'We both partake of the cinematic principle [...] Advertising & montage, Mr. E., – Eisenstein has nothing on us.'[30] Whether or not Pound had been conscious in his adoption of a montage principle that belonged more to D. W. Griffith than Homer is beside the point; what matters is that his *Cantos* 'safeguarded' that exhilarating principle against its commercial trivialisation in the movies. While Hollywood kept the structural possibilities of the film medium at a low simmer, the fullest extent could be explored in texts that were not circumscribed by capital. A montage aesthetic can be seen at work in any number of texts across the twentieth century, perhaps culminating in the 'cut-up' technique of William Burroughs. But so too, for that matter, can we make out a 'radio voice' technique in the 'noir' novelists' proclivities towards 'voice-over' narrative devices, and a 'phonograph' technique in the repetitions and vocal verisimilitudes of Dos Passos and others. This migration of the technical elements peculiar to a given medium but underdeveloped there, to literary texts desperate to remain *au courant* in a media climate where they must inevitably appear slow and demanding, is a constant of twentieth-century literature.

Nor did it stop at mid-century, when the literary star was arguably at its last zenith in Western history, but continued through the era of television and into the digital hegemony of today, as that star sank lower and lower in the cultural firmament. The transposition of the unique formal quality of television – its capacity for instant channel-surfing – to literary form can be felt in the fashion for 'multi-channel' story-telling in Julio Cortázar, Georges Perec, Thomas Pynchon and others, and textual construction in John Ashbery, Frank O'Hara and the Language Writers; while the possibilities of hypertext and variable construction in contemporary literature have been partially mapped by N. Katherine Hayles in a series of riveting studies.[31] However, while the transpositions that took place during the fifty or so years of modernism reaped for literature a series of high aesthetic rewards, the rate of return in these later speculative transferences has arguably been considerably lower. Since the heyday of postmodernism at the end of the 1960s (the moment at which both televisual and cybernetic models proved most propitious for literary work), there would appear to have been a relative decline, both in the cultural status of literature in advanced capitalist societies, and in the aesthetic ambition and realisation of individual texts – particularly in their ability to feed laterally off the media ecology that surrounds them. If cinema and radio drove writers to unprecedented formal audacities, the digital media – while they have certainly raised the quality of 'information' internal to literary textualisation – have appeared to degrade the average level of literary aesthetic achievement.[32]

## HISTORY OF THE SENSES

At stake in the colossal transformation of the media ecology triggered by the new technologies at the end of the nineteenth century is not only the question of what constitutes a message, but the very human sensorium itself, whose cultivation, it has been suggested (by the young Marx), 'is a labour of the entire history of the world'.[33] 'The manner in which human sense perception is organized', Walter Benjamin wrote, 'the medium in which it is accomplished, is determined not only by nature but by historical circumstances as well.'[34] If the senses have a history, then, because media work through sense perception, not only can these technologies be described as sensory 'extensions of man' (in McLuhan's formulation), but the senses themselves must of necessity have been 'cultivated' and 'organised' by those very technologies. Benjamin's thesis was that the technological basis of modernity had subjected 'the human sensorium to a complex kind of training'.[35] David Wellbery remarks in a similar spirit that:

> The body is the site upon which the various technologies of our culture inscribe themselves, the connecting link to which and from which our medial means of processing, storage, and transmission run. Indeed, in its nervous system, the body itself is a medial apparatus and an elaborate technology. But it is also radically shaped and reshaped by the networks to which it is conjoined.[36]

Given this, it is clear that literature not only has before it the tasks of 'remediating' the new media as content, and of transposing their techniques into its own substance, but, perhaps even more profoundly, of attending to the transformations of the human senses that have accompanied these technical revolutions. What Sara Danius calls the 'senses of modernism' are senses that have been permanently modified by their subjection to a relentless barrage of mechanical and electronic mediation[37] – since, in Pound's telling phrase, '[y]ou can no more take machines out of the modern mind, than you can take the shield of Achilles out of the *Iliad*'.[38] As Danius puts it, the novel was faced with an entirely unprecedented aesthetic problem: 'how to recover and represent the immediacy of lived experience in an age when modes of experience are continually reified by […] the emergence of technologies for reproducing the visual and audible real'.[39]

The prostheses of modern media 'extend' the senses only to transform them from within; first by separating them, one from another, as so many incompatible 'data-streams' – Jameson once wrote that under the pressure of rationalisation and alienation, the senses of modernity had undergone a 'fragmentation, reification, but also production, of new semi-autonomous objects and activities';[40] while Kittler observes that the mechanical triad 'gramophone, film, typewriter' corresponds to the Lacanian triad 'Real, Imaginary, Symbolic', and so drives a sense-perceptual wedge into the 'universal medium of the imagination' that was poetry[41] – and then by pushing each to untold levels of stimulation, speed and saturation. Modern sense perception is specialised and radicalised in ways that would have been incomprehensible to Jane Austen, and is so thanks to the media colonisation of communications. Photographic time-and-motion studies profoundly altered and made more 'efficient' the traditional processes of manual labour; telegraphy first trained the ear to hear infinitesimal distinctions between the long and short tones of Morse code; film, in Benjamin's fine phrase, had burst the 'prison-world' of everyday perception 'asunder by the dynamite of the tenth of a second', laying bare 'an unconsciously penetrated space and introducing us to "unconscious optics"';[42] radio sensitised the ear to musical and vocal materials otherwise inaccessible to the peripheries and accustomed listeners to the static hiss of white noise; television trained the eye to withstand untold amounts of information without succumbing to reactive inertia.

Twentieth-century literature is rife with evidence of a traumatic 'history of the senses' that both attests to unparalleled kinds of expertise and efficiency in the refashioned mediatised acts of looking, hearing and touching, and indicates symptomatic points of implosion, dissociation and derangement among them. By reading literature for evidence of this progressive material transformation of its fundamental phenomenological elements (smells, appearances, sounds, textures and so forth), we can better learn how the media have shaped our sensory history, and how literature in turn has acted to codify and make known a range of otherwise inexplicable, anxiety-inducing experiences most often pushed into the domain of the unconscious.

## THE MEANS OF CULTURAL PRODUCTION

Briefly, in conclusion, it needs to be affirmed that literature's historical realisation of its own status as a medium among media is also a categorical transformation of the very horizon of cultural production itself:

> Capitalism, and the modern age, is a period in which, with the extinction of the sacred and the 'spiritual', the deep underlying materiality of all things has finally risen dripping and convulsive into the light of day; and it is clear that culture itself is one of those things whose fundamental materiality is now for us not merely evident but quite inescapable. This has, however, also been a historical lesson: it is because culture has *become* material that we are now in a position to understand that it always *was* material, or materialistic, in its structures and functions.[43]

The emergence of the media in our modern and postmodern sense has fomented a radical materialisation of culture *tout court*, and a retroactive sense that all the time-honoured genres and categories that have preserved literature as an autonomous and 'spiritualised' exception to the means-ends rationality of capitalism have always and already been absorbed into the economics of cultural production, exchange and consumption. Print capitalism is and always has been but one branch of the cultural means of production that typify our way of life. In that sense, it, and the various institutions that attend it (the apparatuses of education, criticism, reviews, prizes, bookstores, marketing and so on), are essentially no different from the means of cultural production that we designate via the epithets Hollywood, Silicon Valley, the Hit Parade and all the other mediatic branches of the entertainment and information economy today.

To conceive of literature as a constituent element of the cultural means of production as a whole is to grasp its function in the broader economy. There is a steady conversion of hard-won cultural values into simple profits in the market for books, such that writers as diverse (and diversely critical of capitalism) as William Faulkner, Thomas Pynchon and Karl Marx, end up as positive entries in the accounts of publishers like Vintage, Penguin and Verso. But it is also to alert ourselves to the fact that this is already exactly how literature is treated within our economy, with ever increasing literalness. If once upon a time publishers had tended to be satisfied with profits of 3 to 4 per cent, the large-scale corporate takeover of the publishing industry in the last twenty years has put paid to such modest returns. The 'new conglomerate owners wanted returns much closer to those they had gotten from their other media holdings – newspapers, TV networks and so on. The pressure to earn at least 10 to 15 per cent, if not more, profoundly altered the output of the major publishing houses'[44] from the turn of the present century.

So a potential cost of being revealed as one medium among many is that literature has been stripped of the relative autonomy permitted by the modest rate of return that somehow lasted as an industry standard till the end of the last millennium, and consequently been shorn of its more experimental and aesthetically ambitious moments. The CEOs of Time Warner or Bertelsmann, conceiving of publishing companies as tributary enterprises within their vertically integrated media conglomerates, are showing us what the 'equalisation of materials' looks like: authors today, however they may conceive of themselves, and however old-fashioned criticism may choose to classify them, are objectively defined by their own industry as media 'content creators', akin to programmers and film producers, only cheaper and more economically precarious. Books are mere aspects of aggressive marketing campaigns that involve advertising, book tours, festivals, film adaptation rights, radio appearances, talk shows and so on; all novels increasingly seem much the same; poetry is neglected. In the world of late, or multinational capitalism, culture is in the hands of 'the communication business – not the movie, book, or television business'. Media may once have stimulated the aesthetic upsurges of literary modernism; today, they are too often simply 'ways to build new pathways to the consumer's door', with no thought of any enduring quality or truth.[45]

Perhaps poetry's neglect can here stand for its long-term potential as a renovator of literary fortunes, at a qualitative if not a quantitative level. In the work of contemporary poets such as Keston Sutherland, Rachel Blau duPlessis, Kevin Davies, Andrea Brady, Claudia Rankine and others, the media-saturation of daily life is taken for granted, and subjected to extraordinary formal protocols whose fundamental impulse is often enough the televisual, digital and informational wellsprings of all 'data' today. Contemporary radical poetry is the melancholy, sometimes exhilarating transcription of utopian messages hauled up from the 'deep web' of our collective political unconscious by Argonauts of the postmodern media ecology. With them hang the fortunes of literature itself.

## FURTHER READING

Bolter, Jay David and Richard Grusin. *Remediation: Understanding New Media.* Cambridge, MA: MIT Press, 2000.

Danius, Sara. *The Senses of Modernism: Technology, Perception, and Aesthetics.* Ithaca: Cornell University Press, 2002.

Gitelman, Lisa. *Always Already New: Media, History, and the Data of Culture.* Cambridge, MA: MIT Press, 2008.

Hayles, N. Katherine. *How We Became Posthuman: Virtual Bodies in Cybernetics, Literature, and Informatics*. Chicago: University of Chicago Press, 1999.

Kittler, Friedrich A. *Discourse Networks 1800 / 1900*, trans. Michael Metteer, with Chris Cullens. Stanford: Stanford University Press, 1990.

Kittler, Friedrich A. *Gramophone, Film, Typewriter*, trans. Geoffrey Winthrop-Young and Michael Wutz. Stanford: Stanford University Press, 1999.

Murphet, Julian. *Multimedia Modernism: Literature and the Anglo-American Avant-Garde*. Cambridge: Cambridge University Press, 2009.

Stewart, Garrett. *Between Film and Screen: Modernism's Photo-Synthesis*. Chicago: University of Chicago Press, 2000.

Trotter, David. *Literature and the First Media Age: Britain Between the Wars*. Cambridge, MA: Harvard University Press, 2014.

Wollaeger, Mark. *Modernism, Media, and Propaganda: British Narrative from 1900–1945*. Princeton: Princeton University Press, 2008.

## CHAPTER 4

# Translation

Thomas O. Beebee

The first person in the Western world to have left behind written translation criticism was St Jerome (c. 347–420 CE), who was responsible for rendering the Bible into Latin. Naturally, as someone concerned with transmitting a text's divine meaning and spirit, Jerome's memorable statements on translation had little direct bearing on what today we know as literary history. Translation theory had to wait another 1,400 years to develop ideas of translation that defined the activity's role vis-à-vis a literary corpus: Johann Wolfgang von Goethe's famous distinction of approaches to translation in terms of the relative familiarity of the target culture with the text, published in the 1819 *Noten und Abhandlungen zu besserem Verständnis* that conclude his *West-östlicher Divan*.[1] Goethe's three stages ('*Epochen*') are: prose rendering; parodistic rendering (the famous 'free translation' for which the French were known); and finally, a third stage of close imitation of the formal aspects of the original. He makes it very clear that the first two stages prepare the latter, with first- and second-stage translations educating a public in how to read translations in a process of positive feedback. Not coincidentally, Goethe's essay comes just six years after an epochal shift in German self-identity with the end of Napoleonic occupation and the beginning of attempts at forming a national literary and cultural canon by Jacob and Wilhelm Grimm.

In contradistinction to Goethe's approach, writing on translation has tended to focus on individual works of literature, on individual authors, or on the activities of individual translators (for example Anne Dacier, Lin Shu, Ezra Pound) rather than on translation's effect on literary history, or on the history of translation. Conversely, and with the important exceptions of translations of the Bible and of Greek and Roman classical texts into modern European languages, literary historiography has been far more apt to consider operations of transmission, influence and change as these occur within languages than as they do between one language and another. Translation critique has been too ad hoc to form the basis of literary history, in other words, while literary history has been too oriented towards national canons to take interest in investigating translation as a driving force in literary development.

To state the last point more precisely, the 'invention' of modern literary history

tends to go hand-in-hand with the need for a national canon. Hence, even translations that played a large role in the development of literatures are nearly always
excluded. We should remember that this bracketing of translation works in both
directions: translated literature is excluded from the national canon; and the
national canon is supposed to interest only those who can read its works in the
original. Translations are frequently excluded from the collected works of authors,
and authors whose one and only activity was translation, such as the legendary Lin
Shu of China, enjoy second-class status at best.

One would think that histories of world literature, such as Adolf Stern's 1888
effort, *Geschichte der Weltliteratur in übersichtlicher Darstellung*, would need to account
for translation as fundamentally bringing world literature into being, but in fact
this is not the case. These and other attempts to write histories of world literature
construct a taxonomy of literatures as coherent, mostly self-contained wholes: world
literature is additive rather than exponential, and the whole is simply the sum of its
parts. 'Influence' is mentioned often in these histories, translation only rarely.[2]

It is hard to overestimate the deficit created by the continued scholarly neglect
of translation as an aspect of authorial and textual reception. European literary
history since the Enlightenment (when Latin began to decline as a lingua franca),
for example, has undergone its various movements through the circulation of texts
that get translated from one language into another. Fania Oz-Salzberger has given an
excellent overview of this process as it unfolded during the Enlightenment:

> Many of the works conveying Enlightenment ideas could be written only in
> vernaculars; this was especially true of popularized science and philosophy,
> national histories, new imaginative literature deeply stamped by local
> landscape and idiom, travel books, and ethnography. Moreover, not all
> Enlightenment readers knew French, and many of its authors could not write
> it. [...] Thanks to translations, the Republic of Letters could slowly evolve
> in some parts of Europe into an embryonic democracy of letters, where
> numerous people could read, but only in one language. Having survived
> the loss of its universal language [Latin], Enlightenment thought became
> increasingly sensitive to linguistic and cultural differences and ever more
> dependent on translation.[3]

Latin, of course, had for centuries been no one's mother tongue, and thus the tie
between the individual situations and lived experiences of writers and their literary
expression had been relatively loose. The increasing emphasis on vernacular
languages for literature since the late middle ages eventually created a new problem:
untranslatability, the other side of the coin of terms such as 'genius' and '*Volksgeist*'.
Untranslatability then became a major excuse for bracketing translation as belonging
to an author's oeuvre or to a national canon.

Nor does the recent appearance of the multi-volume *Oxford History of Literary
Translation in English*, valuable though its contributions are, really provide an alternative history of English literature as shaped significantly through translation. Rather
than write a history, the series makes visible a valuable historical record. This can be

seen from its subject matter being parcelled out to dozens of contributors, and from the table of contents of the published volumes, which atomise the history of translation into a variety of sub-topics. Volume 4, for example, edited by Peter France and Kenneth Haynes, begins with four panoptic articles (for example, 'Translation in the United States'), followed by a section on Greek and Latin literature, followed by others on the literatures of medieval and modern Europe, Eastern literatures, popular culture, texts for music and oral literature, sacred and religious texts, and ending with biographical sketches of the translators.[4] The major sections named above are further sub-divided into, for example, the different source languages of Europe or of the East, hindering the development of any overarching narrative of how English literature has evolved under the influence of its surrounding literatures.

We may contrast such an approach with that of Lawrence Venuti, who provocatively subtitles his book *The Translator's Invisibility* as 'A History of Translation'. Venuti's history is not a listing of one translation after another. It is a detailed system analysis, based on sampling rather than comprehensiveness, of how Anglophone publishing markets have created and sustained translational invisibility, and of how they have shaped the techniques translators must use in order for their product to be distributed. Venuti describes his method of translation history as intervening

> against the translator's situation and activity in contemporary Anglo-
> American culture by offering a series of genealogies that write the history
> of the present. [...] This book is motivated by a strong impulse to *document*
> the history of English-language translation, to uncover long-obscure
> translators and translations, to reconstruct their publication and reception,
> and to articulate significant controversies. [...] What domestic values has
> transparent discourse at once inscribed and masked in foreign texts during
> its long domination? How has transparency shaped the canon of foreign
> literatures in English and the cultural identities of English-language nations?
> Why has transparency prevailed over other translation strategies in English,
> like Victorian archaism (Francis Newman, William Morris) and modernist
> experiments with heterogeneous discourses (Pound, Celia and Louis
> Zukofsky, Paul Blackburn)?[5]

My deployment of Venuti's approach to the role of translation in literary history as a contrast to that of the Oxford series is not intended as an endorsement, nor to imply that we should take his approach as our model for composing a literary history that includes translations. I find, for example, that a claim for the uniqueness of a particular cultural approach to translation can only convince when made comparatively against other cultures. Said comparisons reveal a generalised preference for 'transparent' over disruptive language for translation – making the exceptions all the more interesting moments in literary history. More accurate than a hypostasised 'clash of translation approaches' would be the dissection of a particular book market into its various niches within any particular publishing culture. The virtue in Venuti's idea of 'history' is its grounding in a notion of cultures as cybernetic systems for the creation, transfer, modification, storage and destruction of meaning.

Cultural and literary history is not the listing of details, but the explanation of how systems undergo dynamic change. Venuti's approach shows that a number of overall developments in the practice of literary theory, methodology and history have given us better tools for unlocking the mysteries of literary history than in the past. I have selected three of these, to wit: (1) book history and bibliomigrancy; (2) polysystems theory; and (3) postcolonial studies, for extended discussion in their relation to translational literary history. The order in which I discuss these three developments reflects the dialectical relationship between (1) and (2): book history is more about individual facts and 'case histories' of the creation and migration of texts, whereas (2) is more about the *Gestalt* against which we discover those facts, or that we create out of the accumulation of such facts. I conclude with a discussion of postcolonial approaches to translation, which in my opinion supplement the abstractions of poly-systems approaches with specific and detailed examples, and give a political dynamic to the elements of book history.

## BOOK HISTORY AND BIBLIOMIGRANCY

The first field I will describe, which is generally called 'book history' for lack of a better term, has brought a much-needed materialist approach to literary history. Its relatively recent origins can be seen from the fact that a journal with the title *Book History* debuted as late as 1998. The very first issue of this journal included Shef Rogers's piece on the translation of *Robinson Crusoe* into Maori in the late nine-teenth century.[6] Opposed to criticism's romantic image of the spiritual handing-off of the literary *logos* from the father-poet to his son or daughter – where the model for circulation and reading show little difference from that for oral transmission or for the Socratic method – book history concerns itself with how texts actually get into print and from there into people's hands, and with what readers then do with them. For translation, of course, book history implies tracing the methods and infrastructure by which non-native texts appear within a coherent local system, thereby revealing the forces of production and distribution that encourage or discourage translation. B. Venkat Mani has dubbed this last step 'bibliomigrancy', a process whereby 'shelf lives of books are created beyond their points of origin in libraries without walls'.[7] When these books migrate to areas where the dominant vernacular differs from that of the book – in colonial situations, for example – and when these afterlives of books are created in other languages through translation, we witness the formation of world literature, which I will address more extensively in my conclusion.

In general, book history reverses or 'undoes' what we generally think of as intel-lectual history. A historical event becomes such due to the significance it acquires when compared to earlier and later events, which may not be present in the inten-tions of the actors of the event. Intellectual history or *Geistesgeschichte* tends to treat its events differently: ideas are by definition self-present to their originators, who become the 'fathers of logoi'. Literary history was seen either as simple reception, or at its most complicated, in Walter Jackson Bate and Harold Bloom, as a struggle against the burden of tradition or an active resistance and misreading of one writer by another.

Two very simple questions illustrate the way that book history can undo this notion of literary history: (1) who (if anyone) is listed as the author on the title page of a book?; and (2) how does the book characterise itself, especially in terms of form and genre? From the beginning of printing through the early nineteenth century, it was extremely common for books to appear without an author's name – even when almost the entire reading community knew who the author was. A variety of clues and traditions leads modern literary historians to construct canons that often later must be undone. Two opposing examples are Shakespeare (denial of authorship and attribution to another name) and Daniel Defoe (wildly inflated canon). Similarly, the author only gradually came to be recognised as having moral rights in his or her work (for example, through copyright legislation that begins in the early eighteenth century), as opposed to those of printers or booksellers. In terms of the second point, numerous masterworks in the history of the novel were published under another rubric, such as a 'life' or a 'true history'. The messy, granulated view that book history provides tends to work against both literary history and authorship. 'Decidedly', writes Roger Chartier, 'authors [in the early modern period] did not write their books, even if some did intervene in some editions of their works and were aware of the effects of the material forms of their texts.'[8] Within the team of producers behind a published book, the translator takes up a certain position, neither more nor less inclined to fidelity or infidelity than the publisher, bookseller, or government censor. 'Translated from the _____ (insert language here)' was another identifier frequently found on title pages: at times a true statement, while at other times a deliberately misleading clue intended to raise the prestige of a text or to deflect concerns about its innovative qualities. Our ability to track what is happening 'on the ground' in terms of textual production and transfer reveals a wide spectrum of translation practices, ranging from pseudotranslations, through tradaptation, to the *belles infidèles* notion favoured during the Enlightenment, to the most careful and literal translations usually reserved for scripture prior to the establishment of a professional class of secular academics.

Book history thus reinvigorates the original meaning of the Latin *translatio*, which the Romans never applied to textual translation (using instead verbs like *interpretare* or *vertere*). *Translatio* is, quite simply, transfer, the movement from one location into another, thus bibliomigrancy. Transfer occurs at every stage of the publication process. What happens to our sense of literary history when we recognise that eighteenth-century German book fair catalogues list about one third of the titles on display at such fairs as translations?[9] Further, if we consult the periodical *Das belletristische Ausland*, published from 1843 to 1865, we count a total of 3,618 titles of literary works translated into German.[10] Here, the role of translation confronts another aspect of literary history, namely the question of how to deal with the fact that the mass of books read at any time remains invisible and unread to those writing literary history today. Translations constitute only a portion of that overall invisibility.

## POLYSYSTEMS THEORY

Despite its many valuable contributions, book history never developed a coherent theory concerning the patterns of *translatio*, or the ability of these to change dynamically through time. Book history therefore calls out for its theoretical complement, which it finds in polysystems theory (PT). PT was developed primarily by Itamar Even-Zohar, and is associated with translation theorists Susan Bassnett, Theo Hermans, José Lambert, Gideon Toury and André Lefevere, among others. Fundamental to PT is the idea of a cultural cybernetics that determines the placement, function and value of various types of literary phenomena. PT considers translation as its own literary subsystem, subject to coherent and sustained rules governing both its internal rules of production and also, dialectically, its interaction with other subsystems. This approach attempts to model the conditions under which a particular cultural system will value or devalue, affirm or negate, allow or prohibit translation. Even-Zohar famously identified three situations of literature that would cause translation to move from its usual peripheral position to the centre:

> (a) when a polysystem has not yet been crystallised, that is to say, when a literature is 'young', in the process of being established; (b) when a literature is either 'peripheral' (within a large group of correlated literatures) or 'weak', or both; and (c) when there are turning points, crises, or literary vacuums in a literature.[11]

By the same token, mutually autonomous literary systems may remain in a constant state of interference with each other, not only through translation but through other mechanisms such as abstract models that can be adapted (for example, the detective novel, magical realism), personalities that make an impact in other media or through personal contact, international literary institutions and so forth.

One sign of the novelty of this approach to translation issues has been its concept of 'pseudotranslation', by which is meant the presentation of a translation for which no original exists. From the point of view of literary history, pseudotranslation may be the functional equivalent either of translation from the original, or of an original piece in the target language. If any of the conditions listed by Even-Zohar obtains, and no adequate models can be found in other languages, then translations will be manufactured in order to deal with the deficit. For 'traditional' translation critique, which amounted mostly to a credit-debit accounting of the relation between source and target texts, pseudotranslation would be an absurdity and worthy of condemnation but not study; the effect of a pseudotranslation on the literary system, however, is frequently indistinguishable from that of a genuine translation. Pseudotranslation is thus a device for innovating within the literary system without claiming responsibility for doing so.

According to Gideon Toury, pseudotranslations serve the purpose of 'cultural planning', that is, of the attempt by an individual or an institution to alter the literary repertoire and to escape the shackles of convention.[12] For his own bit of cultural planning in *Don Quixote* (1605), Miguel de Cervantes resorted to the biographical invention of the Arab historian Cide Hamete Benengeli who supposedly had first immortalised the exploits of Don Quixote in Arabic. Toury gives the example of a text that stands at the origins of literary expressionism, Arno Holz and Johannes Schlaf's *Papa Hamlet*, which they published in 1889 using the pseudonym of Bjarne P. Homsen, the supposed author of an original Norwegian version. Toury argues that the publication of *Papa Hamlet* within the cultural space of translation served as camouflage for the innovations that Holz and Schlaf were making to German-language literary expression. The text's provocative oddity was disguised as being due to another literary culture and to the alienation effect of translation. Toury generalises from such examples that if

> translational norms differ from the norms of original literary writing in
> the target culture [...] and if the difference is in the direction of greater
> tolerance for deviations from sanctioned models [...] then the translational
> norms can also be adopted [...] for the composition of original texts, which
> are introduced into the system in the guise of genuine translations and, as a
> result, have a lower resistance threshold to pass.[13]

On the other hand, pseudotranslation can also be used to reinforce dominant norms, as in the case of translations of a Kazakh singer's songs of praise for the communist regime that began to appear in Russian 'translation' in the Soviet Union's first decades. Dzhambul Dzhabayev supposedly sang only in Kazakh, yet no originals of his singing in that language could be located. In fact, the pseudotranslations were being produced by a team of writers well placed within the Soviet authorities. Toury interprets the motives thusly: '[T]he poems had to praise "the great leader" and his deeds in a way deemed appropriate. [... A]n author for the concoction had to be found in the national republics such as Kazakhstan, and not in the Russian centre; and in case a suitable one couldn't be found, one had to be invented.'[14] The lesson for literary history may be that studies of translation should not confine themselves to 'genuine' translations, but should consider the entire notion of how translation as a cultural phenomenon can affect literary systems. One such effect that seems to be constantly increasing as the twenty-first century unfolds is the appearance of translation, translators and interpreters, and translation effects in fiction and drama. (The scholarly articles in the 2014 edited collection *Transfiction* give some notion of the wide range of contemporary practices in this field).[15] I will return to this topic in the next section.

Beyond pseudotranslation, Susan Bassnett gives another example of how polysystems theory should change the way that literary historians go about their business. Peter Dronke's *The Medieval Lyric*, first published in 1968 and into its third edition by 1996,[16] seems to say all there is to say about its topic, dealing as it does with all of the major poetic languages of Europe at the time, the fusion of Roman and Christian traditions, and the interaction between religious and secular lyric. But, observes Bassnett,

What is striking about Dronke's study [...] is that at no point does he ever discuss the role played by translation in the development and dissemination of the lyric. Yet unless we assume that all singers and poets were multilingual, then obviously translation was involved, as a fundamental activity. A translation studies approach to the medieval lyric would use a similar comparative methodology to Dronke's, but would ask different questions. It would also look at the development of a literary form in terms of changing sociological patterns across Europe (the end of feudalism, the rise of the city state etc.) and in terms of the history of language. For the development of vernacular languages in Europe was bound up with translation, just as several centuries later, in the Renaissance, the rise of vernacular languages to a status equal to that of the classical languages was also accompanied by a ferment of translation activity. Far from being a marginal enterprise, translation was at the core of the processes of transformation of literary forms and intimately connected to the emergence of national vernaculars.[17]

Even if Bassnett does not deploy the standard vocabulary of PT here, her discussion could nevertheless be framed in terms of 'strong' versus 'weak' literary systems as provided for by Even-Zohar, though 'high-prestige' (literatures in classical languages) versus 'low-prestige' (literatures in vernacular languages) may be a more useful vocabulary for framing the distinction she draws.

The collection *Translation Under Fascism*, edited by Christopher Rundle and Kate Sturge,[18] can be thought of as deriving from the attempt to define 'strong' literatures through a relatively well-defined, secularly political filtering mechanism. Totalitarian systems are one example of the close imbrication of political and literary systems that is a relative rarity in the modern world, where ever-increasing complexity causes subsystems to acquire increased autonomy vis-à-vis each other. Since totalitarian systems sought unsuccessfully to simplify social processes that were irreducibly complex, their attempts at controlling the literary subfield were frequently self-contradictory. Kate Sturge begins her essay on translation in Nazi Germany, for example, by directly invoking Lefevere's reading of translation as a sign of the relative openness of a literary system.

It makes sense to assume that a closed and xenophobic regime like Nazi Germany would be wary of [translated literature...] And indeed, National Socialism's official discourse on translation was marked by suspicion, often portraying translated literature as an insidious channel of dangerous ideas or a failure of patriotism on the part of German readers.[19]

This official position turns out not to give the whole picture, however: translations continued to appear in Nazi Germany, although the presence of English originals was greatly reduced. Modernist and avant-garde works were published less often, with some notable exceptions such as Faulkner and Joyce. This discrepancy between theory and practice can be thought of as a dynamic engine of literary history in the case of societies where the disposition towards literature takes on programmatic aspects, for example when governments subsidise the exportation of 'their' national literatures through translation. Let us now turn to a development in translation studies that problematises the idea of national literature, and turns our attention to the intra-national literary translation that takes place in postcolonial societies.

## POSTCOLONIAL STUDIES

We may think of postcolonial translation studies as a particular instantiation of the frequently abstract modelling of polysystems theory, and also of the investing of book history with particularly clear fields of force. In my study titled *Transmesis*, I asked the question of why translation and translators have become such familiar figures in contemporary postcolonial fiction, from Serbian author Milorad Pavić's 1986 *Dictionary of the Khazars* to Mozambican writer Mia Couto's 2000 *Last Flight of the Flamingo* and beyond. My hypothesis is that by making translation a theme of their works, postcolonial writers are compensating for the deficit of having to choose a single literary idiom to describe societies that are deeply divided between local and official languages.[20]

'Postcolonial' has many definitions; I am using the term here to indicate literature that deals with the cultural legacies of colonialism. 'Postcolonial' does not indicate a temporal sequence. Postcolonial literature may begin to appear as 'anti-colonial literature' while European colonial regimes still hold power, while at the other end of the spectrum colonialism may be said to continue into the present day under altered forms of domination. For example, an important book-history datum to keep in mind when contemplating the literary history of a former colony is the date of its first printing press, and the how and why of how it got there. Brazil did not acquire its first press until 1808, for example, Portuguese colonial policy having successfully prohibited its importation until that date. This fact complicates the question of what can count as 'Brazilian literature' in the colonial epoch, since every book and periodical in the dominant literary language had to be imported from the metropole.

Douglas Robinson posits three overlapping but sequential roles for translation in postcolonial studies: as a channel of colonisation; as a lightning-rod for cultural inequalities after the collapse of colonialism; and as a channel of decolonisation.[21] Colonial and postcolonial situations demand translation – colonial control is brought about or maintained through translation. In (post)colonial situations, two or more language systems are brought into contact and mutually perturb each other, resulting in a stratifying, enforced bilingualism and resulting hybrid literary forms. Curiously, the issue of pseudotranslation emerges under such conditions in a rather different modality, when the mimesis of events occurring in vernacular languages is conducted in a European one (for example, Salman Rushdie's 1983 novel *Shame*, written in English but where the characters are speaking Urdu almost exclusively, an example of what I call 'transmesis', where translation is part of the mimetic process). When postcolonial texts enter literary history, the discussion of translation can no longer be ignored. Furthermore, the topic of translation must be approached with an eye to the systematic nature of the power relations between languages – PT's binary 'strong' versus 'weak' attains almost literal relevance in such situations.

Stefanie Stockhorst claims that postcolonial studies stimulated the broader innovation to translation studies that resulted in its inclusion within the broader concept of 'cultural transfer':

> Transfer studies, by contrast [with traditional translation studies], cannot be modeled as 'autonomous' or 'hermetic' entities, but rather as dynamically interrelated systems. Furthermore, the paradigm of European national cultures and their independent origins appears no longer sustainable in the light of the manifold interrelations in politics, economics, science, philosophy, religion, and literature, which constitute the ensemble of European history: what is alleged to be a genuine part of the 'own' culture, on closer inspection often turns out to be imported, and *vice versa*.[22]

Stockhorst goes on to add a series of axes for transfer studies: the permeability of political and cultural boundaries, integral analysis of selection, reception and acculturation, and a comprehensive concept of culture familiar from cultural studies.

Yet even 'cultural transfer', as a neutral term, fails to convey one of the most powerful, and applicable, aspects of postcolonial theory for translation studies: the relationship between language and power.[23] As is well known, the official language of many nations has little to no purchase in the daily lives of the majority of its citizens. Laws may be debated and passed in a European language inherited from colonialism that has failed to be adopted for daily use by the population. A strong division between written and spoken language may accompany the official/local language split. In his study *The Promise of the Foreign*, Vicente Rafael has shown in the case of the Philippines how the presence of Castilian Spanish, the coloniser's language, appeared as a 'promising' technology for communication across linguistic divides that fragmented the colony – a necessary condition for literary history if it is to be rooted in a culturally unified base.[24] At the same time, use of the coloniser's language called forth a counter-technology of translation to manage and control its proliferation. One of the most interesting examples of the study concerns the 1838 proto-national Tagalog epic, *Florante at Laura*, by Francisco Balagtas. Rafael cites a Balagtas stanza where Spanish phrases are echoed by ones in Tagalog that do not exactly 'translate' the former. In Rafael's reading, Balagtas's practice 'flattens' the two languages and thus points towards a third, missing language that would provide the basis of nation: '[Balagtas] acknowledges that the origins of his poems lie elsewhere. He then comes across like the [Catholic] missionary as a medium for conjuring that elsewhere, bringing it closer in the language of his readers.'[25]

The idea of a 'minor literature', as developed by Gilles Deleuze and Félix Guattari, has also proven fruitful to postcolonial thinking. Interestingly, at one point they revert to PT vocabulary to pin down the slippery concept borrowed from Franz Kafka: 'the majoritarian as a constant and homogeneous system; minorities as subsystems; and the minoritarian as potential, creative and created, becoming'.[26] Translated literature as minority literature can never 'be' at the centre of national literary history, but it is continually in the process of 'becoming' national literature, and may represent the latter's potentiality, as in the concept of pseudotranslation discussed above. To give one example, Sean Cotter has coined the concept of a 'minor Romania' as a basis for asking questions that can usefully be applied to many postcolonial situations:

> Romantic nationalism depends on, but must occlude, translation. Under what conditions, however, could literary translation move to the center of the national imagination? How much would the idea of the nation have to change, in order to create a national translator? The idea is almost a contradiction in terms: a national idea based around a secondary literary practice, authorship without authority.[27]

This contradiction actually happened in Romania under Soviet hegemony, where a variety of political forces caused a national literature to be created in translation: one interesting example is the fact that prominent writers forbidden from publishing original works could at least publish translations.

## CONCLUSION

In conclusion, it is worth looking to the future in considering how two trends may join forces with translation studies to influence literary historiography: comparative and world literature studies; and digital humanities. The fundamental importance of translation to comparative and to world literature needs no elaboration here. World literature in particular can only come into existence through translation. Or, to give the more comprehensive picture, translation is a crucial mediation that transforms what Alexander Beecroft calls the 'epichoric' and 'panchoric' modalities into cosmopolitan literatures.[28] Cosmopolitanism, in its aspects of intercultural communication and critique, polyglottism, and of course translation, represents one of the most important shared spheres of interest between comparative and world literature, one that, in chronological terms, predates the idea of nation that has come to seem intuitive for the construction of compartmentalised literary histories. The twenty-first century has seen a consistent rise in interest in world literature, which naturally brings with it the question of whether we are approaching the edge of a further stage in the process, the attempt at a world literary historiography. If so, then two interrelated questions arise: how to account for translation?; and, how to manage the huge dataset of world literature so as to apprehend it as a gigantic polysystem?

Digital humanities, meaning here the use of 'big data' in humanities research, has developed a variety of methods for visualising the relationships obtaining between literati, a first step in modelling (as opposed to merely theorising) the systematicity of literary interactions. It may be that the kinds of visualisation allowed through computer mediation will turn the abstractions of PT into something more graspable. Prominent studies include Franco Moretti's comparative *Graphs, Maps, and Trees*, Matt Erlin and Lynne Tatlock's *Distant Readings*, which focuses on the German literature and culture of the nineteenth century, and the online *Republic of Letters* project that emphasises French, Italian, English and Spanish writers and scientists of the Enlightenment period.[29] The latter is actually a group of interrelated projects that visualise the relationships between writers of the Enlightenment, or between writers and their publics. Figure 4.1, for example is taken from the interactive, graphic representation of the 'true stated' places of publication of the works of Voltaire from 1712 to 1800. The static screen-capture shows only the places his works were actually published, with the relative size of the circles indicating the relative amount of publication occurring in different places. We see that these include Barcelona, Istanbul, Lisbon and Palermo. On the actual website, a user may apply other filters, such as: the places given on the colophon of the books whether true or not; places of publication known but not stated; places of pseudo-publication and so forth.

Figure 4.1    *Places of Publication of Works by Voltaire, 1712–1800*[30]

One can easily infer that a number of the publications originating outside of French-speaking areas represent translations, an insight that can be confirmed by searching *WorldCat* or the catalogue of the *Bibliothèque Nationale Française*, where the data was extracted in the first place. We find, for example, a translation of the play *Zaïre*, first performed in Paris in 1732, into Portuguese by Pedro Antonio and Antonio Rodrigues Galhardo, published in Lisbon in 1783, and a translation of the same play into Danish by Barthold Johan Lodde that appeared in Copenhagen in 1766.

In sum, the graphic above visualises the diffusion of Voltaire's works, which to some extent involves their translation into other languages. We can discern in this visualisation both the continued invisibility of translation – there is no button for showing translations versus publications in French – and the potential for expansion of the algorithm so as to incorporate translation studies' concerns and interests. One can also imagine a visual that would reveal the publication of Voltaire's works in sequence, as these occur through time. One can imagine additional programming that would get at some of the questions raised by PT. At the same time, it is not entirely clear what questions this particular visualisation is intended to answer, or in what way it may provoke a reprogramming of previously fixed considerations of Voltaire's work – except, of course, that we may return to a point made near the beginning of this entry, concerning the false considerations of a 'national' author. While Voltaire's publications cover nearly the whole of the French hexagon, they also pop up in places spread far and wide. Translation helps make that happen, and reminds us that Voltaire has always been more than just a French author.

Visualisation, for which the above example stands, is but one method in the digital humanities toolbox. Topic modelling, on the other hand, as its name implies, could allow us to compare an original with its translation in terms of how closely the topics identified through machine analysis of the vocabulary in source and target match each other. Translation studies came into being partly due to scholars' dissatisfaction with the individualised critical readings of translation, which proceed text-by-text or at times author-by-author. Judgements on the relative faithfulness or appropriateness of a translation should be foregrounded against the matrix from which it arises, which possesses both synchronic and diachronic aspects. Digital humanities provides convenient methods for describing this matrix, though not the only ones. What is important is that we continue to rethink our methodologies for apprehending the translation effect in literary history.

## FURTHER READING

Bassnett, Susan and André Lefevere. *Constructing Cultures: Essays on Literary Translation*. Clevedon: Multilingual Matters, 1998.

Beebee, Thomas. *Transmesis: Inside Translation's Black Box*. New York: Palgrave Macmillan, 2013.

Dingwaney, Anuradha and Carol Meier, eds. *Between Languages and Cultures*. Pittsburgh: University of Pittsburgh Press, 1995.

Hayes, Julie Chandler. *Translation, Subjectivity and Culture in France and England, 1600–1800*. Stanford: Stanford University Press, 2009.

Hung, Eva, ed. *Translation and Cultural Change: Studies in History, Norms and Image-Projection*. Amsterdam and Philadelphia: J. Benjamins, 2005.

Kaindl, Klaus, and Karlheinz Spitzl, eds. *Transfiction: Research into the Realities of Translation Fiction*. Amsterdam and Philadelphia: J. Benjamins, 2014.

Lowe, Elizabeth and Earl E. Fitz. *Translation and the Rise of Inter-American Literature*. Gainesville: University Press of Florida, 2007.

Robinson, Douglas. *Translation and Empire: Postcolonial Theories Explained.* Manchester: St. Jerome Press, 1997.

Simon, Sherry and Paul St-Pierre, eds. *Changing the Terms: Translating in the Postcolonial Era.* Ottawa: University of Ottawa Press, 2000.

Tymoczko, Maria and Edwin Gentzler, eds. *Translation and Power.* Amherst: University of Massachusetts Press, 2002.

# PART II

# Subjects/Objects

## CHAPTER 5

# Subjects

## Ortwin de Graef

An early draft of the American Declaration of Independence shows a strange smudge. A good number of words in the draft were just crossed out and replaced, but there is one word Thomas Jefferson took pains to fully erase, carefully hiding its trace under the new word 'citizens'. Recent reconstruction using advanced spectral imaging technology has finally solved the mystery of the smudge: the evidence Jefferson tried to destroy in 1776 is the word 'subjects', whose overtones of subservience to monarchical authority evidently jarred with the Declaration's central intent.[1] Around the time Jefferson was busy covering up subjects like a dirty secret, Immanuel Kant was drafting his *Critique of Pure Reason* (1781), the work which arguably consolidated the alternative standard sense of the word 'subject' as denoting free and conscious agents capable of conceiving, articulating and performing an awareness of themselves and other beings – agents distinguished by intentional dispositions and as such receptive in principle to the inalienable rights Jefferson claims for citizens freed from subjection.[2]

The historical coincidence that when the 'modern' subject as an autonomous agent appears to emerge, the subject as a being subservient to autocratic rule begins to fade obviously does not mean that this modern subject actually comes into being for the first time in what we call modernity, nor that its emergence spells the end of subjection. It is not the case that Kant, or Descartes, or whichever alternative master of modernity, produced the modern subject as a being capable of holding, expressing, receiving and acting on intentional dispositions out of the blue and into a future forever free. For if so defined, there is massive evidence of subject activity in premodern times stretching back at least as far as the record of human symbol-crafting skills runs, and much of it occurring under conditions of extreme subjection. What does mark out modernity as different is a substantial modification in the material conditions for subject formation, entailing also a shift in the shades of subjection.

These conditions involve the symbolic technology (prototypically language) humans use to sustain and service intentions. Inasmuch as this technology produces material available for unrestricted circulation through time and space, it alienates humans from their natural condition as animals and institutes the differential possibility of an unrealised future elsewhere. Though unpredictable in principle, in practice the actualisation of this possibility is always circumscribed by the hegemony of homogeny re-naturalising human history. The human animal is a subject of history in at least two distinct but related senses: as a thinking agent projecting itself through time and space by means of symbolic technology, it interferes with the natural order of things and makes history; as a being responsive to the naturalising force of the already-made, it is subject to history – including the history of the technology facilitating its production of unnatural difference, and it is in this respect that Enlightenment modernity in the West can be said to register a decisive difference, encapsulated in the semantic shift between Jefferson's and Kant's use of the term 'subject'.

As a result of processes we need not reconstruct in any real detail here, modernity is distinguished not just by the appeal to *all* humans to boldly take hold of the means of subject-formation (arguably that appeal is also legible in Christianity and most likely in other historical ideologies too), but by the emergence of material conditions that render such an appeal both plausible and compelling. While the identity of the vast majority of individuals in premodern times was sufficiently determined (and rendered uninteresting) by whichever niche of society they happened to be born into, the modern dynamics of destratification, desegmentation and functional differentiation create a society whose subjects are credited, and burdened, with the potential to determine themselves and the duty to register the determination of others.[3] This is not a wishful fantasy of happy harmony and unlimited opportunity for self-made subjects: self-determination indeed imposes a considerable burden on the modern subject. Not only must every attempt at self-determination always negotiate for social space with other such attempts, but the very technology the subject uses to determine him- or herself also always determines her or him in ways that exceed the subject's control. As is already trivially evident in the gendered pronouns in the preceding sentence, language itself pre-formats the subject's field of opportunity – and the apparent binary assignment to gender is only one of the many ways in which the subject's potential for autonomous self-determination is compromised by the heteronomous agency of symbolic structure broadly conceived.

Language is not just a neutral tool with which a putatively pre-existent subject communicates itself to itself and to the world. Rather, it is a system for the circulation and exchange of symbols which performs subjects into existence and makes them available for social inspection, competition and cooperation. Again, the mere fact of this subject formation is not distinctive of modernity; what does characterise the modern condition is the speed and the spread of symbol circulation, the unprecedented increase in the sheer number of participants in the practice of public self-presentation and representation, and the proliferation of ideological apparatuses regulating the interpellation of individuals as subjects.[4] While participation in individual public self-determination under conditions of liberty, equality and reciprocal respect is in principle open to all citizen subjects, the history of the past two centuries or so is not quite the story of the achievement of this regulative ideal – partly because enlightened conditions harbour pockets of darkness where what is other is denied voice, partly because not all that is human can bear being brought to light. The discourse we call literature offers a rich record of this story of subject formation and dysformation. It explores new forms of acting and being human, but also seeks to sustain the shock to human being as the spectre of universal equality takes on differences in class, gender, race and species. Most importantly, perhaps, literature typically effects this work of mediation and exploration in the mode of performative simulation rather than analytical conceptualisation: instead of describing agency and reflection in general, it approximates the embodied experience of singular acts and thoughts of subjects exemplifying only themselves but always also signifying others.

## CLASS

William Wordsworth's Preface to the 1800 edition of the *Lyrical Ballads* (1798) is a poetical manifesto for literature as an experimental engagement with the modern condition. The challenge Wordsworth sets himself is to use 'a selection of the real language of men' to explore 'incidents and situations from common life' with a view to producing poetic 'pleasure' as well as a sense of 'worthy purpose' true to 'the primary laws of our nature'. Resolutely rejecting the 'arbitrary and capricious habits of expression'[5] characteristic of all-too-sophisticated salon culture, Wordsworth proposes to reinvent literature as the representation of common humanity in common language, and the subjects he rounds up for these experiments bear witness to his democratic sympathies at the time: a vagrant, a beggar, a mad mother, a childless father, an idiot boy, a forsaken Indian woman and the wandering Jew, to name just a few. Yet the dominant subject in the *Lyrical Ballads* is the middle-class poet himself. Most of the texts in *Lyrical Ballads* stage a middle-class speaker, while those poems that do impersonate the voice of their marginal subjects also largely do so for the purpose of middle-class moral-sentimental therapy. To simply accuse Wordsworth of self-serving bourgeois bad faith would be to miss the point, though. As is most obviously clear from poems like 'Simon Lee' and 'We Are Seven', the risk of falseness in the appropriation of the supposedly natural voices of 'low and rustic life'[6] is a critical challenge Wordsworth's experimental method precisely aims to address. The extent to which he fails to fully avoid such falseness is less an accidental shortcoming than a structural symptom of the intractabilities of cross-class identification which underscores the restricted access to public speech space for the dispossessed and thereby qualifies the fantasies of full equality lingering on in the aftermath of the French revolution. Some two centuries on, it is the uncomfortable legacy of Wordsworth's failure that gives novels like Irvine Welsh's *Trainspotting* (1993) or Alan Warner's *Morvern Callar* (1995) the critical edge distinguishing them from the middle-class slumming spree they flirt with.

While the participation of the underprivileged in public practices of subject-formation remains a challenge rather than an achievement, the successful accession to self-expression for middle-class subjects is not quite self-evident either. Arguably the central literary vehicle here is the *Bildungsroman*, the novel of formation or education, which typically features a slightly naïve young adult negotiating compromises in social space that end up yielding a sense of chastened selfhood or 'character'. The model of the genre is Goethe's *Wilhelm Meister's Apprenticeship* (1795–96), but it is instructive to also recall Goethe's earlier *The Sorrows of Young Werther* (1774), even if only because its hero's notoriously infectious self-termination dramatically emphasises the risks attending self-determination and the extent to which successful subject-formation involves discipline and the abnegation of both desire and despair. The successfully formed middle-class subject is not only a citizen of character but also subject to society, and although such slightly wistful subjection in classic *Bildungsromane* like Dickens's *Great Expectations* (1861) generally appears as the reasonable price to pay for social stability and respectability, post-classic variations on the genre tend to dispel this ideological accommodation. An unashamedly overwrought case in point is Alasdair Gray's *Lanark: A Life in Four Books* (1981) which wraps up a dispiritingly bleak rewrite of James Joyce's *A Portrait of the Artist as a Young Man* (1916), ending in the artist-protagonist's suicide, inside a dystopian fantasy of an eerily familiar dysfunctional SuperState.

If the commitment to a narrative arc approximating closure that informs the realist novel makes it particularly receptive to accounts of society's compromises with its subjects, the relative looseness of the long introspective lyric allows sustained explorations of uneventful unhappiness lived by badly finished subjects inheriting the curse of the Beautiful Soul ridiculed by Hegel in his *Phenomenology of Spirit* (1807). The great Odes written by John Keats in the final years of his short life are poignantly ironic instances of such abortive introspection, modulating the more spasmodic moans they inherit from S. T. Coleridge's 'Dejection' (1802) and fading into the weary lassitude of Matthew Arnold's 'The Buried Life' (1852). It is noteworthy that both Coleridge and Arnold give up poetry fairly early in their career and instead of further indulging in the painful pleasures of failed subject-formation turn themselves into public intellectuals writing on education and the State with a view to designing a civic curriculum intended to achieve at the level of public institutions what their poetry failed to deliver and what a genre like the *Bildungsroman* envisages in the privacy of reading. As Coleridge writes in *On the Constitution of Church and State* (1830), the task of the intellectual is 'to form and train up the people of the country to obedient, free, useful, organisable subjects, citizens and patriots, living to the benefit of the state, and prepared to die for its defence'.[7] Coleridge's vision of patriotic self-sacrifice partly bespeaks the hangover of his initial enthusiastic support for the (French) revolution but it also captures the nineteenth-century upsurge of nationalism as the ideology of collective subject-formation in imagined communities facilitated by the increased circulation of print.[8] Arnold's programme for the formation of subjects in *Culture and Anarchy* (1869), in contrast, is an early instance of the resistance to nationalism in the name of culture (Arnold's translation for the notion of *Bildung*) and favours support for what he calls the 'aliens', humans who configure their identity not in terms of nation or class but with reference to their 'best self' – a royally vague notion rendered intriguingly more productive and democratic through the specification that whatever is 'best' depends on a subjective judgement inviting assent or objection, engaging and affecting the subject of judgement and thereby cultivating difference instead of fostering sectarian dissent, imposing national identity or subjecting judgement to the certitude regime of natural science.[9]

## GENDER

The lyric as practised by Coleridge, Keats, Arnold and many romantic and post-romantic poets, in line with the genre of the lyric going back to antiquity, typically features a first-person voice you could be forgiven for mistaking as the voice of the poet. Most *Bildungsromane*, too, at least keep plausible the uncritical assumption that the central protagonist is somehow close to the author and thus feed the notion, as with the standard lyric, that the subject under formation in its discourse is one its author identifies with as a version of him- or herself which the reader, in turn, is invited to identify with vicariously. Drama is different: a typical modern play gives up the authorial commentary of the chorus in ancient tragedy and must make all characters comprehensible and credible in their own right, no matter how nasty. We admire Shakespeare for giving vivid voice to the vicious piece of shit Iago in *Othello*, but we identify his voice as our own in his love sonnets. Who is this 'we', though? Mostly men? Gay men are arguably included, because the sonnets entertain heterodox sexual leanings. But women? Because Shakespeare somehow speaks meta-gender love language? Says who? That is the question.

The genre of the dramatic lyric or dramatic monologue takes up that question. It is basically a lyric whose author explores and exploits her or his difference from the lyrical I. Much as Shakespeare can be imagined not wanting to be confused with Iago while still taking credit for his voice, authors of dramatic monologues engage in a complicated dialectic of impersonation and responsibility. Yet in the dramatic monologue there is no developed cast of further *dramatis personae* through which the author can configure discursive space: just one voice performed into a subject in the language of a text produced by a subject self-deprived of counter-voice. The most demanding and rewarding dramatic monologues are those in which the assumed distance between author and character is inversely proportional to the fit between language and character. Robert Browning's 'Porphyria' (1836), for instance, gives voice to a man recounting how his secret lover, a woman of higher social status, left a party she was attending that night to visit him, upon which he strangled her. We don't need Browning to tell us strangling girlfriends is not nice. Instead, he invites us to entertain the desire that drives to murder. Humans, if given the chance, are driven by desire more than need – as is Porphyria's lover, who kills his girlfriend precisely because he is in need and desires requited desire, no matter how imaginary, to achieve subjecthood, the power to say 'I am'.[10] Or more specifically: 'I attain masculinity when I overcome subjection to female agency and become the man I always already was.'[11] The poem stages male subject-formation as a violent claim to recognition: in its minimal narrative set-up, the male lover recovers from his initial condition of passive neediness by usurping Porphyria's agency, literally killing her in the process. What makes the poem arresting is the precision of its inscription in the long history of aestheticised gynocide: initially remarkably unremarkable in diction, the speaker waxes 'poetic' as soon as Porphyria is dead and available for re-imagination as an object of his deadly desire. To recall a chilling pun Browning plays in another of his murder monologues, 'My Last Duchess' (1842), the speaker's 'skill / In speech'[12] is achieved as killing speech: the male subject articulates his gendered identity as dominant agent and arbiter of discourse in a disarticulation of the female into figments of his imagination. The poem ends on the speaker's exclamation 'And yet God has not said a word!'[13] – echoing the absence of an authorial judgement on the part of the poet which would only cover up his uncomfortable implication in the gender trouble the poem performs. A later version of the poem is retitled 'Porphyria's Lover' and presented as a record from a 'madhouse cell', possibly in a belated attempt to make up for this missing cover-up, but effectively diagnosing the darkly underexamined undercurrents informing heterogendered sane subjectivity.

Literary discourse here unfolds as an experimental environment for the performance of gendered subjectivity as a coded protocol of repeated ritual positionings. The extent to which this experiment can or should spill over into felt experience depends as much on the design of the experiment as on the identificatory faculties and flexibilities of the participants, on their relation to current and abandoned gender regimes, on crossed lines creating sparks of enlightening difference, on lines that cannot or must not be crossed, on limits to liberties taken and denied. Like 'Porphyria', D. H. Lawrence's dramatic monologue 'Cruelty and Love' (1913) registers the unsettling insistence of death in desire but complicates the set-up by re-imagining the violence in gendered subject-formation as anxious gynosuicidal fantasy. The voice of the poem is given to a woman waiting for the return of, presumably, her husband as twilight falls. She imagines him sauntering home striking fear in the wildlife around, snapping the neck of a rabbit he has snared, and then he enters and she is snared in turn:

> And down his mouth comes to my mouth! And down
> His bright dark eyes come over me, like a hood
> Upon my mind! His lips meet mine, and a flood
> Of sweet fire sweeps across me, so I drown
> Against him, die, and find death good.[14]

His dark invasion of her being is deepened in Lawrence's masterful occupation of her mind as he wills her to want this, confirming ideological stereotypes of the female as the naturally submissive animal, while lending her the high language of courtly oxymoron to draw her death desire as an agent of drowning. To dismiss this as merely a typical male fantasy of female desire is to miss the point; to understand it as an ideologically compromised exploration of what it might mean to be female by an agent of penetration is better; the challenge is to read it as one attempt to experience sexual difference in the making. The original title of the poem seeks to pre-empt the first and the second response but remains in the ambit of the judgemental; the ironical title Lawrence gave it in 1928, 'Love on the Farm', leaves the text to the reader: inviting him to participate in its audacious test of the imagination, enabling her to register resistance to its brutal appropriations, demanding both to at least entertain its attention.

For all its engagement with the darknesses in desire, Lawrence's language is confidently assertive in its assumption of the purchase of the imagination on the other. J. M. Coetzee's 1999 novel *Disgrace*, in contrast, exposes the abject facilities and failures of the identificatory imagination, most harrowingly in its protagonist's traumatic non-experience of the rape of his daughter by a group of men: 'he can, if he concentrates, if he loses himself, be there, be the men, inhabit them, fill them with the ghost of himself. The question is, does he have it in him to be the woman?'[15] The question is also: does he have it in him to be the men as the black men they are.

## RACE

We're all classed somewhere in society; we're all somewhere on the gender spectrum, off and on; and then there is race – or rather, the unstable raft of biological and cultural features socio-ideologically configured as innate group identity affecting subjectivity. Just as gender does not reduce to biological objectivity, so race does not boil down to natural fact, though that is precisely what happens in the fantasmatic naturalisations of difference as objective hierarchical distinction informing sexism and racism. Both these ideologies of othering involve a sinister systematic restriction of the claim to autonomous subjecthood: women and non-whites are denied the self-determining speech of the white male subject, leaving non-white women doubly deprived. As Gayatri Spivak remarks in her seminal essay in postcolonial theory 'Can the Subaltern Speak?' (1988): 'If, in the contest of colonial production, the subaltern has no history and cannot speak, the subaltern as female is even more deeply in shadow.'[16] Spivak's work is a sustained deconstruction of the wishful fantasy that well-meaning white civilisation is in and of itself the light that will dispel these shadows to bless the subaltern with speech, a fantasy often taking shape in the name of women's liberation, and for which she has coined the sentence: 'White men are saving brown women from brown men' – a slogan reflecting colonialism's all too human face.[17]

As the modern white West expanded its colonial reach, both imperially and accidentally, it predictably encountered the shadows and the darkness of non-speech produced by its own pretensions of enlightened enterprise. It found what its science had already invented as the unintelligible non-subject and set about its business of subject-engineering: both subjecting native populations under colonial rule to facilitate resource exploitation, and forcing selected natives into routines of subject-formation rooted in white culture, consigning others to the darkness of their own unculture. Joseph Conrad's *Heart of Darkness* (1899, 1902) remains one of the most unreadable records of this unfinished business. Its central character is Marlow, who entertains his four companions on board a boat anchored in the Thames with reminiscences of his employment as a captain working for a Belgian colonial trading company, leading to an expedition up the Congo river to meet a Mr Kurtz, a high-ranking employee of the company with a remit from the International Society for the Suppression of Savage Customs. As it seems to turn out, Kurtz has gone native with a difference, setting up some sort of cult in his own honour involving various excesses of violence. When Marlow reaches Kurtz, he finds him terminally ill and manages to get him on board for the journey home, but Kurtz dies before they have cleared the Congo and Marlow is left with the mission to break the bad news to Kurtz's fiancée.

The novel or novella is unreadable for the racism it exudes, for the unavailability of a clear perspective in the text which judges this racism, and for the space it reserves for the unracist speech it withholds.[18] In his powerfully contentious lecture 'An Image of Africa: Racism in Conrad's *Heart of Darkness*' (1975), the Nigerian novelist Chinua Achebe diagnoses racist streaks in the text in compelling detail. As a creator of fiction himself, Achebe is obviously aware that attitudes in a text's narrator need not coincide with convictions held by its author, and he acknowledges Conrad's complex construction of multiple nested narrators. Yet in the absence of 'an alternative frame of reference by which we may judge the actions and opinions of his characters', for Achebe Conrad nonetheless stands revealed as 'a thoroughgoing racist'.[19] His prime evidence is that the text withholds 'human expression' from its black characters, most significantly so in the pointed contrast between Kurtz's white fiancée's articulate mourning when Marlow visits her upon his return and the 'savage and superb, wild-eyed and magnificent [ ] brooding'[20] of Kurtz's presumed African mistress who watches from the bank of the river as they take Kurtz away: 'It is clearly not part of Conrad's purpose to confer language on the "rudimentary souls" of Africa.'[21] Achebe's noble indignation is entirely justified as far as the narrators are concerned, and as in the dramatic monologue it is fuelled by the absence of articulate authorial judgement. But even if Conrad was indeed a racist, as he may well have been, his text includes a scene that interrupts its racist streaks of speech-deprivation. It may not meet Achebe's requirements for a clear and adequate 'alternative frame of reference', but it very precisely questions the very notion of conferring language on the '"rudimentary souls" of Africa' that haunts Achebe's own postcolonial thought.

Just after the scene with Kurtz's 'savage and superb' mistress, Marlow recounts how one of Kurtz's dubious associates hinted at his earlier conflicts with this woman:

> She got in some day and kicked up a row about those miserable rags I picked up in the storeroom to mend my clothes with. I wasn't decent. At least it must have been that, for she talked like a fury to Kurtz for an hour, pointing at me now and then. I don't understand the dialect of this tribe. Luckily for me, I fancy Kurtz felt too ill that day to care, or there would have been mischief. I don't understand... No – it's too much for me. Ah, well, it's all over now.[22]

Covered in three layers of uncomprehending narration, this scene does deliver an image of Africa Achebe's denunciation denies: a black female subject speaking her own language in a passionate demand for justice from a white man who understands her and whom she trusts to protect her from another white man who knows he has reasons to fear retribution. White man fails to save black woman from white man.

The subaltern does not speak directly, but her unreadable speech opens the undecidable space of promise compromised by oppression and exploitation but also always still awaiting the encounter of subjects in human justice.

## SPECIES

If subjective self-determination is considered the inalienable right of human beings, and racism, sexism and classism are violations of our common humanity, the comfortable humanism that denounces these violations and champions the right to subjecthood for the non-white non-men non-rich may yet have to face charges of speciesism. Moreover, in its very denial of subjecthood to other species, it tends to set up a normative understanding of subjectivity that excludes many beings with a good claim to humanity.

There is of course a long and weird history of non-or-not-quite-human subjects in human culture, ranging from mythical animism over mainstream monotheism to all manner of fantasy fanfare involving zombies, vampires, aliens, androids, cyborgs, hobbits and rabbits. Yet the vast majority of these imagined others are more of the same: the non-human subject is either a part of the real onto which the anthropomorphic imagination projects itself, or it is a standard human subject in fancy dress. But what exactly constitutes a standard human subject?

Current cognitive science suggests that one distinctive feature of the neurotypical human subject is the ability to entertain thick representations of the mental state of other humans as keys to understanding their behaviour: we explain what we see someone do by making up what this behaviour means to them. We read their mind, as they say, where 'reading' can mean mirror neurons firing in the sadness sector of our brain when we see tears bringing us to tears, or the intricately articulate construction of spite or suspicion scenarios to overrule our kneejerk neuro-reactions, or anything in between and beyond. That humans typically have this so-called 'Theory of Mind' or 'ToM' (the assumption that other humans do indeed have a mind worth knowing) indicates it is an evolutionary adaptation: without some means of monitoring what our conspecifics mean and feel, we just wouldn't be the hypersocial animals with highly developed mental time-travelling faculties we are. But once more: who is this 'we'?

The commonly accepted conceptualisation of 'mind-reading' or 'Theory of Mind' is in large measure influenced by research on autism as a condition in which this faculty is deficient.[23] The extent of this deficiency varies widely, so it has become customary to speak of 'autism spectrum disorder', but the disorder does always appear to involve some impairment in the processing of mental states. Understanding this impairment is an important therapeutic imperative, but it also raises theoretical issues about standard cognitive processing that may bring about, quite literally, a change of mind. This, in turn, can feed back into the regime of therapy, but it also affects the study of the sustained exercises in mind-reading we call fiction.[24]

A more sophisticated understanding of the ways in which human beings in general construct scripts to capture and manage their interaction with other human beings in a jointly mentifactured world is obviously valuable to narratology as a discipline that seeks technical descriptions of the architecture of fiction. If fiction is to achieve the suspension of disbelief it needs to work, it must trigger tried and tested cognitive routines involving intuition, second-guessing, *skepsis* and trust. Increased psychoscientific precision in the understanding of these routines helps to upgrade the narratological toolkit to trace them. As it happens, and ultimately unsurprisingly, this toolkit often turns out to be pretty sophisticated already: after all, in a discipline that took shape in formal analyses of the morphology of folk tales[25] and was decisively formed in a sustained reading of Proust's *A la recherche du temps perdu* (1913–1927)[26] you would expect a certain amount of expertise in the nuts and bolts of human worldmaking.

Yet the cognitive turn in cultural scholarship does offer rich challenges for literary studies. In terms of literary history, a good instance of this is the study of the emergence of a public discourse to articulate autism. As Ian Hacking has argued, over the past decades fiction has proven to be a remarkably powerful tool to explore what it is like to be mind-blind.[27] While much of this writing is in danger of simplification and typecasting, it does also contribute to the creation of a genuinely public non-specialist language enabling the expression of neurodiversity. Literary scholarship is ideally suited to trace the fine detail of these new languages and to map their interaction with alternative discourses across diverse media. Moreover, as autism spectrum disorder is substantially a genetic condition, it must have affected subjects living before it was diagnosed: the challenge here is to reread the record of human mind-writing to recover traces of insight into the precariousness of mind-reading – evidence for the extent to which an engagement with thoughts and feelings of self and others is far from self-evident. This is not just a matter of hunting for identifiable 'idiots', 'imbeciles', 'retards' and other 'misfits' in prediagnostic literature; instead, the task is to read writing that avoids such confining classifications and attempts characterisations of neurodiversity that do justice to difference by denaturalising the same.[28] Rather than denying subjectivity or indeed humanity to humans with mind-reading deficiencies, such writing makes real again the fictitiousness of the psycho-social fabric enveloping all human subjects yet which humanist ideology typically serves to deny.

Like the study of any impairment, autism spectrum disorder research yields insight into processes we take for granted and has the potential to defamiliarise neurotypical routines of empathy and identification. Yet conversely, cognitive neuroscience investigating these routines in their own right tends to court neuronormalisation, containing the unlikeliness of sophisticated intersubjective attending in essentialist constructs developed under controlled conditions. Here the challenge for literary studies is to insist on raising the bar by demanding appraisals of the complexities of human consciousness in overdetermined conditions outside the laboratory. Such insistence will only work when literary scholars take time to study the wealth of experimental evidence that has been produced inside the laboratory – pretty much like literary scholars in the 1970s engaged with late-Freudian Lacanian psychoanalysis to the point where they could productively find it wanting in the name of writing, as in Shoshana Felman's *La Folie et la chose littéraire* (1978). For instance, literary scholarship should take seriously recent cognitive science research indicating that reading literary fiction improves 'Theory of Mind' and enhances brain connectivity.[29] But it should take it seriously enough to resist inflated neuro-ideological claims for literary 'ToM'-training as a programme for planetary empathy and eternal peace. Not because literary discourse does not exercise mind-reading but because indeed it does and has been doing so for a very long time – as an exercise in *reading*, precisely, and that practice, if sustained, does not reproduce the comforting common sense of how alike we all are but rather invites us to acknowledge how unlikely we are as a species of subjects.

Not all literature solicits such acknowledgement. Much of the cultural production we call literature rehearses and rehashes what we have come to expect of ourselves and others, thereby consolidating a largely unreflective common sense humanism sufficiently flexible to allow pragmatism to suspend prejudice so we can pretend we're all human. Literary scholarship must recognise the vast amount of socio-cultural labour this consensualist humanist literature has achieved, but it cannot afford not to investigate the first principles of this pretence. The data for such investigations are available in literary writing that eschews what we have come·to expect and applies itself to inventing new registers for recording subjectivity, responding both to inadequacies in standard practice and to the changing configurations of culture. A standard example of such deviation from the standard is the so-called 'stream of consciousness' in modernist writing from the early decades of the twentieth century, notoriously instantiated in Molly Bloom's long reverie at the close of James Joyce's *Ulysses* (1922) and in the various minds voiced in William Faulkner's *The Sound and the Fury* (1929). Literary scholarship can trace the lineage of such techniques back to earlier modern experiments with consciousness like the dramatic monologue, measure the extent to which these techniques enter the mainstream, document resistance and alternatives, and in doing so record the emerging posthumanism always under deconstruction in writing, testing, reading, interrupting, under-standing. Such testing occurred, for instance, in William Gibson's *Neuromancer* (1984), whose explorations of cyberconsciousness are much easier for the third-millennium matrix-literate readers it helped to form than for its initial audience. Prepped though it might have been by Philip K. Dick, David Mitchell's *Ghostwritten* (1999) disconnects the trope of disembodied consciousness from the matrix and plugs it back into the ancient discourse of spectres and souls by inventing a 'noncorp' narrator reminding its readers that the unlife of language, and therefore humanity, is not a twentieth-century consequence of cybertechnology but rather its condition of possibility; more recently, audacious revampings of non-non-human streams of consciousness in works like Will Self's *Umbrella* (2012) and Eimear McBride's *A Girl Is a Half-formed Thing* (2013) have further made strange our appearance in print as a species whose being is being read.

## FURTHER READING

Cadava, Eduardo, Peter Connor and Jean-Luc Nancy, eds. *Who Comes After the Subject?* New York: Routledge, 1991.

De Libera, Alain. *Archéologie du sujet, I: Naissance du sujet.* Paris: Vrin (Bibliothèque d'histoire de la philosophie), 2007.

De Libera, Alain. *Archéologie du sujet, II: La Quête de l'identité*. Paris: Vrin (Bibliothèque d'histoire de la philosophie), 2008.

Hall, Donald E. *Subjectivity*. New York: Routledge (The New Critical Idiom), 2004.

Hayles, N. Katherine. *How We Became Posthuman: Virtual Bodies in Cybernetics, Literature and Informatics*. Chicago: University of Chicago Press, 1999.

Robbins, Ruth. *Subjectivity*. Houndmills: Palgrave Macmillan, 2005.

Spivak, Gayatri Chakravorty. *A Critique of Postcolonial Reason: Toward a History of the Vanishing Present*. Cambridge, MA: Harvard University Press, 1999.

Taylor, Charles. *Sources of the Self: The Making of the Modern Identity*. Cambridge, MA: Harvard University Press, 1989.

Thiel, Udo. *The Early Modern Subject: Self-consciousness and personal identity from Descartes to Hume*. Oxford: Oxford University Press, 2011.

Zunshine, Lisa. *Why We Read Fiction: Theory of Mind and the Novel*. Columbus: Ohio State University Press, 2006.

## CHAPTER 6

# Senses

## Michel Delville

Western culture has not treated the senses equally. For a long time, the 'lower' senses of smell, taste and – to a lesser extent – touch were relegated to the lowest positions in the hierarchy, excluded from the realm of aesthetic judgement, and disqualified by the vast majority of thinkers on account of their proximity to the object studied or described. The lower or 'proximal' senses, it was felt until recently, were just too close physically to their objects to produce valuable, shareable knowledge. Thus, for Kant, the eating or smelling subject is barred from any real knowledge of things comestible or smellable because it belongs to the realm of the private and the subjective and cannot lead the mind to universal truths such as would be required in the development of aesthetic judgement. According to such a view, all our taste buds and olfactory receptors can do is convey fugitive impressions and sensations which are too intimate and private to carry any broader, transpersonal significance; only the 'superior' senses of sight and hearing are deemed capable of transcending particular sensual experience. For Hegel too, the exclusion of the proximal senses from the realm of cognition, meaning and representation is justified by their lack of distance from the objects studied. Typically, Hegel's idealism prioritises the theoretical senses of sight and hearing to the detriment of the practical and bodily operations of the proximal senses: it is the physical intimacy shared by subject and object which disqualifies smell, taste and touch from any claim to spiritual or conceptual apprehension. The sense of closeness one experiences when smelling scents or tasting food precludes the critical distance between the subject and the object, the perceiver and the perceived, which allows objective pronouncements to be made, especially in the context of Hegel's conception of art as an operation of the spirit becoming conscious of itself. This open disdain of philosophy for everything connected with the proximal senses characterises all forms of philosophical idealism (Plato went so far as to accuse food of distracting man from thought); it presupposes the belief that gustative sensations and stimuli are, to a large extent, circular, intransitive and self-directed; that they can only refer us back to what the world tastes or smells like, not to what it means; nor can they contribute to our sense of who and what we are.[1]

The general valorisation of visual perception and verbal representation from Plato to Hegel and beyond is hardly challenged by the main branches of empiricist and sensualist thought: for all his insistence that existence and knowledge are rooted in sensation, Locke still regards vision as the noblest sense, and even Condillac's *Traité des sensations* dismisses smell and taste as unable to distinguish between self and world unless they are combined with sight, hearing or touch. It was not until recently that cultural historians and literary critics began to challenge dominant auditory- and ocular-centrist models. At a time when the body has clearly moved to the centre stage of gender theory, anthropology and cultural studies alike, it is hardly surprising that literary historiography has been impacted by the ever-expanding corpus of post-Freudian, post-Bakhtinian and post-Deleuzian theory about corporeality, from Foucault's *History of Sexuality* to Judith Butler's *Bodies That Matter*, both of which argue, in different but related ways, for a reconsideration of the body itself as a discursive and social construct in the field of exercise of dominant institutions of knowledge and power. Other related examples include Donna Haraway's posthuman biopolitics, not to mention the emergence of new research fields specifically related to the study of the human sensorium such as food studies (Madeleine Ferrières, Carole Counihan), affect theory (Gregory Seigworth and Melissa Gregg) and sensory studies (David Howes, Constance Classen). The recent publication of monographs stressing the importance of representations of bodily experience and sensory materialism in a particular period of literary history (e.g., William Cohen's *Embodied: Victorian Literature and the Senses* and Timothy Morton's *Cultures of Taste/ Theories of Appetite: Eating Romanticism*) and of diachronic accounts devoted to a particular sense (e.g., Hans J. Rindisbacher's *The Smell of Books*, Charles Bernstein's *Close Listening: Poetry and the Performed Word* and Denise Gigante's *Taste A Literary History*) indicates that scholars are increasingly drawn to the representation of the body and the functions of the senses and emotions in the production and reception of literary meaning as well as in the development of new theories and models of literary historiography.

## BEYOND AND BENEATH SOUND AND VISION

The history of literature is full of evidence that the world cannot be experienced exclusively through sight and that it can resist the power of the eye to become what Wordsworth describes in the 1805 *Prelude* as 'the most despotic of the senses'.[2] Although certain literary forms have participated more than others in apprehending the full range of the human sensorium (e.g., literary representations of olfactory and gustatory perceptions are more likely to abound, say, in the French realist or naturalist novel as handled by Balzac, Hugo or Zola than in other genres and movements), literature in general throughout its history has drawn attention to how the lower senses have an unequalled potential to overwhelm and destabilise, but also to enrich and complexify human perception. In a cultural environment which privileges the 'verbivocovisual' (or what Hegel called 'the two theoretical senses of sight and hearing'[3]), the proximal senses of taste and smell return with a vengeance once they begin to invade our body and consciousness: one can close one's eyes or block one's ears to avoid seeing or hearing something unpleasant, but smells and flavours invade the body's sensory organs in a way which cannot be easily and promptly warded off.

This is particularly true of the second half of the nineteenth century and the first half of the twentieth, when the desacralised body begins to be perceived by some as an 'organic factory' whose capricious whims and demanding cries must be heard and cannot be contained or controlled. (One is reminded of Plato's foundational attempt, in *Timaeus*, to contain the excesses of the body by confining aesthetic experience to the head and partitioning the body off the mind through the isthmus of the neck.) Literary examples abound of this kind of exploratory, 'materiological' writing of the viscera. One might think, for instance, of the 'Lestrygonians' chapter of *Ulysses*, which exposes the body's peristaltic mechanisms with a meticulous irony, describing man as an unfinished creature dominated by chemical and mechanical processes beyond his control. More generally, Joyce's *Ulysses* investigates the full potential of the five senses as potential gateways to (self-)knowledge. More often than not, such a perspective conveys the failure of self-possession and psychological integration in a context which inevitably questions the boundaries of self and world, nature and culture, at the same time as it forces us to consider ourselves as unfinished creatures. Over the last centuries, many writers have recognised a similar process of demystification of the boundaried self which results in a struggle between the longing for freedom and the need for containment and, more generally, between closed and open form. This realisation, which necessarily upsets our sense of ourselves as self-contained living beings, reveals the impact of the perverse and the abject and unearths the full complexity of the human body's mechanics. Like Rabelais', Swift's or Joyce's scatological grotesques, it confronts the crass effects of incorporation and expulsion, engaging in obscene (in the literal sense of what is usually hidden from sight) speculation about the shifting boundaries and destinies of self and world.

## SEEING IS BELIEVING

Constance Classen has remarked that 'the photographic nature of much of twentieth-century representation helps maintain [an] aura of objectivity by appearing to provide the viewer with direct access to reality, rather than only mediating reality'.[4] The dominance of visual models and representations thus seems to be linked with an attempt to create the illusion that visual imagery can provide viewers with an unmediated, transparent access to knowledge, which is a curious notion when one considers that, unlike the lower 'contact senses' of touch and taste, sight necessarily functions at a distance from its object and requires an external medium (light) to operate. Clearly, these are some of the assumptions that recent developments in sensory studies – whether of the aesthetic (Gigante, Cohen), philosophical (Korsmeyer) or cultural-historical (Howes, Classen) variety – have sought to invalidate by stressing the necessity to rehabilitate the lower senses as organising principles in our conceptualisation of perceptual experience. As Classen and others have shown, however, this is not a completely unprecedented phenomenon. Aristotle, who associated the five senses with the four elements (sight with water, hearing with air, smell with fire and taste and touch with earth), hypothesised the existence of a 'common sense' responsible for collecting and 'relating together the data from all the senses and produc[ing] an impression of an entire object'.[5] Even though he maintains a (highly gendered) hierarchical distinction between the higher arts of sight and hearing (the visual arts, poetry and music) and the lower, physiological arts of cooking, fashion and perfumery – whose main function is to provide immediate sensory gratification – Aristotle, unlike Plato, does not dismiss bodily pleasure as an obstacle to knowledge. In his *Spiritual Exercises* (1522–24), St Ignatius of Loyola also urges his followers to use all their senses in apprehending the multisensorial atrocities of hell:

> The first [exercise] will be to see with the eyes of the imagination those great fires, and the souls as it were in bodies of fire. The second will be to hear with the ears of the imagination the wailings, the howlings, the cries… The third will be to smell the smoke, the sulphur, the filth, and the putrid matter. The fourth will be to taste with the taste of the imagination bitter things, such as tears, sadness, and the worm of conscience. The fifth will be to feel with the touch of the imagination how those fires touch and burn the souls.[6]

A full-length account of practical and theoretical contributions to a counter-history to the hierarchical sensorium would have to consider not only Loyola but a whole range of works as diverse as Rabelais' *Gargantua and Pantagruel* cycle (1532–53), Helen Keller's *The Story of My Life* (1903), F. T. Marinetti's manifestoes of 'Tactilism' (1921) and 'Futurist Cooking' (1930) and Gertrude Stein's *Tender Buttons* (1914). Whereas the culinary experiments of the Italian futurists took food into the domain of the performative and the theatrical, Stein's 'cubist' literary still-lifes stimulate the reader's appetite for things which are neither completely inside us nor completely outside us and therefore address a number of fundamental issues related to the boundaries of the lyric self and its discourse. Through its exploration of the senses of smell, touch and taste, Stein's idiosyncratic use of abstraction in *Tender Buttons* challenges the then dominant visual and auditory modes of poetic expression, which of course included imagism – which was at its heyday when Stein began to work on her collection – and the more radical 'verbivocovisual' experiments of the modernist avant-garde. As Stein reminds us, 'a clatter is not a smell',[7] and 'Roastbeef' – the opening poem of the 'Food' section of the collection – pronounces itself in favour of a kind of writing which seeks to capture the transsensory metamorphoses of objects and whose main subject matter is less the object itself than the very mechanics of perception and meaning. Christopher Knight has contended that Stein's prose largely follows the 'classical premises of perception', an 'episteme which privileges analysis and discrimination' as well as a three-dimensional view of space and a linear view of time.[8] The main textual 'evidence' provided by Knight to support the privileging of looking in the book is the special status it bestows upon 'appearance and color':[9] 'Repeatedly, Stein […] speaks of things as being seen. For example, in "A Piece of Coffee", she writes, "The Sight of a reason, the same sightslighter, the sight of a simpler negative answer, the same sore sounder, the intention to wishing, the same splendor, the same furniture".[10] Surely one would expect ocular perception to play an important part in a collection essentially devoted to the 'observation' of everyday objects. But a closer look at this passage from 'A Piece of Coffee' suggests that the poem, far from privileging visual perception to the detriment of other senses, shows that any attempt to separate vision from other ways of apprehending the world is ultimately pointless and self-limiting. Only a 'sightslighter' (the word would seem to suggest an indifferent or careless observer) would separate sight from reason because perception is always already an act of interpretation leading to more or less simple or complex 'answer[s]'. In the same passage, this recognition of the necessary interaction between the senses extends to the senses of touch and hearing (at least if we assume that the words 'answer' and 'sounder' refer to the production of sound). The establishment of such a democracy of the senses in Stein's *Tender Buttons* is strengthened by the use of multiple puns and alliterations which tend to mix and 'level down' the different sense levels and registers. It emerges as the opposite of the hierarchical system promoted by the classical episteme Knight defines, via Foucault's *The Order of Things*, as 'a space of order'[11] in which sight is 'the means to an analysis *partes extra partes* acceptable to everyone'.[12] In order to achieve these goals, Stein develops a micropoetics of sensory experience which investigates the very fabric of edible objects. Once the inanimate becomes animated, the relation between materiality and meaning becomes a relation in movement, a system of 'spreading', a description in the act of becoming meaningful, poised between an atomist view emphasising the irreducible integrity of matter and a metapoetic stance which confers meaning to things through their physical interaction with the observer/feeler/smeller/taster. Stein's vignettes thus focus on the physical properties of objects at the same time as they insist on their potential for being abstracted from the world of matter and transformed into sense impressions.

## FROM TASTE TO GASTROESTHETICS

The growing success of food studies and its various 'gastrosophical' extensions over the last quarter century is bound up with a theory of consciousness which falls halfway between knowing and tasting; a theory which encompasses those moments when food crosses over into discourse and thus leads to a fundamental reconsideration of the relation between body and world. Timothy Morton and Denise Gigante's respective transdisciplinary examinations of the culture of consumption organising romantic literature interrogate the connections between incorporation and introjection while redefining orality as the space where speech and food meet and interact. Whether they are carried out within the realm of cultural studies, anthropology or literary criticism, such projects are aimed at a global, transdisciplinary poetics of the lower senses, attempts to tease out a particular relation to consciousness, a relation characterised by a desire not simply to report on sensory experience, but also to render it intelligible to the reader. As Gigante programmatically puts it, the sheer scope offered by the literary history of taste extends beyond the mere study of 'food in literature' and forays into broader cultural and ideological terrains:

The expansion of the field through gender studies has revealed how the virile *homo aestheticus* was constructed against such feminized concerns as food and diet, as well as such historically feminized genres as the novel. Questions of empire have become inextricable from the politics of colonial foodstuffs, such as sugar, spice, and tea, and cultural studies have revealed the ways in which the social landscapes of Romantic-period fiction took shape against all-too-real panoramas of crop shortages, bread riots, and Corn Laws. Revisiting central moments of British literary history through the metaphorical lens of consumption may help to initiate a dialogue among these diverse fields of research and recall the power of literary history as a methodology for grounding such disciplinary diversity within literary studies.[13]

Lastly, of all the senses, taste is the only one which is associated with considerations of survival – it is not the deprivation of taste, however, but the absence of food itself which has prompted the birth and development of 'hunger fiction', a genre which has traversed the last two centuries from Melville's 'Bartleby the Scrivener' to Knut Hamsun's *Hunger*, Kafka's 'A Hunger Artist' and countless post-apocalyptic narratives such as Cormac McCarthy's *The Road*. A typology of hunger narratives lies outside the scope of this chapter as it would have to address hunger and disgust not only as sensations but also as the object of philosophical and political ruminations about identity, poverty, food deprivation or mental illness. Kafka's hunger artist and his obsession with absolute fasting come to mind, as do Huysmans's dysphoric meals, where dyspepsia becomes an obstacle to the freedom to choose between life and death, boredom and the release from boredom through the life of the senses.

## THE SYNAESTHETIC MOMENT

Synaesthesia emerges as a useful model against sensory hierarchies and a popular trope in genres and modes as varied as French symbolist poetry (a classic example of this is Rimbaud's poem 'Vowels'), decadentism and naturalist fiction. Zola's *The Belly of Paris* (aka *The Fat and the Thin*, 1873) is replete with descriptions of tastes and smells interacting with sights and sounds, sometimes to the point of saturation, as occurs when the food market of the *Halles*, with its smelly overabundance of meat, fish, cheese, wine and fruit stalls, is likened to a pulsating belly whose mechanised parts embody the disquieting synthesis of the organic and the mechanical, 'some huge central organ beating with giant force, and sending the blood of life through every vein of the city', 'doling out the daily food of its two million inhabitants' and causing an 'uproar [...] akin to that of colossal jaws'.[14] For Zola, as for many other realist and naturalist practitioners of the city novel, the teeming sensuous diversity of the city becomes perceived as the site of corruption and inhumanity. Whereas the smell of the poor invades the pages of much naturalist fiction, thereby signifying the threat of social pollution and contamination, one of the functions of the food market in Zola's novel is to signify the 'too much life' identified by Aurel Kolnai as a basic disgust elicitor.[15] More often than not, this sensory overload leads to dense, synaesthetic descriptions such as in the famous 'cheese symphony' scene taking place in Madame Lecoeur's cheese storeroom where 'each [piece of cheese] add[s] its own shrill note in a phrase that was harsh to the point of nausea'.[16] (To contemporary readers, the word 'nausea' inevitably invites a comparison with Sartre's Roquentin, who starts to feel nauseous 'as soon as objects start existing in [his] hands' and begins to suffocate as 'existence penetrates [him] from everywhere, through the eyes, the nose, the mouth'.)[17]

In J. K. Huysmans's *Against the Grain*, Des Esseintes' 'mouth organ' is a device for creating multisensorial analogies, 'each and every liqueur, in his opinion, correspond[ing] with the sound of a particular instrument'.[18] Des Esseintes's invention (a bachelor machine which inspired Boris Vian's 'pianocktail' in *Froth on the Daydream*) has the capacity to summon interferences, fusions and confusions between sound, smell taste and touch ('Dry curacao, for instance, was like the clarinet with its piercing, velvety note; kummel, the oboe with its sonorous, nasal resonance; crème de menthe and anisette, the flute, at once honeyed and pungent, whining and sweet'[19]) in a way which returns us to Baudelaire's sonnet 'Correspondances', in which the poet establishes a parallelism between scents, colours and sounds. More recently, the 'typographical thickets' appearing in Francis Ponge's object poem 'Blackberries', from *Le parti-pris des choses*, sought to discover phonemic and iconic analogies between words and things, a project mitigated by the poet's awareness of the 'miserable coincidence' and the 'desperate approximation' of sound and sense.[20]

## THE GROTESQUE AND THE UNFINISHED BODY

Mikhail Bakhtin's analysis of grotesque realism, his preoccupation with the 'low' and his anti-idealistic stance ('the essential principle of the grotesque is degradation, that is, the lowering of all that is high, spiritual, idea, abstract'[21]) did a lot to rehabilitate the lower senses in literary studies. Bakhtin's approach to embodiment neutralises any claim to a unique, self-present or transcendental nature and combats the classical (and bourgeois) myth of the self-present, self-contained body. By contrast, Bakhtin's grotesque body is an open, unfinished unit which 'transgresses its own limits',[22] opening itself up to the outside world, 'that is, the parts through which the world enters the body or emerges from it, or through which the body itself goes out to meet the world'.[23] Such an organism, which is constantly traversed by the world in the process of traversing it, can only be adequately represented from a polysensory perspective and calls for a global theory of the body's depths, surfaces and orifices which displaces the centre of attention from traditional idealistic notions of selfhood to the visceral and the teratological. More than any other representational mode, the grotesque appears as the most historically significant alternative to the dominant paradigms of the closed body. Any attempt to develop an aesthetics which seeks to encompass the complexities and intricacies of the unfinished body necessarily challenges the traditional hierarchies between the senses.

## THE SMELL OF BOOKS

Hans J. Rindisbacher's 1993 *The Smell of Books: A Cultural-Historical Study of Olfactory Perception in Literature* was a foundational attempt to re-evaluate the history of nineteenth- and twentieth-century literature through the lens (if one may say so) of smell, pausing importantly with Dostoevsky, Baudelaire, Fontane, Huysmans, Rilke and others. Inspired by Alain Corbin's study of the French 'social imagination' of smells, *The Foul and the Fragrant*, Rindisbacher records the 'perceptual revolution' that took place in the eighteenth century with a view to understanding our current obsession with hygiene and the gradual deodorisation and sanitisation of private and public spaces. The third and final part of Corbin's volume explores the ways in which smell can act as a social marker stigmatising the horrid stench of the poor which, by the mid-nineteenth century, had become one of the bourgeoisie's worst nightmares.[24] Corbin's study of the social representations of smell echoes Stallybrass and White's suggestion that the price to be paid for the bourgeoisie's attempts to construct itself as stable, boundaried and inodorous bodies is the construction of the socially or racially inferior/different as 'grotesque otherness'.[25]

The repression of smell as a marker of the lower class or an indicator of savagery climaxes in the aseptised environment of Aldous Huxley's *Brave New World* (1932), which explores the disastrous consequences of an over-hygienic society in which the technological reduction and manipulation of the olfactory spectrum has become a means of social control so that unpleasant smells (those which prevail in the Savage Reservation) are experienced as a threat to civilisation itself. Another striking literary example of a dystopian narrative centred on the repression of smell is to be found in Mynona's 1911 'On the Bliss of Crossing Bridges'. The story features Dr Krendelen, a dystopian scientist who sets himself the goal of purifying the whole planet's atmosphere in order to establish a 'paradise of the lungs', a world purified of bad air and stench which would prove to be 'the surest way to improve humanity, better than all philosophical moralizing!'[26] Krendelen's project ends in the spreading of new diseases and the annihilation of humanity, the bodies of the deceased burning 'without a trace of corrupting odor in the delightful air of early spring'.[27]

Patrick Süskind's *Perfume* (1985) is one of the most memorable attempts to carnivalise the hierarchy of the sensorium. A rare case of a novel originating in an academic book, Süskind's novel was itself inspired by Corbin's cultural historiography. One of the problems encountered by writers in their attempts to represent the olfactory is that the lexicon of smell is very limited and is usually confined to adjectives describing not the smell itself but 'the pleasantness or unpleasantness of the smell, most of which merely mean bad or good smell: fetid, foul, stink, stench, rancid, vile, revolting, nauseating, sickening'.[28] As for the vocabulary of disgust, it requires that we concentrate as much on sensations as on the metaphorical value of nausea. Sartre's reflections on the 'viscous' in *Being and Nothingness*, for example, extend the notion of disgust to the sense of touch, the inbetweenness conveyed by the slimy – that which is neither solid nor liquid – a form of existence which resists objectification and becomes a threat to the integrity of the self. Located between the 'in-itself' (the world of objects which exists independently from human consciousness) and the 'for-itself' (the capacity of human beings to be self-conscious), the viscous enacts such an impossible compromise between subject and object, being and consciousness, action and inaction. The threat of a dissolution of the boundaries between self and world is not metaphorical but rooted in a direct, unmediated experience of the body's capacity to become simultaneously fascinating and repellent and to generate disgust from within, as illustrated by Roquentin's attempts to identify with 'the little pool of whitish water' sliding down into his throat and coming up into his mouth, 'grazing' his tongue.

## HAPTIC PERSPECTIVES

The conjunction of taste and touch in Sartre's description of the viscosity of mucus returns us to the issue of the ambivalent status of touch within the hierarchy of the senses. Both Aristotle and Kant consider that it occupies an intermediary position between the low and the high, the subjective and the objective, the bodily and the mental, because of its capacity to interact with vision in the subject's apprehension of the world outside.[29] Likewise, Herder's haptic model does not so much set out to 'eliminate optics but to restore touch to seeing, and bodily substance to knowledge', being 'convinced that the establishment of the haptic paradigm of aesthetic experience against the oculocentric paradigm of the Enlightenment opens up a dimension of depth behind what is now only the surface of appearances'.[30]

Be that as it may, the sense of touch is less represented than taste or smell in literary studies of the lower senses – it is also less prominent as a mode of representation or characterisation in literature itself and at the time of this writing, the great novel about touch which would be the tactilist equivalent of Süskind's *Perfume* has yet to be written. It is only very recently that scholars have started to show an interest in how the sense of touch deploys itself in literary texts from a synchronic or diachronic perspective. Abbie Garrington's 2013 *Haptic Modernism: Touch and the Tactile in Modernist Writing* concentrates on selected writings by James Joyce, Virginia Woolf, D. H. Lawrence and Dorothy Richardson and identifies the advent of a haptic culture with the birth of modernist literature in response to technological innovations such as film and the motorcar. That same year saw the publication of Trish McTige's *The Haptic Aesthetic in Samuel Beckett's Drama*, and one expects more studies to appear in the next few years which will enrich the emerging field of haptic studies. As for Milena Marinkova's recent examination of Michael Ondaatje's *Haptic Aesthetics and Micropolitical Writing*, it is more indebted to affect theory (Marinkova studies affects produced by writing whose embodied character 'parallels the immediate and metaphorical meanings of "touch"'[31]) and Deleuzian film theory with its emphasis on texture, grain and 'skin' and argues for a revaluation of the proximal senses over the distal senses, the word 'haptic' suggesting ways in which 'vision itself can be tactile, as though one were touching with one's eyes'.[32]

William A. Cohen's *Embodied: Victorian Literature and the Senses* draws upon the theories of Merleau-Ponty, for whom sight should be lent the haptic, embodied qualities of the proximal senses and be converted from 'an objective, distant sense into a corporeally-grounded and reciprocal one'.[33] The book deals with topics as varied as Dickens's tendency to present interiors as 'permeable through sensory organs',[34] Trollope's investigations of the cultural and theoretical significance of skin 'both as a [...] sensory surface and a marker of social identity',[35] and the porous relationships of body and landscape in Hardy's *The Return of the Native*. Cohen's discussion of Hopkins's tactile metaphors investigates the poet's conversion of formulations of visual sensations into a proximate sense which physically incorporates the outside world and inscribes it on the surface of the body (the author cites the 'yellowy moisture' and the 'trambeans truck[ing] at the eye' of 'The Candles Indoors' as an example of Hopkins's 'tactile visuals').[36]

When the sense of touch becomes central to a literary text (say, from H. G. Wells's 'Country of the Blind' to José Saramago's *Blindness*) it is often as a result of the deprivation of the sense of sight. Diderot's 1749 *Letter on the Blind For the Use of Those Who Can See* was the first substantial text which challenged the central Enlightenment assumption that moral and intellectual insight is reliant on seeing. The implications of this can be further explored in the context of the life of Helen Keller, the famous deaf-blind woman whose autobiography, *The Story of My Life* (1903), has been immensely important to the development of an understanding of the complex process of collaboration and remediation between the senses. Having lost her sight and hearing at the age of nineteen months, Keller recovered an ability to perceive her environment through the sense of touch. Thanks to the manual alphabet that her tutor, Anne Mansfield Sullivan, herself partially blind, began to teach her just before her seventh birthday, she was able to attend Radcliffe College, manually communicating through the hands of Mrs Sullivan, who remained at her side during lectures. In the absence of direct visual and auditory stimuli, the development of Keller's consciousness and identity was carried out with the help of her three remaining senses, of course, but also, and above all, through language itself. Recalling the moment when her teacher spilled cold liquid over her hand while spelling the word 'w-a-t-e-r' on the other, Keller describes the awakening of the 'strange, new sight that had come to [her]'[37] as a result of her learning of language. 'Everything had a name', she writes, 'and each name gave birth to a new thought [...] every object which I touched seemed to quiver with life.'[38] Keller's life presents an extreme case of sensory deprivation leading to a renewed coordination between person, body and world, one which is directed towards the re-creation and the re-naming of that world.

The examples examined above suggest that studying the body and the senses in a way which does justice to the complexities and limits of perception and representation has important implications for future literary histories, not only in terms of the representation of characters, settings and atmospheres, but also in the experience of readers and writers and their subjectivities. Perhaps one important future avenue of research lies in the application of affect theory to literary studies. Such an approach is sketched out in my brief analysis of Sartrean disgust elicitors and Huysmans's aesthetics of boredom. Winfried Menninghaus's comprehensive history of the significance of disgust across the disciplines has led to extensive discussions of

Kafka, Bataille and Sartre against the background of a wide range of theories about the aesthetic stimulation of the affects.[39] Another such move has been spawned by Eve Kosofsky Sedgwick's analysis of shame and paranoia as social emotions in their relationship to male homoerotic sub-plots and queer performativity in the works of Henry James.[40] Because of its intermediary status between the physiological and the psychological, affect evokes states of being which address a double problem of representation. What is at stake here is not only how literature is likely to convey 'feelings' in terms of bodily sensations but also how the description of the senses can represent or suggest aspects of identity and interiority in their interaction with material forms of existence.

## FURTHER READING

Ackerman, Diane. *A Natural History of the Senses*. New York: Vintage, 1991.

Bernstein, Charles. *Close Listening: Poetry and the Performed Word*. Oxford: Oxford University Press, 1998.

Classen, Constance, David Howes and Anthony Synnott. *Aroma: The Cultural History of Smell*. London: Routledge, 1994.

Delville, Michel. *Food, Poetry, and the Aesthetics of Consumption: Eating the Avant-Garde*. London: Routledge, 2007.

Garrington, Abbie. *Haptic Modernism: Touch and the Tactile in Modernist Writing*. Edinburgh: Edinburgh University Press, 2013.

Gigante, Denise. *Taste: A Literary History*. New Haven: Yale University Press, 2005.

Gregg, Melissa and Gregory J. Seigworth, eds. *The Affect Theory Reader*. Durham, NC: Duke University Press, 2010.

Korsmeyer, Carolyn. *Making Sense of Taste: Food and Philosophy*. Ithaca: Cornell University Press, 1999.

Marks, Laura. *Touch: Sensuous Theory and Multisensory Media*. Minneapolis: University of Minnesota Press, 2002.

Rindisbacher, Hans J. *The Smell of Books: A Cultural-Historical Study of Olfactory Perception in Literature*. Ann Arbor: University of Michigan Press, 1993.

## CHAPTER 7

# Animals

## Carrie Rohman

The question 'what is an animal?' seems easy to answer in one precise sense: a creature that is not human. The recently heightened dissatisfaction with this routine, 'common sense' distinction, however, lies at the foundation of work in literary animal studies. What the common sense answer reveals to us is that 'the animal' is a – perhaps even *the* – constituting difference or ground upon which the human erects itself, understands itself, defines its own idea of itself. Animal studies and literary animal studies, in its various permutations, are interested in the aesthetic, cultural and ethical stakes of the figuring of animals, the figment of the non-human, the particular animal fabrications that often lie at the core of our narratives about human experience. Part and parcel of this interest are, inevitably, the actual animals in our midst and in our histories, what we are able to know about them and how we can engage with them in ways that don't simply reproduce an unthinking notion of 'the animal'.

It is worth beginning this discussion of the inventive or fabricated, which all literature enacts, by noting that Jacques Derrida plainly reveals the absurdity of our standard linguistic notion of 'the animal', this conceptual category against which humans define their own exceptional status. Derrida, in his influential essay, 'The Animal That Therefore I Am', identifies the staggering lack of precision inherent in our general notion of 'The Animal', as if 'all nonhuman living things could be grouped within the common sense of this "commonplace"'.[1] Derrida immediately describes the interestedness of this designation in ethically loaded terms:

> Confined within the catch-all concept, within this vast encampment of
> the animal, within the strict enclosure of this definite article ('the Animal'
> and not 'animals'), as in a virgin forest, a zoo, a hunting or fishing ground, a
> paddock or an abattoir, a space of domestication, are *all the living things* that
> man does not recognize as his fellows, his neighbors, or his brothers.[2]

Despite the 'infinite space that separates the lizard from the dog' and so on, humans heuristically rely upon the blunt instrument of the general concept 'animal'. This

reductive conceptual strategy shores up an almost cartoonish notion of living creatures residing in two categories ('human' and 'animal'), and allows an easy dismissal
of any ethical call that might issue from the neighbour or stranger beyond human
fraternity. The consolidation of all or even most living things into the general
singular 'animal' also enables a kind of willed blindness to the proliferative capacities, the almost infinite *Umwelten* or life-worlds of non-human creatures. Their vast
differences from one another and from humans, their singular life experiences, their
infinitely variable and ethically relevant ways of being and acting in the world
hence remain undetected. Lumping non-human creatures into one opposed category
encourages us to see ourselves as wholly unique and discourages us from seeing the
complexities of other creatures.

The challenging of such intellectual habits helps to explain the emergence of a
philosophically and ethically engaged literary animal studies over roughly the last
fifteen years.[3] To some degree, our intellectual habit as readers of human texts has
been to see only the human. In many cases, we didn't see or acknowledge animals
in texts at all.[4] They were completely ignored, not even viewed as accessories in
the work of textual interpretation. Moreover, when non-human animals were
acknowledged in literature, critics often saw them as only a cipher for, a gloss upon,
a comment about, an elaboration of or occasion for human concerns. This problem
of seeing or recognising the 'animal question' in literary studies can be productively
explored in relation to another of the most often cited moments in recent animal
theory, the moment in which Derrida is arrested by the gaze of his household cat.[5]
Critics have examined innumerable ideas and problems that emerge from Derrida's
account. In this case, I want to suggest that the anecdote usefully evokes the way
that literary animal studies testifies to the fact that we – critics, humans, readers
– have recently been caught, or exposed, in a particular manner. That is, while
explorations of our humanness in literary texts have always been intimately coiled
around questions of other animals – albeit in various and historically marked ways
– until very recently, that question in our *study* of literature has remained rather flat.
Animals thus persisted in a relatively unseen or unthought manner, simplistically
understood as mirrors, 'reflections' of some quality, struggle, or daemon that was seen
as ultimately human.[6]

In addition to this exposure of our own narcissism, the moment when Derrida's cat
'looks back' is also suggestive of the current disciplinary moment in literary animal
studies (happening right now) in terms of a charge or a summons. The recent inten-
sification of interest in literary animal studies attests to the need for an accounting,
the counting of animals, the recounting of animality, that needs to take place across
all our literatures. As a scholarly community, we are right now reckoning with all
the animals, the animalities, and the human enmeshments with animal being(s)
that were not seen or tended to in literature until very recently. This tending to, this
particular kind of 'care-ful, close reading', if you will, has distinct ethical parameters
that are infused with questions of intimacy, as we shall see. One of the challenges
of writing this chapter at this moment is that the immensity of the task at hand
– to account for animals and animality in literature – threatens to eclipse in its
magnitude the work that has already been done to prise open the species question

for our critical attention.[7] And I would suggest therefore that the work of tending to and paying attention to animals in literature may have more of an inherent ethical dimension than critics have previously acknowledged, and I count myself among them. Thus while I still agree with Cary Wolfe that we can often make clear distinctions between what work goes about its business without troubling humanist presumptions, and what work unsettles them,[8] I am recently persuaded that bringing animals in to the realm of the 'seen' in literary studies inevitably contributes to our responsibility in thinking about animals. Another way of saying this is that *what* we tend or attend to may, over time, inevitably impact *how* we attend, so the emerging visibility of animals in literary studies may inexorably cross into more ethical terrain, in general, as the field matures. Thus the distinction between animal studies and 'critical' animal studies in literature may eventually be less crisp.

To date 'critical animal studies' has operated as an ethically charged interdisciplinary undertaking that addresses the histories of human violence against animals and often endorses a poststructuralist dismantling of the human subject that is wrongly seen as exceptional in its abilities to think and speak.[9] 'Animal studies' more generally is sometimes viewed as less interested in these ethically inflected questions, and as having a more structural perspective about when and how animals operate in human discourses. Michael Lundblad has also suggested the term 'animality studies' in order to highlight how views of animals have shifted over time and resulted in different 'identity categories' within the human.[10] There have been a number of related debates in animal studies recently around questions of empathy or affective identification with animals, the difference or relation between activism and scholarship, and whether 'animal rights' discourses are compatible with a kind of progress in moving beyond speciesist forms of violence. Cary Wolfe, for instance, suggests that while standard 'rights' discourses based on expanding liberal subjecthood may be strategically useful at times, they nonetheless replicate a fidelity to 'human' capacities that fundamentally leaves intact unjust and often biologically insupportable species hierarchies that are normative in most industrialised, contemporary cultures.[11] Other scholars like Traci Warkentin have carefully troubled the strident calls for 'ethical veganism' in animal studies and thus complicated assumptions about the relations between ethical action and scholarship.[12] Moreover, I have suggested, as has David Clark in his compelling essay on animals in theory, that animal studies scholars ought to embrace 'high' theory and new theoretical developments, partly in order to enliven the field's ethical engagements.[13]

As the above discussion intimates, the ubiquity of animals and the particular 'otherness' or alterity of animals means that the breadth of work now being undertaken in literary animal studies can only be glimpsed at here. Wolfe has elaborated Derrida's claim that the animal may pose the 'most different difference' to our human-centred knowledge systems, detailing throughout his recent work how animals stand as the '"hardest case" of our readiness to be vulnerable to other knowledges'.[14] Moreover, Timothy Morton's term for the non-human, 'strange stranger', has been proliferating in work on animals. In a slightly different register, David Clark asks whether humans are 'the unwitting vow to bear witness to the absolute precedence of animal lives'[15] even though, and also because, the animal seems to be the 'paradigmatic case of the

Stranger'.[16] So too, as Marianne DeKoven has noted, it is imperative to 'avoid a reductive, ahistorical approach that lumps all literary animals together'.[17] Thus the range and specificity of work on animals being done across traditional literary periods could hardly have been imagined by those of us who were taking up the animal question fifteen or so years ago, as Robert McKay implicitly notes in his recent reflections on the field.[18] My canvassing here will ideally provide a cartography of questions and frameworks that the reader can locate and find elaborated in literary animal studies work that is not specifically detailed in these pages.

## KNOWING SUBJECTS

What are the implications of rendering animals in language?[19] How do animal figures in literature affirm or rattle the ways we think we know, both within language and beyond language? The question of representation is always hovering near the core of the literary project, but in the case of animals, it has an especially double-edged quality. This is partly so because of a tension between the assumption that only humans have the capacity to re-present, to re-create, in essence, to be symbolic and to produce the symbolic, and the suspicion that animals might be engaged in similar kinds of tracings, codings and interpretings. Thus what we think we know, a kind of *ersatz* phenomenology, is both predicated upon the reductive othering of non-human animals and, at the same time, is often 'undone' by the traces and markings of animals in our 'human' texts.[20] There is a parallel acrobatic exchange between the exclusion of animality from the domain of 'human' subjectivity, which often allows the human to posture as internally coherent in its own self-representations, and the impossibility of this exclusion since, after all, the 'animal' is internal to the human as well. This partly explains why animality in literature is often figured as an eruption.[21]

So much thinking about the species barrier hinges on the question of language and its use, its sophistication, its seeming correlation to 'higher order' capacities such as self-presence, self-knowledge, pretence, intentional forms of erasure, etc. In *Thinking Animals: Why Animal Studies Now?*, Kari Weil pays careful attention to how questions of representation and epistemology have been developing in the 'animal turn' in the academy. As Weil indicates, queries about language and species can revolve around the notion that non-human animals exist outside of language and thus embody some 'unmediated experience', or rather that they do speak in various ways and can describe 'however imperfectly [...] their lives and their traumas'.[22] Weil uses Kafka's ape, Red Peter, to explore the relation between language and self-knowledge and to analyse the ways in which speaking about the self is linked to erasures of that very self: language gives Red Peter 'access to knowledge that he was an ape, but it does not allow him to represent that life' so that his '"report" takes the place of that former life that exists only as an aporia, a knowledge lost along with that of his ape life'.[23] Weil observes that animal studies, like trauma studies, 'stretches to the limit questions of language, epistemology, and ethics'.[24] Moreover, we might want to ask whether literature, because its medium is language – that with which humans have so virulently insisted upon their exceptionalism – is particularly freighted with the 'traumatic' question of our own animality, our duty to non-human animals, and our own vacillating recognitions that we are both like and unlike other animals.

Weil and other critics have repeatedly returned to the question of 'giving' voice to others who are in some respects marginalised from mainstream discourses: Weil ruminates upon the problems of 'how to understand and give voice to others or to experiences that seem impervious to our means of understanding; how to attend to difference without appropriating or distorting it; how to hear and acknowledge what it may not be possible to say'.[25] Moreover, Alice Kuzniar usefully turns the anthropocentric framing of the language question on its head by posing the following reversal: 'The question then becomes not "do *they* have language?" but "do *we* have an adequate language to speak to them and about them?"'[26]

Questions of language, knowledge and subjectivity have been especially central in the recent proliferation of new work on Virginia Woolf's *Flush*. Traditional readings of that text have understood it as especially 'domesticated' or anthropomorphic, such that the dog is 'granted a Victorian sensibility'; but recent work asks whether the text 'raises the dog to the status of a "fellow-creature"'.[27] Kuzniar further suggests that Woolf, in acknowledging the gulf between species in various ways throughout the novel, engages 'the brilliant paradox that estrangement can [...] lead to intuitive comprehension – to intimacy'.[28] Furthermore, Derek Ryan's recent work on *Flush* deftly employs Derrida's discussions of nudity, subjectivity and the gaze to suggest that Woolf's dog may experience far more than even Derrida imagined. According to Ryan, Woolf may be 'opening up the possibility that Flush looking at himself naked [...] may be where thinking begins',[29] positing an even more animal 'source' for philosophy than Derrida himself. Given what Ryan calls this book's 'underdog' status, such questions provide important ways to begin re-mapping received ideas about particular animal 'portraits' in literature that may have seemed overly human-ised.[30] In another recent re-reading of *Flush*, Karalyn Kendall-Morwick reconfigures an anthropocentric understanding of the *Bildungsroman* tradition to ask how the dog's own aesthetic education and self-cultivation are central to Woolf's text, concluding that 'Flush's epiphany, like the novel itself, affirms not a narrowly humanist project of self-cultivation but an ongoing process of intersubjective becoming that exceeds the boundaries and potentials of the individual human' and that 'understands char-acter as contingent and relational'.[31]

A final set of questions in this segment would inevitably circulate around how animals and animality pose limits upon the knowing human subject and, to put a finer point on it, how literature imagines animals inviting us to move beyond a classic 'human' engagement with the world. In my own reading of Djuna Barnes's *Nightwood*, for instance, I discuss the character of Robin as a figure who refuses to adopt a human identity that is founded upon the abjection of her own animal being, and who remains suspicious of language and the various human subjectivities that language attempts to support.[32] Robin's final entanglements with a dog in this novel, famously ambiguous and much-analysed by critics, point not to her 'degenerate' status, but rather to the way that Robin transgresses the symbolic as a limit upon her phenomenality. The most traditionally 'human' characters in Barnes's novel are the most thwarted, alienated and distraught. Robin, however, refuses the false fixity of 'human' subjectivity and knowledge. By moving, changing and embracing a kind of animality, her character revises the category 'human' in a manner that challenges language and the symbolic as forms of knowledge, at their core. Readings such as this lead us to ask whether the animal turn in literary studies is figuring the traditional anthropocentric humanist as disabled. Such a 'disability' seems based on the disavowal of animality that distances the conventional, vertical human from its deep evolutionary lineage, from the forces of life and death, from understanding its own ontological and phenomenological positions as constitutively enmeshed with those of other animals.

Thus in many ways, work in literary animal studies is holding up a new mirror to the human, and asking it to rearticulate figures of itself that engage with the question of species. As we are being asked to consider what exclusions the 'human' is predicated upon, and whether these exclusions are in various ways insupportable, we are able to see both humans and non-human animals in new ways, new relations and new assemblages. This is why animal studies often goes hand in hand with post-humanism. As Cary Wolfe elaborates in his landmark book, *What is Posthumanism?*:

> the question of posthumanism [...] enables us to [...] rethink our taken-for-granted modes of human experience, including the normal perceptual modes and affective states of *Homo sapiens* itself, by recontexualizing them in terms of the entire sensorium of other living beings and their own autopoietic ways of 'bringing forth a world' – ways that are, since we ourselves are human animals, part of the evolutionary history and behavioral and psychological repertoire of the human itself.[33]

## NARRATING CREATURAL LIFE

How is narrative a more-than-human procedure? How does literary narrative recount and situate what it means 'to cross paths with life', as David Clark so distils it?[34] Susan McHugh's work urges us to understand narrative 'as a zone of integration, one that does not end in literary studies so much as it begins to explain how story forms operate centrally within shifting perspectives of species life'.[35] McHugh also acknowledges the way in which developments in science insist upon the 'interdependence of life forms even below the cellular level', such that the 'pervasive companionship of human subjects with members of other species appears even more elemental to narrative subjectivity, a dark matter of sorts awaiting literary analysis'.[36] McHugh emphasises the participation or agency of animals, especially in modern and contemporary fictions, with a particular eye on cross-species companionship and the ways in which human and animal actions are co-constitutive, rather than supplementary.

In demonstrating how to answer the 'creative imperative to elaborate new forms of agency' across species lines and in relation to literary aesthetics, McHugh articulates a 'queer camaraderie' in J. R. Ackerley's memoirs.[37] Ackerley's texts, like those of J. M. Coetzee, are becoming increasingly fruitful for critics interested in an ethical enmeshment of species that has as one of its signal effects the challenging of human exceptionalism. In Ackerley, the levelling of sex acts 'among all sorts of social animals'[38] promotes a kind of 'queer counterpublic'[39] that is organised around 'nonstandard intimacies'.[40] Within Ackerley's 'triangulation' of gay men, bitches and 'their preferred mongrel (here meaning alternately human bisexual or canine mixed-breed)', sexual agency becomes reconfigured through what McHugh calls 'pack sexualities'.[41] By figuring a queer solidarity with his pet bitch, Ackerley seems to distribute the burdensome expectation to couple across species lines, sharing and perhaps mitigating the failure to 'reproduce' a heternormative erotic life.

David Herman also addresses literary accounts of human 'failure' in some of his most recent work, in which he calls for a 'narratology beyond the human'. Herman brings narrative theory and work in animal studies into dialogue with other disciplines, such as anthropology, in order to explore questions of self-narrative and self-hood within a species matrix, questions that heretofore have not occupied a central place in narrative studies. In his work on the contemporary short story 'Above and Below' by Lauren Groff, Herman suggests that this story 'highlights how "humans" understanding of their relations to other kinds of selves takes on special salience when self-narratives come under pressure, or no longer find purchase at all'.[42] In Groff's account of a woman who becomes homeless after having imagined a future as an intellectual, the protagonist re-shapes her sense of self horizontally, within 'a wider world of selves, nonhuman as well as human'.

One of the fascinating implications of Herman's new work is that when a human's self-narrative becomes disrupted, that disruption may often trigger transspecies identifications. In Groff's text, the protagonist variously sees herself as akin to frogs, snakes and rats, particularly when she is experiencing certain kinds of estrangement from normative human behaviours and forms of community. Herman productively links these fictional moments to the recent 'ontological turn' in anthropology. For instance, Eduardo Kohn explains how some human communities regard all beings as having a point of view, such that humans understand their own position within an 'ecology of selves'.[43] As Herman points out, Groff's protagonist has anything but an easy transition during her 'biocentric becoming', as she moves from an anthropocentric self-narrative to a more interspecies notion of self. Nonetheless, she begins to understand 'her place within another, wider community, transhuman in scope and opening up new narrative vectors leading to a different future'. In this trajectory, the protagonist begins to see herself as one creature among many, having moved from a 'parsimonious' ontology to a more 'prolific' one. Herman situates this human narrative by evoking broad questions of biodiversity and the enmeshment of life forms, noting that the text 'suggests that the most sustainable self is one that insists least on its own sovereignty'.[44]

## BIOPOLITICAL FRAMES

While sovereignty has become a truly fetishised concept in biopolitical theory, critics in literary animal studies have only recently begun to engage with the set of concepts that Foucault put in motion, and that have been taken up by thinkers like Agamben, Hardt and Negri, and Esposito.[45] However, new work that links the concerns of biopolitics with those of animal studies and literature is providing compelling trajectories for thinking about how the imaginative operates alongside and through various power structures. Colleen Glenney Boggs usefully explains that biopower 'depends on regulating representation and affect' because imagination and desire are potential sources of resistance to the 'totalizing aspirations' of imperial power.[46] Yet she is most interested in the strand of affirmative biopolitics that has emerged around Esposito's emphasis on kinds of *bios* that are not limited to the conscious subject, which allows us to see animals 'in a position that need not always be abjected'.[47] Continuing the sort of troubling and recalibrating of subjectivity that has been at the heart of animal studies work in the last decade, Boggs investigates the 'fundamental plurality' of subjectivity, and elaborates its specific relation to animals in American literature and history. She also asks whether the 'maintained animal' within language and writing might provide an opportunity for founding community, opening up the possibility for imagining 'an alternative biopolitics that does justice to animals'.[48]

Emphasising the fraught history and implications of 'representation' both in political and linguistic terms, Boggs insists that we ought to approach literature as 'a means of encounter' where we can move beyond the duality offered by what Laura Brown describes as the alterity/anthropomorphism choice, and engage with the 'complex nature of the imaginary animal'.[49] A good example of this complexity emerges in Boggs's work on Emily Dickinson, which explores affective interspecies relations as they are depicted and resisted in animal representations. Focusing her analysis through Locke's 1693 *Some Thoughts Concerning Education*, widely acknowledged as 'inaugurating the fields of pedagogy, child psychology, children's literature, the sentimental novel, and American literature as such', Boggs discusses the didactic project of developing children's abilities, and notes that the relationship to animals 'forms the nexus between the body and mind that is requisite for liberal subject formation, but it also challenges the very parameters of that subject formation'.[50] First articulating the way that humanity itself is a 'sentiment' that 'hinges on compassion for animals' in Locke's text,[51] Boggs goes on to examine how and why animals become central to the way children learn to read through her analysis of 'didactic ontology', or the practice of 'teaching children how to be human by teaching them how to be humane'.[52] Boggs elaborates her discussion of these questions by considering the 'animation of orthography' in eighteenth- and nineteenth-century pedagogical techniques and texts.[53] Dickinson takes up the alphabetical animal and the question of pedagogical disciplines that make us human in a number of poems and poetic correspondences. In her examination of these texts, Boggs shows how Dickinson 'makes language itself the locus for relating animal and human subjectivity'[54] but at the same time 'silences the pedagogical voice' that tends to separate human from animal in the creation of a humane posture.[55] Boggs suggests that Dickinson makes 'poetry itself animate': so too, she reads animal 'noise' or utterance in Dickinson's poetry as positing a 'liveness of a natural language beyond social silencing'. Dickinson's employing of 'animetaphor' (Akira Lippit's term) creates a poetry that is not fully calculable within the social, reflecting Esposito's emphasis on potentials for 'resistance' within biopolitical frameworks.

Boggs's discussions of metaphor bring to the surface an interesting tension or torsion around the framing of animality in relationship to language or the trace. Animals are seen as, according to Lippit, 'the unconscious of language, of *logos*',[56] or in Derrida's terms, *logos* 'is engendered by a *zoon*, and can never entirely efface the traces of its origin'.[57] Here animality is overdetermined as the 'real' or material- ised 'thing' around which human languages arrange themselves and organise their remainders. But as Wolfe has been keen to emphasise in much of his recent work that evokes Derrida as well, human and animal are alike 'subjected' to the radically ahuman trace structures that frame all forms of coding and communicating among life forms. If animals have language or languaging as well, then what unconscious, outside, or *zoon* are their own codes displacing and tracing? Such a question reveals a potential facile-ity in our own animal renderings. The animal is quintessentially like us yet different: an animated being with a perspective, yet one that offers enough alterity to stand as an 'exemplary' or 'originary' metaphor, in Lippit's terms. But does this association of the animal with the trope too easily foreclose or flatten animals' complexities, putting under erasure their own enmeshment with marks and traces both human, animal and (otherwise)?

Some of Cary Wolfe's very recent literary work asks similar questions as it demar- cates a 'lameness' or weakness in Wallace Stevens's poetry. This lameness goes hand- in-hand with a blotting out of Heideggerian *Being* and 'overcomes epistemology', or radically recalibrates the traditional ways that humans think they know things.[58] The 'sovereignty' at issue here is one that circulates around the human's putative ability to respond rather than react, and the trite association of animality with mere 'reaction'. Wolfe suggests that Stevens's emphasis on the performative *factum* in his poetic works alongside his broader anti-representationalist poetics make 'available to us a logic that is "heterogeneous" to idealism' and also emphasise that the finitude or prostheticity enacted in all autopoetic systems (both human and non-human) is best understood as revealing epistemology itself to be necessarily environmental (and not natural). Wolfe emphasises the weakness of human foundations and mediations in Stevens's work as its strength, which flags his broader insistence that a 'shared subjection to an "arche-materiality"' or semiotic system 'binds the human to (at least some) nonhuman animals'.[59] Thus Wolfe shows how Stevens's work offers a 'deconstruction of the sovereign power of the imagination'.

## CREATIVE BECOMINGS

Critical animal studies have as a major strand running through them the replacement of a logic of verticality with a horizontal ethics. As we have seen to some degree already in this chapter, such an ethics attempts to see animals as subjects, chal- lenges human exceptionalism, and investigates the ways that humans and animals are companionate,[60] can 'get on together',[61] and are deeply coexistent along lines of ontology, finitude or vulnerability, but also share certain abilities or capacities.

Deleuze and Guattari's concept of becoming, which in their terms progresses from a becoming-woman, through a becoming-animal, -molecular and -imperceptible has, not surprisingly, been productive for new thinking about human-animal assemblages that are not reducible to questions of mimesis. Indeed, becoming in Deleuze's framework is an alternative to fixed forms: it emphasises process, the hyphenated passage between points or entities, and not a simple 'change' from one end point to another.[62] Deleuze and Guattari are at pains to emphasise that becoming is not about mimesis:

> Becomings-animal are basically of another power, since their reality
> resides not in an animal one imitates or to which one corresponds, but in
> themselves, in that which suddenly sweeps us up and makes us become – a
> *proximity, an indiscernibility* that extracts a shared element from the animal far
> more effectively than any domestication, utilization, or imitation could.[63]

The emphasis on becomings in literary animal studies thus operates as a kind of counter-logic to the insistence on representation in textual analysis.

Broadly speaking, literary critics are interested in these potential animal 'proximities' or passages because they disrupt the coherence of both the human and the symbol. I have argued elsewhere that Deleuze and Guattari's continual return to the creative involution found in the works of modernists such as Lawrence, Woolf and Kafka should be seen less as demonstrating the creative 'genius' of these writers and more as native to that era because of the post-Darwinian specificity of humanism's crisis vis-à-vis the animal.[64] Here I want to note that medievalist critics have made recent use of these concepts in reorienting our readings of Chaucer's body of work, for instance. As Carolynn Van Dyke notes in her introduction to *Rethinking Chaucerian Beasts*, certain generalisations have long held sway in medieval studies and often more broadly:

> that medieval thinkers drew rigid doctrinal boundaries between human
> beings and other creatures; that attributions of intention and consciousness to
> nonhuman animals must be naively anthropomorphic, fanciful, or lopsidedly
> figurative; that all sophisticated thinkers, medieval and modern, reflexively
> preface 'agency' with 'human'.[65]

Van Dyke's volume collects Chaucerian readings that counter these assumptions. Christopher Roman, for instance, opens his discussion of Chaucer's *The Book of the Duchess* in this fashion: 'If we read the dream in an imposed, linear fashion, the dreamer is affected by birds and their song, rides a horse, follows a deer, is led by a dog, and is immersed in a forest full of animals. This continual assemblage results in a reconsideration of the Black Knight himself – is Chaucer making an animal of him?'[66] Roman goes on to invoke Derrida's question, 'What would being-with-the-animal mean?'[67] and discusses the poem's 'saturation' with animals, its engagements with the problematics of hunting, the absorption of vitality, and questions about finitude within Chaucer's 'hauntology' – a kind of huntology – in this poem. Roman goes on to characterise the Black Knight as having become-animal in the text: 'immersed in the wood, [he] has been infected by the animals, their *being* a contagion'.[68] Roman ultimately suggests that critical animal studies enables a reading of Chaucer's poem that shows 'how the animal assists us in thinking about finitude in all of its openness and complexity',[69] as our 'sense of death is reshaped as we are immersed in the animal and as the placeholder represented by the hyphen in "becoming-animal" erodes'.[70]

Roman makes a number of comparisons between Chaucer's text and J. M. Coetzee's novel *Disgrace* throughout his essay. As I have already mentioned, Coetzee's work is of particular interest to those working in literary animal studies. Weil insists that her experience of being 'haunted' by the novel *Disgrace* propelled the writing of her book *Thinking Animals*, and critics like Robert McKay have examined the literary 'performance' of animal ethics in Coetzee's *The Lives of Animals*. My own recent reading of *Disgrace* takes a Deleuzian approach that is informed by the work of Elizabeth Grosz. There, I suggest that the aesthetic becomes framed in Coetzee's text as a tendency of the living in general, a bio-impulse towards superfluity, display and participation in broad organic forces. This 'becoming-artistic of life' profoundly exceeds the domain of the human and should be viewed as a creaturely orientation of life to other life, and to the pulsations to which all life is exposed.[71] By analysing the productive 'devolution' of David Lurie's opera in the novel, and his willingness to include a dog's voice in his newly horizontal musical venture, I show how the species barrier is rendered porous through a becoming-animal of art. This process leads Lurie away from a controlling, entitled anthropocentrism, towards an 'appreciation of the erotico-artistic that is more marginal, and more creaturely, yet ultimately more legitimate'.[72] In this reading, the novel proposes that the life we share with animals is indeed the only life, a life that has at its core the artistic, the metamorphic and the improvisational. Thus in my view, Coetzee's text reveals how the 'very artistry of art brings us back to the animal, and humans must humbly acknowledge the proliferation of the aesthetic across vast manifestations of nonhuman life'.[73]

## HUMILITY

Around the time that literary animal studies was starting to coalesce, which I often mark by citing the conference 'Millennial Animals', organised in 2000 by Robert McKay and Sue Vice, critics like Cary Wolfe regularly noted that literary studies lagged behind other disciplines in recognising that animals pose theoretically and ethically acute questions.[74] Why was this the case? The likely answer is that the linguistically aesthetic is seen as one of the last strongholds of human pre-eminence, for all the reasons we have already rehearsed around humans imagining their exceptionalism as based in unique capacities for language, self-knowledge, creativity, etc. It may be, therefore, that literary studies is especially in need of humility, of acknowledging the 'unbearable' questions that David Clark suggests non-human animals pose to humans. And if Clark is right, that animals tend to 'dispossess' our discourses,[75] then we ought to look forward to and embrace that dispossession as something which rightly mitigates our arrogance, but also affords us the opportunity to pursue what Clark calls 'the most arduous occasion of difficult knowledge'.[76] One way of answering this difficulty is in continuing to ask what makes animals knowable within literary frameworks, and in turn, how that interchange makes humans knowable to themselves – but in a much more capacious way that takes us beyond the human we thought we knew.

## FURTHER READING

Armstrong, Philip. *What Animals Mean in the Fiction of Modernity*. London: Routledge, 2008.

Crane, Susan. *Animal Encounters: Contacts and Concepts in Medieval Britain*. Philadelphia: University of Pennsylvania Press, 2013.

Fudge, Erica. *Brutal Reasoning: Animals, Rationality, and Humanity in Early Modern England*. Ithaca: Cornell University Press, 2006.

McHugh, Susan. *Animal Stories: Narrating Across Species Lines*. Minneapolis: University of Minnesota Press, 2011.

Miller, John. *Empire and the Animal Body*. London: Anthem Press, 2012.

Rohman, Carrie. *Stalking the Subject: Modernism and the Animal*. New York: Columbia University Press, 2009.

Shannon, Laurie. *The Accommodated Animal: Cosmopolity in Shakespearean Locales*. Chicago: University of Chicago Press, 2013.

Steel, Karl. *How to Make a Human: Animals and Violence in the Middle Ages*. Columbus: Ohio State University Press, 2011.

Wolfe, Cary. *Animal Rites: American Culture, the Discourse of Species, and Posthumanist Theory*. Chicago: University of Chicago Press, 2003.

Woodward, Wendy. *The Animal Gaze: Animal Subjectivities in Southern African Narratives*. Johannesburg: Wits University Press, 2008.

## CHAPTER 8

# Objects

## Timothy Morton

This chapter contemplates the possibility of an alternative literary history, one in which we bid the idea of Nature farewell, and consider the ramifications of a more object-centred or posthuman ecology for literary studies. The first part of the chapter, as sketched here, outlines the theoretical and historical framework for such an approach. Starting out from a reconsideration of 'nature' and 'ecology', this outline leads, perhaps surprisingly, to a reconsideration of non-natural objects. In the second part, I will apply these theoretical insights to a select number of literary works from the modern period.

### LITERATURE WITHOUT NATURE

In rethinking literary history, we can no longer afford to ignore the links between literature and the environment, between cultural and natural time. Just when Western philosophy had decided that direct access to reality is impossible, after all, humans began to deposit a thin layer of carbon in Earth's crust, directly intervening in reality. This is the beginning of what is now called the *Anthropocene*, a period in which human history intersects with geological time or what some critics have called 'deep time'.[1] This disturbingly ironic combination brings to an end the concept Nature as it generally manifests itself in literary texts. In order to activate ecological awareness, such works show, we must drop Nature, which I capitalise to emphasise how it is not 'natural', but rather an artificial construct.

Much eco-inflected literature, in fact, thematises this descriptive conundrum. Simply put: I see rabbits, I see thunderstorms, I hear the mewing of cats, but I fail to see or otherwise sense Nature. Perhaps then Nature is the totality of a certain set of things: birds, fish, mammals... Yet the set must exclude something. Let us add non-living forms such as iron deposits and chalk hills, which are made of life forms – as are most of the top levels of Earth's crust. This set still excludes what lies below the crust and the electromagnetic shield around Earth that protects it from solar rays, and so enables life to evolve. So let us now include non-life in our set. I must then include the Sun, without which the chemical soup could not have developed into strands of complex proteins. And there is no way to stop the inclusion arbitrarily at the Solar System, since comets containing organic chemicals and the sheer fact that stars are made of all kinds of other materials prevents the set from being closed. Yet once Nature covers absolutely everything, it also includes human-made objects like spoons, computer software and traffic cones. As this train of reasoning indicates, Nature only works as a concept when it is *normative*, and this normativity is predicated on a difference between Nature and non-Nature. Since I can't decide in advance what to include in the Natural set, Nature as a category becomes useless. Boundaries between life and non-life, and furthermore between sentience and non-sentience, are not thin or rigid enough to produce distinctions that count beings as Natural or non-Natural. Darwin's devastating insight – which soon seeped into the very tissue of literary texts – was that life forms arise from non-life, and that life forms are made up of other life forms. Furthermore, he demonstrated that there is no rigid boundary between a species, a variant and a monstrosity. Thus we encounter a vast assemblage of 'weird' entities or objects. And this assemblage, I will argue, has actually been the domain of literature.

In the rest of this chapter I will examine how such paradoxes animate and complicate our understanding of inanimate things, drawing upon an object-oriented view of causality, which argues that if things are not reducible to their perception or uses, they can only re-emerge as traces and footprints, or as archaeological evidences of themselves. It is from this aesthetic dimension that I intend to map out a trajectory for literary history which gives voice to unspeakable and speechless things.

## EXPLODING CONTEXT

We usually – and this means for the last hundred years or so – read poems, plays and novels, or examine art or music, and other cultural artefacts, to find out what they tell us about the people who made them. We might be inclined to study the way the poem (or whatever) expresses the author's life. Or the way in which it says something about another context, such as the social and historical conditions in which it was made.

The trouble with this approach is, it is difficult to know where to draw the line – or perhaps impossible. You may find out about where a poem was written, but is that really where it was written? The poem was written in a guest house in a small town. But the poem was also written in England. The poem was also written in Europe. The poem was also written on Earth. I don't mean to sound flippant here. It is genuinely difficult to draw a line, a thin rigid one at least, around a context. There seems to be the possibility of a contextual explosion. Consider the question of *when* a poem is written. In 1805? In the nineteenth century? (Of course we already run into trouble here – is the poem a product of the eighteenth or nineteenth centuries, for instance?) In the time of global warming? As we know now, 1805 is about fifteen years into what is now called the Anthropocene. Surely this might be relevant, and if it isn't relevant directly, that's also interesting. In the time of capitalism? Modernity?

The last millennium? The time of Axial Age religions such as Christianity? The time of agriculture – a boundary that goes back to 10,000 BC?

What seems strange is that the injunction always to find a context for what is being read often contains some kind of implicit *limitation* on exactly what sorts of context count as correct or relevant. One would have thought that the enjoyment of context is that it might be a limitless explosion. However, most scholarship that promotes the idea of meaning as a product of context seems to want to draw the line somewhere.

We can study this quite simply by considering contextualism as a single sentence: *All sentences are contextually determined.* Now the trouble is that for those sorts of sentences to be true, they must include themselves in their truth claim. Which means that they are also contextual. Which means that they cannot be understood outside of their context, which means they cannot tell the truth on their own and so on. *All sentences are contextual* is false, or it implies an infinite regress. So you can get around this by the usual method, which is the Russell and Whitehead way of containing the contradictoriness of Cantor, or the Tarski way of containing contradictory sentences, which Tarski called metalanguage. You can invent a rule:

*All sentences are contextual* is not a sentence.

Then I can blow up your silly rule by making this kind of sentence:

*This sentence is false.*

Then you can try to arrest me like the policeman in Monty Python's 'Argument Clinic' sketch and say

*This sentence is false* is not a sentence.

Then I can make a nice upgraded virus that says:

*This is not a sentence.*

For every metalinguistic disinfectant soap you make, I can evolve an even more virulent sentence.

I do not mean to reject contextualism. I am simply saying that the forms of humanistic contextualism we have on offer try to contain the contextual explosion. And this is something you just can't do in an ecological age. Switching from logic to empirical evidence for a moment, where are we? When are we? Where exactly is here? Glasgow? Europe? The Solar System? I could go on like Stephen Dedalus in his elementary school. When are we? The twenty-first century? The Anthropocene? The agrilogistical age? The time of humans? The Cambrian explosion? The moment when the bacteria created their own ecological catastrophe we call oxygen, which is why you are able to read this without keeling over? The point being, that these temporalities are all happening right now. Which means that now is not an atomic point of whatever size – be it a femtosecond or a billion years. There are so many different scales such that we have lost track of what counts as the right one: think of all those scale tools on the Internet where you can zoom from the Planck length to the extent of the universe in a few seconds like scrolling back and forth through a Mahler symphony movement on iTunes in a couple of seconds. The perhaps supposedly callous technology that enables this speed, itself a product of accelerated agrilogistics, provokes an ontological crisis of scale that forces us to realise that we are not progressing at all, but rather that we are beings among other beings just as important as us. Weirdly, anthropocentrism is over because of anthropocentric hubris.

So there are contexts, but no top, bottom or final one, no 'in the last instance'. Funnily enough, contextualism so far (for the last two centuries, that is to say the Anthropocene so far) has been a rigid, desperate attempt to *contain* contexts. If we allow context to erupt, we find that place or context can't possibly be a small bounded region.

Unlike in a classic realist novel, there is no one narrative frame to rule them all, some kind of human-flavoured top level where it all makes sense, as if we were watching the writhings of the others (including our physical bodies) in some kind of VIP lounge of being. Rather than rejecting it because it's contradictory and therefore meaningless, we allow *All sentences are contextual* to go into an infinite regress, while remaining true, which is also saying that we allow it to express its quintessential loop form, like a Möbius strip or the ouroboros, the kind of serpent you have to kill before you get to plant the seeds. It isn't possible to achieve escape velocity from the phenomenal world, such that thinking can do without its poor phenomenological host. Which is kind of where we've been at, and increasingly so, for 12,500 years.

I hope that by now you can see that there are troubles with a fundamentalist approach to context, the idea that context is somehow *more real* than the poem (or what have you) at hand. This thought is very significant if we are going to start thinking about objects. The poem, after all, is some kind of object, and we are trying to explain it away by its context rather than look at it for what it is. Even thinking this thought is taboo in the context of the contemporary theory class, such that theory often contains dogmatic blind spots, despite its claims to be about loosening our conceptual grip on things. Theory has too often become the opposite of its name, which implies a quizzical, questioning attitude.

Boundaries between periods and places are never thin or rigid. Jacques Derrida very elegantly argued throughout his career against the idea that boundaries could be thin or rigid in any case whatsoever. Derrida's approach was primarily epistemological, having to do with how we understand the world. Quite rightly, because he is trying to avoid the kind of violence often associated with saying what the world is, he avoids talking about what is. However, his work deeply implies some thoughts about how things are. His later work, for instance on justice and forgiveness, and in particular his work on animals, suggests that how things are is such that they are ungraspable, yet not totally without existence. For instance, there is the case of the *arrivant*, the strange arrival from the future – and the arrival of the future as such – that exists, but can't be grasped in advance. This poem I'm holding was indeed written in 1805. And it's a Wordsworth poem, not a Coleridge poem. It has definition. But that doesn't mean that we can completely grasp it.

Indeed, that is what is, for want of a better word right now, fun about poems and other cultural documents. They seem finite, yet somehow inexhaustible. We shall revisit this thought constantly, since we are going to use it as if it seems to suggest something about how things are in general. In the meantime, let us summarise what we have explored so far. It can be summed up quite briefly. We usually read poems to find out what they say about some kind of *subject*: the person who wrote the poem, its place in history, the economic relations at the time, its place in literary history and so on. But what about the other term that comes up when we say *subject*? What about objects?

## MYSTERIOUS ESSENCES

Objects are the neglected twin sister of subjects. They go way back at least to Aristotle, but in fact this notion of objects as rather bland or as blank screens for (human) desire has all kinds of even deeper social and historical determinants. One might argue, for instance, that the transition from hunter gathering to agriculture brought about a severe impoverishment of human conceptions of objects, and of those objects themselves. Rather than being viewed as ready-to-manipulate lumps of extension, objects were, quite simply, seen as alive, no matter whether they were animals or trees or rocks or stars. We are likely to dismiss the idea that they are alive as a thought that we couldn't possibly think. Even pointing it out is regularly dismissed as primitivism. But the agricultural logistics of the Neolithic age, along with its axial religions (which replaced indigenous animisms), already treated objects as inert: an implicit substance ontology was in effect, long before it was formalised by Aristotle.[2] This impoverishment has only grown more severe as agriculture of a certain sort has taken off and accelerated, giving rise eventually to the industrial revolution and the information age, let alone global warming and mass extinction.

Our traditional ways of talking about objects in art is quite limited. This is mostly because we are reluctant to say anything that sounds 'ontological' – anything that sounds like the question of what exists and how it exists has been outsourced to physics and biology. We are wary of the very term *ontology*: it sounds 'medieval', to name another abject poor relation. Since about the later eighteenth century, in Western philosophy, epistemology has reigned supreme, inhibiting access even to talk about objects, before that talk is put through various security screens to make sure it is not talking 'nonsense' – to wit, not stepping outside the bounds of accept-able scientistic (not scientific) parameters: there are fundamental units of matter, and they compose everything else, and things are lumps of whatever decorated with accidents.

Running parallel with this knee-jerk scientism – which really just repackages Aristotle for a decidedly post-Aristotelian age – is an insistence that we cannot talk directly about things, only about (human) access to them. It started with Kant, who argued that what we can think is extension, time and space and so on – but not the actual things in themselves. The Kantian subject is like someone who opens the fridge to check whether the light is on or not. Since Kant, all kinds of substitute fridge-openers have been proposed: spirit (Hegel), will (Schopenhauer), human economic relations (Marx), will to power (Nietzsche), *Dasein* (Heidegger), and on and on.

Rather than an intrinsic lump, we have another kind of lump, a sort of blank screen onto which the (human) subject projects her or his desires. This has given rise to the predominant mode of art and of art criticism in the last two centuries. Art is what I make of it, and interpretation is practically limitless, or at least not bound by the thing to be interpreted. Interpretation is perhaps bound by ideology, or the limits of language, or something else, but not by the 'object' in question. So many people, despite what Derrida and others argue, enter and leave theory class with the same idea, a telling idea when it comes to objects: *art is whatever I make it mean*. Art can be anything. Duchamp practically formalised this: everything is a urinal, waiting to be signed by the artist. The signature makes it art. Or the signature questions the status of art and of signatures and so on – in a potentially infinite regress of a certain kind of very popular irony.

This large-scale philosophical and cultural background helps to explain why we are in quite bad shape when it comes to talking about objects in art. We talk about representations of things in poems – only to see those representations as indicative of a human social or historical or cultural context. We talk often about object relations – only to shadow and detail some thought about human meaning. Sometimes we now talk about *things*, and how these things interrupt our expectations when they malfunction, and how poems and other kinds of art show us this. Yet this malfunctioning is always for someone, to wit, a human.

Despite all this, we are fascinated by things, and by things in poems. Studies of 'imagery' just don't quite reach them, and studies of imagery themselves are a dying breed. It appears the humanities have inherited and are reinvigorating and reproducing the general modern tendency to want to explain things away. That tendency was part of the initial reaction to Kant. Kant's startling insight that there really are things in themselves, lights in fridges to use the image I used just now, without me needing to make them real by checking them – that thought needs to be covered over, even by Kant, other inclinations notwithstanding. So for instance, Hegel: I am thinking the fridge and its light, so there is no 'actual' fridge; the fridge in itself is my fridge-thought. The uneasy way in which Kantian things are not just blank screens has been erased over and over again, in all kinds of different ways.

This has literary critical ramifications. A poem is 'merely' a cultural construct, which means that the context in which one finds the poem is more real than the poem as such – the context makes it real. It's taboo and disturbing to say that there are poems, hanging there, 'naked' – you get accused easily of essentialism, and such statements are absolutely inadmissible in theory class, in which the one totally unquestioned (non-theorised, indeed) assumption is that one must never, ever appear to be talking about essences of things. Let's face it. On the whole, things are seen as mere adjuncts of some human drama, like props, and mentioning them at all risks a certain unseemliness.

Aristotle himself was interested in texts as objects. What is a play? What is a tragedy? What can we expect from a recognition scene, or a jug, or a duck? Aristotle's answers are now unacceptably teleological: ducks are for swimming, tragedies are for making us cry, Greeks are for enslaving barbarians... But at least he is giving objects a try. Post-Kantian philosophy and evolutionary theory (among others) have made this kind of teleological approach illegal, which isn't a bad thing. We can never quite tell what some entity is for. Darwinian evolution is so drastically anti-teleological that some Darwinians at the time were anxious enough to insist that Darwin insert phrases such as 'survival of the fittest' into the manuscript, as if evolution theory really were just an extension of the dog-eat-dog politics of Social Darwinism (not the same thing at all). Being well adapted in Darwinism doesn't mean having six-pack abs or outsmarting your enemies. It means being able to pass on your DNA before you die. The bar is set unbelievably low, which is why there is so much diversity and so much clunky and wonderful non-functionality in life forms, including sexual selection, something so expensive that no self-respecting selfish gene would ever consider it. If it's efficiency you want, cloning is the way to go.

What if objects were not static or bland or lumpy at all? There is something profoundly strange about objects, which tells us something profoundly strange, yet intuitive, about poems. And what if that something was found to be quite explicit in all kinds of art? What would it do to criticism? Take out a coin. Look for the 'other' side of the coin. When you turn it over, what you have is always going to be 'this' side. Not the other side. Something about the coin withdraws from you. But it's much deeper than that. Even if you could see all sides of the coin at once, or all the uses to which the coin has and will be put, you will not see the actual coin. Imagine the dollar coin is sentient. It goes on Oprah and says: 'Well, I first came to consciousness in this philosopher's pocket. I was just an object to be used in his presentation. I had a bad childhood...' That wouldn't be the dollar coin either!

A thing is deeply mysterious, even to itself. Yet it is none other than itself. We usually think that kind of weirdness applies only to us. But it's dollar coins and microphones too. Haim Steinbach talks about how things talk to him, and how he talks to them. I think he also allows things to talk to one another. And indeed, laugh with one another. A Steinbach display seems to be full of giggles emanating from the entities that are already there. There is an overall sense of huge smile. It's a joyful laughter of coexisting, non-violently. And when I say *thing* here, I mean anything – maybe I should just say *entity*. You are an entity, a frog is an entity, a chorus of frogs is an entity, the meadow with all the frogs in it is an entity, the biosphere is an entity, Brazil is an entity, thoughts about frogs are entities – and on and on. It's crowded in here. And these entities, they can talk with one another – amongst themselves, when we're not listening.

## POETRY, ONTOLOGY, TEMPORALITY

How might one go about reading a literary text with regard to what I am here calling objects? One principal way would be to see how the text *times*. I mean this verb in a transitive sense, in so far as according to the view I am outlining here – object-oriented ontology – an entity emits time, time is an aesthetic property of things, rather than a neutral, blank container of things. Time is secondary to things. Why? This is really straightforward Humean science, at least at first. Causality has been shown to be a correlation among data, not some pregiven realm existing underneath objects. Time and space, the parameters of causality, are ontologically 'in front' of things. And this is borne out by relativity theory, in which spacetime is indeed an emergent property of things. We call this 'in front', if we are humanists, the aesthetic dimension. So when an artist makes an artwork, she is tampering directly with cause and effect. And when someone studies or appreciates it, she is studying or appreciating causality. Art is in no sense about some kind of decorative candy sprinkled on top of the boring cupcake of scientism.

A poem *times*. In what sense? To the general modern scientific environment in which time and space are in front of things, we must add the object-oriented desire to speak about things without a metaphysics of presence. Since an object cannot be reduced to its parts, or to some larger whole, or to some effect of some other entity such as a (human) subject or other 'decider' (history, economic relations, will, *Dasein*), and since it cannot even be reduced to some bland, lumpy version of itself, an object defies presence. Being is not presence, as Heidegger argued, and this is as true of fish and fish forks as it is true of human beings.

In practice, this means that what we call *present* is in some sense a fiction. It doesn't disappear altogether, but collapses into a shifting, unstable *nowness*. What the present can't be is a bounded, specific unit, an atom of time – whether we think that atom as a nanosecond or as a billion years. It doesn't matter, since *present* can be determined to arbitrary specifications. What is less arbitrary is the sliding of the past over the future, without touching, giving rise to the relative motion I am calling *nowness*.

This view, that there is no present but only past and future sliding over one another, sounds astonishing, but it's really an everyday experience. It's just that we are not well designed culturally, at this moment in the developed world, to understand it or appreciate it. Yet we can understand why this is the case simply by looking at an artwork such as a poem. A poem is a certain form: just this lineation, just that rhyme scheme, just this stanza form, just those images. Poems are records of causal–aesthetic decisions. To read a poem is to be an archaeologist. For OOO, the physical form of an object is a form-as and a formed-by. A glass is shaped the way the breath and hands of a glass blower, a tube and a blob of molten glass, interacted. Its shape is the trace of what happened to it. Freud argues that the ego is just the record of 'abandoned object cathexes'.[3] What if we inverted this phrase, and assert that the form of objects is their ego? If ego is object-like, then the inverse applies. The identity of this glass is the way it was shaped as a glass. Form is *memory*, as in a memory stick: your face, your hard drive, your chipped coffee mug, records what happened to it. What is called the past is really other objects that coexist with the object in question. When we hold a glass, we are holding the past. There is a profound *rift* between the *appearance* of the glass and the *essence* of the glass, which is not the same as the difference between an undifferentiated blob and a defined shape with stem, neck, weight, sparkle and so on. For lack of a better way of putting it, it's *the difference between the glass and the glass*. ('What is the difference between a duck? One of its legs is both the same.') The glass is a glass and an uncanny not-glass.

What then of the present? What is existing, or continuing, or persisting? It just means being in-difference from oneself. Existing thus is futural. It is not-yet. Consider a poem. Its meaning is its future. At some point we will read it and decide on its meaning. Then we re-read it and another meaning might emerge. The only reason we return to a poem is that it might release a different meaning this time. Since the aesthetic dimension is the causal dimension, what does this basic fact about what we do as literary scholars tell us about time itself? It tells us that the 'present' is not a bubble between past and future, or a blinking cursor, or a point. The present is a construct imposed on an uncanny intermeshing of appearance and essence. Presence is hollowed out from the inside by 'past' and 'future'. We are approaching an OOO interpretation of the end of Shelley's 'A Defence of Poetry', in which Shelley regards poets as 'the hierophants of an unapprehended inspiration, the mirrors of the gigantic shadows that futurity casts upon the present'.[4]

Because causality is aesthetic, it's legitimate to use poetry to think causality. Only consider what Harold Bloom says about a poem: 'the meaning of a poem can only be a poem, but *another poem – a poem not itself*'.[5] Likewise, the meaning of an object is another object. We can slightly modify this to argue that the 'other object' could uncannily be the very same object, since objects are dialetheic. This is not a limpid, naïve givenness: not WYSIWYG meaning (in an age before Microsoft Windows, this meant 'what you see is what you get'). This is a shifting, deceptive, illusory meaning. The past just is appearance. Contrary to the commonly held belief that appearance is 'now', the formal cause of a thing just is its pastness. That must mean that *the future is the essence of a thing*.

How startling: *appearance is the past, essence is the future*. We commonly associate the *essence* of a thing with the past: what was this thing before I looked at it, before it interacted with that other thing? Science is now beginning to confront the limitations of this default ontology. The quantum-theoretical definition of 'measure' is 'deflect with another quantum'. At this level, the link between perceiving and causing is undeniable, though many consider this to be an invitation to idealism or New Age fantasy. Many of the problems of Aristotelian–scholastic substance theories and post-Kantian correlationism (the Standard Model of quantum theory just is correlationist) stem from thinking essence as the past. Thus is born the light-in-the-refrigerator anxiety of the correlationist and the idealist. When you close the door, how can you tell if it's off?

The meaning of a poem is (in) the future. This future is not a now-point that is $n$ now-points away from the current one: it is withdrawn, it is withdrawal. This future is what Derrida calls *l'avenir*, the to-come, or what I call the *future future*.[6] In a strict sense, poetry does come from the future, just as Shelley argues. A weird Platonism is in effect, beaming the shadows of objects down from the future future into sensual – aesthetic – causal coexistence. The future future is not some transcendental beyond: this would be a top object par excellence. Nor is the future future a 'time in which' the object 'resides'. The future future is the pure possibility of the object as such.

Withdrawal is futurality, not as a predictable time that is ontically given. Nor is futurality a poststructuralist '*excess*', since this implies a thing for-which the object is excessive (this could be a telescope or a teabag as much as it could be a human or a fish). Excess is an appearance, belonging to the realm of an object's pastness. Nor is futurality a void, a gap or empty nothingness. Perhaps the term *openness* expresses it best. Withdrawal is openness, a shadow of futurity 'cast into the present' (Shelley).[7] Now we can discern more clearly the *chorismos* between essence and appearance. It is a rift between openness and pretence. An object persists and moves for as long as it can maintain its inner lie. If it is forced to speak nothing but the truth, destruction ensues: the rift collapses. On this view, the death of tyrants and the overthrow of oppression is the exposure of tyranny to its truth. Marx writes that the revolution to come must 'draw its poetry [...] from the future'. I wonder whether he had Shelley's 'A Defence of Poetry' in mind.[8] The very workings of causality as such are the shadow play of the future's poetry, vibrating the strings and surfaces and hollows of wind harps, egg cups, cathedrals, underwater gas pipelines, poems, neutron stars, PDFs and grains of salt.

On the event horizon of the black hole into which I have fallen, you see a slowly fading photograph of my horrified face.[9] A black hole is the densest possible object in the universe, an object from which no information escapes. In their appearance aspect, all objects are like the photograph on a black hole's event horizon. Fancifully, *appearance just is the event horizon of an object*, the point ontologically 'in front of which' causality becomes meaningful. Yet even black holes eventually evaporate. They exist because they do not coincide with their appearance. Eventually essence collapses into appearance, which is how an object ends. When I die, I become your memories of me, the crumpled pieces of paper in my waste paper basket.[10]

Samuel Beckett replies to someone that the reason why he writes in French is that 'There is a need to be ill-equipped', a phrase that also means 'There is a need to be Mallarmé'.[11] Mallarmé broke the hammer of poetry by stretching the space on which it was written like a rubber sheet, treating the paper as part of the poetry. The space stopped being a blank container for words, and started to be for humans what it already was: an entity in its own right. Paper can tear. Ink can spill. Lines of poetry can burst asunder. Trees can be pulped to form paper and wind harps. To write poetry is to force the reader to coexist with fragile phrases, fragile ink, fragile paper: to experience the many physical levels of a poem's architecture. Since there is no top object, no bottom object, and no middle object, sheer coexistence is what there is. To write poetry is to perform a non-violent political act, to coexist with other beings. This coexistence happens not in some eternal now, or in a now-point however expansive or constrained. The 'nowness' of a poem, its 'spaciousness', is the disquieting asymmetry between appearance and essence, past and future. With remorseless gentleness, a poem forces us to acknowledge that we coexist with uncanny beings in a groundless yet vivid reality without a beyond.

A literary text is as substantial as a butterfly, yet this substantiality means that it is not constantly present, but shimmering or flickering, without being pushed mechanically by anything else. All beings, whether they are butterflies or poems or thoughts, are considered to have the properties of withdrawal-yet-manifestation, according to the view I've outlined here. The question then becomes, what kinds of temporality does the poem afford us? What kind of meeting place is this?

## FURTHER READING

Bennett, Jane. *Vibrant Matter: A Political Ecology of Things*. Durham, NC: Duke University Press, 2010.

Bogost, Ian. *Alien Phenomenology: or What It's Like to Be a Thing*. Minneapolis: University of Minnesota Press, 2012.

Brown, Bill. *A Sense of Things*. Chicago: University of Chicago Press, 2003.

Gee, Henry. *In Search of Deep Time: Beyond the Fossil Record to a New History of Life*. New York: Free Press, 1999.

Harman, Graham. *The Quadruple Object*. London: Zero Books, 2011.

Harman, Graham. *Weird Realism: Lovecraft and Philosophy*. London: Zero Books, 2012.

Latour, Bruno. *We Have Never Been Modern*, trans. Catherine Porter. Cambridge, MA: Harvard University Press, 1993.

Mao, Douglas. *Solid Objects: Modernism and the Test of Production*. Princeton: Princeton University Press, 1999.

Morton, Timothy. *Ecology Without Nature: Rethinking Environmental Aesthetics*. Cambridge, MA: Harvard University Press, 2009.

Morton, Timothy. *Realist Magic: Objects, Ontology, Causality*. Ann Arbor: Open Humanities Press, 2013.

## CHAPTER 9

# Politics

David Ayers

Since recent years have been characterised by a return to a certain kind of historicism in literary studies, the question of politics has been opened up in a manner that requires analysis. Literary scholars invariably make reference to 'history', perhaps more now than ever before. However, the notion of what history is or what it can mean has become elusive. For that reason, some clarification of the manner in which the term 'history' has shifted is essential for literary scholars. As ever, any attempt to address a contemporary topic requires a review of the more long-term processes that can help to show us where we are now. The terms 'history' and 'politics' seem always to be implicitly associated, yet the relationship between these two terms or domains is of a peculiar complexity. When many years ago the Marxist literary theorist Fredric Jameson declared that we must 'always historicize', the very phrase implied a body of objects which were somehow *not* 'historicised', to which some process of 'historicisation' should be applied. The demand to historicise was, very evidently, made in the name of a politics, in this case a modernised and Americanised Marxist politics, which associated itself loosely as to objectives, internally with the social movements of women and so-called minorities, and externally with the decolonisation process in the Eastern hemisphere. The 'historicisation' of literary studies was inaugurated then in a particular political moment of which the two initial stimuli were probably the decolonisation process itself, and the much-celebrated moment of workers and counter-cultural revolt in Europe of 1968. The working assumption was that literary studies as then constituted served to obscure history in a manner that, intentionally or otherwise, concealed the ideological functions of both literature in its own times and of literary and cultural criticism as a university practice. The assumption was that really any form of historicisation would serve to uncover a variety of concealed social functions, and that in particular Marxism in its then modern form would avail itself of these resources to demonstrate that the broad function of literature as instituted in universities, and in other contexts of its transmission and mediation, could be shown to constitute a kind of ideological masking which served to protect the status quo from a development of human consciousness(es) which would otherwise overthrow existing conditions and allow for a fuller development of human potential and a movement from oppression to freedom.

This, in sum, was the manner in which a Marxist or Marxist-influenced criticism advocated a 'return' to history, as if literary and cultural history had hitherto ignored history for conscious or unconscious political ends, and the 'return' to history would complement and serve to further the aims of a global liberation movement in which workers, women, students and young people, and the majority world would be the bearers of the consciousness of a new, freer future. This is not to say that these bearers of consciousness necessarily looked to literature, literary studies or, indeed, to Marxism for inspiration or support, although in different ways they often did. American feminist groups would often use literary reading groups as a mode of what they called 'consciousness-raising'; African-American authors such as Richard Wright and Ralph Ellison had in the 1940s and 1950s created novels designed to articulate and intervene in the African-American political situation; Anglophone former colonies questioned the pedagogic role of English literature in school curricula; Scottish nationalists mapped a Scottish literary tradition as the necessary cultural underpinning of their own national liberation movement. These examples can be multiplied, although it is not clear that every brand of literary historicism active today lends itself to the process of political liberation. Indeed some of that activity is indistinguishable from varieties of biography and antiquarianism which the 'left' broadly speaking had earnestly wished to sweep away. Jameson's slogan referred less to a process of historical documentation than to the need for a historiography informed by Marxism. It is striking though that in Jameson's phrase 'history' is substituted for 'politics': the injunction is not to 'politicise' but to 'historicise'.

## THE POLITICS OF HISTORICISING CRITICISM

The governing assumption of the model, which saw some kind of historical unmasking as a political process, is that politics and history are broadly the same thing. This is a profoundly modern assumption with clear roots in the thought of Hegel. What is meant by the term 'politics' is not that series of questions regarding governance, constitution, formal electoral process and so on – that set of things which are the domain of governments and their administrations, whether shaped by a party-political electoral process or not – but rather the total ensemble of human relations. 'History' implies not simply that set of things which happen to happen, so to speak, but a process in which the general human condition is increasingly enlightened and improved. This totalising view of history was set out by Hegel in the lectures gathered and published as *The Philosophy of History*.[1] The view of history which Hegel sets out in those lectures is profoundly political in terms of the role which it accords to the state in the process of the attainment of human freedom, what Hegel calls 'the *freedom* of spirit', where by 'spirit' is meant not simply the world of ideas but the 'substantial world', that is that which is realised in the totality of human practical existence. The objective of spirit is both to be conscious of its own freedom and to realise it, something that Hegel claims has indeed taken shape in certain Christian, European states. 'World history' has continually aimed at this freedom, and this 'idea of freedom' is the 'final aim' which is 'God's purpose with the world'. Hegel does not accept that the state is a constraint on the freedom of individuals, but argues the contrary, that the state is the realisation of the project of human freedom. It is not enough to arrive at the simple idea of freedom in the abstract; 'to introduce the principle [of freedom] into the various relations of the actual world, involves a more extensive problem than its simple implantation; a problem whose solution and application require a severe and lengthened process of culture'.[2] So the political objective of freedom is only attained through a historical process, and history itself *is* this process: despite the appearance of chaos in certain periods of human affairs, as individuals rationally pursue their individual goals, there is at work another rationality, in which individuals grasp that their freedom can only be realised in the whole.

Hegel's general argument is not widely accepted today, and indeed much of recent theory is in effect an attempt to find alternatives to the Hegelian notion of history which is presumed to have been exploded. Yet Hegel's arguments are not easily dismissed without in effect disavowing his general desire to see human history in terms of ethical progress, regardless of the accident of events, and regardless of the accidental differences between peoples. This resistance to Hegel is partly evidenced by the frequent recourse of modern theory to the term 'difference' as the marker of unclosable gaps which cannot be swept away by progress and which it cannot be assumed will finally be subsumed under a universal or absolute, which might presumably take the form of a world government. This question of world order and of global governance, though, remains at the front of everyone's minds today, and if there is a perpetual sense of crisis in world affairs which rotates continually around the ethical leadership role of the United States and the legitimacy of supranational bodies such as the United Nations, in terms of literary studies, and reflected in what is only apparently a wholly different way, there is a gentle and mainly unspoken crisis concerning the rejection of Hegelianism and the loosening of the bonds between history and politics – that is, the loss of confidence in the politics of a historicising criticism.

Hegel was well aware of the prima facie objections to his optimistic vision of the slow but inevitable progress in human affairs. His case for what the state is as a collective venture is carefully reasoned. The essential being of the individual, he argues, is a union of the subjective and of rational will, and it is the 'moral whole, the *state*, which is that form of reality in which the individual has and enjoys his freedom; but on the condition of his recognizing, believing in, and willing that which is common to the whole'. The state is not that which denies freedom through its laws but its laws are the realisation of freedom. The State is the 'actually existing, realized moral life'. In his most abstract formulation, Hegel asserts that 'truth is the unity of the universal and subjective will; and the universal is to be found in the state'.[3] This carefully reasoned account runs into two principal difficulties, both of which Hegel attempts to deal with.

First, how can the claim that the state (or what Aristotle calls the *polis*) is the summit of a process of long historical evolution, in which reason as such leads to an end of history in freedom, be reconciled with the fact that the individual actors in the supposed historical process have acted without envisaging this final goal, which is indeed not yet fully anticipated, let alone realised? Hegel's attempted answer is, famously, to argue for the 'cunning of reason', which is his term for the operation of supra-individual reason in the background, as it were, even where individuals are pursuing only selfish or localised goals. So reason will always arrive at its single, universal end, no matter the accidental, particular outcomes which may befall it along the way.[4]

Second, if the state is the realisation of absolute reason, how does one deal with the fact that the world is filled with a multiplicity of states or peoples which are actually different in nature? Hegel answered this question by asserting that 'each particular national genius is to be treated as only one individual in the process of universal history' and, while insisting that each national development represented a 'grade' of development (that is: as if there were still only one, single developmental 'scale'), glossed over the reality of differences by concluding that 'to realize these grades is the boundless impulse of world-spirit', and that 'this division into organic members, and the full development of each, is its Idea'.[5] While the logic of Hegel's position regarding cultural difference may prove unpersuasive to many, it is those points at which he reveals his dependence on Eurocentric and (as we would see it) racist paradigms that will lead many readers to find that his view of a universal historical development is fundamentally flawed, or at least very much 'of its time', as when, examining questions of comparative national/racial development, he asserts: 'A mild and passionless disposition, want of spirit, and a crouching submissiveness towards a Creole, and still more towards a European, are the chief characteristics of the native Americans; and it will be long before the Europeans succeed in producing any independence of feeling in them.'[6] Yet Hegel is the great theorist of the state as the realisation of freedom. Freedom arises from the drives and desires of individuals, and the state, through a complex process of ethical development, allows these desires to take shape and human potential to be realised. This is a dramatic reversal of the viewpoint which sees human desires as only individual and the state then merely as the normative container of anti-social desires and the arbiter of conflicts of interest. Yet Hegel's vision of a universal history clearly stumbles when it attempts to deal with national difference, and the Eurocentrism of his model tends to equate European and universal history in a way that satisfies few thinkers today.

Yet the world we inhabit is the very one which Hegel attempted to describe. Politics does not for us have simply the restricted meaning of the form of government, but extends to the notion that there is a politics of everyday life – that the form of the family, interpersonal behaviour, religion, literature and arts, sexuality, wars, environment, all aspects of individual identity, all have a politics, are all political, and are all given shape not within the individual existence but within the whole, not merely within the whole which is the state we happen to inhabit, but also in the whole world. So if Hegel's view of a universal history has come to be doubted, his grand view of the universal and dialectical nature of ethical life has many elements in common with what – often invisibly – passes for common intellectual sense today. Hegel's view of politics, though, depended on his model of history, and the governing question of the inquiry in this essay – which involves many more steps backward than forward – is: what is the consequence for theory's practice of historicism, which is undertaken implicitly in the name of a universalistic ethics, when the view of history as a progression towards a universal ethical end has been abandoned?

It is clarifying when addressing this to look back to the ancient world, where the notion of history as progress was unavailable. When Aristotle attempted to describe the function of the state in the documents collected as his *Politics*,[7] he had around him the world of the Greek city-states, in which quite contrasting forms of government existed side-by-side. Aristotle's study is comparative, that is, he contrasts different forms of government, such as oligarchy and democracy, and does indeed ask how changes in form of government come about, but the net contrast with Hegel is very evidently that Aristotle does not see freedom as the desideratum of government, he does not share Hegel's idea that freedom must be for all, including slaves, and he certainly has no notion of history as the process of unfolding of human self-realisation. Yet it is the Greek world which gave us the term politics. The term *polis* in Greek refers to the city-state. It is related to the terms *polit¬ēs*, citizen, *politeia*, constitution, and *politikē*, politics (whether as practice or theory). Politics for Aristotle is mainly concerned with the question of the form of government, yet he takes a key step which is influential on Hegel and which forms part of the common intellectual sense which steers contemporary theory: he views the city and the citizen, that is, the state and the individual, as a unity. While in Aristotle's view only those qualify as citizens who participate in the administration of the state, with others such as slaves and labourers allotted a lesser role,[8] his view nevertheless creates the ground for the modern view of the state developed by Hegel. Yet when it comes to the question of political change – that is, of changes not merely in government but in modes of government – since Aristotle has no view of progress he can only argue that factional conflicts regarding the constitution arise from differences of opinion, so democracy arises from the opinion that people are equal in every way, oligarchy from the opinion that people may be equal in some ways but not in every way.[9] Aristotle takes a particular view of equality, preferring a middle way between democracy and oligarchy which he believes reflects the reality that human beings are not absolutely equal, but his answer to the question how and why constitutional changes occur is that they are driven by the conflict of different views of, and interests in, equality.[10]

Aristotle's view of the state tolerates the difference between states that Hegel, as we have seen, struggled to account for. Yet Aristotle's *Politics*, which settles in the main for a simple comparison of different forms of state without any notion of progress, also struggles, in that it cannot account for changes to the state except as the accidental result of conflict between factions arising from opinion and interest. In Hegel, history is going somewhere; in Aristotle it is not. It should not be thought, though, that the subsequent rejection of Hegelian goal-oriented or teleological history has arisen from a merely intellectual process. Marx and Engels criticised Hegel's belief that history had reached its end in the form of the modern state. They argued that a further inevitable stage of conflict between classes would lead the world into a true final phase, communism, in which states themselves would disappear. While Marx and Engels were the first and most important of the intellectual opponents of this aspect of the Hegelian view of history, they basically shared Hegel's view of history as collective, human progress. It was not just intellectual arguments concerning Hegel, though, which account for the broad rejection of his view of history, but the attempt to realise the project of Marx and Engels which took place in Russia in 1917.

## COMMUNITY AND ALTERITY IN LITERARY HISTORY

In 1920, one of many foreign visitors to Russia keen to witness the effects of the 1917 revolution, the British journalist H. N. Brailsford, visited the Russian Workers' Soviet (council) in the town of Vladímir, some 120 miles from Moscow. One of the things that Brailsford noted was the massive extension of the role of the state:

> The word 'administration' suggests to our Western experience an important but limited conception. One thinks of roads and police, public health and elementary schools. It means under Communism the entire organisation of life. The State is manufacturer and merchant, farmer and railway director, and on the brains at its head, and the bureaucratic machinery below them, every detail of the citizen's welfare depends. The work of every counting-house and bank has been concentrated [...] The banker's cashier and the book-keeper have now become civil servants. The young women who would have been typing and calculating in a hundred separate offices are now working at rather similar tasks in a few big rooms. Nearly everyone in what we call the 'middle class' (Russians with more dignity describe it as the 'intelligentsia') is now a public servant on salary and rations. Only the big capitalists and landlords have fled.[11]

Brailsford's observation encapsulates the shift that was taking place at that time in the early Soviet state which was to be replicated later in the ambition of many modern states to subject to state control every aspect of human life. This tendency is confirmed in the writings of Leon Trotsky. Trotsky had been the leading orator of the revolution and was the commander of the Red Army during the period of Allied Intervention and the Civil War which followed. He had been a highly competent military commander and produced extensive writings on military theory. Trotsky was no stranger therefore to effective organisation, and once the Civil War had been concluded he turned his analytical skills to domestic matters in a series of essays published in 1923. One group of essays deals with questions of everyday life, the other with literature and art. The second group of these was published in book form in English as *Literature and Revolution* (1925), a famous collection which has had an influential role in the history of literary theory; the first group was published in English as *Problems of Life* (1924), and is barely known at all. These essays manifest the same desire, to bring control of cultural life, whether culture is taken to mean art or simply everyday life, under the influence of the state. In the essays on literature, Trotsky evaluates the existing literary currents, themselves shaped by theoretical considerations – symbolism, proletarian literature, formalism, futurism – and assesses their ability to contribute to the as-yet-unrealised communist future. Divided between his recognition of the need for autonomy in art and his sense of the necessity that art must serve progress, Trotsky remarks:

> Our policy in art, during a transitional period, can and must be to help the various groups and schools of art which have come over to the Revolution to grasp correctly the historical meaning of the Revolution, and to allow them complete freedom of self-determination in the field of art, after putting before them the categorical standard of being for or against the Revolution.[12]

While states had frequently employed censorship before, this notion that the state would require a certain function of all art evidences a new ambition for an unprecedented integration of cultural functions with the steering mechanisms of the state. This step towards state control of the arts is paralleled by Trotsky's essays on everyday life, notably in his account of the manner in which socialism must socialise women's work, thus removing the economic motives for marriage, thereby not only making marriage a more free choice but also creating the conditions for the emergence of a new and as yet unanticipated form of family life.

The total administration of life becomes a theme of Trotsky's writings. This theme of absolute administration would also become a dominant strand in the writings of Adorno and Horkheimer who, in the published text of *Dialectic of Enlightenment* (1944), pointedly created a vocabulary which treated communist administration and capitalist trusts and governments in the same analytical breath. While Trotsky in orthodox Marxist fashion views the total administration of life as a desirable, rational necessity, Adorno and Horkheimer view the fulfilment of reason in history not as the realisation of freedom which Hegel anticipated, but as the subjection of the individual to the domination of the whole. 'The Enlightenment has always aimed at liberating men from fear and establishing their sovereignty. Yet the fully enlightened earth radiates disaster triumphant.'[13] The manner in which the domination of all aspects of life has taken hold not only in the workplace but in culture is outlined by Adorno and Horkheimer in their discussion of the culture industry. Using the US culture industry as their model, they argue that the technological means at the disposal of culture – which has now become a mass industry – allow it to standardise the consumption of culture and ensure the complete identification of the individual with the general society.

In this pessimistic analysis, the culture industry is the form in which the path of reason is perverted into one of a new domination, and in which therefore the path of history towards freedom is not only thwarted but reversed. Despite the resonance which this account has gained with many readers, the significance of the Russian revolution – and, on many measures, its evident failure – should probably be regarded as the key moment in which the apparent realisation of a Hegelian-Marxist historical vision turned into something else. One consequence of this is that it became necessary to formulate a new theory of history – one which did not depend on a progression to absolute reason – and at the same time to begin to reconceptualise society – in terms which would not presuppose an inevitable ethical onward march. The modalities of this rethinking have been various and uneven, and it is in this uneven and, it might be said, frequently unacknowledged philosophical and practical context, that the present dominance of historicism in cultural scholarship and analysis now functions.

## HISTORY AFTER THE GRAND NARRATIVES OF HISTORY

One example of the philosophical revisiting of the theory of history can be found in the work of Jean-Luc Nancy. His *The Inoperative Community* (1990) begins from the premise that the Hegelian notion of a progressive history had not only suffered a devastating blow from the perversion of the hope of the Russian revolution into the reality of the totalitarian state, but that it was in any case a philosophically incoherent position. One consequence of the real failure of communism, Nancy argues, has been the loss of any ability to think about community, and about all of the ideals of liberty and justice which had been espoused by communism. Politics and the theory of history are therefore closely intertwined. According to Nancy, for us, now, history is suspended or finished; it no longer progresses towards a goal, and can no longer be imagined in terms of its meaning. Yet he argues that we cannot go back to the ancient view, as found in Aristotle, of history as the simple reportage of successive events, even though we can no longer believe in history as what Hegel called the 'ruse of reason', working to deliver freedom behind the scenes.[14] While it was once possible to imagine ourselves as taking part in a historical grand narrative, we no longer belong to history, or indeed to time, in the same way. Nancy claims that in this post-Hegelian world, history is without an idea and cannot be theorised.[15] Now, history is not the pattern of inevitable events in which we participate; instead our way of being in history lies in the process of reabsorbing history. History for us is now the history of history, and Nancy argues that this end of history gives us to ourselves in a new way, requiring us to formulate a new concept of community which can properly respond to the fact that the Hegelian or Marxist collective narrative no longer holds.

Nancy operates at an abstract theoretical level. It is possible to object to the airy manner in which he presents the notion that history is suspended – as a consequence, he argues, of 'total war, genocide, the nuclear arms race, technology without mercy, famine and absolute misery, all these apparent signs of the self-destruction of the human race, of the self-annihilation of history'.[16] We would be right to be cautious of the haziness of this narrative. War, genocide and famine are not new, and from the perspective of the 2010s the 1980s assumption that the potential of nuclear annihilation or – though Nancy does not mention it here explicitly – the holocaust have changed history itself would require further analysis to say the least. Yet Nancy is surely right to focus on the failure of the Russian revolution as the demise of the hopes of communism and as a crisis therefore for any project of social justice in the absence of a credible grand narrative of historical progress.

Nancy's own response to this dilemma has the advantage, for us, of making explicit the shakiness, now, of the theoretical underpinnings of the attempts to think about politics in philosophical terms, and by extension the latent problems for a contemporary historicism which seeks to put itself at the service of a collective politics – that is, of community. Nancy draws on two sets of vocabulary: the interrogation of the question of Being in the work of Martin Heidegger, and the working-through of difference in the work of Jacques Derrida. Community is no longer a unity, according to Nancy: 'There is not *a* common *being*, there is a being *in* common, or being one *with* the other, or being *together*.' In the space of being together, difference appears: 'The alterity of existence arrives only as "being together". [...] Being together is alterity.'[17]

The philosophy of difference or alterity on which Nancy draws here is also commonly found in that contemporary literary-theoretical work which is routinely grounded in the term 'difference', except that such work very frequently has recourse also to the notion of identity. It is worth pausing over this, since the point of Nancy's model is to suggest that community only exists in difference, *without* there being any subject or essence which differs from any other subject or essence. In other words, as in Saussure's *Course in General Linguistics*, there are only differences without positive terms. By contrast, the cultural-theoretical discussion of identity – in such contexts as the politics of gender identity, sexual identity, racial or national identity and so on – oscillates awkwardly between the assertion of a common subject identity (for example, lesbian) and the notion that such an identity is marked by difference (for example, from a patriarchal, heterosexual norm). Nancy is therefore more rigorous in discerning that the abandonment of a philosophy of history as progress now requires a politics based on difference without any recourse to identity. Literary scholarship tends to step over this difficulty, though, in a more pragmatic manner, as it finds a constant stream of subordinated or eclipsed identities which must be liberated from the menace of totality, from the supposed normative tendencies of the state, and from the related assumption that a single state (the USA) or grouping of states (the 'West') can and must embody the highest realisation of ethical or political progress which other states or peoples should seek to attain.

This observation, which necessarily generalises across a range of domains and activities and which could be applied more or less differently in the many different contexts of cultural studies, and even then only in certain (though dominant) areas of scholarly work, could nevertheless be documented across a series of examples. What begins to be seen now is that the failure of the Russian revolution, combined with the tendency of developed states and their cultural machinery to extend their power over human life, has led broadly to a pessimism regarding both progress and the state which, on the one hand, requires a fairly rigorous (though abstract) reworking, but which also requires a pragmatic response on the part of those elements of cultural studies which are engaged in any way in any politics of ethical revaluation – politics which would be construed as progressive were it not for the simple fact that the notion of progress has had its philosophical underpinnings swept away. What this means in practice is that cultural studies themselves tend to share the view of philosophy that they exist in the aftermath of the philosophy of history. They evoke the typical vocabulary of 'difference', and also seek to unearth subordinated histories which are said to have vanished beneath the dominance of imperial or Western powers. Yet just as philosophy has failed, really, to provide a true alternative to Hegelian and Marxist models – and, indeed, as real-world political practice has so far proved little able to escape from the model of the state, with new states created in abundance since 1917 – so too cultural theory has tended to do little more than evoke a kind of pathos around difference as the symbol of its desire to escape the aftermath of the fall of the theory of history, even while its activities serve quite practically to give space to differences and give life to previously hidden or marginalised narratives.

## BIOPOLITICS, PESSIMISM, CHANGE

The situation of politics after Hegel then is complicated for everyone. There is, though, an unfortunate contrast between the progressive optimism of Hegelian theories of history and the state, and a contemporary recourse to theoretical pessimism which has been such a strong thread of social and cultural theory since the 1930s and the rise of Adorno and the Frankfurt School. This style of pessimism can be seen in the attention paid to biopolitics. Biopolitics takes the pessimism of Adorno and Horkheimer one step further, by arguing that not subjects – in the classical sense of the self-knowing entity intended by philosophy – but the body itself, or bodies themselves, have become the object of totalising administration. This strand of thinking relies heavily on Michel Foucault, who in a series of books examined the scientific administration of mental health (*Madness and Civilisation*, 1961), medicine (*The Birth of the Clinic*, 1963), crime (*Discipline and Punish*, 1975), and sex (*The History of Sexuality*, 1976–84). Each of these areas concerns the control of the body. This pattern of thinking was elaborated by Foucault in the context of a rejection of the notion of history as progress in favour of a model which suggested that changes in societal norms were akin to paradigm shifts in the sciences, which are in effect more-or-less abrupt changes from one episteme, or model of knowledge, to another. Change, in other words, does not represent progress and does not ensure any human liberation. If anything, in Foucault's vision, things are getting worse. Madness is now no longer in dialogue with modern reason, but is its object; medical science has made an object of the body, divorced from the subjectivity which it embodies; prison transforms the aberrant into bodies; scientific and social discussions of sex are a key element in the disciplining of all bodily and psychological functions in modern society – and not at all the liberation of the body or the progressive discovery of any truth about sex.

Biopolitics in the wake of Foucault has tended to emulate this pessimism. In *Homo Sacer: Sovereign Power and Bare Life* (1995), Giorgio Agamben returns to Aristotle's *Politics*, noting Aristotle's celebration of the good life as the objective of all men, individually or in community. Life, says Aristotle, is an end in itself. Men create and maintain communities with the goal of simply living. Most people are attached to life as if there were, just in that, a sort of serenity and natural sweetness.[18] This simple natural life, notes Agamben, was even in the ancient world considered separate from the world of the *polis*. Turning to the modern world, he endorses Foucault's claim that here, by contrast, natural life does not stand outside the *polis*, but is included in the mechanisms and political calculations of the state, and what for Aristotle was politics is in the modern age now biopolitics. So the classical style of examining power in terms of the legal and political structures which govern an otherwise natural life which they cannot penetrate now shifts into the analysis of a new style of sovereignty – the biopolitical – which is nevertheless continuous with and not absolutely dissociable from the old, since each treats naked life as an exception or exclusion.[19] Agamben argues that while Foucault made a key move in examining power in terms of institutions such as psychiatry, medicine and incarceration, he did not take account as he might of the connections between such institutions and state power, and he did not take account of the most glaring example of the exercise of state power over naked life: the Nazi extermination camps. So biopolitics returns to the theory of the state, revisiting Aristotle and renouncing the optimistic Hegelian view of the state as the site of the realisation of human potentials and desires. Indeed the focus on the concentration camps tends to carry biopolitics into an almost absolutely pessimistic vision of the exercise of power over life. In the extermination camps, Agamben claims, biopolitics has become thanatopolitics – death-politics: 'In this perspective, the camp, as pure, absolute and unsurpassed biopolitical space [...] will appear as the hidden paradigm of the political space of the modernity whose metamorphoses and disguises we must learn to recognise. The camp, and not the city, is today the biopolitical paradigm of the West.'[20] The focus of biopolitics on the extermination camps in a way replicates and reverses the Hegelian notion of the grand narrative of history; not liberation but increasing subjugation is the *telos* of this narrative.

Alert to the risks of such organised pessimism, Alain Badiou has argued that philosophy should step away from accounting for history, especially if that has caused leading philosophers to declare that philosophy is powerless to account for such apparently unthinkable realities as the extermination camps.[21] Philosophy, though, can still take responsibility for providing an account of the nature of change, even if changes in the state and society can no longer be attributed to progress. 'History does not exist', states Badiou, but this does not mean that communism – which he desires – cannot exist, rather that it must be regarded as an idea, not a simply available reality, where an idea has a multivalent form as simultaneously real, symbolic and ideological.[22] To follow through the manner in which Badiou creates a theory of change in the theory of ontology which he presents in *Being and the Event* (1988) is beyond the scope of this chapter, except to note that Badiou has set himself the task of erecting an entire machinery which can account for change without any recourse to a Hegelian notion of progress. The notion of communism as an 'idea', involving the redefinition of what an idea is in its relation to political reality, can be viewed as symptomatic of the difficulties in which the desire for a really different political reality (communism) now finds itself once the notion of progress has been abandoned.

## THE POLITICS OF LITERATURE

It is not surprising that other thinkers have opted for simpler models than that offered by Badiou. Jacques Rancière, for one, has adopted a much simpler model of democratic social change. Making recourse to Aristotle – though with some indebtedness to Badiou[23] – Rancière defines the existing state of things, and in particular the available forms of common understanding which he calls the 'sensible', as the 'police', playing on the Aristotelian notion of *polis*. In Rancière's reading of Aristotle, the *demos* or common people are perpetually excluded from representation. Democracy, or the rule of the people in general, cannot ever be a reality, instead it must be a principle which operates every time an unarticulated group or desire attempts to achieve political articulation. Politics is thus always an eruption of the *demos* against the controlled set of representations made available by the actually existing state, the 'police' or *polis*: 'Politics exists when the figure of a specific subject is constituted, a supernumerary subject in relation to the calculated number of groups, places, and functions in a society. This is summed up in the concept of the *demos*.'[24] That is, politics is defined in terms of the excluded, and not in the terms of any political science or any philosophy of the state. The aesthetic enters this frame as a key point of intervention against the existing state and its official representations, the 'sensible':

> An aesthetic politics always defines itself by a certain recasting of the distribution of the sensible, a reconfiguration of perceptual forms [...] The dream of a suitable political work of art is in fact the dream of disrupting the relationship between the visible, the sayable, and the thinkable without having to use the terms of a message as a vehicle. It is the dream of an art that would transmit meanings in the form of a rupture with the very logic of meaningful situations.[25]

Literary politics, then, would amount to the intervention of literature *as* literature (and not as political discourse) in the process which decides what is visible or invisible, what is a voice or what is merely noise, an intervention therefore in the forms of the visible and the sayable. Modernity in literature is not, he argues, a matter of the breaking away of the arts from the tyranny of representation in favour of the autonomy of language, as traditional accounts of literary modernism have asserted. Instead, the literature of modernity takes its effect not from its own formal break with the past but from the democratic levelling implicit in the forms of art. So Flaubert is the example of a writer who is personally anti-democratic, but whose fixation on the materiality of language and indifference to his subjects ushers in a new regime of the art of writing in which the writer or the reader could be anyone. This new regime offers a literature which opposes the literature of the classical age, which sustained the representative order of the status quo, and offers instead a neutral writing in which the real can present itself and be available to any reader.[26] Rancière develops this model in his writings on literature and on the visual arts in the spirit of answering a kind of pessimism which considers that art has failed or retreated following the failure of the grand political project of revolutionary socialism. Democracy is in a constant state of emergence, is his underlying claim. Politics, he writes, 'is not about the exercise of power or about the struggle for power', but concerns the struggle over who can speak and what can be spoken about.[27] For thinkers and teachers, this implies a whole pedagogy centred around the surrender of mastery, a breakdown of the division of labour between those who know (and are empowered, the 'police') and those who do not know (the excluded *demos*).[28]

Rancière's work is just one manifestation of a contemporary desire to articulate a politics of literature free from the demands of party politics and the state, one which would be free of the burden of the failure of communism and, with it, the corresponding pessimism about progress, and about art's own failure to instantiate liberation or respond to the tragedies of the last century. In general, contemporary literary commentary steps away from the rigorous theoretical examination of the state and, while it gestures against the totalising and imperialist state, has tended to concentrate on more local goals – such goals as the rights of native Americans; the uncovering of lost working-class or gay histories; the ecological impact of industry; the preservation and reanimation of eclipsed cultures and languages; the cultural mediation and effects of discourses of science, medicine, consumerism, fashion, race, lifestyle. These typical topics of literary commentary are in general addressed to local political issues, and they will always claim to speak in the name of a politics in the post-1917 sense, in which it has been increasingly assumed that every aspect of everyday life belongs to the political in some fashion. Yet while such work is in general intended to interdict the machinations of capitalist and state power – and will commonly employ what is purportedly an anti-Hegelian rhetoric against the state and in defence of difference – it perhaps thankfully does not replicate the kind of political pessimism which has been identified here in a current running from Adorno to Agamben. This perhaps results in tensions and contradictions within such work, which usually fails to embrace the necessary working-through of political philosophy which, as appears in the example of Nancy, is necessary in the wake of the demise of Hegelian optimism and the evident impasse of the theory of history. And yet, it may be that the politics of much cultural commentary today implicitly embraces a Hegelian vision, even though Hegel has become the principal object of the critique of 'Western' thought. The politics of theory today – and of the types of historicism it embraces – still stems from an optimism about ethical practice, from the assumption that ethical questions are political in nature and can indeed be in some way progressed, even when the theory of progress has been abandoned, by giving voice to the unvoiced. In this sense, and in spite of itself, cultural commentary today retains a Hegelian style of faith in the progression towards freedom implicit in the process of realising human desire not in the form of individual needs, but in the form of change and development in the numerous institutions and the polyvalent cultures which indeed still do – in a dialectical fashion – continue to act on and transform the nature of states.

## FURTHER READING

Adorno, Theodor W. and Max Horkheimer. *Dialectic of Enlightenment*, trans. John Cummings. London and New York: Verso, 1986.

Agamben, Giorgio. *Homo Sacer: Sovereign Power and Bare Life*, trans. Daniel Heller-Roazen. Stanford: Stanford University Press, 1998.

Aristotle. *Politics*, trans. Ernest Barker. Revised edition with an introduction and notes by R. F. Stalley. Oxford and New York: Oxford University Press, 1995.

Badiou, Alain. *The Communist Hypothesis*, trans. David Macey and Steve Corcoran. London and New York: Verso, 2010.

Foucault, Michel. *Discipline and Punish: The Birth of the Prison*, trans. Alan Cumming. Harmondsworth: Penguin, 1977.

Jameson, Fredric. *The Political Unconscious: Narrative as a Socially Symbolic Act*. Ithaca: Cornell University Press, 1981.

Hegel, Georg Friedrich Wilhelm. *The Philosophy of History*, trans. J. Sibree. Preface by Charles Hegel. Introduction by C. J. Friedrich. Mineola: Dover, 2004.

Marcuse, Herbert. *One Dimensional Man: Studies in the Ideology of Advanced Industrial Society*. London and New York: Routledge, 2002.

Nancy, Jean-Luc. *The Inoperative Community*, ed. Peter Connor, trans. Peter Connor, Lisa Garbus, Michael Holland and Simona Sawnhey. Foreword by Christopher Fynsk. Minneapolis: University of Minnesota Press, 1991.

Rancière, Jacques. *The Politics of Aesthetics: The Distribution of the Sensible*. Translated and introduced by Gabriel Rockhill. London and New York: Continuum, 2004.

# PART III

# Temporalities

## CHAPTER 10

# Time

## Tyrus Miller

A t the outset of this chapter, I consider the broad topic of time and the 'poetic imagination' – or, stated even more broadly, the concept of a 'productive imagination' intrinsically engaging a temporal dimension, the synthesis and manifestation in time of new cognitive, figurative or linguistic complexes. In a necessarily cursory treatment, I refer to a few key figures in German philosophy – Gotthold Ephraim Lessing, Immanuel Kant, Wilhelm Dilthey and Martin Heidegger – who provide conceptual background for my more specific discussion of temporality in literary history, which constitutes the main subject of this chapter. Accordingly, following this initial exposition of the imagination's temporal nature, I go on to discuss three aspects of temporality in literary history as conceived by key literary and aesthetic thinkers of the twentieth century, including Erich Auerbach, Hans-Georg Gadamer, Mikhail Bakhtin, Paul Ricoeur, Gérard Genette, Walter Benjamin, Paul De Man and Gilles Deleuze. First, I consider time in its relation to interpretation: as an integral element of interpretative acts, as a medium of human experience articulated and qualified through interpretative processes, and as a defining component of a broad range of textual hermeneutic theories. Second, I discuss time in its relation to narrative, in particular, the technical features of narrative that allow time to be articulated, reordered, and in some cases played with or refigured in ways that diverge radically from objective chronology or the intuitive everyday experience of time. Third and finally, I consider time in its relation to the historiography of literary history: primarily, the periodising notions of literary history that arose with modern historicism, and various alternative concepts of literary period, context and historicity implied by modern critiques of historicism.

## TIME AND POETIC IMAGINATION

In 1766, Gotthold Ephraim Lessing published his *Laocoön*, subtitled *An Essay on the Limits of Painting and Poetry*. Having first dealt with what he conceived as the spatial essence of the expressive signs used in paintings, which represent actions indirectly by depicting bodies in single poses, he turns in chapter sixteen to poetry, which, he argues, is suited by the successive nature of its signs to represent actions directly, in their unfolding in time. Actions, he writes, 'are the true subjects of poetry',[1] and if poetry also represents bodies, it is not through direct depiction like painting, but as inferred from the characteristics of action. He goes on to point to the example of Homer, whose writings, Lessing claims, represent 'nothing but progressive actions. He depicts bodies and single objects only when they contribute toward these actions, and then only by a single trait'.[2] Lessing thus drew an influential distinction between arts of simultaneity in space and arts of succession in time. In turn, this distinction framed his influential critical attack on descriptive pictoriality in poetry and on allegory in painting, which he saw as inadmissible admixtures of the proper essential characteristics of the arts. In this foundational work of modern literary and art criticism, thus, artistic categories and critical judgements intertwine in an exemplary fashion with philosophical reflection on the nature of language and its relation to time.

Less than two decades after Lessing's seminal work appeared, Immanuel Kant, in his *Critique of Pure Reason*, provided a ground-breaking philosophical definition of time, both distinguishing it from and relating it to space as an 'intuition-form' that structures all possible experience. Time, Kant argues, must be understood as our '*inner* intuition-form' (as space is the outer intuition-form) of experience, which means there is a particular intimacy between temporality and our awareness of our own mental activity. Moreover, though at first postulating them as complementary forms of intuition, Kant goes on to discern an asymmetry between space and time, which ultimately leads him to claim time's predominance as the most general form of intuition. Even our intuitions of the spatially extended world outside of us, Kant notes, are ultimately available to us only as inner representations; therefore, both our spatial intuitions as well as our inner, aspatial, temporal intuitions are mediated by the inward temporality of subjectivity.[3] In his larger system, Kant arrayed the stream of pure intuitions on one side (sensibility) and pure concepts (understanding) on the other. In order to bring these together in knowledge, intuitions had to be previously brought together in coherent unities. This took place, Kant argued, through the spontaneous activity of the *imagination*.

In trying to understand Kant's view of how perception and concept could be joined in knowledge of beings, Martin Heidegger argued that the Kantian imagination possessed a special, originating capacity for 'spontaneity'. This 'spontaneity' of the imagination, which is not easily understood as being either passive or active, is more of the nature of an intransitive 'event' that originates itself in its very occurrence. For Heidegger, this rather mysterious capability of the imagination indicates the trace of another, more original time at work in Kant's system:

> The interpretation of the transcendental power of imagination as root, i.e.,
> the elucidation of how the pure synthesis allows both stems to grow forth
> from out of it and how it maintains them, leads back from itself to that in
> which the root is rooted: to original time. As the original, threefold-unifying
> forming of future, past, and present in general, this is what first makes possible

the 'faculty' of pure synthesis, i.e., that which it is able to produce, namely
the unification of the three elements of ontological knowledge [apprehension,
reproduction, recognition], in the unity of which transcendence is formed.[4]

Heidegger goes on to explicitly equate Kant's 'imagination' with 'original time',
suggesting that time is, at root, transcendence itself:

> Only because [the] modes of pure synthesis are originally unified in the
> threefold-unifying of time, is there also to be found in them the possibility
> for the original unification of three elements of pure knowledge. For
> that reason, however, the original unifying which is apparently only the
> mediating, intermediate faculty of the transcendental power of imagination,
> is in fact none other than original time. This rootedness in time alone
> enables the transcendental power of imagination in general to be the root of
> transcendence.[5]

Time, in Heidegger's reading of Kant, is an original power, co-founded with subjectivity itself, a power to transcend. It is this transcendence that expresses itself in
the subject's temporal constitution of experience: in time's differentiation into past,
present and future; in the relations between these dimensions in remembrance,
recall and anticipation; in the velocities and stases, durations and interruptions that
constitute the qualitative aspects of experience 'in time'.

While neither Kant nor Heidegger intended the term 'imagination' in a restricted
artistic or literary sense, nevertheless their formulations have powerful implications
for our understanding of time's relation to literature. If Lessing already discerned an
intrinsic resonance between the signifying capabilities of poetic language and the
temporal phenomena of human action, Kant (and subsequently, Heidegger reading
Kant) discovers time as the transcendental capacity of the constitutive subject
for original world-making in an act of *poesis*, the ability to constitute new 'worlds'
through imaginative syntheses of feeling, thinking, acting and creating. Between
Kant and Heidegger, Wilhelm Dilthey, a key figure both for modern philosophy
of history and theory of literary interpretation, argues that literature is, in fact, an
epitome of *historical* world-making, and that careful study of literature can reveal how
the law-like regularities of creativity, which Dilthey rooted in human psychology,
and historicity are related. This, in Dilthey's view, derives from a peculiar temporal
characteristic of written literature: its capacity as a product of the past to be brought
back fully to life in the present-tense imagination of its reader, which thus makes
it a particularly rich and complete object of historical understanding. Specifically,
Dilthey argues, we have greater access to the cultural and experiential worlds of
the past through literature than through religion or ethics, which remain opaque
to us and resistant to imaginative reanimation. As he argues in his 1887 essay, 'The
Imagination of the Poet: Elements of a Poetics':

> In no other area except that of science have the products of human activities
> been so perfectly preserved. The history of literature has preserved them as

successive strata. Active powers still appear to pulsate vigorously in such products. Today poetic processes occur in just the same way as in the past. The poet is alive before our eyes; we see evidence of his creative work. Thus the poetic formative process, its psychological structure, and its historical variability can be studied especially well. [...] Our philosophical conception of history was developed from literary history. Perhaps poetics will have a similar significance for the systematic study of historical expressions of life.[6]

For Dilthey, literary history (or 'philology', a term Dilthey uses interchangeably) stands in a complementary relation to poetics in its contribution to modern historical understanding and the advance of the human sciences, which are defined by their historical object as opposed to the natural sciences that take nature as their object. Philology, he argues, 'first produced an understanding of the inner coherence among the literary products of a nation and their relation to the vitality of the national spirit',[7] yet it also reveals that this historical creativity employs a limited range of expressive devices that span historical periods. Poetics are thus tasked with discovering the basic psychological and technical components of literary expression subject to historical variability; literary history groups these variances into linguistic, national and period categories sequentially organised in historical time. The poetic 'genius' is for Dilthey the factor that turns historically changing content into the impetus for the invention of new expressive forms: 'On the basis of the norms of poetic creativity as well as the principles of the poetic impression, it is the *achievement of the poetic genius* to produce a *form* and thus the *technique* of a *literary genre* from the factual *multiplicity of the given life of a period*; this form is thus *historically conditioned and relative*.'[8] Literary history has, therefore, in this perspective, an intrinsically temporal dimension rooted in the historicity – the capacity of the 'genius' to originate change in time – of the productive imagination. Aside from its external aspect of periodisation, literary history is thus premised on an inner dynamic of change that discloses shifts in the 'poetic' structure of experience over time, which themselves are related to different constellations of past, present and future in any given world-making synthesis.

## TIME IN INTERPRETATION

Interpretative acts, and the interpretation theories that take them as their object, put to work a wide range of temporal structures, but have in common a focus on how temporal difference generates narrative and other rhetorical figures that require explication of their meanings. Whether offering ways of relating Old and New Testament histories, correlating sacred and worldly events, disentangling archaic myths and modern histories, connecting moments of textual creation and moments of reception, or distinguishing naïve and mature perspectives in an autobiographical text, acts of interpretation take the figural articulations of time in texts as a primary object for exposition and elaboration. In addition, many interpretation theories self-reflexively foreground how the interpretative act is itself situated horizontally *in* time – hence also, implicitly, constituting its own secondary temporal figure in rela-tion to a text whose origin lies in the past – and how its unfolding of the interpreted text's meaning *takes* time, thus further implicating interpreted meaning within a multi-faceted temporal structure.

In his celebrated essay 'Figura' (1938),[9] Erich Auerbach offered a rich historical account of one mode of interpretation, 'figural interpretation', that was originally developed as a way of creating correlations between the Hebrew Old Testament and the New Testament gospels and prophecies. In distinction to strictly allegorical interpretations of biblical texts, which explained stories, personages or descriptive details as emblems of abstract philosophical or conceptual contents, figural inter-pretation insisted on the literal, historical reference of the biblical texts. However, across the historical gap between the Old and New Testaments, there pertained a particular symbolic relation of anticipation in the earlier text of a historical event that would 'fully' occur only later, as part of the Christian gospel story. Both the earlier and the later text referred to real, historical personages or events; but between the two, figural interpretation discerned a spiritual relationship of both continuity (the history of the Jews, as God's chosen people, prepares and issues into the Christian age) and transcendence (the birth of Christ as a one-time event that divides time into a 'before' and 'after'). Auerbach, in fact, uses the tropological analysis of *figura* historiographically: to set apart the medieval historical formation from the classical pagan age, from which, he argues, the allegorical method of interpretation derives,[10] as well as from the modern, in which historical figures are depicted within 'the concrete life of the world – as Shakespeare did for Caesar or Schiller for Wallenstein'.[11] The medieval is characterised by its representation of historical personages and events not realistically but *figurally*, as a fulfilment of an earlier anticipatory sign or as the prefiguration of a fulfilment yet to come, in a Providential history of salvation.

In Auerbach's analysis of *figura*, notably, it is not only because of the rough chronological relation of 'before' and 'after' that the figural structure is historicising. The interpretative act itself correlates two historically actual events referenced in different coordinated textual corpuses, thus first *constituting* the medium ('history') of union between them, the temporal continuity in which these could be seen as different figural modalities, qualified by degrees of historical realisation, of the 'same' event. This salvational history, in short, can be seen as a projected *institution* of figural interpretation, which *configures* a body of textual documents into a continuous story of prefiguration and fulfilment in historical time. This productive capacity of the interpretative act – productive of 'historicity', the form of temporal relationality that founds the possibility of writing 'history' – is, in the view of metahistorian Hayden White, what is most momentous in Auerbach's analysis. Indeed, White overrides Auerbach's confinement of figurality to the medieval epoch to discover in it a more general figural logic of 'epochalisation' itself, essential to modern historicism.

In his essay, 'Auerbach's Literary History: Figural Causation and Modernist Historicism',[12] White proposes an understanding of modern historicism structured by a network of figural relations of prefiguration and fulfilment. Figuration and the relations between figures are, for White, the basic medium of historicising thought and discourse, because figuration itself is subject to historical change, to 'epochalisa-tion'. We might note that 'schema' and 'epoch' have a common etymological root in the Greek verb *echein* (to hold, to be in a condition), with *schema* being a synonym for 'figure' or 'arrangement' and *epochē* meaning 'cessation, pausing, holding back'. Figures are, so to speak, the 'schemata' of any possible historical experience, while the tropological relations between historical 'epochs' are articulated by the fluctuating events of configuration and refiguration of the past that arrange figures within and across time. Hence, *figura*, in Auerbach's sense, may at once define a characteristic epochal ('medieval') tropology, while also representing only one epochal variant of a more universal, perhaps even transcendental 'figural' structure.

For White, in experiencing their historical epoch and seeking to render that expe-rience in writing, authors stand in a horizon of figures that are temporally disposed and that are relatively more or less 'legible', more or less available for appropriation and reapplication. As White notes, the mediation of context and text in Auerbach's account is the domain of *experience*, which he conceives as historically mutable, but capable of being suspended in a kind of *epochē* and figurally expressed: 'In his actual hermeneutic practice, Auerbach tends to present the text as a representation not so much of its social, political, and economic milieus as of its author's experience of those milieus; and as such, the text appears or is presented as a fulfillment of a figure of this experience.'[13] This concept of experience, understood as the subjective mediation between text and context, or between two scales of figuration, also thus roots historicity in human agency: human beings produce history as a work on, and work of, figuration. This horizon of figures, with its variable regions of clarity and obscurity, is composed of multiple figurations of time: figures arriving from the past, to be fulfilled by the present writing; the figural relation of the present writing to the experienced present ('context'); and in the 'incompletion' of the present writing with respect to its possibility for its future 'fulfilment', its projective 'prefiguration' of new meanings in a future that will appropriate this present as *the past of a future present*. These acts of appropriation of the horizon of figures are, moreover, fundamentally acts of interpretation analogous to textual readings. The more that the formative 'experience' of an author is mediated by a corpus of literary texts, the more that the writer's life is shaped by the practice of literary reading – the literary tradition and contemporary literary community in which an author situates herself – the closer the figural appropriation of the epoch in her writing will approximate to an act of literary *interpretation*.

In an analogous way, Hans-Georg Gadamer, in *Truth and Method*, mapped a textual hermeneutics onto the temporality of existence first expounded by Martin Heidegger in *Being and Time*.[14] Heidegger had focused his 'fundamental ontology' on the temporal problematic of *Dasein* (human existence). In Heidegger's exposition, *Dasein* is uniquely that being for which the question of (its own) being is posed by time: by its own inescapable finitude, by the limitation of its possibility for being to relatively brief spans of time, by the immanence of death, whether affirmed or disavowed, in all its experience. 'Thrown' into a framework of being that precedes it and drawn towards a horizon that forecloses it, each individual existence experiences its own being as a singular, potentially 'authentic' ('my own') story unfolding in time. This experience is profoundly bound up with time, because our understanding of existence, and by derivation, our ways of understanding the whole of being, is circumscribed by finite horizons of disclosure. All that we can know and understand of our existence is delimited by time, as articulated in reiterated circles of projective, reappropriative and retrojective interpretation.

In *Truth and Method*, Gadamer argues against viewing literature as simply the occasion of aesthetic experience, which is fundamentally subjective, and instead draws the verbal work of art back into the hermeneutic structure of understanding which, in Heidegger's view, reveals the temporal nature of human existence. Accordingly, having eliminated the aesthetic criteria for identifying a work of literature, Gadamer extends the category of 'literature' to a vast domain of written texts that exist in unity with works of poetry, fiction and drama, and engage us in the same hermeneutical structure of time-bound understanding:

> An entire written tradition partakes of the mode of being of literature – not only religious, legal, economic, public and private texts of all kinds, but those writings in which these texts are scientifically treated and interpreted: namely, the human sciences as a whole. Moreover, all scientific research has the form of literature, insofar as it is essentially bound to language. If words can be written down, then they are literature, in the widest sense.[15]

The understanding of texts, Gadamer argues, occurs in a temporal process involving 'effective history', the way that the past affects the present as a kind of fate, and the 'fusion of horizons', in which commitments and expectations of the present seize upon the received past and project it towards the future as 'application'. As Paul Ricoeur has neatly summarised it: 'Effective-history, we might say, is what takes place without us. The fusion of horizons is what we attempt to bring about.'[16] Yet Gadamer draws a further conclusion from the third term, 'application', which he sees as a crucial future-oriented dimension of our relations to texts: that historical understanding has an inescapable *critical* element to it, which does not merely passively receive the effective-history of the past, but also responds to it and redirects it in light of its applicability to concerns yet to be resolved. It is thus, too, that he sees the activity of the historian and the literary critic not as essentially different disciplinary practices, but simply as two different emphases within a single hermeneutic process of relating to texts of the past. 'Historical understanding', Gadamer writes, 'proves to be a kind of literary criticism writ large.'[17] Gadamer clarifies that he does not mean that the historical process 'has as perfect a meaningful form as has a text',[18] but rather that both the reader of the text and the scholar of history grasp the effective-history of the past from a finite perspective within historical meaning, a perspective focused by a future horizon of 'application'. Not only does this emphasis on application allow Gadamer to argue against positivistic methods of history and philology, which seek to establish once and for all the 'facts' in which, supposedly, the meaning of a historical or literary phenomenon exhausts itself; nor does it only underpin his argument about the unity of the activity of historian and critic. Since application derives from an open, future-oriented horizon of concerns that renders impossible any complete, definitive statement of the meaning of a text or documented historical phenomenon, application also implies the finitude of any possible historical or critical interpretation.

## TIME AND NARRATIVE: EMPLOTMENT AND CHRONOTOPE

In *Time and Narrative*, Paul Ricoeur traces a fundamental relation between narrative and the appropriation of time for human purposes. 'Time becomes human', he writes, 'to the extent that it is articulated through a narrative mode, and narrative attains its full meaning when it becomes a condition of temporal existence.'[19] In Ricoeur's view, this takes place by means of narrative emplotment linking the prefigurative field of action, through the mediation of a narrative text, to its 'application' (in Gadamer's sense) to the field of action of the reader. Or to put it another way, the configuration of narrative time through 'emplotment' opens a temporal relation between a prefigured field of action received as 'effective history' and a refigured field of action projected as 'application'. Understood in this light, then, the concepts of narrative temporality developed by structural narratology, although seeming to abstract from literary history, help to deepen historical understanding when placed in this larger hermeneutical context of human involvement in time through narrative, which – as Ricoeur argues – is mediated by the structural articulations of narrated time. It is in this sense that we may understand Roland Barthes' well-known apothegm regarding structuralist methodologies: 'I shall say that a little formalism turns one away from History, but that a lot brings one back to it.'[20]

Narrative can be understood as a temporal configuration in several senses. First, it takes shape from a differential between the time of action and events within the narrated world and the temporal organisation of the narrative representation by which this narrated world is evoked. This distinction – referred to as *'fabula'* and *'sujet'* in Russian formalist theory, *erzählte Zeit* and *Erzählzeit* in German narrative theories, and story and discourse in structuralist narratology – is fundamental to all modern theories of narrative. The time of narration may (and usually does) diverge from narrated time in three key ways, identified in Gérard Genette's fundamental studies of narrative discourse: order, duration and frequency.[21]

*Order* involves not merely the *sequence* of narrative segments in relation to the sequence of narrated events, but also sequence as a means of representing temporal distensions and protensions of the consciousness of characters within the narrated world: for instance, representations of memory that give rise to 'flashbacks' or imaginative visions expressed as proleptic narration of events to come. *Duration* is a more complicated concept, signifying the relative proportion of the time that passes in a given sequence of narrative events and the time that is devoted to narrating those events. Although every reader will take a different amount of time to read any set of pages or a whole book, there is an intuited 'pace' of reading against which 'accelerations' and 'decelerations' of narration can likewise be discerned – and gauged against the temporality of the events passing in the narrative. Narrative techniques such as the condensation of large spans of narrated time into a short span of prose or large ellipses between events can give the impression of narrative acceleration; whereas, in contrast, the accumulation of details, especially descriptive details which do not represent action but serve to dilate the reading time relative to the narrated events, can create the sense of the slowing down of time, or even, as in the modernist novels of James Joyce or Virginia Woolf, suggest the incommensurability of inner, psychological time with the outward temporality of events. *Frequency* designates how many times an event or event-sequence is narrated with respect to how many times it occurs in the narrated world. According to Genette, there are three basic modes of narrative frequency: 'singulative', in which an event that happens once is narrated once; 'repeating', in which an event that occurs once is narrated more than one time; and 'iterative', in which an event that occurs repeatedly is narrated once. Notably, the categories of 'repeating' and 'iterative' frequency offer examples of how a choice of narrative technique in one dimension may affect others such as order (the repetitions of a repeating narrative may be interspersed with other narrative sequences, thus changing the order) or duration (an 'iterative' narrative may condense a large span of time in a small sequence of narrated events). It is even possible for individual repetitions of a repeating narrative to employ variations of both order and duration, yet still be perceived as 'repeating' in the dimension of frequency.

The study of narrative techniques for managing time in stories reached a new level of sophistication with the formalist- and structuralist-influenced narratology of such theorists and critics as Roland Barthes, Gérard Genette, Tzvetan Todorov, Algirdas Greimas, Julia Kristeva, Christian Metz, Seymour Chatman, Thomas Pavel and Mieke Bal. Yet Roland Barthes' maxim was only to a limited extent borne out, as history remained elusive to this astonishing development of narrative theory in the 1960s and '70s. Its theoretical power at the level of structural analysis was seemingly bought at the cost of an impoverishment of its understanding of the larger context of time and history in which narrative is embedded and which, ultimately, lend literature and other storytelling a vital human interest. Attempts to rediscover historical contextuality for narrative theory include Peter Brooks's influential study *Reading for the Plot*,[22] which related narrative structure to the temporality of psychic drives and desires as expounded by Freudian psychoanalysis; and Fredric Jameson's pathbreaking work *The Political Unconscious*,[23] which ambitiously aligned shifts in narrative form (from realism to modernism) with epochs of social history. Jameson argues that narrative functions *ideologically* in relation to history by encoding it in narrative figures, in historically variable ways. All narratives, in Jameson's view, at once disclose, expressively distort, and repress the socio-historical reality embodied in society's modes and relations of material production. But different narrative types do this to varying degrees and in changing configurations, depending on their specific stylistic and structural features.

Dissatisfaction with this deficit of historical understanding in structural narratology also led literary critics and historians to reappraise the work of earlier, Marxist-influenced critics such as Walter Benjamin and Mikhail Bakhtin, who developed suggestive analyses of the interrelations of narrative structure, the 'historicity' of literary figuration, social history and literary history. In his 1936 essay 'The Storyteller', for example, Benjamin analysed the short stories of the Russian nineteenth-century writer Nikolai Leskov in light of broad historical transformations of narrative structure, which in turn were, in his view, indices in the mutations in the structure of 'experience' and memory, which, finally, pointed to social phenomena such as the rise of information media, urbanisation, the technologisation of labour and the atomisation of social interaction.[24] In his long essay of 1937–38, 'Forms of Time and of the Chronotope in the Novel: Notes Towards a Historical Poetics', Mikhail Bakhtin analogously advanced the philosophically rich notion of the 'chronotope', a 'formally constitutive category of literature'[25] in which, he argues: 'spatial and temporal indicators are fused into one carefully thought-out, concrete whole. Time, as it were, thickens, takes on flesh, becomes artistically visible; likewise, space becomes charged and responsive to the movements of time, plot, and history.'[26] Bakhtin goes on to explain that chronotopes are the constituent elements of literary genres, and the determinants of the 'image of man' in works of literature – thus carrying valences of human agency, morality and the relation of human activity to mortality and eternity.

In a footnote, Bakhtin suggests that chronotopes are analogous to the transcendental 'intuition forms' that in Kantian philosophy structure any possible experience, but which are now de-transcendentalised and related to historical and social reality. 'We shall attempt', Bakhtin writes, 'to show the role these forms play in the process of concrete artistic cognition (artistic visualization) under conditions obtaining in the genre of the novel.'[27] Referring to our earlier discussion of Auerbach and White, we might understand Bakhtin's 'chronotopes' as generic clusters of figures, mediated by literary tradition, that shape the author's experience of reality and facilitate its transformation into literary form. At the conclusion of his essay, Bakhtin offers examples such as 'the road', 'the castle' (Gothic novels), 'the idyll', 'the provincial town' (*Madame Bovary*), 'salons and parlours' (Gogol, Turgenev and others), 'crisis and break in life', 'mystery- and carnival time' (Dostoyevsky), and 'biographical time' (Tolstoy).

Bakhtin's examples span a vast literary historical range from the Platonic dialogue and the Greek novel through the chivalric romance and Rabelais up to a wide range of eighteenth- and nineteenth-century European romantic and realist novels including those of Sterne, Walpole, Swift, Voltaire, Rousseau, Goethe, Jean-Paul, Chateaubriand, Stendhal, Gogol, Pushkin, Balzac, Flaubert, Dickens, Goncharov, Dostoyevsky, Turgenev and Tolstoy, among others. The transnational and transhistorical span of his examples suggests that Bakhtin's interest in the chronotope as a tool of literary history is not 'historical' in a positivistic sense or even in a historicist sense of explaining the features of a literary work by reference to its 'historical context', but rather *historico-phenomenological*: revealing how the figural articulation of experience, via chronotopic schemata, constitutes the *epochal* character of a work. Chronotopes have a genesis and evolution in history, but also take on a quasi-transcendental stability that allows them to submerge and re-emerge across large gaps of chronological time and national context. They are, in a sense, schematic vehicles of historical *transmission*, which means that their historicity operates on a different time-scale and rhythm than the chronological succession of historicist 'literary periods'. In fact, Bakhtin's reorientation of literary history towards the chronotope suggests the basic irrelevance of historicist notions of 'period' to his thinking. Instead, implicitly, he reconceives literary history as a stratification of chronotopes and their cross-period, transnational evolution and interanimation. The differential rhythms of emergence, disappearance and revival of chronotopes lend their various qualities to any particular moment in literary chronology, which is necessarily a complex, contradictory and manifold present in which multiple chronotopic 'voices' strive and contend.

## TIME AND LITERARY HISTORIOGRAPHY

Literary history has deployed various sorts of periodising concepts in order to define relevant notions of context, delineate interrelations between authors and/or texts, legitimate possibilities of comparison, and trace out pertinent patterns of evolution or emergence of new tendencies. Such periodising frameworks deploy – sometimes explicitly, sometimes only implicitly – conceptions of historical time with important implications for the practice of literary history. In conclusion, I will briefly discuss three explicit critiques of the historicism that still underlies much modern and contemporary literary history – those of Walter Benjamin, Paul De Man and Gilles Deleuze. In light of their work, I will consider not simply how texts might be 'historicised' by their being incorporated into a literary historical framework, but also how they might be actively involved in the work of 'historicising' literature: offering temporal models critical of inherited conceptions of historiography and contributing to the formation of alternative historical imaginaries. Understood in this post-historicist way, literature and literary history may serve as an open-ended repertoire of counter-historical 'time images' spurring us to write, and eventually to experience, collective and individual histories in a new way.

Walter Benjamin attempted to recast literary (and cultural) history by eschewing the concepts of epochal periodisation and related temporal ideas of progress, decline and repetition as characteristics of historical periods. His historiography took into account, as he writes in his study of nineteenth-century Paris, *The Arcades Project*, 'the differentials of time',[28] meaning not only the different stratifications of time in a single synchronic moment in history, but also (and relatedly) the different horizons of legibility of elements of the historical past in the mobile perspectives of the historical present. Benjamin calls the montage-like constellations of past and present elements 'images', which he distinguished from phenomenology's *epochē*, as well as from the periodising and contextualising concepts of the historicist cultural, artistic and literary scholarship of his day. Benjamin writes:

> These images are to be thought of entirely apart from the categories of the human sciences, from so-called habitus, from style, and the like. For the historical index of the images not only says that they belong to a particular time; it says, above all, that they attain to legibility only at a particular time. And, indeed, this acceding to 'legibility' constitutes a specific critical point in the movement at their interior.[29]

Benjamin relates this historiography to a particular idea of 'truth', which was neither removed from time and related to a phenomenological 'essence' nor the speculative becoming of an idea as in Hegel, but rather a differential, unpredictable *event* occurring in time, constellating in a disclosive 'now' the transmitted past and the receiver in the present: 'Resolute refusal of the concept of "timeless truth" is in order. Nevertheless, truth is not – as Marxism would have it – a merely contingent function of knowing, but is bound to a nucleus of time lying hidden within the knower and the known alike.'[30] Benjamin thus ontologises time as a force that realises itself in events of historical disclosure that are neither 'subjective' (as in idealism) nor 'objective' (as in certain versions of materialism) but rather immanent actualisations of historical understanding as an event comprising both 'effective history' and 'application'.

Although the *Arcades Project* was a very broadly conceived work of cultural and material history, Benjamin's historiography was arguably forged in the crucible of his earlier *literary* historical work, including his study of baroque tragedy, *The Origin of German Tragic Drama*, and his methodological essays related to commentary, translation, criticism and literary history. In his essay on Goethe's *Elective Affinities* and his essay 'The Task of the Translator', Benjamin put forward a view of the 'life' and survival of a text dependent on the passage of time, the decay of its immediate relation to its context, and an ongoing, 'historical' transformation of its meaning through successive acts of commentary, criticism and translation into other languages. In an important programmatic essay of 1931, 'Literary History and the Study of Literature', Benjamin summed up his thinking, emphasising the effective afterlife of texts as the ground of historicity upon which any authentic literary history must be founded. This approach implies downplaying the typically privileged chronology of the genesis of literary works (composition and publication) and instead focuses on the temporal differentials of material transmission of texts in reception, criticism and translation. It also thoroughly rejects readymade idealist constructs of period based on style, national spirit, or 'spirit of the age', which in turn map the individual work into 'literary history' by the chronological date of their composition rather than through the extended duration of effective history that may fluctuate across wide chronological gaps:

> The entire life [of works of literature] and their effects should have the right
> to stand alongside the history of their composition. In other words, their
> fate, their reception by their contemporaries, their translations, their fame.
> For with this the work is transformed inwardly into a microcosm, or indeed
> a microeon. What is at stake is not to portray literary works in the context
> of their age, but to represent the age that perceives them – our age – in the
> age during which they arose. It is this that makes literature into an organon
> of history; and to achieve this, and not to reduce literature to the material of
> history, is the task of the literary historian.[31]

In an analogous way, Paul De Man carried on a resolute polemic against the spurious status of most 'literary historical' periodising concepts and what he, like Benjamin, took to be a false opposition of literary criticism and literary history. In one of his most important programmatic essays, 'Literary History and Literary Modernity', De Man argued for a thorough 'revision of the notion of history' underlying literary history, and, 'beyond that, of the notion of time on which our idea of history is based'.[32] 'It would imply', he specifies, 'abandoning the pre-assumed concept of history as a generative process [...] as a temporal hierarchy that resembles a parental structure in which the past is like an ancestor begetting, in a moment of unmediated presence, a future capable of repeating in its turn the same generative process.'[33] De Man's suggestion, based on his reading of hermeneutical theorists such as Heidegger and Gadamer, is to reconceive literary history through the temporal ontology of existential hermeneutics, which in turn means understanding it as closely aligned with literary criticism. In this conception, literary historical time is neither linear nor mono-dimensional, but rather complexly articulated by acts of interpretations of the past, critical returns and repetitions, and future-directed projections of expectations, wishes and aspirations. 'All the directives we have formulated as guidelines for a literary history', De Man writes, 'are engaged in the much more humble task of reading and understanding a literary text.'[34] The urgent tasks of literary history, in De Man's view, are to shatter the crust of received pseudo-historicising concepts and attend closely to the philological and rhetorical historicity of texts and their interpretations. 'To become good literary historians, we must remember that what we usually call literary history has little or nothing to do with literature', he writes, 'and that what we call literary interpretation – provided only it is good interpretation – is in fact literary history.'[35]

Beyond Benjamin's and De Man's critical disclosure of a philologically stratified time that undoes imposed categories of literary periodisation, we might also imagine a still more radical possibility of active *experimentation* with alternative 'times' to recast the writing of literary history. Gilles Deleuze, in the second volume of his study of cinema, *The Time-Image*,[36] considers the possibility of reversing the typical classical cinematic derivation of time as implied by the movement of bodies and objects in space and by the unfolding of narrative ('the movement-image'), and instead seeking the dynamics of narrative and action from the explication, in cinematic narratives, of direct 'images' of time. Some of the time-models Deleuze considers include: 'sheets of time', time as continuous duration that can be folded and gathered or slackened and released; 'time-crystals', which capture different facets of a moment, giving rise to proliferating narrative threads; 'stratified time', narrative time as overlapping and in-folded layers; and 'peaks of present', in which the discontinuous events picture time as a series of intensities, of accents and troughs of concentrated duration. Although Deleuze offers a rough 'historicisation' of cinema as predominantly organised around 'movement-images' prior to the Second World War and shifting towards 'time-images' after it, his simple 'historical' schema is not nearly as suggestive for our purposes as his notion of the time-image itself. The time-image, as Deleuze conceives it, can serve not only as a way of thinking about modernist innovations in cinematic narrative but also as a critical notion extending to the reading of literary works of all sorts and their modelling of time and as a historiographic model opening up new ways of writing history. Elsewhere I have suggested what such a historiographic practice might look like:

Particular qualities and types of time express themselves in singular occurrences and mixtures, through particular images, artifacts, spaces, and movements. The historian may not be searching for direct links of narrative and causality between the different elements, which might even derive from diverse chronological or cultural contexts. Rather s/he seeks in them a virtual conceptuality that will be methodologically disclosed through techniques of montage, multimedia assemblage, play between documentary and personal memory, interpenetration of fictional and factual frameworks, or other experimental modes of figural thought typically associated more with the arts than with the discipline of history.[37]

Walter Benjamin suggested this sort of reciprocity between artistic form and historical time when, in his essay on literary history, he argued that the work in its effective life constituted a 'microeon'. If we understand the form of works not just as a set of received forms, but also as a continually evolving set of emerging forms, forms that can be the object of intentional artistic experimentation, then the creation of 'microeons', specific historical 'images' of time, may be as open-ended as the practice of literary invention itself. That means, however, that we cannot just unreflectively assume chronological time as the primary organising factor underlying literary history. Time, in its manifold and revisable images, is an active force of creation of literary histories. Its proliferating forms of manifestation disrupt any fixed conception of literary historicity, compelling at once the invention of new literary forms and the adaptation of literary understanding, again and again, to each new metamorphosis of literature.

## FURTHER READING

Bakhtin, M. M. *The Dialogic Imagination: Four Essays*, ed. Michael Holquist, trans. Caryl Emerson and Michael Holquist. Austin: University of Texas Press, 1981.

Benjamin, Walter. 'Literary History and the Study of Literature', trans. Rodney Livingstone. In *Selected Writings*, vol. 2, ed. Michael W. Jennings, Howard Eiland and Gary Smith. Cambridge, MA: The Belknap Press of Harvard University Press, 1999.

Deleuze, Gilles. *Cinema 2: The Time-Image*, trans. Hugh Tomlinson and Robert Galeta. Minneapolis: University of Minnesota Press, 1989.

De Man, Paul. 'Literary History and Literary Modernity'. In *Blindness and Insight: Essays in the Rhetoric of Contemporary Criticism*. Second revised edition. Minneapolis: University of Minnesota Press, 1983.

Dilthey, Wilhelm. *Poetry and Experience*, ed. Rudolf A. Makkreel and Frithjof Rodi. Princeton: Princeton University Press, 1985.

Genette, Gérard. *Narrative Discourse: An Essay in Method*, trans. Jane E. Lewin. Ithaca: Cornell University Press, 1980.

Jameson, Fredric. *The Political Unconscious: Narrative as a Socially Symbolic Act.* Ithaca: Cornell University Press, 1982.

Porter, James I., ed., and Jane O. Newman, trans. *Selected Essays of Erich Auerbach: Time, History, and Literature*. Princeton: Princeton University Press, 2014.

Ricoeur, Paul. *Time and Narrative*. 3 vols, trans. Kathleen Blamey and David Pellauer. Chicago: University of Chicago Press, 1984–88.

White, Hayden. *Figural Realism: Studies in the Mimesis Effect*. Baltimore: Johns Hopkins University Press, 1999.

## CHAPTER 11

# Invention

## Jed Rasula

*Invention* is a very old category in Western aesthetics, deriving from the conceptual repertoire of the Greco-Roman world. In ancient rhetoric, *inventio* was the first of five parts, the others being arrangement, style, memory and delivery. *Inventio* encompassed *thesis* (or hypothesis) and extended to the structure of an argument. For the greater part of Western oratory – encompassing what we now call literature – the substance was passed on by tradition, and the artistry involved in making a speech, telling a story, or exclaiming a lyric was restricted to the ingenuity with which the author 'invented' or reanimated the primary – and inherited – material.

When John Milton adopted the form of elegy to mourn the loss of Edward King, his friend appears as Lycidas in a poem abounding with references to Greco-Roman pastoral. What Milton added to the conceit was a Christian element, lamenting 'Lycidus sunk Low' while envisioning him 'mounted high, / Through the dear might of him that walked the waves'.[1] In a poem of nearly two hundred lines, Milton's *inventio* is dutifully unobtrusive; the ancient topos of mourning is preserved, even as the Christian resurrection subtly trumps the mythological source. The poet's reverence for tradition provides him with a template on which to introduce minor variations within long established parameters. Milton participates in a practice spanning millennia, in which such changes as occur unfold very gradually, especially to a modern eye.

We find a comparable principle at work in Renaissance painting, which lavishly retains the full array of pagan myth transposed to scenarios suffused with Christian motifs and allegorical detail. Such practices conformed, however loosely at times, to the principle of *inventio*. But Titian and Signorelli and their fellow masters consolidated another element – perspective – that would jolt invention out of its ancient pedigree. Second nature to us now, the laws of perspective were in fact a revolutionary eruption in painting, presaging a series of transformational paradigms in the arts that would culminate in modernism.

The exceptional range and cultural prestige accruing to the achievements of modernism by the twentieth century imposed an unsustainable standard of invention on the individual practitioner – hence the so-called postmodern turn to styles of pastiche and derivation. To raise the issue of modernism, however, casts invention in an unprecedented light. For it's clear that the principle of development in all the arts in modernity is predicated on a different model of invention than the older model inherited from ancient rhetoric.

Ever since the revolution of perspective pioneered in the Renaissance, visual art has been understood in terms of stylistic progress. Each new style – from impressionism to cubism – is presumed to improve on or at least challenge an older one. This assumption spread to other arts as well. The sonata form revolutionised musical composition in the eighteenth century, and the concurrent rise of the novel not only convened the paradigmatic modern literary genre, but had an impact on older genres. But by the time English artist Wyndham Lewis wrote *The Demon of Progress in the Arts* (1954) as the postwar society of designed obsolescence was getting underway, he cursed the 'pathological straining after something which boasts of a spectacular *aheadofness*' which he saw run amok in the arts and in commerce alike.[2] Although 'originality' has continued to be a conceptual gold standard in the intervening fifty years, it too has been debased by over-use, and compromised by the constantly available alternative, *novelty*.

Novelty and originality alike were antithetical to the venerable neoclassical outlook, aptly summed up in the eighteenth century by Sir Joshua Reynolds: 'The Invention of a Painter consists not in inventing the subject, but in a capacity of forming in his imagination the subject in a manner best accommodated to his art, though wholly borrowed from Poets, Historians, or popular tradition.'[3] The eminence of the Greco-Roman heritage in the West cast a long shadow over the prospect of invention as artistic prerogative. Even the unavoidable singularity of a Dante, a Cervantes and a Shakespeare was regarded as an unrepeatable outburst of creative abandon, worthy of respect but not a model to be perpetuated.

Eventually the neoclassical model came under suspicion, inasmuch as it appeared to sanction servile imitation. The very notion of servility was itself borrowed from the traditionally subordinate domain of the crafts. But as Stefanie Buchenau helpfully elucidates in *The Founding of Aesthetics in the German Enlightenment*, a different understanding of invention began to emerge in the eighteenth century, modelled not on manual dexterity but on mental alacrity. 'To invent', she writes of the emerging view, 'is to discover *unknown* objects' – an experimental attitude proceeding without distinct expectations of what might be discovered in the creative process.[4] Ostensibly this could impose on the artist 'the paradoxical task of producing a copy before coming to know the model'.[5] By means of this curious prolepsis, the imagination was no longer subordinate to a model, and the mimetic obligations of the artwork fell away. Art was now in the position of disclosing *original objects* without precedent. This venturesome prospect was outfitted with paradigmatic contours by the German philosopher G. W. F. Hegel in his lectures on aesthetics from 1820.

Hegel outlined three modes of art, ostensibly corresponding to states of mind, but also mapped onto stages of human history in his account. The first mode, which Hegel calls 'symbolic', is identified by its characteristic discordance between concept and execution, between the idea and the formal material. The artwork points to (or symbolises) its idea rather than embodying it. In the second mode, the 'classical', the artistic means achieve proportionate unity with the desired end. But the classical solution is compromised by according archetypal status to the human form. Hegel's prototype here is derived from ancient Greece. In the classical model, art too easily becomes a mirror for human vanity. The third mode overcomes this anthropocentrism as well as the material shortcomings of the symbolic mode.

In its pursuit of higher aims, Hegel's third stage – 'romantic' art – demolishes the classical unity. Because sensuous immediacy is no longer an adequate complement to inner serenity, the material profusion of the world which had been so imposing in the symbolic stage now returns, but as raw material for a self-transfiguring subjective mastery. The artist, no longer seeking mimetic concord with unruly material, and resisting the alluring mirror of anthropomorphic vanity, is now free to dispose the artistic means in any direction whatsoever. The unprecedented is now the aspiration of true artistry.

## THE ANXIETY OF INVENTION

By the twentieth century, Hegel's views had so deeply permeated aesthetic discourse that they could be replicated impromptu, without intended reference or homage – as in the case of American poet Wallace Stevens. In a lecture given at the Museum of Modern Art in New York in 1951, he proposed that for modern artists 'our revelations are not the revelations of belief, but the precious portents of our own powers'.[6] This was Stevens's affirmation of an existential condition that had been a source of consternation, even anxiety, in his 1940 poem 'Of Modern Poetry'. The opening lines are what concern us:

> The poem of the mind in the act of finding
> What will suffice. It has not always had
> To find: the scene was set; it repeated what
> Was in the script.
>      Then the theatre was changed
> To something else. Its past was a souvenir.[7]

There's much to unpack here.

At the outset we're confronted with a sentence fragment, as if to foreshadow the theatrical scenario with which the poet illustrates the dilemma facing a modern poet. Since this is a 'poem of the mind' it's not necessary to be given a complete sentence, of course – a lesson made vivid in modern fiction, like Ulysses and Mrs Dalloway. But when it comes to poetic utterance, Stevens implies, the tradition provided script and stage together, the poet being little more than a thespian of the occasion. But this convenience was revoked, changed ambiguously to 'something else', the past no longer of help. Much of the character of modernism has been conflated with the rhetoric of defiance and liberation associated with the avant-garde. But Stevens offers another prospect, in which radical change may not be actively sought, but is nonetheless unavoidable.

To start from scratch, without playbook at hand for prompts, is the daunting new world of modern poetry. 'Of Modern Poetry' is a lament for the loss of meaningful context, such as the ancient arrangement whereby *inventio* played a familiar if strictly subordinate role. Charged now with *finding* – making or identifying the New – the poet discovers that invention is magnified beyond all precedent. What's more, this magnification is played out against a backdrop of deprivation.

Stevens's mere sufficiency seems contrite relative to other modern confrontations with invention, like the 'dark dictations' of *duende* (Edward Hirsch's term for the Spanish model of inspiration embraced by Federico García Lorca). The extremities of fateful encounter as inspirational touchstone are abundant in modern culture. In 1871 Arthur Rimbaud expressed his desire to become a seer in these terms: 'the soul must be made monstrous' by means of 'a long, gigantic and rational *derangement of all the senses*'.[8] He goes on with prescriptive emphasis: 'let us ask the *poet* for the *new* – ideas and forms'.[9]

When Ezra Pound presented the famous modernist mantra *Make It New* as the title of a 1934 collection of his essays, he was in effect reaffirming the Hegelian model of *invention* as romantic prerogative, inasmuch as his real focus was not on the adjective, but the verb. Pound's verb *make* has a raw force, imposing an exorbitant pressure on the individual artist, and reaffirming the auspiciousness of Stevens's stage set, where a solitary agent is the lone bulwark against chaos.[10]

Emboldened by the nightly activities at *Cabaret Voltaire* in Zurich, 1916, in the throes of giving birth to Dada (with due deference to Rimbaud), Hugo Ball affirmed: 'The distancing device is the stuff of life. Let us be thoroughly new and inventive. Let us rewrite life every day.'[11] With this, the *new* is extended as broadly as possible from its basis in aesthetics; but this extension is obtained by means of a 'distancing device'. What, precisely? Two influential suggestions come from nearly concurrent theories by Victor Shklovsky and Bertolt Brecht.

In 1917, the Russian writer presaged the coming revolution by outlining a theory of confrontation by interruption. 'A work is created "artistically"', Shklovsky proposed, 'so that its perception is impeded and the greatest possible effect is produced through the slowness of the perception.' So 'estrangement' came to be regarded as a positive quality, and poetic language verified as 'a roughened, impeded language'.[12] A political aspiration was encoded in Skhlovsky's view that 'art removes objects from the automatism of perception'.[13] This is another version of *make it new*, line by line and even by syllable. The sub-semantic, phonemic and syllabic repertoire of the Russian futurists had familiarised Shklovsky with the potential of works that reframe the model of communication, shifting the emphasis from form to deformation, from recognition to defamiliarisation, and from mimetic to materialist registers of perception.

The German playwright Brecht inaugurated a similar initiative in order to renovate performance practices in the theatre. His 'alienation effect' (*Verfremdungseffekt*) sought to disrupt the illusionistic fourth wall, to dispel the aura of theatrical credibility and, in doing so, disclose a principle at work in everyday life, where the givenness of the world was subject to ceaseless framing events – conveyer belts of ideology, as it were. 'Before familiarity can turn into awareness', wrote Brecht in the vein of

Shklovsky, 'the familiar must be stripped of its inconspicuousness; we must give up assuming that the object in question needs no explanation.'[14] But Brecht was no champion of halting the performance in order to explain it; so the alienation effect required yet another layer of invention, *performing* the explanation.

The 'distancing device' of Hugo Ball, like Shklovsky's 'defamiliarisation' and Brecht's 'alienation effect', attest in their way to the radical reorientation of the human sensorium as it absorbed new technologies like telephone, radio, audio recordings, cinema, as well as transport networks under, on, and above the ground. An emphatic lesson broadcast by the rapidly transforming urban environment of the early twentieth century was that invention thrived everywhere, compared to which the fanciful adumbrations of art (and even the avant-garde) struggled to keep up. The communications revolution – 'encompassing the multiple circuits of exchange and circulation of goods, people, and messages'[15] – imposed repeated bouts of defamiliarisation in the public sphere, albeit masked in the jargon of beneficent improvements. The net effect, by the twentieth century, was a generalised view of invention as a universal norm, a legacy of Enlightenment rationalism, cultural liberalism, and a free market political economy.

## THE PERSISTENCE OF INSPIRATION

With the historical past relegated to the status of souvenir, as in Wallace Stevens's poem, the anticipatory prow of human consciousness was now pledged to invention as the defining trait of the species. As technological invention became increasingly conspicuous and acquired considerable social eminence, the arts often held tenaciously onto premodern prototypes of agency. Foremost among these was the role of *inspiration*. Potentially antithetical to the notion of originality in its manifest dependency on an empowering source like the Muse or other external support, inspiration retained the ancient power invested in *genius*.

The *genius loci* of antiquity celebrated the uniqueness of certain locales, elevating geophysical properties into the status of sanctuary, commemorating sites in which human nature is charged with some transformative dimension. Extended to persons, *genius* acquired a range of human characteristics, demarcated as good and evil in the Christian era. The satanic and demonic petitions pervasive in *fin de siècle* decadence reflect this legacy of an ambiguous bounty, the antiquity of which can be dated to Faust, the tragic medieval figure whose unrivalled powers of invention come with the ultimate price.

The notion of inspiration has a considerable legacy, dating back to Hesiod if not to primal chants that petition divine aid. And as that legacy discloses, the gift of tongues afforded by the Muses has no certificate of authenticity or even veracity. 'We know how to speak many false things as though they were true', the Muses concede, 'but we know, when we want to, how to tell the truth.'[16] The prerogative of invention, in the communications network, has always been compromised by this legacy: inspiration as ambiguous empowerment.

The persistence of inspiration in modernity attests to the power of tradition, but it also says something about the continuing appeal, in D. H. Lawrence's line, to accredit as source of art 'not I, but the wind that blows through me'.[17] Rainer Maria Rilke's famous angelic supplications in his *Duino Elegies* have been paradigmatic of this legacy in which artistic genius entails a subservient relation to extra-human promptings. The atavistic inclination exposed in such retentions of the Muse tradition has often been countered by the procedural tactics of the avant-garde.

A famous and flamboyant charter of the anti-Muse comes courtesy of Dada impresario Tristan Tzara. Performed to the accompaniment of a jazz band (consisting of Jean Cocteau with composers Darius Milhaud and Georges Auric), Tzara read his 'Manifesto on Feeble Love and Bitter Love' at a vernissage for Francis Picabia's work at Galerie Povolozky in Paris, December 1920. In section VIII, Tzara issued this impeccably provocative formula:

> To make a dadaist poem
> Take a newspaper.
> Take a pair of scissors.
> Choose an article as long as you are planning to make your poem.
> Cut out the article.
> Then cut out each of the words that make up this article and put them in a
>     bag.
> Shake it gently.
> Then take out the scraps one after the other in the order in which they left
>     the bag.
> Copy conscientiously.
> The poem will be like you.
> And here you are a writer, infinitely original and endowed with a sensibility
>     that is charming though beyond the understanding of the vulgar.[18]

The penultimate line sounds like it could have been accompanied by a cymbal crash and a thump on the kick-drum. But the final line aims the whole procedure at the figure of the poet, reproachful of any purported superiority derived from inspiration. Directly addressing the writer, and making an appeal to the originality presumed to be the writer's prerogative, Tzara mocks invention by suggesting a comparable result might be obtained randomly.

Randomness courted the spectre of the automaton, as did the pursuit of the 'shadow mouth' by the surrealists, whose embrace of the unconscious was pursued by means of automatism in the 'sleeping fits' and the *vague des rêves*. The random and the serendipitous, those freakish concoctions of Dada extended into surrealism, made explicit the sort of agency always already implied by the role of the Muse. The half-truth/half-fiction gift of the Muses can be shifted formulaically to the entirety of the material world.

Any bit of rubbish plucked off the pavement has a fifty-fifty chance of being serviceable. Kurt Schwitters behaved as if the ratio were even higher, favouring chance by a considerable majority, in his peregrinations of city streets collecting refuse for his 'Merz' collages and constructions. Schwitters proceeded with the ecumenical principle of equal opportunity. Why, he wondered, should oil paint take precedence over a thousand other means of conveying visual information?

With chance legitimated as an acceptable method for producing art, personal agency and the stamp of individuality would seem to have been revoked. Yet that taunting remark of Tzara's lingers: 'The poem will be like you.' There may be mockery in the message, but it anticipates the prospect for artistic creation outlined as common sense by Kenneth Goldsmith, opening his book *Uncreative Writing*:

> In 1969 the conceptual artist Douglas Huebler wrote: 'The world is full of objects, more or less interesting; I do not wish to add any more.' I've come to embrace Huebler's ideas, though it might be retooled as 'The world is full of texts, more or less interesting; I do not wish to add any more.' It seems an appropriate response to a new condition in writing today: faced with an unprecedented amount of available text, the problem is not needing to write more of it; instead, we must learn to negotiate the vast quantity that exists. How I make my way through this thicket of information – how I manage it, how I parse it, how I organize and distribute it – is what distinguishes my writing from yours.[19]

It could be argued that Goldsmith's scenario – writing as organisation of pre-existing texts – has been part of the tradition all along, albeit under the name of tradition itself, with its expansive domain of *topoi* and *tropoi*, its *loci communes*, its store of tales and myths. What he reaffirms, however, is a basic inheritance from Tzara and Schwitters onward, opening up the creative venture to the immense exigencies of the material as such.

A decisive modern modification to the notion of inspiration emphasises the material means, the foundation of any artistic practice. The traditional model was implicitly neoplatonic, a species of idealism, for which the material was accidental, while the concept was paramount. By contrast, the materialist orientation ceded initiative to the medium of a given art, anticipating that unforeseen creative possibilities would emerge from a playful immersion of the artist in the means at hand.

In a short text called 'Monologue', German romantic writer Novalis entertained the prospect that language has a mind of its own, sometimes aiding but often impeding the intentions of a speaker. By recognising intransigence in the material, Novalis opened the way to a modern interest in the pre-expressive initiatory propensity of the medium as such. This contributed to a modern view of the artwork as autotelic – that is, self-generating, autonomous, compelled by internal necessity.

As the artist Wassily Kandinsky observed, 'every genuine work says, "Here I am!"'[20] Kandinsky was intent on making a practical distinction between the terms 'abstract' and 'concrete', favouring the latter because it signals the advent of a new phenomenon rather than a derivative extraction from some pre-existing template. For him, as for many others after him, a non-objective work was not abstracted from a visual model, but precipitated by material means in the form of an emergent visual sensation without precedent. No longer mimetic, the artwork passed from re-creation to creation.

Kandinsky, preoccupied with synaesthetic interchange between the senses, did not restrict his aspirations to visual experience alone. Instead, he was alert to the way any sensory experience is modulated by the other senses. So he came to speak of the *inner sound* of a painting as a way of indicating its force was not strictly visible. For a visual artist to forswear allegiance to sight as primary to his art was not a gesture of renunciation, however, but a pledge of faith in the medium itself as inherently generative.

Kandinsky's outlook was reaffirmed from another angle altogether by his Bauhaus colleague László Moholy-Nagy, who warned photographers of the danger of presuming the eye itself was the standard of reference: *'why should the photographic camera conform to the human eye?'* he wondered. Instead, '[w]e should use the camera for performances not otherwise conceivable'. 'We do not want to subordinate the lens to the insufficiencies of our faculty of seeing and perceiving: it must help us to open our eyes.'[21]

As an institution dedicated to the practical efficiency and social applicability of arts and crafts alike, the aims of the Bauhaus were in striking contrast to the institutional sanctuaries of art as a higher calling, in which students were immersed in time-honoured techniques. In the atmosphere of the arts academy, the past was ever-present, and personal achievement was strictly correlated to precedent. Not surprisingly, such institutions were regarded by vanguard artists as little more than finishing schools for the practice of art as social décor, a prerogative of the wealthy. The Bauhaus was a product of the countertrend, in which the reverential attitude was directed more to the future than to the past. This drew the attention, and wrath, of the Nazis, who forced the closure of the Bauhaus in 1933.

Nowhere is there a more pronounced contrast, artistically speaking, than what could be seen in Munich in 1937 in simultaneous exhibits of 'Degenerate Art' (in a building formerly occupied by the Institute of Archaeology) and 'Great German Art' (housed in Haus der Deutschen Kunst, the first official building erected by the Nazis). The *Entartete Kunst* show was a comprehensive gathering of modern art, seized from municipal museums throughout Germany. The nationalist exhibition, by contrast, consisted of art deliberately eschewing any developments after 1850, and in its choice of subject matter placed Nordic race pride on a Greco-Roman pedestal.

The service-oriented model of art promoted under the Third Reich restricted invention to pre-ordained roles. Art could be a medium of consolation, in which slaughtered soldiers were *fallen heroes*. It could also provide continuity with the past through genre paintings (nudes and landscapes, for the most part), in which the aesthetic experience of *recognition* was paramount. Officially sanctioned German art consisted of all that the dadaists had rebuked as 'a large-scale swindle' and 'a moral safety valve'.[22]

Writing from the safe haven of America in 1936, to which he had recently escaped from Germany, Richard Huelsenbeck reaffirmed that Dada was 'forever the enemy of that comfortable Sunday Art which is supposed to uplift man by reminding him of agreeable moments'.[23] After the apocalyptic collapse of the Third Reich, Theodor W. Adorno continued in this vein, railing against 'Sunday institutions that provide solace', with their clichés that 'rub against the wound that art itself bears'.²⁴ Adorno insisted on perpetuating the wound, not the Sunday consolation.

## OPEN FORMS

The antitheses outlined by Adorno as comprising the options of modern art – accommodation versus non-compliance – are not altogether applicable outside the historical catastrophes overshadowing his generation. In fact, the kernel of dissidence had been innocuously ventured at the end of the eighteenth century, when artistic purpose began to be theorised not by opposing prevailing practices but by embracing the unforeseen, and extolling the *potentiality* of the artwork. In the bold formula of Hegel's contemporary, Friedrich Schlegel: 'Every poem is a genre unto itself.'²⁵ Such a prospect upends the inherited structural relation between genre and work, in which the latter is an instance of a type convened by the former. To imagine the work as inaugurating its own category makes every work literally *sui generis*. With this, *invention* is elevated to an unprecedented legislative norm.

An important initiative in this tradition can be traced to the poet Stéphane Mallarmé, who sought behind the work 'la scansion rythmique de l'être', a primal prompting, as it were, subtending the unique work but not in the way a genre frames and forecloses its applications.²⁶ In pursuit of the rhythmic scansion of being, the 'open work' identified by Umberto Eco becomes the model of artistic invention.²⁷ Incentives to the open work are implicitly conceptualised in the autotelic mission of Schlegel's model of the poem convening a genre unto itself. Eco understood the open work as surmounting aesthetic contemplation of the static object with the sensation of movement.

For Eco, the polyvalent realm of the open work had been augured in baroque aesthetics, in which 'for the first time, man opts out of the canon of authorised responses and finds that he is faced (both in art and in science) by a world in a fluid state which requires corresponding creativity on his part'. Although Eco concedes 'it would be rash to interpret baroque poetics as a conscious theory of the "open work"', his evocation implicitly renders it so: the artwork in the baroque was no longer 'an object which draws on given links with experience and which demands to be enjoyed'. Instead, it is 'a potential mystery to be solved, a role to fulfil, a stimulus to quicken the imagination'.²⁸

A recent model of open format composition is by Canadian poet Darren Wershler-Henry. His small book-length poem *The Tapeworm Foundry* goes on for fifty pages without punctuation or capital letters. In their place he used a revolving-door neologism, 'andor', to propel the text through a cascade of speculative scenarios for producing art, broadly conceived. A characteristic sample:

> imagine a poem called ideas for poets consisting of pithy epithets that
> describe the personalities of literary notables so that for example christopher
> smart might be a thin one forever patrolling the edge of the sidewalk smelling
> of vegetable crates and cat food andor avoid the habits of another artist andor
> fill a steamer trunk full of it and then let your friends edit it while you sleep

off the drug of your choice andor make a western about the group of seven starring yul brynner as emily carr andor write all of your misgivings about your work in ballpoint pen along the edges of your collated manuscript doing so in the same way that you might have written on the edges of your highschool math book and then shuffle the pages before you bind them andor write haiku noting that stonehenge is actually a circle of big pi symbols made out of rock andor massmarket it as if it is both obtainable by all and producible by all andor remove random keys from your typewriter before you begin to write and then forget which ones have been removed andor write with your head between your hands andor posit a novel in which a time traveller first appears at the denouement and then proceeds backwards to the beginning through a series of non sequiturs andor smoke your manuscript page by page when you run out of rolling papers[29]

As some may recognise, the last suggestion about rolling papers is drawn from the annals of history: it was the fate of a manuscript written by Russian theorist M. M. Bakhtin during the Second World War. Earlier, Wershler-Henry has merged the Canadian modernist artists known as the Group of Seven with the Hollywood western, *The Magnificent Seven*, starring Yul Brynner. By citing Emily Carr, however, he draws attention to her exclusion from the Group of Seven, a point made emphatic by the suggestion that her role be played by a man. Wershler-Henry's tapeworm text, drawing equally from history, legend and imagination, is nothing if not inventive.

The inventions that abound in the serial format of *The Tapeworm Foundry* are conceptual in nature, and the 'andor' hinge linking them permits endless supplementation. Like the tour de force poem 'Sunset Debris' by Ron Silliman – forty pages of nothing but questions – there's little sense of internal shaping, no dynamic of rise and fall. Both works go on until they end, and once the reader catches the general drift, reading to the end (or even reading from the beginning) becomes optional. Invention in an open format, then, may have little to do with larger questions of form and structure.

This was precisely the problem that nagged Ezra Pound, who struggled to articulate his vision of a ground plan undergirding his *Cantos*. In any case, after fifty years, old age – along with personal and historical calamity – overtook Pound's epic, ending fitfully in 'Drafts and Fragments'. Yet the dream of creative persistence was not dispelled. Addressing the final fragments of *The Cantos*, American poet Robert Duncan avowed the exemplary character of Pound's engagement:

he remains for me a primary – the master of his craft, yes; but also, in the art at large the creator of a mode, projecting beyond his work new considerations of the meaning of form (as, indeed, our idea of sidereal orders, of cosmos, is no longer that of a creation by paradigm but of a creation in process, and our own experience thereof an ideogram).[30]

Duncan's homage to Pound instructively, if parenthetically, aligns the poet with nothing short of a cosmological spectrum in which open form is sidereal destiny.

With the burden of invention relegated to the stars, the poet can resume a practical engagement with the work at hand, unconcerned – like Pound – with whether it all coheres.

## EVERYDAY INVENTIONS

*The Cantos* was indebted to nineteenth-century aspirations of cultural authority, predicated on the grandest designs, whether a poem in 800 pages or a series of operas like Richard Wagner's Ring cycle. Wagner's dream of an integration of all the arts in a transcendent festival – with the potential of curing mankind from the derelictions of history – cast *invention* in the largest possible scale. Such grandiose aspirations, enticing as they were, proved unsustainable. And the emergent view of a post-Newtonian cosmos to which Duncan refers provided artists with another model, in which what might be called the Brownian movement of particles in the system alleviates the artist from unmanageable claims of world-historical consequence.

The theory of agency proposed by Michel de Certeau in *The Practice of Everyday Life* (1984) provides a coherent outline of this downsizing initiative. Facing the hegemonic triumph of global capitalism, fantasies of the artist as Promethean personality strutting the stage of history are outmoded. Certeau tacitly merges the figure of the artist into the more modest compass of the citizen, the ordinary person negotiating small triumphs in an overdetermined public sphere, committed to 'moves, not truths'.[31] Movement is survival skill predicated on the moment, in which 'we can create networks of connivance and sleights of hand', suggests Certeau.[32]

Certeau's paradigm opposes 'strategies' – the art of power – with 'tactics', a realistic option only tenable outside official quarters, as it were, beyond the prerogative of power. In the agora of the public sphere, 'strategies are able to produce, tabulate, and impose these spaces, when those operations take place, whereas tactics can only use, manipulate, and divert these spaces'.[33] The spaces to which Certeau refers can be any locale in which an expected result obtains, in which a strategy delegated from on high convenes the space in the first place.

Tactics are the renegade practices of the upstart, the outsider, or anyone not seeking official approval or status. Certeau strikes a balance between invention as the tolerated augmentation of a secure order of things, and invention as exploratory option without obligation to any schematic. Like the 'rhythmic scansion' of Mallarmé, Certeau regards the tactic as a temporal activity rather than a determinate manifestation. 'Tactics are procedures that gain validity in relation to the pertinence they lend to time', he writes, 'to the circumstances which the precise instant of an intervention transforms into a favorable situation, to the rapidity of the movements that change the organization of a space, to the relations among successive moments in action, to the possible intersections of durations and heterogeneous rhythms.'[34] This passage evokes nothing so much as the art of jazz, although Certeau's focus is not primarily on artistic practices, but on the role of invention in everyday life.

Writing at a moment when Michel Foucault's model of the complicity of knowledge with power was omnipresent, Certeau wanted to outline a model of agency not always already forestalled by the prevailing institutions in which power reigned. His molecular solution followed promptings from aesthetics like those described here, in which (following Schlegel), as every poem convenes its own genre, every act establishes its own territory, however fleeting, however minute.

Invention is henceforth alleviated from exaggerated claims of efficacy, and reassigned to a domain of practical engagement, its use value reckoned not in prestige or tradition but by its expedience in the moment, one person or context at a time. Certeau returns the model of invention to its more modest origins. In the process, it is detached from the heroic modes of modernism with its insistence on making new. Disburdened of the absolute – absolute artwork, absolute originality – invention is now reassigned to the quotidian as pragmatic exercise, no longer apocalyptic destiny.

## FURTHER READING

Adorno, Theodor W. *Aesthetic Theory*, trans. Robert Hullot-Kentor. Minneapolis: University of Minnesota Press, 1997.

Buchenau, Stefanie. *The Founding of Aesthetics in the German Enlightenment: The Art of Invention and the Invention of Art*. Cambridge: Cambridge University Press, 2013.

Certeau, Michel de. *The Practice of Everyday Life*, trans. Steven Rendall. Berkeley: University of California Press, 1984.

Eco, Umberto. *The Open Work*, trans. Anna Cancogni. Cambridge, MA: Harvard University Press, 1989.

Gilbert, Katharine Everett and Helmut Kuhn. *A History of Esthetics*. Revised edition. Bloomington: Indiana University Press, 1954.

Mattelart, Armand. *The Invention of Communication*, trans. Susan Emanuel. Minneapolis: University of Minnesota Press, 1996.

Moholy-Nagy, László. 'Sharp or Fuzzy?' In Krisztina Passuth, ed. *Moholy-Nagy*. New York: Thames and Hudson, 1985.

Schlegel, Friedrich. *Literary Notebooks 1797–1801*, ed. Hans Eichner. Toronto: University of Toronto Press, 1957.

Shklovsky, Victor. 'Art as Technique'. In *Russian Formalist Criticism: Four Essays*, trans. Lee T. Lemon and Marion J. Reis. Lincoln: University of Nebraska Press, 1965.

Stevens, Wallace. *The Necessary Angel: Essays on Reality and the Imagination*. New York: Knopf, 1951.

## CHAPTER 12

# Event

## Scott McCracken

Early on the morning of 18 March 1871, two French army brigades, led by General Lecomte, entered the working-class quarter of Montmartre in Paris. Two months earlier the French government had capitulated to the Prussians on humiliating terms. Lecomte's aim was to take control of a cannon paid for by the district to defend the city during the Prussian siege. He did not expect the quarter to hand over its arms easily to the disgraced authorities. *Mitrailleuses*, an early form of the machine gun, were trained on the local streets in case of trouble; but Lecomte was too slow. So concerned was he about local resistance that he had forgotten to bring the means to remove the cannon. It took two hours to find suitable horses and by then the quarter had awoken. Local women surrounded the machine guns. A handful of men from the National Guard, a conscript force composed largely of working-class Parisians, sounded a call to arms. More people arrived, pressing on the troops. The General ordered his men to fire. They refused. The crowd advanced and Lecomte and his officers were arrested. The local Vigilance Committee issued orders that due process be followed, but later that day Lecomte was seized from his captors by an angry mob and executed.

The defence of the Montmartre cannon was by any standards an event. In popular histories of the period, such as Prosper Lissagaray's *Histoire de la Commune de 1871*, the defence of the cannon, initiated by working-class women, was the first act of the Paris Commune, a revolutionary experiment that lasted only a few weeks before its ruthless suppression in the last 'Bloody Week' of May.[1] Despite its short duration, the Commune held an important significance for socialist historians of the twentieth century, who saw it as the first revolutionary event led by the urban proletariat. But what exactly is an event and why might its conceptualisation be an issue for literary history?

Theories of the event have proliferated in contemporary literary theory.[2] For many critics, the work of literature is itself an event rather than an unchanging object: its production is an historical act and its reception has the capacity to change its readers. However, and before the idea of the literary work as event can be considered, it is necessary to give an account of the event as a concept in its own right. This chapter will give an outline of Paul Ricoeur's useful definitions of the event before discussing the problem the event creates for narrative. That problem is often seen in relation to the difficulty of representing the newness the event brings into the world; but not everyone experiences an event in the same way. The outcome of a battle, for example, will create winners and losers. For the winners, the future will indeed open up to the new; but for the losers, such as General Lecomte on 18 March or the Communards in the last week of May 1871, it closes down. Virginia Woolf's *Jacob's Room* and Chinua Achebe's *Things Fall Apart* can be read as responses to two events which seemed to close down the future: the First World War and colonialism. Both texts devise narrative strategies that attempt to re-open futures that the logic of defeat has obscured. Both novels, in fact, might be described as literary events, because they participate in re-opening the world to the new. In the modern period, the event has often meant revolution. But as the final part of this chapter shows, while both bring newness into the world, the relationship between the literary event and revolution is far from straightforward.

## DEFINING THE EVENT

For most commentators, the event is defined by its singularity. It is a unique occurrence, not defined or necessitated by what happened before. Most theorists invest the event with what Martin Jay calls 'the pathos of disruptive innovation, either as a moment of freedom, radical surprise, libidinal energy, the appropriation of being, or the undermining of conventional meaning'.[3] In this respect, the event represents a problem for the historian: its origins are not certain, its timing is unpredictable, and its consequences cannot be foreseen. The event marks the point where the known past ends and the unknown future begins. As Alain Badiou writes in his philosophical work *Being and Event*: 'the evental site is on the edge of the void'.[4] Paul Ricoeur offers three useful definitions:

1. Whether a physical or an historical event, the event is something which has happened in the past, and 'the pastness of what has happened is taken as an absolute property, independent of our constructions and reconstructions'.[5]

2. Historical events, as opposed to physical events, are what 'active beings make happen or undergo'.[6]

3. To the notion of the human past, the event adds an absolute difference, which is an obstacle to our understanding of it.[7]

Ricoeur suggests that we are only able to come to an understanding of the past event when we recognise its absolute difference from our own experience. Thus, what happened on 18 March 1871 was an historical event because: (1) it actually happened; (2) it was initiated by human agents and the consequences were the result of their actions; and (3) the radical otherness of what happened makes it difficult to represent in our own time.

Ricoeur then matches his three ontological definitions of the event, 'absolute having been, absolutely past human action, and absolute otherness',[8] to three problems that the event poses for knowledge:

1. The singularity of the event means that it is the opposite of a universal law: 'an event is what only happens once'.[9]

2. The event is not governed by logical or physical necessity: 'An event is what could have been done differently.'[10]

3. The otherness of the event has its 'epistemological counterpart in the notion of the gap between an event and any constructed model or invariant'.[11]

The epistemological problems posed by the events of 18 March 1871 are therefore:

1. That the defence of the Montmartre cannon was unique and cannot be explained by models or theories of history. Even if we were to apply a theory of revolutions to it, the event still has its own unique characteristics. It is for this reason that Terry Eagleton maintains that there is 'something almost oxymoronic about a theory of the event'.[12] Its singularity means that it is not easy to draw conclusions that have a more general application.

2. The day need not have turned out as it did. Despite Paris's history of urban insurrection, what happened was not wholly predictable, nor were its consequences easy to foresee. An event introduces something new into the world, and that newness will be difficult to assimilate and rationalise. (It is worth noting here the parallel between the event and an act of creation, as this parallel will become important when we consider the question of whether a work of literature can itself be characterised as an event. A historical event is an act of creation in the sense that human action produces something new, which cannot be explained by what has happened before. The origins of contemporary literary events are creation myths and the idea of divine creation continues to resonate in modern conceptions of making the new.)

3. Even the most innovative and sophisticated historical narrative will struggle to represent the singularity of the event. The radical break introduced by the event creates a moment of narrative crisis: a point at which the narrative can no longer proceed smoothly, where it either has to evade the event or to stumble and stop, because what has occurred cannot be explained by the events narrated thus far. There is therefore always a gap between the historical event and the narrative event and that gap may bring the very actuality of the historical event into question.

It is therefore to the narrative event that we must now turn.

## THE NARRATIVE EVENT

When questioned about what was most likely to blow his administration off course, Harold Macmillan, British Prime Minister (1957–63), replied with aristocratic panache: 'Events, dear boy. Events!' The phrase has become a cliché of political journalism, recycled whenever a politician stumbles in the face of the unforeseen. However, there is a wide gap between the anecdote and a verifiable historical event. No documentary evidence exists to substantiate either the question or the reply. Macmillan was well known for his quick wit, but this only makes the story plausible, not verifiable. It contributes to the myth of Macmillan's political intelligence, and more generally to the truth that the progress of even the most adept politician can be upset by the unexpected; but in these respects, the anecdotal narrative removes, even as it evokes, the singularity of the event, transforming its freshness and unique-ness into a gloomy universal law: everything goes wrong eventually.

The story exemplifies the problem the singularity of the event poses for narrative. As Ricoeur argues: 'events receive an intelligibility derived from their contribution to the development of the plot. As a result, the notions of singularity, contingency, and deviation, have to be seriously modified.'[13] It is a paradox of the event that the more one strives to understand it, the more it loses the singularity that marked it out as an event in the first place.

For one school of history, the problem lies not with narrative, but with the concept of the event itself, the ephemerality of which acts as a distraction from the larger explanatory power of long historical narratives. The Annales School of history in France reacted against the empirical, facts-based, approaches of nineteenth-century historiography, arguing that the *longue durée*, the 'long duration', was more important than single and necessarily fleeting events. Their argument was put most succinctly by the historian Fernand Braudel, who argued that events were superficial distractions. They work

> on the scale not so much of man in general as of men in particular [...] a surface disturbance, the waves stirred up by the powerful movement of tides. A history of short, sharp, nervous vibrations. Ultrasensitive by definition, the slightest movement sets all its gauges quivering. But through its nature the most exciting and richest in human interest of histories, it is also the most perilous. We must beware of that history which simmers with the passions of the contemporaries who felt it, described it, lived it, to the rhythm of their brief lives, lives as brief as are our own. It has the dimensions of their anger, their dreams, and their illusions.[14]

In his most famous historical work, *The Mediterranean and the Mediterranean World in the Age of Philip II*, Braudel puts events to one side and begins instead with the geography of the Mediterranean – the sea, its shores, the mountains, which surround it and the plains that lie beyond – as the proper frame for historical work.[15] This establishes the first level of a *longue durée* that creates the conditions in which human history takes place: 'It is a history that unfolds slowly and is slow to alter, often repeating itself and working itself out in cycles which are endlessly renewed.'[16] Only once this level is established, does Braudel move to the second level: the shorter time of institutions, of 'economies and states, societies and civilizations'; and only then, coming a poor third, is he prepared to countenance events, the brief histories of key characters and dramatic happenings.[17]

The advantage of Braudel's *longue durée* is its productive distance from the froth of immediate happenings and a consequent ability to analyse long-term trends. From a distance, what may at first appear as singular and unpredictable reveals itself to be an effect of a structural development that has been unfolding over a much longer time span. The disadvantage is that Braudel's prioritisation of the long duration produces the illusion of scientific objectivity. All events have to be explained in terms of what happened in the past: 'cycles which are endlessly renewed'. This means that the Annales school squeezes out the possibility of the new, or indeed the impact that their own time had on their historical narratives.

Paul Ricoeur suggests that in turning away from the event, the Annales school failed to realise that the concept of the *longue durée* was itself a response to an historical occurrence: the Great Depression that began with the stock market crash of 1929. In the face of that event, they sought 'a means of long-term analysis that would divest it of its catastrophic singularity'.[18] For Ricoeur, it is not possible to disentangle narrative and events. Events are 'not necessarily brief and nervous', but a 'variable' of the narrative that renders human experience understandable.[19]

However, this raises the awkward question of whether the event is just an invention of the narrative historian. If we return for a moment to Montmartre on 18 March 1871, it has to be asked whether socialist historians such as Lissagaray have given it a significance that bolsters a narrative of the Paris Commune as a justified uprising of an oppressed people. An alternative narrative might (and many did) focus on the summary executions of General Lecomte and General Clément-Thomas as evidence of the brutality of the mob and the need for its suppression. Narrativising the event also raises the question of where it begins and where it ends. Does the event in question begin at 3 a.m., when the troops set off for Montmartre, or when the women confront the soldiers, or should its origins be traced further back? An historian such as Braudel might want to focus on longer term trends in urban geography and political institutions to explain the uprising.

To make clear the gap between historical events and narrative events, Ricoeur writes of 'quasi-events', positioned within 'quasi-plots'. 'All change', he goes on, 'enters the field of history as a quasi-event.'[20] For Ricoeur, the quasi-event appears in the narrative as a moment of concentration or emphasis on particular kinds of historical or ideological change. The quasi-plot configures the quasi-event, rendering it understandable and making it safe for consumption within the ideology of the time in which the story is told. As with the apocryphal anecdote about Harold Macmillan, narrative is both a device for configuring the reader's understanding of time and a form of ideological containment.

However, perhaps because Ricoeur attempts a comprehensive understanding of the event, he succumbs to the paradox described above: even though his theory of narrative as the configuration of human temporal experience includes the configuration of future time, as well as the past and the present, his attempts to explain the event appear to close down the very things that give the event its uniqueness, depriving it of its singularity, its novelty and its creativity. What is lost is the notion that the event opens up the future. The question then for literary history is whether, despite this modification, the literary work can still convey some of the singularity and contingency of the historical event: whether the narrated event can break free from the demands of common sense and reveal its future edge. Here literature, rather than history or philosophy, offers us the most innovative ways of (re)configuring the event. Sometimes this means recapturing a sense of the singularity of an event. Sometimes, as in my first example, it means attempting to recreate a sense of the future in the face of a catastrophic event that seems overwhelming.

## JACOB'S ROOM

Virginia Woolf's novel *Jacob's Room* (1922) is a narrative response to the catastrophic event of the First World War.[21] As suggested by the title, *Jacob's Room* and not Jacob *himself*, Woolf writes a narrative that engages with an absence, the death of the novel's protagonist, Jacob Flanders, and through his absence the void created by the millions killed in the conflict. While the novel is an attempt to come to terms with the past, to bridge the gap that exists between the present and the historical event, it employs narrative techniques that resist the powerful version of the First World War as an inevitable disaster rather than as an event that could have happened differently. Through such techniques it attempts to keep the future open, as still full of possibility, rather than as doomed only to dwell in or, at worst, to repeat the past.

To achieve this, the narrative returns to those moments of Jacob's life before the war when the future still seemed open, the last moments when what otherwise seems an inevitable, predetermined march towards war and Jacob's death might have been averted. To resist this sense of inevitability, the novel is suffused with the language of chance and probability. The word 'probably' is deployed frequently, and the word 'perhaps' is used over a hundred times. Certainty on the other hand is always ironised. The phrase 'no doubt' is never inserted except in a syntactical structure that brings it into question. Yet while chance and opportunity cluster round him, the only character in the novel that does not seem subject to uncertainty is Jacob himself. From the opening passage, where as a young boy he is drawn ineluctably towards an animal's skull on a beach, it is Jacob's masculine certainty that draws him to war and death. However, the structure of the narrative, which is written around Jacob's absence, his 'room', rather than his presence, means that the attention of the reader is directed away from Jacob's march towards death to those he leaves behind: those who were and still are subject to possibility.

These characters survive while Jacob does not, and with them survive all the undecided wagers made before the war, all the chances and probabilities from which Jacob kept himself distant. Thus, the novel operates not as a memorialisation of Jacob, but more as a critique: a critique of his certainty, the mistaken confidence which took him to war. A certainty that his friend, Richard Bonamy, staring at Jacob's room after his death, suddenly finds incredible: "'He left everything just as it was,' Bonamy marvelled. 'Nothing arranged. All his letters strewn about for any one to read. What did he expect? Did he think he would come back?' he mused, standing in the middle of Jacob's room.'[22] Jacob leaves behind him a scatter of things – 'Such confusion everywhere!'[23] his mother exclaims – but also a scatter of people: people who still have the potential to activate the possibilities inherent in the past, while he does not.

We might understand Woolf's response to the event of the First World War not so much as a redemption of the possibilities inherent in the war itself – Woolf is anti-war, and not interested in redeeming it – but a redemption of the possibilities inherent in all the minor events in the lives of those whom the war has touched but spared. The narrative of Jacob's Room opposes not just war, but the war as a certain kind of narrative event, one which closes down rather than opens up the future. In the midst of national grief, it would be too much to consider the social changes the war brought about. So the narrative opens up to the 'minor' characters and the little events that represent a life that will go on. The future can be found, the novel suggests, in those little events rather than a catastrophic narrative of heroism and sacrifice.

Jacob's Room shows that it is possible to construct a narrative in which the event does not lose its singularity and become part of a retrospective logic of causality, although it is a paradox that in order to achieve this, the novel directs the reader's attention away from the single event, demonstrating its position in a constellation of events and hence multiple possibilities rather than a single narrative outcome. One way of viewing its narrative strategy might be as a critique of the event as a singular occurrence, one which belongs to those modern narratives that privilege stories of great events and great men. This raises the question of whether, as François Hartog suggests, the concept of the event is relatively new: an invention of modernity.

## THE EVENT AS A MODERN INVENTION

For Hartog, the problem the event poses for narrative is specific to the modern period. Only within the temporality peculiar to the modern age does the idea emerge that the event is 'unique'.[24] The 'modern historical sense' then responds to the challenge that its novelty 'cannot be apprehended or controlled',[25] by integrating it into the teleological perspective required by modern ideas of progress and development. If there was nothing in the past that allowed the event to be predicted, then at least its multiple future consequences can be charted. In the words of François Furet, 'If it had no past, it will have a future.'[26] The catastrophic events that bring about modernisation – industrialisation, war, colonialism – may seem unprecedented, but a narrative of progress aligns them with a movement forward into the future even if, as in Walter Benjamin's metaphor of the Angel of History, inspired by Paul Klee's picture, Angelus Novus, history then becomes a retrospective on the wreckage that piles up behind us. Klee's painting:

shows an angel looking as though he is about to move away from something
he is fixedly contemplating. His eyes are staring, his mouth is open, his wings
are spread. This is how one pictures the angel of history. His face is turned
towards the past. Where a chain of events appears before us, he sees one
single catastrophe, which keeps piling wreckage upon wreckage and hurls it at
his feet. The angel would like to stay, awaken the dead, and make whole what
has been smashed. But a storm is blowing from Paradise; it has got caught in
his wings with such violence that the angel can no longer close them. The
storm irresistibly propels him into the future to which his back is turned,
while the pile of debris before him grows skyward. This storm is what we call
progress.[27]

However, the definition of the event as a modern invention risks defining premodern
periods as uneventful and therefore without history. A notorious example of this
kind of thinking was the statement by the German philosopher Hegel that Africans
had no history, in other words that African societies were incapable of progress
or development. Hartog does not go this far, but he suggests that the narratives
produced by premodern 'regimes of historicity' represented events as the products of
mythic, divine or cyclical temporalities. For example, the loss of a battle might be
interpreted as the fulfilment of a prophecy, the will of the gods, or as a return to an
earlier archetypal condition. This view is problematic on a number of levels. First,
because it assumes that each particular period is locked in to a single temporality.
Second, because it can be used to perpetuate the myth of European superiority that
began with the colonisation of the Americas and continued until Europe had to
abandon its empires in the face of the anti-colonial movements of the twentieth
century. This myth holds to a false opposition between Europe, as the carrier of
progress and development, and an undeveloped non-European world, still subject to
premodern, mythic temporal modalities. From this perspective, the historical event
is something that the coloniser makes happen, but which the colonised undergoes. It
is not so much that non-European cultures have no future, but that in the coloniser's
discourse their future can only be imagined as either a precolonial repetition of
the same or a postcolonial development towards a version of 'European values' or
'European civilisation'.

   In fact, while narratives of progress and development are specific to the modern
period, it would be wrong to think that earlier periods had no way of representing
the future. In his monumental work *The Principle of Hope*, Ernst Bloch documents
narrative encounters with the 'not-yet-become' from the ancients to the twentieth
century, from myths and fairy tales to modern popular genres such as the detective
story.[28] He argues that the question 'What happens next?' is fundamental to all
narratives; and utopian yearning has always been a part of human consciousness.
Yet even Bloch gives modernity a special status, as a period of heightened temporal
consciousness, when the multiple anticipated futures of the past have reached the
possibility of fulfilment through revolution.

   In the contemporary world, postcolonial narratives written by writers from Africa,
Asia and Latin America have articulated the contradictions between modern and

premodern temporalities. The Nigerian novelist Chinua Achebe's *Things Fall Apart* (1958) was one of the first African novels that questioned colonial discourses' assumptions that indigenous cultures lacked the power to make events.

## THINGS FALL APART

*Things Fall Apart* (1958) is a response to two events: the event of West Africa's colonisation by the British Empire; and the event of decolonisation that followed the Second World War, a process that was far from complete when the novel was published.[29] The novel is set in a small Igbo village and the narrative covers the years just before and just after colonisation.[30] Achebe's narrative is detailed and unromantic. As such, it is written against colonial literature, such as Joseph Conrad's *Heart of Darkness* (1899), that represented precolonial African life as lurid and uncanny in its brutality and barbarism. With great economy, by showing the different characters of fathers and sons, Achebe's novel indicates how the social world of the village is not stuck in a cyclical or mythic temporality, but is in process. The central protagonist, the hardworking, prosperous and martial Okonkwo, is very different from his father, who dislikes agricultural labour and conflict, preferring to spend his time playing music. Okonkwo's son, Nwoye, on the other hand, is sensitive and uncomfortable with his father's martial code and its consequences. These small differences between the generations indicate that the future is not fixed, but open and subject to change.

Yet Achebe's novel displays no nostalgia for the precolonial past. Practices such as leaving newborn twins to die are described impartially and objectively. Some of the consequences of colonialism are also seen as beneficial. Nwoye's conversion to Christianity by European missionaries makes sense in relation to his rebellion against his father's values. However, while it opens one new future, the arrival of colonial rule closes down the alternative future paths contained within the existing social structure, creating a master narrative that suppresses previous experience based on the village's culture and traditions. Okonkwo resists this process and, after getting into a violent confrontation with the colonial authorities, he commits suicide, an act that violates the traditions by which he has lived his life, but which comes about because the new order has left him no place. To emphasise the point, the final part of the narrative is narrated from within the colonial discourse, from the perspective of the local District Commissioner. In it, Okonkwo's own experience and consciousness has been eliminated:

> The story of this man who had killed a messenger and hanged himself would make interesting reading. One could almost write a whole chapter on him. Perhaps not a whole chapter but a reasonable paragraph, at any rate. There was so much else to include, and one must be firm in cutting out details. He had already chosen the title of the book, after much thought: The Pacification of the Primitive Tribes of the Lower Niger.[31]

Like Woolf, Achebe resists a narrative of the event that locks history into an inevitable causal logic. He too returns to what happened before 'the event' to open up the narrative to multiple alternative possible outcomes. For example, Nwoye's conversion suggests the possibility of consenting engagements with the colonial culture, engagements that prefigure new postcolonial cultural forms, such as culturally distinct modern African churches or, indeed, the Anglo-African novel, of which *Things Fall Apart* is one of the first examples. The suggestion is that the event holds more possibilities than the single path originally conceived by its perpetrators. One of these possibilities was the path of national self-determination, an event in which the publication of *Things Fall Apart* took part by giving voice to the anti-colonial movement in Africa.

For some critics, the whole point of the event is that it promises just this kind of social transformation. In its most radical form, this means revolution. If for Woolf and Achebe the First World War and colonialism respectively are negative events, that is, events that close down and obscure future prospects, then for philosophers such as Walter Benjamin and Alain Badiou, revolution is a positive event, one that opens up all the future's possibilities.

## REVOLUTION AS EVENT

Revolution is the modern event par excellence and it is not surprising to discover that for those such as Benjamin and Badiou, for whom the event plays an important role in their thinking, it is the revolutionary event they have in mind. Benjamin, while he does not have a theory of the event as such, is as concerned as Badiou to try to bring to representation the unique moment of change intrinsic to the event. Both writers engage with the event as problem and as possibility. Benjamin's aim is to break out of the evolutionary, linear narratives that characterise the modern ideal of progress. Such narratives, he argues, are essentially anti-historical, in that they only see the past in terms of the present. History presented as 'the way it really was' means a history acceptable to the present, rather than a history that disturbs it.[32] What is required, Benjamin proposes, is a break with this conformist narrative, an event that will 'wrest tradition away from the conformism that is working to overpower it'.[33] For both Benjamin and Badiou, revolution is, in Benjamin's words, 'the leap in the open air of history' that makes 'the continuum of history explode'.[34] It performs a double action of concentrating time and opening up the possibility of new temporalities.

Benjamin is much taken by a story from the July 1830 revolution in Paris, when '[o]n the first day of fighting, it so happened that the dials on clocktowers were being fired at simultaneously and independently from several locations in Paris'. According to one witness, it was as if the revolutionaries wanted 'to make the day stand still'.[35] Such moments are characteristic of what Benjamin describes as 'Now-time', which 'comprises the entire history of mankind in a tremendous abbreviation'.[36] Paul Ricoeur also uses the term 'abbreviation', when he describes the event as a moment of narrative concentration. For Benjamin the event acts as a concentration of historical potential.

For Badiou, on the other hand, the event is more akin to an act of creation. It marks a complete break with the past, but while it appears to come out of nowhere, to be 'on the edge of a void', it draws its power from the social actors whom the pre-revolutionary order has rendered invisible. In the eighteenth and nineteenth centuries these actors were the peasants and the urban poor, later the industrial working class, in 1968 students and young workers, today they include disenfranchised migrants, *les sans-papiers*:[37] those deprived of their rights in the countries in which they live. In bringing these actors into play, the event creates a new truth.

Literature finds it difficult to capture such moments of revelation; but we can find something of Benjamin's 'image' of the past that can be seized only as it 'flashes up at the moment of its recognisability'[38] in Ezra Pound's two-line imagist poem, 'In a Station of the Metro':

> The apparition   of these faces   in the crowd :
> Petals   on a wet, black   bough .[39]

Whatever Pound's aesthetic intentions, a political reading is possible. The faces in the crowd are the faces of the invisible actors who make the event happen. They achieve recognisability through their actions, but the fragmentary nature of the experience that might coalesce into an event is indicated by the gaps in Pound's lines. It is not certain that the individual faces will come together into a collective that will bring about change. It is in the nature of the event that at any time it might happen, but equally it might not.

## THE CREATIVE ACT: THE WORK OF LITERATURE AS EVENT

The attraction of Badiou's concept of the event is that it creates what he calls 'the possibility of possibles'.[40] It opens up a vast field of potential; and for this reason the moment of the event is precious. Badiou stresses the importance of remaining faithful to its moment of truth, even during what he calls 'interval periods', periods of defeat for revolutionary forces.[41] The problem with Badiou's theory, a problem that also applies to some extent to Benjamin, is that it becomes difficult to argue with the truth he claims the event produces, which achieves a status beyond rationalisation. As Eagleton comments, Badiou's notion of the event bears a family resemblance to 'a purely creative act, original and gratuitous, beholden to nothing beyond itself, and as such an imitation of the divine act of creation'.[42] We have already noted the relationship between the modern concept of the event and creation myths. In the modern period, however, creative power comes to be seen as human rather than divine.

A work of literature represents an act of creation, because the possibilities of human agency are *worked* into its form. Yet, the work is a unique event in the sense that it breaks with the past and has a future. By foregrounding ambivalence, as in *Jacob's Room*, or through narrative structures that complicate straightforward resolutions or closure, as in *Things Fall Apart*, the work of literature can take its reader to the edge of the void and provoke them into confronting what comes next as Badiou's 'possibility of [multiple] possibles'. The alternative to regarding the work as an event, as Eagleton points out, is to see it as a dead object complete in itself, as: 'an edifice or architectural structure, complete with various levels and sub-systems, which is supposed to exist in the reader's mind as a synchronic whole, rather than a dramatic or symbolic act with its own evolving history'.[43] If, however, the work is, as it were, a live event, then its structure is strategic rather than a synchronic and self-referential whole. It is a 'socially symbolic act'.[44] Its design, a word that as Eagleton points out means both structure and purpose, is to make the world anew, a project that may in turn 'do something to the reader'. The work must of course have a readable structure, one that can be understood and analysed, but the *work* it does in the world means that it has the potential to change the world.

There are, however, at least two reasons why we should be cautious about claims that overstate the literary work's powers of transformation. First, because its power is weak rather than strong. As Virginia Woolf once wrote, it is unlikely that a poem would ever cause a revolution, even if it were possible that in a pre-revolutionary situation, reading a poem at an opportune moment might be the action that precipitates change. This, however, would be an atypical event. It is doubtful that Pound's 'In a Station of the Metro' would start an uprising. Second, because the 'work' achieved by the work of literature is not done by the literary work alone. It has a 'context', a shorthand term for the complex set of circumstances in which the work is created.

The debate about the relationship between the literary work and its 'context' divides between critics such as Derek Attridge, who focus on the singularity of the literary work and those, such as Rita Felski, who take their inspiration from cultural studies, putting more emphasis on what she calls the 'articulation' of a 'forged connection' between different aspects of the aesthetic, the social, the political and the economic. Felski argues that the 'political import of a text cannot be inferred from its internal form or logic, but derives from its position in a constellation of texts, practices, and interests'.[45] It might be more accurate to say that the political import of a text cannot be inferred *just* from its internal form or logic, as Felski goes on to suggest that cultural studies pays more attention to formal questions than is usually recognised. For Attridge, however, the critic who reads a text for its political import is already too instrumental. The literary work should be read first and foremost on its own terms: as an act of invention which only becomes literary when it is 'experienced by the reader (who is, in the first instance, the writer reading or articulating the words as they emerge) *as an event*, an event which opens up new possibilities of meaning and feeling (understood as verbs), or, more accurately, the event *of such opening*'.[46] The tortured and slightly mystical turn of this sentence is symptomatic of the fraught relationship we have already encountered between the literary and the historical event. The drawback of Attridge's insistence on literature's singularity is that it risks cutting off the literary from other forms of human creativity. Attridge's theory of literature divests it of the capacity to be anything more than a literary event. The danger of 'context', on the other hand, a danger Felski is all too aware of,[47] is that it has a deadening effect not just on the literary work, depriving it of its originality and uniqueness, but on the same human capacity for making the new. In the end, both the literary and the historical event elude us precisely because to pin them down is to deprive them of their power.

In the absence of a clear relationship, we might perhaps deploy a metaphor: the force-field. Modern works of literature, we might say, while events in their own right, seem to participate in and contribute to the force-field created by powerful historical events. It is, for example, difficult to disentangle romanticism from the French revolution or modernism from the revolutionary fervour that came to a head in Russia in October 1917. However, the attempt to identify a clear causality between the event and a particular work (not least because there are romantic and modernist works before 1789 and 1917) will always result in a reductive and instrumentalist reading; and yet, to ignore the vital correspondences between new literary formations and new social formations would be to miss a vital part of what literature is.

## CONCLUSION

We have come a long way, it would seem, from the morning of 18 March 1871. However, it should by now be clear that what connects the historical, the narrative and the literary event is that they are all concerned with the creation of something new. Newness is what makes an event an event: those characteristics which cannot be predicted and therefore cannot be fully explained in terms of what has happened before. As we have seen, this poses a problem for historical narratives, and indeed for any of the human or social sciences whose purpose is to explain the past. While, as Ricoeur makes clear, narratives need events in order to introduce change, there is always a gap between the event and its representation. Even though the event, like History with a capital 'H', cannot be apprehended except through its 'prior textualization, its narrativization',[48] the process of narrativisation modifies the event, and defuses its creative power. Works of literature, less bound by the constraints of science and logic, are more suited to capturing the novel and inventive powers of the event. As creative acts themselves, they draw on its singularity, entering into and contributing to its force-field, making the most of the new multiple alternative futures it offers. Even in the face of catastrophic events such as war or conquest, the literary work can create a space in which alternative futures might be thought.

There is of course a danger of romanticising the event, just as there is a danger of exaggerating the creativity of the literary work. The 'sanctity' of the revolutionary event, in particular, was used after the French and the Bolshevik revolutions to justify acts of state terror. Investing the literary event with too much importance may also inspire fear, although with less serious consequences. Yet, to diminish the awe literature can inspire is to banish from literary study its capacity to show us that things might be different from the way they are; and to give up on that possibility would be to cast out hope, without which literature would lose much of its appeal and all of its point.

## FURTHER READING

Attridge, Derek. *The Singularity of Literature*. London: Routledge, 2004.
Badiou, Alain. *Being and Event*, trans. Oliver Feltham. London: Continuum, 2007.

Badiou, Alain. *The Rebirth of History: Times of Riots and Uprisings*, trans. Gregory Elliot. London: Verso, 2012.

Benjamin, Walter. 'On the Concept of History'. In *Selected Writings, Volume 4: 1938–40*, ed. Howard Eiland and Michael W. Jennings, trans. Edmund Jephcott et al. Cambridge, MA: The Belknap Press of Harvard University Press, 2003.

Bloch, Ernst. *The Principle of Hope*. 3 vols. Oxford: Blackwell, 1986.

Braudel, Fernand. *On History*, trans. Sarah Matthews. Chicago: University of Chicago Press, 1982.

Eagleton, Terry. *The Event of Literature*. New Haven, CT: Yale University Press, 2012.

Felski, Rita. 'Context Stinks'. *New Literary History* 42:4 (2011), pp. 573–91.

Jay, Martin. 'Historicism and the Event'. In *Against the Grain: Jewish Intellectuals in Hard Times*, ed. E. Mendelsohn, S. Hoffman and R. Cohen. New York: Berghahn, 2013.

Hartog, François. *Régimes d'historicité: Presentisme et expériences du temps*. Paris: Éditions du Seuil, 2012.

## CHAPTER 13

# Generation

Julian Hanna

In the English-speaking world the concept of generations is most commonly found in journalism and publishing or in everyday speech rather than in the academy, where its position has been described as 'somewhat marginal'.[1] (As Marius Hentea has observed, this is not the case in other languages: 'French, Spanish, German, and Hispano-American literary scholars have worked with and continue to use the concept.'[2]) Part of the problem is that the notion of a generation is at once extremely familiar to us and yet surprisingly hard to pin down. It is familiar as a means of describing one's peers: of 'talking about my generation' in the words of The Who's 1965 hit song 'My Generation'. It serves as useful shorthand to discuss broad historical groups sharing a similar age cohort and set of formative experiences (Baby Boomers, Generation X), as well as more narrowly defined cultural sub-groupings (the Beat Generation, the Woodstock Generation). In journalism, obituaries typically refer to a public figure's place in relation to his or her generation, for example as a leading figure among political, scientific or literary peers. In book publishing the popularity of the concept is demonstrated by its ubiquity among bestsellers: William Strauss and Neil Howe's pop sociology *Generations* (1991), *13th Gen* (1998), and *Millennials Rising: The Next Great Generation* (2000); Douglas Coupland's zeitgeist novels *Generation X* (1991) and *Generation A* (2010); Tom Brokaw's Second World War history *The Greatest Generation* (2002); and Evan Wright's report from the second Iraq war *Generation Kill* (2004) are all suggestive examples. Strauss and Howe make a broad but compelling case for viewing American history (and America's future) through the generational lens rather than by using the familiar temporal milestones of wars or presidential terms. The cohorts they propose include the Lost Generation (born 1883–1900), the G. I. Generation (born 1901–24), the Silent Generation (born 1925–42), the Boom Generation (born 1943–60) and so on.

In stricter scientific usage, however, the idea of generations presents some problems. The sociologist David Kertzer traced the shift in usage from 'popular to scientific vocabulary' and found evidence of 'considerable conceptual confusion'. 'The term's multivocality', Kertzer observed, which was 'a virtue in popular discourse, became a liability in science'.[3] Another problem is the competing variables of time and space. For example, while some literary movements are referred to in temporal terms, such as the Spanish avant-garde 'Generation of '27' or the Young British Artists of the 1990s, others are referred to by location, as in the case of the Lake Poets or the Bloomsbury Group. Still others refer to neither time nor place but only to a general spirit ('lost' or 'decadent') or are given an arbitrary name ('X' or 'Y'). The writer and artist Wyndham Lewis, who coined the term 'Men of 1914' to describe a literary generation that was born in the 1880s and shaped by the experience of the First World War, but who was also deeply suspicious of collectives of all kinds (shown in his fierce attacks on Bloomsbury and American expatriate circles in Paris[4]), questioned the usefulness of his own label. In a chapter of his memoir titled 'An "Age" Group Meets Itself', Lewis wrote of 'the vanity of classification' when it came to literary generations. He claimed: 'Four people more dissimilar in every respect than [James Joyce,] myself, [Ezra] Pound and [T. S.] Eliot respectively, it would be difficult to find. There is only one sense in which any such a grouping of us acquires some significance – we all got started on our careers before the War.'[5]

So how does thinking about generations help us to make sense of literary history? According to the pioneering sociologist Karl Mannheim, a theory of generations is 'indispensible [...] to an understanding of the social and intellectual movements'.[6] For researchers, generations help to draw boundaries around, for example, writers writing in a certain time and place under specific social and historical conditions. Strauss and Howe argue that each generation 'is shaped by its "age location": that is, by its age-determined participation in epochal events that occur during its lifecycle'. The 'age location', in turn, produces a 'peer personality', 'a set of collective behavioural traits and attitudes'.[7] These characteristics can be applied to writers and readers as much as anyone else. Moreover, a theory of generations enables us to recognise, in Mannheim's words, 'the accelerated pace of social change characteristic of our time'.[8] Mannheim's essay 'The Problem of Generations' (1927) is still considered 'the seminal theoretical treatment of generations'.[9] It was written during a decade that was 'a high-water mark for generational theory', with not only Mannheim but also José Ortega y Gassett,[10] Julius Petersen, François Mentré and others producing a range of influential studies.[11] Not unrelatedly, as we shall see, the 1920s also marked the high point of literary and artistic modernism, a period which saw a veritable explosion of movements, groups and 'isms' in the build up to and the aftermath of the collective trauma of the First World War.

Viewing literary history through the lens of generations remains an illuminating, useful, even vital approach. The Spanish philosopher Ortega y Gasset, part of the Generation of '98 and an influential figure for the next generation of Spanish intellectuals in the Generation of '27, captured the fundamental importance of the phenomenon. He wrote:

The most elemental fact of human life is that some men die and others are born – that lives succeed each other. All human life, in its very essence, is enclosed in between other lives which came before or which are to come after [...] This is not to say, heedlessly, that the youth of today – that is, his soul and his body – is different from the youth of yesterday; but it is inevitable that his life should have a different *framework* than that of yesterday.[12]

More recently, a Pew Research Center study, *Millennials: A Portrait of Generation Next* (2010), offered the following 'caveat' that nevertheless ends in a strong endorsement:

> Generational analysis has a long and distinguished place in social science, and we cast our lot with those scholars who believe it is not only possible, but often highly illuminating, to search for the unique and distinctive characteristics of any given age group [...] But we also know this is not an exact science.
> [...]
> We are mindful that there are as many differences in attitudes, values, behaviors and lifestyles within a generation as there are between generations. But we believe this reality does not diminish the value of generational analysis; it merely adds to its richness and complexity.[13]

This caveat must be kept in mind when approaching the narrower field of literary generations and the at times seemingly arbitrary categories and boundary lines one encounters there.

To lay the groundwork for this chapter, we will start with an overview of Mannheim's landmark essay, which remains the clearest and most fully elaborated treatment of the phenomenon of generations. Many of the examples will be drawn from the modernist period, for the reason that the twentieth century in general, and the first half of that century in particular, with its abundance of traumatic events, rapid technological development in the West, seismic shifts in everyday life, and a pervasive sense of crisis, all caused extreme ruptures between generations ('generation gaps'). It was also during this period that the analysis of generations came to prominence in sociology, history and literary studies.

## MANNHEIM'S THEORY OF GENERATIONS

The origin of the generation concept in its modern usage, to denote members of a particular age cohort who share and are in turn defined by certain experiences, dates back to the French revolution and its immediate aftermath. Those who witnessed the early events of the revolution, including the English romantic poets William Wordsworth and Samuel Taylor Coleridge, were one such generation – and in the case of Wordsworth, he defined himself and his contemporaries by this measure.[14] The next generation, the so-called 'Children of the Revolution' born shortly before or just after the year 1800, included writers and philosophers such as Victor Hugo, Honoré de Balzac, Auguste Comte and others. Comte, one of the founders of modern sociology, was also one of the first theorists of the new concept of generations, and is referred to in the first part of Mannheim's essay, subtitled 'The Positivist Formulation of the Problem'. There Mannheim outlines the contribution of Comte and the French positivist tradition, which was 'anxious to find a general law to express the rhythm of historical development, based on the biological law of the limited life-span of man and the overlap of new and old generations'.[15]

Mannheim found this approach overly simplistic, however, complaining that through it 'the history of ideas appears reduced to a chronological table'. In the second part of his essay, the section titled 'The Sociological Problem of Generations', Mannheim attempts to move beyond the limitations of previous theories. He begins by establishing the primary elements, which for him include both location and social context: 'the unity of generations is constituted by a similarity of location of a number of individuals within a social whole'.[16] (More recently, the importance of location appears to have decreased with the rise of 'global generations'.) Mannheim compares generation to class: in the sense that generation, like class, is 'an objective fact, whether the individual in question knows his class position or not, and whether he acknowledges it or not'.[17] This is true at least of generations in the broadest sense; smaller 'generation units', as we shall see later in this chapter, involve a greater degree of self-conscious agency. Even though Mannheim acknowledged the 'elemental fact' of the biological foundation of generations, moreover, he emphasised, more than contemporaries like Ortega y Gassett, 'extra-biological factors', and in particular 'the prevailing tempo and impact of social change'.[18] This is remarkable given the fact that the 1920s, the decade in which Mannheim wrote, saw an unprecedented surge of faith in evolutionary biology and an interest in the study of eugenics, the science that uses breeding to 'improve' the health or other characteristics of a given population. From the publication of Max Nordau's notorious study *Degeneration* (*Entartung*, 1892; translated 1895), which specifically targeted artists and writers, to the rise of Nazism in the 1930s, there was a widespread fear of racial decline in contemporary and future generations. Degeneration, in other words, was the illness that eugenics sought to cure. The First World War, which decimated an entire generation, was initially welcomed by some as a necessary 'cleansing' force – as the Italian futurist leader Marinetti famously called it, 'the world's only hygiene'.[19] This is important in relation to generational theory because, when generations are not viewed as moving in cycles, they are often seen as going one way or the other: either improving with progressive evolution or experiencing a degenerative decline. Ideas of eugenics and degeneration were extremely popular at the time Mannheim was writing, even (or especially) among progressive thinkers: Aldous Huxley, H. G. Wells, Havelock Ellis, Bertrand Russell, John Maynard Keynes and many other leading intellectuals were ardent supporters of the idea that people should take an active role in improving generations through selective breeding and other biological measures.

Written in the wake of the First World War, it is not surprising that traumatic historical events play an important role in Mannheim's theory of generations. One of the most notable features of the Lost Generation or the Generation of 1914 was the formation of experiential bonds – veterans' groups, for example – to replace traditional biological bonds. In effect this meant a widening of the generation gap and a strengthening of bonds within a generation marked by the shared traumatic experience of trench warfare, for example, at the expense of traditional family ties across generations. Literary depictions of this generation abound, from Ernest Hemingway's protagonists, with their varieties of wounded masculinity, often adrift in a postwar Europe, to Virginia Woolf's portrait of Septimus Warren Smith in *Mrs Dalloway* (1925). Septimus, the innocent, poetic soul who 'went to France to save an England which consisted almost entirely of Shakespeare's plays and Miss Isabel Pole in a green dress walking in a square', returns to London terminally scarred by his experience, shell-shocked and haunted by survivor's guilt.[20] Women after the First World War, meanwhile, were forced back into a feminine role by the masculinist society that had wreaked such havoc: 'Their reproductive function was what mattered. Everything else – votes for women, increased educational opportunities, continuing employment in clerical jobs – came second. First came nurturing the new generation.'[21] This example also shows the gendering of generations, highlighting the different expectations, roles and experiences for men and women. Many generational constructs, like Wyndham Lewis's 'Men of 1914', deny the place of women entirely.

One of the most striking aspects of Mannheim's theory of generations is the insistence that not every generation was a 'true' generation. True generations in Mannheim's view have a unifying spirit; they are not automatic, nor are they merely identical to age cohorts. Only certain generations realise their inherent potential and become significant in social terms. In the historian Robert Wohl's memorable phrase, 'Historical generations are not born; they are made.'[22] As Mannheim himself emphasised, 'The most important point' is that 'not every generation location – not even every age-group – creates new collective impulses and formative principles original to itself and adequate to its particular situation'. In other words, only certain generations will develop a 'distinctive pattern of interpreting and influencing the world'.[23] For Mannheim, the rise of generations is closely linked to the speed of social change. 'The quicker the tempo of social and cultural change [...] the greater are the chances that particular generation location groups will react to changed situations by producing their own entelechy.'[24] This would seem to explain the unprecedented explosion of 'isms' across Europe in the modernist period. Such a period, marked by traumatic conflict and social, political and technological upheaval, was fertile soil for producing the sort of entelechy, or fully realised potential, that Mannheim described.

The idea that generations are 'realised' to greater or lesser degrees, or not at all – that some are 'major' and others are 'minor' – is a very suggestive one for literary historians. The circle of young poets led by W. H. Auden that emerged from Oxford in the late 1920s to flourish in the 1930s as the 'Auden Generation', for example, began very much in the shadow of the 'high' modernist generation of poets like T. S. Eliot and Ezra Pound, and had to work hard to set themselves apart stylistically (and ideologically) from that famous generation.[25] At other times, when the lines of demarcation are very bold, it is hard not to see the phenomenon of major and minor generations as an overly deterministic creation of literary historians themselves. For example, there is the divide between writers who came to prominence before and after the Second World War, very broadly sketched as modernist and postmodernist generations, and the problem of the writers who fall through the generational cracks. As one scholar describes it:

> histories of American poetry have been remarkably consistent in locating the divide between modernism and postmodernism at the end of World War II. On one side of the divide is the generation of modernists who were born in the 1880s and became widely recognized in the 1910s and 1920s, while on the other side are writers born in the 1920s and afterward, writers who first became publicly prominent in the 1950s and 1960s. As a result of such normative definitions of modernism and postmodernism, poets whose literary reputations were formed in the 1930s or 1940s have fit neither of the dominant generational models. They instead have been relegated to such liminal zones as 'the middle generation', 'modern poetry after modernism', or 'the first postmodernists', or they have been shuttled back and forth […] to one side of the divide or the other.[26]

This example illustrates the potentially harmful tendency among some historians to sketch generations or periods too broadly. This tendency ignores subtler patterns in exchange for simple binaries, and forces writers born at the 'wrong time' into one generation, with its accompanying set of characteristics, or the other.

It is not uncommon for a generation to begin in the shadow of the previous generation and to think itself minor in comparison at first, before eventually coming into its own as a major generation. Members of the generation may feel a sense of belatedness; writers and artists may experience what Harold Bloom called the 'anxiety of influence' with regard to their predecessors.[27] In fact most generations of the last century may be seen in this light. The modernists of the Generation of 1914 or the Lost Generation grew up in the shadow of the giants of late Victorian and Edwardian literature, the Auden Generation struggled to assert themselves in the 1930s, and the younger writers of the 1950s, including The Movement, the Angry Young Men, and the Beat Generation, bore the weight of everything produced in the miraculous interwar period. Generation X grew up in the shadow of the Baby Boomers, Generation Y in the shadow of Generation X and so on. Pierre Bourdieu describes the struggle that repeats itself to a greater or lesser extent with each generation:

> The ageing of authors, works or schools is something quite different from a mechanical sliding into the past. It is engendered in the fight between those who have already left their mark and are trying to endure, and those who cannot make their own marks in their turn without consigning to the past those who have an interest in stopping time, in eternalizing the present state; between the dominants whose strategy is tied to continuity, identity

and reproduction, and the dominated, the new entrants, whose interest is in discontinuity, rupture, difference and revolution.[28]

The pattern is similar to that of the *bildungsroman*, the literary coming-of-age story. As Hentea notes, the new form 'emerged [...] around the time that the generation began to take on a sociological meaning'.[29] It begins with isolated rebellion against the values of the dominant culture, followed by an integrative phase in which members of the younger age group find each other and 'join forces' to create a new vision suited to their own artistic and social reality, and from this integration begins the path to artistic maturity and cultural dominance, only to be overthrown by the next generation. Since Mannheim, all of this generation formation – the ability to transform the latent potential of the 'biological fact' of generations into 'a distinctive unity of style' – has been seen as depending largely on social factors. 'Whether a new generation style emerges every year, every thirty, every hundred years, or whether it emerges rhythmically at all', Mannheim argued, 'depends entirely on the trigger action of the social and cultural process.'[30]

## MAKE IT NEW

In 1910, one of the many avant-garde manifestos of the period, the 'Manifesto of the Futurist Painters', concluded with the declaration: 'Make room for youth, for violence, for daring!'[31] It was a typical generation-based appeal to overthrow the old order; it insisted that 'Italy is being reborn.' This sort of performative narrative is typical of the self-conscious effort to shape generations, whether in the present or retrospectively. A generation, as Mannheim demonstrated, is more than a 'chronological table': it is a human construct that can be realised to a greater or lesser extent, and which may be 'chosen' in the sense of choosing to share values with others, though usually with others who share a certain time and place in history. Each generation also represents the chance to encounter the world as if for the first time, to see the cultural heritage with fresh eyes, and to transform it – in the words of Ezra Pound, to 'make it new'.

By performing the 'mental experiment' of envisioning a utopia in which everyone lives forever, Mannheim came up with a list of five 'fundamental facts' about generations.[32] The five principles out of which Mannheim drew his conclusions still represent a useful description of generations. They include: the 'continuous emergence of new participants in the cultural process'; the 'withdrawal of previous participants'; the fact that we 'can only participate in a temporally limited section of the historical process'; the 'necessity for constant transmission of cultural heritage' (if people lived forever this would not be necessary, because there would be an unbroken line of memory); and the continuous 'transition from one generation to another', with several generations in existence at any one time.[33] What all of these characteristics together suggest, more than anything, is the cultural dynamism that comes from the constant rejuvenation of new generations replacing old ones. Each new generation must reinterpret the cultural legacy it is given, deciding what to keep, what to reject, and how to 'read' the material. It must also add a new layer. 'The phenomenon of "fresh contact"', as Mannheim calls it, 'is a productive force: it ensures the continuous renewal of culture'.[34]

Of course, the process is not always a smooth one. The new generation may well reject the old, as the futurists did. In Henry David Thoreau's *Walden* (1854), for example, the American ideal of self-reliance clashes with the ideal of respect for one's elders. Thoreau provoked and challenged his readers by rejecting at the outset of the book the idea that we have much if anything to learn from our elders. Far from seeing a gentle continuity from one generation to the next, he saw that in rapidly changing times '[o]ne generation abandons the enterprises of another like stranded vessels'. Thoreau states plainly: 'The old have no very important advice to give the young [...] I have yet to hear the first syllable of valuable or even earnest advice from my seniors. They have told me nothing, and probably cannot.'[35] Generational theory after Mannheim, however, formed as it was in a period of revolution and upheaval, would see this rejection as being on a natural spectrum of reactions to the inherited culture. Thoreau's generation, with Ralph Waldo Emerson and the other American transcendentalists, added a new layer to the American cultural heritage that emphasised, among other things, self-reliance and the questioning of authority.

Even within the same generation there are different attitudes towards the inherited cultural legacy. Before the First World War there was the brief period of cultural upheaval that Wyndham Lewis evocatively described as the 'big bloodless brawl prior to the Great Bloodletting'.[36] Many artists and writers across Europe followed the example of the Italian futurists and sought to break with the cultural heritage of the past altogether, becoming futurists of one kind or another. It was perhaps inevitable that Italy's artists, feeling suffocated by the weight of an especially rich cultural history, would react most violently against previous generations. In their first manifesto the Italian futurists famously urged people to 'set fire to the library shelves! Turn aside the canals to flood the museums!'[37] In the same manifesto they also commented directly on the passing of generations, welcoming their own inevitable displacement by the next generation as strongly as they sought to overthrow the last: 'When we are forty, other younger and stronger men will probably throw us in the wastebasket like useless manuscripts – we want it to happen!'[38]

But the futurist-inspired vorticists led by Wyndham Lewis and Ezra Pound took a different approach to the cultural heritage of past generations. Despite the high degree of iconoclasm expressed in their magazine, *BLAST* (1914–15), the vorticists set themselves apart from their futurist rivals. While the vorticists agreed that the new generation of artists and writers should not dwell on the past, they nevertheless argued that the past was an inseparable part of the present (which they preferred to the future). Two days before the first issue of *BLAST* appeared, Lewis published 'Kill John Bull With Art', in which he declared on behalf of the vorticists: 'We, like Mr. Marinetti, or rather much more than he, are happy, and can well do without the Past. *Our fathers are part of us*, and the more we live instead of idling about their ashes the more we honour them, as of course we ought to do.'[39] (The poet Guillaume Apollinaire sided with Marinetti, declaring even before the War, in 1913: 'You cannot carry around on your back the corpse of your father. You leave him with the other dead.'[40])

More than in any other era, perhaps, the modernist era brought into question the value of cultural transmission. In the case of Anglo-American modernism, especially for writers such as Eliot and Pound, the path through the present crisis to 'cultural renovation' was 'a return to the values of a previous age': as Peter Nicholls has argued, 'this modernism sought to correct the apparently amnesiac tendencies of modernity by reconnecting it to a valued cultural tradition'.[41] The example of Anglo-American modernism is also reminiscent of Mannheim's caution against assuming that each generation is inherently more progressive than the last, which is often not the case. 'Whether youth will be conservative, reactionary, or progressive', Mannheim argues, 'depends [primarily ...] on whether or not the existing social structure and the position they occupy in it provide opportunities for the promotion of their own social and intellectual ends.'[42]

How do we define a 'true' generation? As I mentioned earlier, Mannheim distinguished between 'actual' (fully realised) and merely 'locational' or 'age-based' generation groups. To form a generation 'in its full actuality', he argued, required two factors: 'co-presence in [...] a historical and social region' and '*participation* in the common destiny of this historical and social unit'.[43] By way of example, he asked the rather blunt question: 'Do we put the peasants [...] in a common actual generation group with the urban youth of the same period?' To which he answered: 'Certainly not!' This was not simply class bias: it was because the rural youth, traditionally deprived of much communication with the outside world, 'remain unaffected by the events which move the youth of the towns'. As Mannheim acknowledges, however, this rural-urban division was not even true at all times in the past. Sometimes, people from all classes and regions are caught up in the same events and become part of the same 'actual generation', as often happens in the case of war or revolution.[44] In Mannheim's terms, then, people in the same age group and location are 'only united as an actual generation in so far as they participate in the characteristic social and intellectual currents of their society and period'.[45] But how do we define what is 'characteristic'? Is the concept of a unified social and intellectual body, even in a single nation, becoming foreign to us?

As we have already seen in examples drawn from avant-garde movements of the early twentieth century, within each 'actual generation' there are usually smaller, often opposing factions. These groups Mannheim defines as 'generation units': 'groups within the same actual generation which work up the material of their common experiences in different specific ways'.[46] Generation units may be on different sides of a political question or event, such as the Vietnam War that divided American opinion in the late 1960s and early 1970s, or the Spanish Civil War that divided opinion among European intellectuals in the 1930s (as seen in Nancy Cunard's 1937 *Left Review* pamphlet, *Authors Take Sides on the Spanish War*). Beyond a 'loose participation' in shared events, these more tightly knit groups are united by 'an identity of responses'.[47] An interesting example may be drawn from the Lost Generation, which was a particularly broad 'actual generation' owing to the collective trauma of the First World War. It was also a highly self-conscious generation, documented and analysed by its own members during its formative years. One such chronicler, the writer Malcolm Cowley, described the highly fragmented yet ultimately homogeneous character of his generation in a statement that sums up the odd phenomenon of mass nonconformity being reflected in a mosaic of apparently discrete generational units that add up to an 'actual generation'. In the 1920s, Cowley wrote: 'escape from the mass was becoming a mass movement'.[48]

## ISMS AND SCHISMS

According to Mannheim, 'within any generation there can exist a number of differentiated, antagonistic generation units'.[49] This was particularly true in the modernist era, when 'generation units' proliferated at an extremely high (and highly visible) rate. Here we enter the territory of 'isms' – movements, groups, coteries and cliques of literature, art and politics. In the modernist era manifestos were launched in their hundreds by 'isms' across Europe, and these movements spread to North America and urban centres around the world. 'After 1910', as William Wees has argued, '"groups" became increasingly characteristic features of the intellectual-artistic landscape.'[50] But as Bradbury and MacFarlane observed, 'As in sects, religious or political […] "ism" tended toward schism.' In fierce competition with each other, members of each movement 'rallied followers, mounted displays, [and] enacted themselves in public'.[51] The flourishing of movements under modernism hence represents the clearest illustration of the phenomenon of generation units described by Mannheim.

Alongside the proliferation of antagonistic units within a generation, another crucial feature of generations that stands out in the modernist era is the role the avant-garde plays in generation formation. In 1930, one of Mannheim's contemporaries in generation theory, Julius Petersen, published a study that includes a list of six factors that define a literary generation. According to Petersen, members of a literary generation must be contemporaries, share a similar education, be in personal contact, be defined by a common 'generational event' (such as the First World War), have leading figures among them, and use a common language.[52] In Petersen's definition, as we can see, a literary generation is more or less synonymous with a literary movement. Mannheim and Ortega y Gasset disagreed with Petersen in this respect, insisting on the broader societal impact of generational consciousness. However, they agreed on the importance of elites in forming the core ideology of a generation unit.

'The generation-unit', wrote Mannheim, '[has] as its nucleus a concrete group which has developed the most essential new conceptions.'[53] At the core of each unit, in other words, there is a small elite, or avant-garde. This core group writes the mythology for the broader, more diffuse generational unit, as Ernest Hemingway, F. Scott Fitzgerald, Dorothy Parker and others set the tone for the Lost Generation of Americans in the 1920s. The other members of the generational unit, 'outside the narrow group' in Mannheim's terms, 'find in them the satisfying expression of their location in the prevailing historical configuration'.[54] In other words, the core speaks for the whole. In some cases, isolated members of the older generation act as 'forerunners' for the younger, developing 'the nucleus of attitudes' that will come to define the new generation.[55] Gertrude Stein's role as curator and spiritual leader of the Lost Generation of American expatriates in Paris is one example; William S. Burroughs' role as mentor to the Beat Generation in the 1940s and 1950s is another. Mannheim insists, however, that the relationship between the artist and society is a two-way system: 'The artist certainly lives [...] in his artistic world with its particular traditions, but as a human being he is always linked with the driving forces of his generation even when politically indifferent, and this influence must always transform even purely artistic relations and entelechies.'[56]

## CONCLUSIONS AND FUTURE DIRECTIONS

For Mannheim, as we have seen, '[t]he phenomenon of generations is one of the basic factors contributing to the genesis of the dynamic of historical development'.[57] Generations realise their latent potential to a greater or lesser degree, and within each generation there is a proliferation of antagonistic sub-groups called generation units. What we might call the *Zeitgeist*, the spirit of the age, 'does not pervade the whole society at a given time'; the *Zeitgeist* merely reflects the ability of one particular unit within the generation to put its 'intellectual stamp on all the other groups' – but still 'without either destroying or absorbing them'. The theory of generations, developed by Mannheim and his contemporaries and returned to by sociologists and literary historians over the past decades, remains a useful approach for understanding the development and structure of movements. It helps us to understand the interplay between the rise and dissemination of artistic tendencies and their socio-historical contexts.

Certain aspects of Mannheim's conception of generations, however, are called into question by recent historical changes. For example, how important is location in the Internet Age? Are we now in an era of 'global generations', or is this phenomenon limited to a cosmopolitan elite? Mannheim's insistence that generations are grounded in a particular location, confined by national boundaries, now seems questionable at the very least. However, adapting this aspect of Mannheim to the realities of the twenty-first century may require only relatively minor adjustments. Mannheim emphasised location because of the importance he attributed to the participation by members of a generational group 'in the same historical and social circumstances'.[58] If participating in the same 'historical and social circumstances' is now possible across a much wider, even global, space since the proliferation of the Internet, then location is no longer an essential element in the formation of generations. Global movements such as Occupy (the Occupy Generation?) suggest this to be true. Recently some scholars have argued for the rise of a global '9/11 Generation'.[59] How much does this affect the theory of generations as conceived by Mannheim? There remain, even within Europe, stark differences in socio-economic and historical circumstances. Compare the experience of the current 'twentysomething' generation, for example, in Scotland, Greece, Germany and Ukraine, and it is far from homogeneous. But the argument could also be made that there is a growing sense of greater commonality between members of a certain age cohort across national borders than whatever bonds exist between older and younger generations within a particular national culture.

In a *Guardian* article from 2014 the novelist Will Self questioned 'the very assumption that generations are capable of individuation and of possessing their own *geist*', and argued that if it existed at all, such a phenomenon was becoming more rare in our increasingly complex world.[60] Defining a more stable and persuasive terminology for generations is one of many challenges currently facing scholars of generational theory. Another is to isolate more specific categories and to delineate the differences between them. Yet another challenge is to understand the extent of transnational or even global affinities between generations in the twenty-first century. The growth of 'memory studies' as a field in recent years has also added new layers of complexity to the basic concept of generations. For example, the idea of 'postmemory' – where 'powerful, often traumatic experiences' that precede the birth of the next or 'second generation', such as the memory of the Holocaust, are nevertheless 'transmitted to them so deeply as to seem to constitute memories in their own right', thus creating continuity and blurring generational boundary lines.[61] Or does such a traumatic event have the opposite effect, further widening the gap between generations – as seems to be the case in a text like Art Spiegelman's *Maus*?[62] We might also investigate generations by drawing on empirical social network theory in order to produce a more nuanced understanding of the increasing complexity of generations. Finally, we should seek to go beyond networks of human agents and, as in Bruno Latour's Actor-Network-Theory (ANT)[63] and the 'new' modernist studies, incorporate objects (magazines and journals) and spaces (venues of performance) into a broader understanding of what constitutes and gives a distinct character to a generation.

## FURTHER READING

Bloom, Harold. *The Anxiety of Influence: A Theory of Poetry*. Second edition. Oxford: Oxford University Press, 1997.

Edmunds, June and Bryan S. Turner. 'Global Generations: Social Change in the Twentieth Century'. *The British Journal of Sociology* 56:4 (2005), pp. 559–77.

Hentea, Marius. 'The Problem of Literary Generations: Origins and Limitations'. *Comparative Literature Studies* 50:4 (2013), pp. 567–88.

Hirsch, Marianne. 'The Generation of Postmemory'. *Poetics Today* 29:1 (2008), pp. 103–28.

Hynes, Samuel. *The Auden Generation: Literature and Politics in England in the 1930s*. London: Bodley Head, 1976.

Latour, Bruno. *Reassembling the Social: An Introduction to Actor-Network-Theory*. Oxford: Oxford University Press, 2007.

Mannheim, Karl. 'The Problem of Generations'. In *Karl Mannheim: Essays*, ed. Paul Kecskemeti (1952). Reprint, London: Routledge, 1972, pp. 276–322.

Ortega y Gassett, José. *The Modern Theme*, trans. James Cleugh. New York: Harper, 1961.

Strauss, William and Neil Howe. *Generations: The History of America's Future, 1584–2069*. New York: William Morrow, 1991.

Wohl, Robert. *The Generation of 1914*. Cambridge, MA: Harvard University Press, 1979.

## CHAPTER 14

# Period

Ben De Bruyn

We live in a time when historical periods and literary movements are often dismissed as crude containers, when the practice of periodisation is being contextualised and demystified and when new planetary realities force us to recalibrate the scale of our historical imagination, arguably making debates over particular period terms less pressing. Yet the fact that we can assign these developments to a determinate place in time – or that we can speak about any term in this book in terms of its value at this moment – immediately reveals our indebtedness to the logic of periodisation, and indicates that periods are resilient entities, hard to avoid if not inescapable in any literary history. Often perceived as antiquated throwbacks to an unsophisticated view of history if not as coercive totalities with dangerous homogenising effects, period concepts continue to play a role in our work as students, teachers and scholars, and we ignore their contribution at our peril. In investigating this notion in more detail, we are not just learning about what other people do but also, unavoidably, about the pitfalls and possibilities of our own activities, about the roots of our historical toolkit and about its recalibrated use in the emergent period that is the early twenty-first century.

Before turning to these timely reflections on periodisation, some preliminary remarks are in order. First things first: what is a period? Srinivas Aravamudan offers this succinct definition: 'a period is a boundaried domain that includes events as well as backgrounded [...] conditions that do not [...] possess the distinctiveness associated with an event'.[1] In other words, periods are containers for salient events and their background conditions. Looking for specific examples, one is further struck by the diversity of their names, as period concepts include numerical labels like the twelfth century and the 1990s, political notions like the Restoration and the Victorian age, aesthetic categories like baroque and romanticism, broad phrases like classical antiquity and narrow ones like the roaring twenties, firmly rooted labels like cold-war fiction as well as more free-floating notions like realism or modernism. In contrast to seemingly self-contained terms, some period concepts are also explicitly 'relational',[2] like neoclassicism or *arrière-garde* (a relation which frequently implies a value judgement, as in the middling middle ages), though Fredric Jameson has noted that periods always 'project narratives [...] of the historical sequence in which such individual periods take their place'.[3] All period names hint at what came before and will come after, inevitably sketching the contours of a broader history. Briefly put, every period is a narrative. If the preceding examples illustrate what periods are, they also suggest that, to some extent, different labels come with distinct types of baggage. Realism poses descriptive problems that do not overlap completely with those posed by the 1960s, say. This lesson is worth remembering, because the existing literature on periodisation often treats period terms in a wholesale fashion, criticising their reductive workings *in toto*, ironically, without bearing in mind that these are heterogeneous entities with their own affordances and limitations. This implies that if you want to argue for a newly restrictive definition of modernism, for instance, that doesn't necessarily have implications for other periods. After all, some periods are more equal than others.

That is not to say that general reflections are impossible or that shared problems cannot be identified. Returning to the initial definition, the distinction between event and background conditions is not set in stone. Foreground and background can change places depending on the historian's perspective, who might expand the particular event of 1789 into its own period, as a spate of publications devoted to a single year have shown, or might consider the background conditions of a period as events in their own right (as happens when a classicist focuses on the everyday life of slaves instead of 'major' political events). Reproducing established period labels also encourages various questionable beliefs, as Eric Hayot has noted: that these ages have a unique essence, which is created ex nihilo and later disappears without a trace; that the historical continuum is composed of a fixed sequence of periods with clearly circumscribed spatial and temporal boundaries (a Victorian age that characterised life in Britain between 1830 and 1900, for example); and that recent periods require more attention, as their number increases as we get closer to the present (less people work on the 930s than on the 1930s).[4] Nevertheless, periodisation continues to play a crucial role in literary history, which tries to identify these ages, assign authors, works and other phenomena to the right period, and establish the basic parameters for their appropriately contextualised interpretation. And whether we are classicists, medievalists or postmodernists, as Rita Felski has suggested, our teaching and research routinely draw on these insights, implying that '[u]nderstanding a text means clarifying the details of its placement in the box, highlighting the correlations, causalities, or homologies between text-as-object and context-as-container'.[5] This is a practical view of literary history, but a problematic one too. To do literary history is to encounter this double-bind situation, and that is why we should all reconsider periodisation, its advantages and disadvantages, its institutional history and its potential future.

## DISCARDING PERIODS, TRACING NETWORKS

Trained to scrutinise words for their covert as well as overt functions, it is hardly surprising that literary scholars and other humanists have been sceptical of rigid period boundaries and strict all-or-nothing definitions for a long time. In English, the most famous attack on the attempt to identify isolated periods and literary movements is Arthur O. Lovejoy's 1924 essay 'On the Discrimination of Romanticisms', as it led to a spirited response from René Wellek that I will discuss in the next section. Focusing on the notoriously difficult category of romanticism, Lovejoy notes that existing accounts lead in wildly different directions; at the time, critics argued over when and where this movement started, who originated it (some even mentioned Plato), who developed the legacy and, of course, how it should be described. As a historian of ideas interested in 'a clearer understanding of the general movement of ideas', Lovejoy has little patience with this 'confusion of terminology and of thought'.[6] The solution he proposes is twofold: we should start speaking of romanticism in the plural (an influential suggestion) and we should analyse these romanticisms into their 'unit-ideas'[7] to compare them more adequately. This double procedure is necessary because, as boundary cases allegedly show, it is impossible to define 'a single chronologically determinate Romanticism',[8] a conclusion he generalises at the essay's end: '[t]he categories which it has become customary to use in distinguishing [...] "movements" in literature or philosophy [...], are far too rough, crude, undiscriminating'.[9] As these labels never refer to 'some single real entity',[10] there is no such thing as Elizabethan literature, Victorian literature, modernism or postmodernism. Refusing to believe in a reality that corresponds with such period terms, Lovejoy is a nominalist, not a realist. Exit periods.

Many contemporary critics agree that periodisation is dubious at best. In their view, the use of period labels distorts historical realities by *partitioning* the flow of time with arbitrary boundaries, by *narrativising* history through the use of a linear sequence of pre-packaged periods, by *homogenising* essential differences between authors and works which coincidentally belong to the same age, by ignoring the contributions of certain groups or even *excluding* them from history, and by *naturalising* these conventional instruments, inculcating the belief that these heuristic tools are the actual coordinates of literary history. According to Micah Mattix, for instance, periodisation invariably has a problematic 'leveling effect' on the achievements of individual poets like Frank O'Hara; in contrast to what our concepts should do, she claims, '[p]eriod terms do not make difference apparent' and they should therefore be discarded.[11] Attempting to salvage contingent historical phenomena from homogenising labels, Mattix does not want to be a *periodiser*, but a *particulariser*. Turning to readers, Frances Ferguson has observed that 'literary history has been largely founded on a claim about the importance of acquaintance, in which we take historians to be functioning primarily as readers and offering up descriptions of their own perceptual objects', inevitably setting limits to generalisations (we can only ever read so many works, as Franco Moretti has pointed out) and 'continually challenging stable historical groupings'.[12] In a similar vein, Katie Trumpener observes that '[p]eriod, for us, seldom possesses the same rawness, volatility and vital force as the texts it ostensibly produced and now, retrospectively, groups'.[13] Because of its strong investment in individual authors and close reading, literary history cannot avoid troubling and unworking the periods it creates. As writers and readers, we are all particularisers.

Other critiques have been less directed at how period terms smooth over individual differences than on how they have helped to marginalise certain groups, as the contributions of gender and postcolonial scholars, among others, have shown. As Gilbert and Gubar suggested more than twenty years ago, there is 'a relationship between the apparent coherence of a period and its sexual politics', with boundaries and definitions often derived from the contributions of major male writers, to the detriment of their female peers.[14] More recently, queer studies scholars have attacked the hegemonic, heteronormative understanding of history, which presumes to know, once and for all, what sexual identities and historical periods are and ignores queer experiences and seemingly unhistorical anachronisms. That is why we should start looking for an alternative: '[i]n opposition to a historicism that proposes to know the definitive difference between the past and the present, we venture that queering requires what we might term "unhistoricism"'.[15] Rejecting 'straight temporality', with its teleological orientation and conventional periodisations, these scholars highlight the queer temporality of chronology-defying experiences and identities, which refuse to be consigned to the past and linger promiscuously across canonical boundaries.[16] Orthodox periods do not just help to maintain traditional gender roles but also to invalidate international competitors and to establish European hegemony by creating communities, to paraphrase Benedict Anderson, of imagined contemporaries and non-contemporaries. Periodising schemes are nationalising instruments, one scholar observes, comparing rival accounts of the Spanish and English Golden Ages: '[t]he construction of high moments in literary history [...] often mobilizes national and imperial rivalries, and the retrospective consolidation of that history solidifies both military and cultural distinctions'.[17] In a related vein, Pascale Casanova has described how prestigious literary capitals like Paris and New York define the Greenwich meridian of literary modernity and force everyone to keep up, with their belated romanticisms and modernisms.[18] More generally, scholars like Dipesh Chakrabarty and Bruno Latour have demonstrated how a dubious notion of modernity is used to distinguish enlightened Western experiences from supposedly backward peripheries that are imperiously assigned a premodern status. But as Latour notes, the modern distinction between things and humans and the associated belief in a history composed of distinct periods break down as soon as we attend to the polytemporal quality of the material and discursive actor-networks that compose our more-than-human collectives. How can we assign an academic lecture, for instance, to just one period, given that it juxtaposes brand-new and age-old words and requires ageing computers built with components that will outlast human civilisation?[19] The distinction between progressive moderns and stagnated premoderns only works if these two periods are sealed off and form 'an ordered front of entities sharing the same contemporary time',[20] but the presence of untimely, non-contemporary components shatters this belief in disconnected periods and in a divide between the West and the rest.

Drawing attention to Latour's work makes sense here, for many scholars who have recently criticised periodisation do not just dismiss the work of earlier periodisers like Michel Foucault, Fredric Jameson and new historicist critics including Stephen Greenblatt, but also turn to actor-network theory for inspiration. Indeed, you could argue that we are witnessing a shift from strong periods to weak ones, from reductive boxes to sprawling networks. The tension between the older and newer position can be summarised as follows: '[c]ontext [...] points both to a synchronic structure – a singular constellation of coeval elements, or what New Historicists called "co-texts" – and to an ongoing polychronic process comprising diverse actors functioning at potentially different speeds'.[21] The former is bad, critics like Rita Felski, Wai Chee Dimock and Jonathan Gil Harris agree, the latter good. This position is not radically new, for scholars like Hans Robert Jauss and Raymond Williams, to give but two examples, already highlighted the importance of a work's ongoing reception history and a period's uneven temporal makeup in the early 1970s. Yet it has acquired a new urgency and inflection in recent scholarship. As Felski observes, periods often function like boxes or even coffins that enable us to pack and unwrap texts all too quickly. The moment a work was produced is important, she admits, but an exclusive focus on coeval context ignores the work's agency and individuality as well as 'the ubiquity of cross-temporal networks'.[22] Neither classics nor popular works can be quarantined in a single period; to what century can we assign Shakespeare, to what decade James Bond? Developing her earlier critique of new historicist contextualisation, Wai Chee Dimock similarly maintains that we should distrust fully integrated social fields, where '[p]eriodization can proceed with ease', given the cross-historical 'leakiness' of literary texts and their distributed 'long networks'.[23] Instead of privileging certain genres or authors, we should attend to how every actor and node makes a difference to the network – they are mediators, not intermediaries, as Dimock puts it, using Latour's terms. Like his colleagues, Jonathan Gil Harris discards what he calls 'the national sovereignty model of temporality', 'the notion that history consists of bounded periods with unique constitutions and borders that need to be respected' because it hinders 'an ethics of unboundedness' that acknowledges phenomena working across these divides.[24] Harris does not just embrace Latour's critique of easy contextualisations and emphasis on distributed agency, but also his interest in non-human things – the way in which material objects complicate linear understandings of history. If we want to understand such 'untimely matter', Harris contends, we should replace 'period purification' with an alternative approach, and '[a]ttend to both the production and the erasure of temporal partitions enabled by the actor-networks of matter'.[25] To contextualise properly, in other words, Jameson's call to 'always historicise' should be taken as 'always polychronise'.[26] There are differences between these scholars, but they share a desire to replace disconnected periods and monocausal contextualisations with actor-networks composed of polychronic and nonlinear relations. And even if they might admit that there is no rupture between box and network, Foucault and Latour, they would still encourage us to think in terms of anachronistic connections, not period-bound determinations. The time of literature, they hold, is not a flat tapestry but a crumpled 'handkerchief',[27] not a predictable flow but a set of 'whirlpools [...] in which [elements] from different moments [...] collide',[28] not a fixed map separating Osip Mandelstam and Dante, but a 'fan', which 'can be folded up, putting Italy in the immediate vicinity of Russia and making strange bedfellows out of the fourteenth and the twentieth centuries'.[29]

## HISTORICISING PERIODS, EMBRACING BOUNDARIES

If the case against periodisation is so strong, why do we continue to fit literary history into predesigned boxes? Individuals as well as institutions may be reluctant to change, but mere convenience is a poor explanation given these strong critiques. Why do we not subscribe to a presentism that rephrases Jameson's famous dictum as '[a]lways [a]nachronise!'?[30] For even presentist critics who argue for the importance of contemporary associations in our experience of literature end up saying things like '[h]istory, we can all agree, matters'.[31] And why do queer 'unhistoricists' underline that their project is not 'ahistorical', indeed is 'rigorously historical'?[32] And even that qualification does not suffice for one commentator, who responds that '[t]he wholesale characterization of periodization as a straightening of the past [...] mak[es] light of [...] the ways in which practices [and] discourses happen to gather in specific places and times'.[33] Latour-based models are no different; Harris mentions 'a distinctively Renaissance attitude to time'[34] at one point, reinstating a traditional period, and Elizabeth Outka, drawing on Felski, maintains that a network-model of context allows us 'to reassemble a more vibrant picture of what it might have been like to be alive at [one] particular moment'.[35] Apparently, letting go of the past and its periods is not that easy. Why do we keep returning to these terms, knowing that they are problematic? Should we embrace them after all?

To answer these questions, let us first consult one of the few scholars who has explicitly argued in favour of periodisation, René Wellek, even though '[n]ot even the greatest advocate of this kind of literary history was much at ease with it'.[36] In the influential *Theory of Literature*, Wellek devotes an entire chapter to literary history, a chapter which discusses topics like nation and influence, but also devotes considerable attention to periodisation. Responding to Lovejoy's rejection of terms like romanticism, Wellek concedes that romanticism is not a unitary phenomenon but rejects the nominalist conclusion that such terms are arbitrary labels, for 'the concept of period is certainly one of the main instruments of historical knowledge'.[37] Periods help us to acknowledge both historical evolution and individual originality, after all, if we consider them as successive sets of 'purely literary' conventions; in Wellek's view, a period is 'a time section dominated by a system of literary norms [...] whose introduction, spread, diversification, integration, and disappearance can be traced'.[38] Contra Lovejoy, he doesn't believe such sections should be coherent; the unity of periods can only be relative, as no individual work can realise all of these norms and periods are linked by 'the survival of a preceding scheme of norms and the anticipations of a following scheme'.[39] Wellek emphasises periods, in other words, not complete homogeneity. This approach may ultimately seem 'unduly "purist"',[40] he admits, and most readers have agreed, despite his remarks that literary history should only be studied 'in comparative isolation' from social history.[41] And there is no denying that Wellek's chapter underlines this autonomy. For the first sentence is a simple question: '[i]s it *possible* to write literary history, that is, to write that which will be both literary and a history?'[42] And the chapter concludes not only that, with the help of periodisation, yes, we can, but also that there is still a lot to be done, ensuring 'that literary history has a future as well as a past'.[43] If we start tracing changing norms and successive periods, literary history has an identity and a future. Here, periods are not opposed to the main aims of literary studies, as Ferguson argued by pitting general periods against individual close readings, but are central to its identity.

This argument has old roots, as Ted Underwood has shown in a recent study about the role of periodisation and discontinuity in literary history. Taking the long view, he argues that literary periods mattered in the period between 1840 and 2012 especially, because the division of literary history into ages and movements like transcendentalism, naturalism and postmodernism served two vital purposes: 'historical contrast' allowed middle-class readers to acquire a uniquely *cultural* social distinction and enabled emerging literary scholars like Wellek to establish a form of disciplinary autonomy.[44] Underwood's account of the rise and endurance of 'historical contrast' begins in the early nineteenth century, when genres like the historical novel reveal a gradual shift in the conceptualisation of tradition; instead of the unbroken lineage associated with aristocratic property, writers like Walter Scott promote a historical sensibility that involves a sharp awareness of discontinuity via the horizon-expanding encounter with the norms and customs of a different period. Radically different from aristocratic continuity, this experience of contrast was available for cultivation by characters and readers without established position and therefore created the conditions for an alternative form of social prestige, based on reading rather than pedigree and on the distinction between periods rather than on untroubled continuity. The story continues when early literary scholars like F. D. Maurice, a largely but unjustly forgotten professor at King's College in the 1840s, rejected existing curricula in English literature, devoted to etymology and writing skills, and created the first 'tightly periodized'[45] survey course as well as the first theory that explained 'why periodization was good for you'.[46] Embracing the experience of historical contrast popularised by writers like Scott, Maurice felt that the vivid evocation of former societies was the only way to foster a specifically middle-class form of national pride and collective antiquity in his students. The hegemony of contrastive periodisation was threatened by emerging gradualist approaches in the first half of the twentieth century, Underwood continues, but contrast won because it created a unique rationale for literary history, as Wellek's chapter already suggested; if the causal explanation of transitional moments inevitably involves extra-literary factors, the contrastive description of successive periods limits itself more easily to the discussion of particular aesthetic programmes. Only by stressing the difference between past and present, in short, could middle-class readers and literary scholars defend their claims vis-à-vis other classes and disciplines, creating the familiar situation where the 'cultured individual becomes a temporal cosmopolitan'.[47] This account explains why causality and continuity have such a bad reputation in literary studies and why we keep worrying about those labels and boundaries. Ultimately, the difference between straight and queer periods, boxes and networks might be less important than the shared belief that reading involves the 'ennobling' juxtaposition of historically remote works and experiences.

Although this account helps us to contextualise periodisation, its implications for future research are not obvious. Underwood's position is clear enough. Already in the 1990s, his reading of contemporary literary and theoretical works reveals, 'periodized historicism' seemed to be coming to an end, because '[t]he specificity of the past seemed to be erased by the insistent contemporaneity of journalism, or by challenges to the print medium itself, or by an "end of history" that flattened majestic Hegelian processions into retro style'.[48] That the cultivation of historical discontinuity is losing its prestige is not bad, he adds, for it opens the way for a 'quantitative historicism'[49] in which digital humanities tools break the hegemony of the discontinuity paradigm and open up 'new ways of characterizing gradual change, and thereby mak[e] it possible to write a literary history that is no longer bound to a differentiating taxonomy of authors, periods, and movements'.[50] By increasing 'methodological diversity', we can take 'a fresh look at the tension between continuity and contrast, which our discipline has often treated in a one-sided way'.[51] Maybe quantitative approaches and gradual processes should play a bigger role in literary history. But we should not exaggerate the revolutionary novelty of 'distant reading' either. Even without computers, we can arrive at good gradualist observations, like Underwood's own claim that 'the distinction between "national tales" and "historical novels" is best understood as a gradual transformation perceptible within the oeuvres of several different novelists, rather than as a contrast between authors'.[52] Digital humanities tools may be exciting, moreover, but Richard Grusin has warned that we should not overlook the 'dark side' of the digital humanities, which can be used to contract the scope of historical research, to increase the number of researchers in precarious positions and to privilege institutions with unlimited access to expensive digital infrastructure.[53]

Nor should we forget that periods enable us to do things too. In fact, some scholars explicitly embrace traditional periods, restricting the term modernism to the period between 1890 and 1940, for instance, to counterbalance the spatial expansion typical of recent research. Here, '[p]eriodization [...] amplifies, rather than constrains, scholarly discourse about modernism'.[54] When it functions as 'the site of an engagement [...] of positions', even a seemingly obsolete notion like *Zeitgeist* might have some mileage left.[55] More generally, we can interpret period less reductively, not as a 'uniform shared style or way of thinking' but as 'the sharing of a common objective situation, to which a whole range of varied responses [is] possible'.[56] Alternatively, we can accept the critiques outlined earlier and decide to focus on hybrid periods.[57] A good starting point here might be Caroline Levine's brand of new formalism. In her recent *Forms* (2015), she outlines a position that approximates the one of Felski and company; not only does she give pride of place to networks, but she also rejects 'the very notion of a historically specific time period' and concludes 'that the act of historicizing should mean [...] *refusing* any enclosed, bounded notion of cultural experience in favor of intricately intertwined transhistorical processes of transmission'.[58] But she also argues that most critics are not formalist enough in the sense that, in analysing bounded wholes like periods, for example, they ignore differences between types of wholes and fail to discuss how different wholes collide and counteract each other. Instead of focusing exclusively on how bounded wholes 'exclude and imprison', she wonders, why not consider their power 'to hold things together' or 'to disrupt the controlling power of other bounded shapes'?[59] Including neglected female or foreign writers into anaemic conceptions of romanticism or modernism can be fruitful, and so can the attempt to pluralise periods, not by analysing unit-ideas à la Lovejoy or aesthetic norms à la Wellek but by rubbing together categories like medieval and modern, modernist and postmodernist. If some stories enabled by periodisation are harmful, others may be beneficial too.

## THE PERIOD OF THE PLANET

A contemporary reflection on periodisation should not only consider its origins and limitations, but also factor in a very recent development: the turn to big history and the concomitant embrace of long periods. This scaling up of the historical imagination seems strange from the perspective of the 1980s and 1990s, when many scholars focused on small stories, individualised anecdotes and, if anything, on short periods and individual years. In the microhistory beloved of new historicists, its most famous proponent Carlo Ginzburg has noted, the aim is to expand what would have been a mere footnote in another scholar's work, to zoom in on a particular event, offer 'the minute analysis of a circumscribed documentation, tied to a person who was otherwise unknown'.[60] At the other end of the spectrum, Fernand Braudel famously argued for 'slow history', 'the history of long, even very long, duration (*longue durée*)', which draws attention to geographical constraints, for instance: '[m]an is a prisoner for long centuries of climates, of vegetations, of animal populations, of types of crop, of slowly constructed equilibria, which he cannot transform without the risk of endangering everything'.[61] This seems an unpromising scale for literary historians. Indeed, it doesn't appear to be historical at all. As Franco Moretti argues, in a piece that identifies the thirty-odd year cycles of novelistic sub-genres (and generations) as the proper measure of literary history, we should prefer these cycles to 'the circumscribed domain of [...] the individual case', the scale preferred by critics, as well as to 'the very long span of nearly unchanging structures', the home of apparently unhistorical theorists.[62] But not all critics would agree that *longue durée* equals unchanging structure. As one scholar has noted, this long duration has in fact acquired a new currency in literary studies with the advent of transnational studies, and '[a]ll the uses of the *longue durée* reflect efforts to stretch the concept of the time period', though she warns that this gesture risks becoming 'an automatic response [that] extends conventional chronological divisions without asking new questions about them'.[63] Against such automatic extensions, however, recent research demonstrates that a *longue durée* perspective can lead to exciting new questions.

Several projects are urging us to take the long view. In a recent manifesto, the historians Jo Guldi and David Armitage offer an impassioned plea to move beyond the microhistories of the last decades, however fruitful their lessons, to tell new ambitious stories, cross-period syntheses that abandon the 'horizontal chronology of one age following the next' by dealing with several decades, centuries and millennia simultaneously, because only by scaling up our imaginations can we understand the slow processes behind the unstable world economy and the even more unstable global climate.[64] Literary scholars have offered parallel proposals. Literary Darwinists maintain that an evolutionary perspective avoids narrow contextualisations by testing views of fiction and human nature 'in *real historical depth*, [...] over the millions of years that shaped the human mind'.[65] Even more ambitious is the proposal of Wai Chee Dimock, who invites us to explore not just the national canon but a fully transnational and transtemporal literature. As she suggests in *Through Other Continents*, the space-time coordinates of the nation fail to match the global spatial and temporal relations created by literary works.[66] What if we consider American literature across the 'deep time' of geology, as her subtitle suggests? To be more concrete: what if we compare Thoreau not to Emerson or another coeval writer, but to the Bhagavad Gita and Ghandi? What sort of literary history emerges if we take the planet's extension and duration into account, and consider how very old texts continue to resonate, tracing the 'far-flung kinship'[67] and 'vital nonsynchrony'[68] characterising this globalised conception of intertextuality? Such a longer literary history reveals, Dimock argues, that an old epic sensibility is preserved in 'percentages'[69] in later forms, including the novel. This project appears to broaden the scope of literary history to the age of the planet, but the emphasis ultimately lies on a smaller period, as we only have 'written records going back five or six thousand years'.[70] That is why Mark McGurl has taken issue with Dimock's argument, claiming that we can only address literary history's anthropocentrism if we take 'deep time' seriously and start to analyse how texts and other cultural artefacts take up the formidable challenge of representing processes that operate across inhumanly large timescales – that would be a real 'Big Historicism'.[71] There is again a generic corollary; instead of assigning a privileged place to the venerable epic, this approach draws attention to lowbrow genres like horror and science fiction, forms which court aesthetic failure in their attempt to map the fringes of what science tells us about the deep past and future. The narratives of Dimock and McGurl also culminate in different morals; the former paints a picture of planetary kinship that invalidates racism, sexism and speciesism, the latter one of a cosmic indifference so complete that it nullifies the least trace of anthropocentrism. The latter, you could say, encourages us to imagine a literary history without humans.

This *longue durée* perspective can also be found in recent research on climate change and its cultural meanings, leading, once again, to a fundamental rethinking of basic categories, like our conception of history, of the earth and of humanity. As Dipesh Chakrabarty has observed, first of all, 'anthropogenic explanations of climate change spell the collapse of the age-old humanist distinction between natural history and human history'.[72] When the geological event of climate change has a human cause, human history and its allegedly rapid events are integrated into natural history and its supposedly slower rhythms, and vice versa. Taking this lesson seriously as literary scholars would mean that we no longer contextualise literary works solely in terms of a human history which is disconnected from its supposedly stable natural environment. Drawing on Spivak's work, Chakrabarty notes that climate change also changes our understanding of the earth, creating 'a growing divergence in our consciousness between the global – a singularly human story – and the planetary, a perspective to which humans are incidental'.[73] Studying capitalism, colonialism and consumerism remains important, but this global imagination offers little help when we find ourselves face to face with the otherness of the planet, which simply doesn't care about justice, inequality or humanity. Reminiscent of the Dimock-McGurl debate, global connectivity is important, but planetary indifference shouldn't be ignored. How have literary works represented these two dimensions of our earth-bound existence? Finally, climate change changes our understanding of humans. We should no longer consider humanity solely in terms of shared rights or individual differences, Chakrabarty asserts, but also as a non-human, 'geophysical force' that 'stretches our capacity for interpretive understanding'.[74] As the processes involved have long and complex causes and consequences, how can we assign responsibility, untangle causality and identify agency with any measure of certainty, seeing that they connect poor humans and rich ones, people and animals, invisible gases and toxic things? We live in a period that requires new narratives, an alternative '*geostory*', as Latour has argued, one that can untangle these global and planetary networks and respond to climate change's incremental, anti-narrative pace and 'catachronistic' future orientation.[75] 'The problem for all of us in philosophy, science, or literature becomes', Latour ponders, 'how do we tell such a story?'[76] Right now, we are in need of a planetary narratology, a geological rhetoric, a post- or non-humanities.

That this debate has implications for our modes of periodisation is indicated most clearly by the fact that literary scholars have recently adopted the notion of the Anthropocene, a term launched by ecologist Eugene Stoermer and chemist Paul Crutzen to signal that we are actively if involuntarily changing the global climate, thereby inaugurating a new geological epoch: the human aeon. This notion is especially interesting for my purposes because scholars disagree over when this new epoch started – with the great acceleration, the industrial revolution, the rise of agriculture? Whatever the answer, it is clear that the topic is not just characteristic of 2015 and of the current generation (with climate change taking the place held by nuclear catastrophe), but simultaneously expands the scope of this present to include much older events. As Nicholas Mirzoeff has noted, in an essay that shows how canonical Western paintings by Monet, among others, have helped us to love the panoramas characteristic of an increasingly industrial world: '[i]n the Anthropocene, all past human history in the industrial era is the contemporary'.[77] If we focus on our fossil fuel use, our vulnerability to instable climates, our attempts to alter the course of rivers or our destruction, modification and relocation of animal species, many of us, alive and dead, become imagined (if uncomfortable) contemporaries. And if we want to adapt ourselves to these conditions as cultural scholars, Mirzoeff adds, we will have to abandon the temporal and spatial boundaries that currently define research. Now that the long causes and effects of our environmental impact are revealed, should we still uphold strict boundaries between the modern and the early modern, between the romantic, the modernist and the postmodernist? Maybe we should not discard existing categories altogether, but it is still clear that these long and slow topics create a penumbra around our cherished periods that is much broader than before. When we study late nineteenth-century debates over the global spread of 'human empire', for example, we inevitably see glimpses of longer durations, newly elongated periods. In contextualising writers like Jules Verne,

202 BEN DE BRUYN

William Morris and Robert Louis Stevenson, we should not just attend to slavery, industrialisation and colonialism but also to geological facts like the course of the Loire and Thames, the low and high islands of the Pacific and the polders of the Netherlands.[78] In a similar vein, literary scholars have asked a more general question: 'Instead of divvying up literary works into hundred-year intervals (or elastic variants like the long eighteenth or twentieth century) or categories harnessing the history of ideas (Romanticism, Enlightenment), what happens if we sort texts according to the energy sources that made them possible?'[79]

Recent scholarship urges us to rethink period for different reasons, then, arguing that the unruly phenomenon of literature should be described via anachronistic unhistoricism or polychronic networks rather than synchronic periodisation, that gradual processes should receive more attention than our favoured historical distance, that we should attend to the affordances of particular, productively colliding period terms and that we should scale up our imagination as periodisers and particularisers, lengthening our timeframes and turning older authors, readers and characters into our unwitting contemporaries. If periodisation puts us in a double bind, and comes with disadvantages as well as advantages, our conclusion should hence be unambiguous: understanding periodisation remains a crucial task for students and scholars of literary history in the twenty-first century.

## FURTHER READING

Chakrabarty, Dipesh. 'The Climate of History: Four Theses'. *Critical Inquiry* 35:2 (2009), pp. 197–222.

Dimock, Wai Chee. *Through Other Continents. American Literature Across Deep Time*. Princeton: Princeton University Press, 2006.

Goldberg, Jonathan and Madhavi Menon. 'Queering History'. *PMLA* 120:5 (2005), pp. 1608–17.

Harris, Jonathan Gil. *Untimely Matter in the Time of Shakespeare*. Philadelphia: University of Pennsylvania Press, 2009.

Hayot, Eric. 'Against Periodization; or, On Institutional Time'. *New Literary History* 42:4 (2011), pp. 739–56.

Latour, Bruno. *Reassembling the Social: An Introduction to Actor-Network Theory*. Oxford: Oxford University Press, 2007.

Levine, Caroline. *Forms: Whole, Rhythm, Hierarchy, Network*. Princeton: Princeton University Press, 2015.

Lovejoy, Arthur O. 'On the Discrimination of Romanticisms'. *PMLA* 39:2 (1924), pp. 229–53.

McGurl, Mark. 'The Posthuman Comedy'. *Critical Inquiry* 38:3 (2012), pp. 533–53.

Underwood, Ted. *Why Literary Periods Mattered: Historical Distance and the Prestige of English Studies*. Stanford: Stanford University Press, 2013.

# PART IV

# Aesthetics

## CHAPTER 15

# Beauty

Sascha Bru

As students of literature or literary historians we are sooner or later all confronted with a fundamental question: does this thing I study, literature, have value in and of itself? Many have claimed that in recent decades this question was raised insufficiently by literary historians and theorists. Far more energy instead was invested in showing how literature always forms part of a larger discursive network of (dominant) views and ideas, or in illustrating how even the history of modern aesthetics, the discipline which reflects on the very value and experience of art and literature, is itself an off-print of the history of modern society's power structures. In so doing, some argue, literary historians come close to reducing the aesthetic to external factors. For precisely the aesthetic aspect of literature is what makes writing of value. It may well be true that literature can enlighten us about the social and cultural context in which it emerged and circulates. Yet it is undeniably also the case that people enjoy reading literature, that they find literature interesting on its own terms and appreciate it in an aesthetic manner that differs from the way in which they experience other, non-aesthetic artefacts. For these reasons, many critics since the turn of the millennium have argued, attention again has to go to the aesthetic aspect of writing. The present chapter cannot possibly cover all the approaches developed of late to qualify literature's aesthetic value. Providing a selective survey of such approaches, this chapter goes on to highlight how beauty, as an aesthetic category, has returned to the realm of literary (historical) interpretation, and how that return is itself of potential historical significance.

## NEW FORMALISMS AND NEW AESTHETICISMS

There are those who claim that in order to come to terms with the aesthetic value of literature, literary scholars need to reconnect with the discipline of aesthetics. These critics are frequently gathered under the label of the New Aestheticism. In the often-cited introduction to their anthology of essays, *The New Aestheticism* (2004), John Joughin and Simon Malpas proclaim the need to trace the origins of literary theory back to the philosophy of art and to the discipline of aesthetics. This discipline shows us that there are several ways of coming to terms with the singular experience of modern art and literature, but it above all makes us aware of the fact that for ages literature, like art in general, has been endowed with particular, if not, singular aesthetic values. This is a fact all too often forgotten, proponents of the New Aestheticism claim. Joughin and Malpas, for instance, assert that in 'the rush to diagnose art's contamination by politics and culture, theoretical analysis has tended always to posit a prior order that grounds [...] a work's aesthetic impact, whether this is history, ideology or theories of subjectivity. The aesthetic is thus explicated in other terms, with other criteria, and its singularity is effaced.'[1] Against this tendency, the New Aestheticism brings the aesthetic aspect of writing back into focus through philosophy and its reflection on the value of art in general. As such, this movement in recent theory principally proves to be a renewed aesthetics. Yet by opting for the label of Aestheticism – recalling art-for-art's sake poetics – it makes little effort to hide its polemical agenda.

A similar project can be found among those who advocate a return to the text and an updated form of close reading so as to better understand the aesthetic of literature. These critics are often gathered under the banner of the New Formalism – a somewhat unfortunate label as we will see, first coined by Heather Dubrow.[2] A movement rather than a uniform school of criticism propagating a distinct method for reading, the New Aestheticism counts a great variety of proponents who I cannot discuss individually here.[3] In broad terms, however, the New Formalism falls into two groups of critics. A minority, harking back to Kant's conception of aesthetic experience as disinterested, pleasurable and consensus-generating, upholds that history and literature need to be radically separated. Literature has to be met on its own, aesthetic terms, the argument goes, because those terms make manifest that the immanent value of literature resides in its capacity to add, in a transhistorical manner, aesthetic pleasure to our world. The beauty and complexity of a literary work is in a way universal and timeless; it can always be reactivated and has cognitive value in itself. The beauty of a text can enhance our humanness, for example, as it shows us a shared sense of wonder across the ages, forces us to adopt different subject-positions, or puts us in touch with the key roles of bodily sensation, emotion and affect. It is the task of the literary scholar to isolate and analyse the constitution of this aesthetic experience of literature. The material conditions for literature's aesthetic are constituted by its form – often still understood here as the organ-isation of the linguistic components and, occasionally, the paratextual features (page design, typography, ...) of a work intentionally constructed as a piece of literature – and so this first minority group of New Formalists sets out to analyse textual form as that what defines literariness. This is arguably a not so new variant, then, of an old Formalism.

The second group of New Formalists, the majority, does not imply that the aesthetic experience of textual form somehow takes place outside of history or the world that surrounds us; we never experience writing in a state of total disinterestedness, nor is there a universal ontology of literary form. This second group accordingly tends to distinguish the basic linguistic material of a text more clearly from its form proper, as form in their view is not a given but the experience of that material as it arises in the act of reading. Form, in other words, is a dynamic phenomenon as well. With the advent of cultural studies and new historicising approaches to literature, however, our scholarly attention has moved too far away from the specifics of literary form, this second group argues. The experience of this form indeed cannot be separated from other experiences; matters of taste are firmly shaped by social and cultural forces. Yet special about literary texts is that those social and cultural forces are also mediated through or by forms. Literature, as a result, by grace of its ever changing form, is a dialectical or historical yet above all aesthetic force. In order not to eradicate litera-ture's aesthetic peculiarity, many here claim, the goal of literary scholars should not be to show how aesthetic form can or has been put to use in a culture, but to describe how forms allow for such use in the first place through the aesthetic experience texts trigger.

As just noted, the label New Formalism, like that of the New Aestheticism, hides a not so new approach. With the minority of New Formalist critics we encounter a somewhat sterile, backlash Formalism – indeed, a remarkably old Formalism. We could say that the majority of New Formalists trace the conditions of the slippage from what Prague Structuralist Jan Mukařovský called the 'artefact' (the stable mate-rial form and structure of a specific text) to the 'aesthetic object' (the historically variable actualisation of that artefact in the mind and imagination of a reader). In so doing, among others, an attempt is made to restore 'the individual literary work as a significant object of study' while avoiding reduction of that work to the factors that helped shape it historically.[4] Most New Formalists do not oppose historical interpre-tation per se, however. In fact, they often call upon materialist critics like Adorno and Macherey or Jameson to strengthen their arguments, because those critics too closely scrutinised literature's form as a socially (over)determined yet also mediating force whose aesthetic aspect always incites a complex mixture of other (emotional, ethical and moral as well as political) judgements. Much like Susan Sontag, in her 1960s essay 'Against Interpretation', the act of interpreting texts is not denied by the New Formalism – interpret we do, always – but an argument is raised against over-interpretation and for limiting our scope to the surface effects of literary texts. In their view, after all, the surface is more valuable than whatever depth we later ascribe to it. If anything, New Formalists claim, identifying and experiencing these formal features makes us better and more skilled readers. It can further help us to appreciate how beautiful and rich literature is in and of itself.

Whatever else we make of the New Formalism and the New Aestheticism, both must be read as responses to the ubiquity of the 'historical turn' in literary studies which this book as a whole seeks to chart. The basic argument in both movements is that we have come to pay too much attention to context and history, burying literary texts under layers of discourse that obscure what is on the page. In this process, according to some New Formalists, certain critics do not just end up denying the intrinsic value and process of mediation encountered in the object we study, but also plainly ignore the complexity and ambivalences triggered by the text. To remedy this, the New Aestheticism seeks to 'philosophise' literary studies and raise aware-ness of the aesthetic aspect of literature by reconnecting theory with the reflection on art in general within aesthetics. The New Formalism aims to 'formalise' research, valuably advocating a return to close reading and the development of the skills required for this – not least among students, for the New Formalists are not alone in asserting that various university curricula might have gone too far in downplaying the significance of reading up close. Yet both movements are at the same time more than responses to some of the excrescences of the recent 'historical turn' in literary studies. By drawing renewed attention to the aesthetic value of literature, they also highlight the need to revaluate the aesthetic categories with which literary studies operates – beauty perhaps first and foremost.

## THE RETURN OF BEAUTY

If, as the majority of New Formalists claim, our experience of aesthetic objects and texts is always related to other types of experience, then the aesthetic categories we use to voice our experience of literature are tools with which we organise not only our encounter with writing but also with the world surrounding us. These tools are malleable and the forms to which they correspond are also subject to change. To put it simply: a poem we call beautiful, ugly, sublime, magnificent or interesting today would not necessarily have been called that a thousand years ago. This illustrates in a rather mundane way that we cannot content ourselves with studying the (processes) of a literary form; to gauge the aesthetic value of a text we should also look at what people within a given context call beautiful, ugly and so on. When we apply this to our own moment in literary studies, then it quickly transpires that to speak of the aesthetic, and of beauty in particular, is always political. In their earlier cited anthology, Joughin and Malpas stress that the New Aestheticism does not 'present a rearguard defence of [...] the notion of art as a universally and apolitically humanist activity presided over by a benign council of critical patriarchs'.[5] A similar note, a veritable political programme for literary studies even, can be found in Isobel Armstrong's The Radical Aesthetic (2000), a book mentioned as often in discussions about the New Formalism as in those about the New Aestheticism. If we do not take the aesthetic aspect of literature seriously and come up with new ways to deal with it, if left-leaning critics 'remain silent about the politics and poetics of "beauty"', Armstrong asserts, then we leave literature 'to the reactionaries'.[6]

Such claims suggest that the aesthetic category of beauty tends to be equated with conservative or right-leaning politics. A brief look at self-proclaimed conservative critics who also advocate the virtues of beauty allows us to explain why this should be so. Take the British philosopher Roger Scruton. Scruton defends the transcendental status of beauty in the secularised West. He never encounters beauty in abstract forms of art and suggests that it belongs more or less exclusively to its figurative or mimetic variants. Such art, he avers, forms an antidote to the meaninglessness of the ugly world – and the supposedly ugly art – that characterises contemporary, Western, democratic society. In our democratic society, which stresses equality, apparently all types of art have come to be treated on equal terms. The stress on equality has managed to welcome the least talented of artists and writers as the most ingenious ones, adding further to the proliferation of the ugly in our world. Only great artists, by contrast, make the world beautiful and show us how things should be. Hence, to restore order (in art, but also in society, which for Scruton has a natural penchant for inequality) we should accordingly reinstall beauty at the centre of our lives.

This brief and admittedly simplifying résumé of Scruton's defence of beauty[7] uncovers some of the major reasons for equating attention to beauty with conservative politics. Scruton twice draws on a premodern tradition in Western aesthetics to make sense of the modern or contemporary. First, he reintroduces a premodern conception of beauty today. While the discipline of aesthetics only comes into being as a distinctly institutionalised form of philosophy in the eighteenth century – Alexander Gottlieb Baumgarten is often credited with this modern 'invention' – reflection on the aesthetic is of course as old as writing itself. And specifically the premodern reflection on beauty is what informs Scruton's take. In a nutshell, from Plato to early modernity or the Renaissance, a transcendental approach to the beautiful was propagated whereby beauty was always defined in some way or another as the earthly, sensuous, if not sensual, expression of the divine. This left the value of art and beauty unquestioned. As secularisation took over in modernity, however, the precise nature of literature's transcendental beauty became unclear; the category of the sublime, perhaps quaint to us today, for a while came to take beauty's place. Now, with the moment of premodern aesthetics long behind us, thinkers still drawing on beauty are often positioned on the conservative side, because it is felt they deny the variability and changeability of things, or defend some kind of religious return, if not an aesthetic upholding of the social and political status quo. Scruton's assertion that only figurative or mimetic forms can be beautiful reveals that he is a tributary to premodern aesthetics in a second way. For simultaneously in premodern aesthetics, from Greek antiquity onward, the assumption that art always imitates reality and human behaviour became standard, the notion of mimesis figuring centrally both in Plato's and Aristotle's thought. The idea that a figurative, mimetic art or writing is also the most beautiful and consensus-building cultural practice followed suit. This in part explains the anachronistic presumption still at work in Scruton when he implies that a more mimetic type of art or writing would also be more conservative, as opposed to formally experimental, 'avant-garde' work, which is allegedly progressive. This is of course highly debatable, countless examples attesting to the opposite.

As it is not hard to see how in thinkers like Scruton politics takes the upper hand at the cost of art and the aesthetic, beauty, Isobel Armstrong argues, cannot remain the domain of conservative intellectuals alone. More progressive critics too should lay claim on beauty and develop alternative approaches that make this category meaningful in the modern and contemporary world, and not just as a remnant of a long-gone past. Armstrong is not an isolated case here. In fact, a veritable return of beauty, and a wager over this notion, seems to mark reflection in aesthetics of the past two decades. Elaine Scarry's *On Beauty and Being Just* (2001) is often referred to in this context as a key text initiating that wager. Theorists and analysts of literature and the arts appear to have put beauty under a taboo, Scarry observes. They argue that beauty distracts us from real issues like injustice; it is said that only a handful of people can produce beauty and thus that beauty is always in the hands of the privileged, thereby serving political rather than aesthetic goals. This is an oversimplification, Scarry objects. The domain of beauty is neutral terrain in so far as it is democratic: the perception of beauty brings us to a forgetting of ourselves, leads us to perceive more, equally beautiful objects, and at best incites us to produce beautiful objects ourselves. By analogy, she argues, this 'fairness' of objects also makes us fair in an ethical sense: we become susceptible to beautiful behaviour and justice. There is no convincing evidence available for Scarry's second assertion here – that beautiful objects, artworks or literary texts make us better equipped to recognise beautiful (and always potentially immoral) behaviour. But it would also be incorrect to claim that Scarry is a conservative per se. As the author of *The Body in Pain* (1985), a poststructuralist study of the rhetorical exploitation of pain, covering Marx, Greek tragedy and Francis Bacon as well as war reportage, Scarry had also treated outright abject or ugly phenomena in art and writing to argue that our experience of such aesthetic phenomena also always entails an ethical dimension. What we can say, therefore, is that in her subsequent *On Beauty* she perhaps overemphasised the positive experience of beauty, thereby ignoring other categories of the aesthetic such as the abject and the ugly discussed in her own earlier book. More generally we might argue that Scarry's take on beauty shows how difficult it is today to articulate what things we find beautiful and precisely why.

In Dave Hickey's *The Invisible Dragon: Essays on Beauty* (1993, revised ed. 2009), yet another landmark publication in the defence of beauty, we even find that the aesthetic and beauty fully overlap. To highlight the democratic ethos of beauty, and to peel off the institutional discourse circulating in the art world from artworks proper so as to be able to appreciate them for what they are, Hickey draws out the subversive pull of Caravaggio and Robert Mapplethorpe's photography, in particular his *Helmut & Brooks* (1978), as prime examples of art's beauty. Some viewers will certainly appreciate the balanced configuration of body parts in this work by Mapplethorpe, but many might also object that not everyone will find the term 'beauty' apt to describe it. Here, then, looking more closely at the 'return of beauty' in recent decades, we come to see, in T. E. Hulme's droll phrase, that 'the lexicon of the beautiful is elastic'.[8] The term 'beauty' apparently is often used in rather general ways denoting literary texts and artworks alike that many would not necessarily characterise as beautiful – often to the point of equating 'beauty' with 'the aesthetic' as such. Could this be evidence of the fact that our contemporary culture lacks the means to properly evoke or at least describe beauty? Does beauty still exist? In what remains I aim to show that there is an argument to be made for the maximalist definition of beauty encountered in Hickey – beauty understood as the aesthetic as such, and hence encompassing what would traditionally be seen as the 'non-beautiful' – when we turn to the history of modern writing. That history, today more than ever, shows that we need to turn to literature's aesthetic with renewed vigour.

## LITERATURE AND THE ANAESTHETIC

So far in this chapter our attention has been on how aesthetic categories such as beauty are used for evaluating the experience of literature (*aesthesis*) and form, yet we can also turn the table and look at things from the point of production or creation (*poiesis*). What aesthetics of writing were developed in modern literature from, roughly, 1800 onward by writers? And what place do these aesthetics of writing allocate to beauty? It does not take long to see that in modern literature 'beauty', in an increasingly secularised world, became synonymous with the entire realm of art or aesthetic production, circulation and appreciation.

It is a truism to argue that with the advent of the Enlightenment and romanticism writers claimed the transcendental notion of beauty for art in general. In the ever more secularised modern world, not some divine entity, but the worldly entity of art and literature alone came to function as the bringer of transcendental relief. Art and literature became the new religion. In this process something else happened as well. In a letter to Goethe of 7 July 1797, Friedrich Schiller expressed his concern at the fact that beauty dominated art. Without ugliness, he felt, neither ancient art nor the specific art of Schiller's own time could be understood. This echoed Friedrich Schlegel's *Über das Studium der griechischen Poesie* (1795), which above all stressed the role of beauty in art, yet also had a few important things to say about the ugly in this context. Schlegel implied that art only became truly modern with authors like himself, writers who also paid attention to the ugly. To Schlegel beauty was the norm in art, and its true counterpart was neither the sublime nor the interesting, but the ugly, that which simply was not treated or seen as art. A modern writer, self-conscious of his practice, was therefore also to plunge headfirst into the ugly, to explore it, and to consider whether advances in writing could be made by bringing aspects of non-art – and the non- or anaesthetic – into the realm of beauty.[9]

Hans Robert Jauss has pointed out that with Schlegel the insight emerged that the entire dynamic of change in modern art and writing could well be summarised by an endless exploration and domestication of non-art.[10] Indeed, the ugly in modern aesthetics from romanticism onward came to be broadly defined as those forms and topics which, at a certain point in history, challenge what counts as art and litera-ture. The ugly, the name given to the anaesthetic or non-art as it is introduced into art, thus came to be depicted as a category always broadening the domain of beauty within a specific historical constellation. The most important consequence of this way of looking at art was that it paved the way for the assertion that true change in modern art always occurs by drawing in ugly contents and forms that at a certain point are not regarded as part of art. This is why, for example, the symbolists' or naturalists' turn to the city and everyday metropolitan life in poetry was received as both distasteful and ground-breaking. It is also why Marcel Duchamp's simplest ready-mades are still remembered by a wider audience as constitutive of modern art. Rupture in art, revolution even, always comes by way of the radically ugly.

We might instantly question this teleological model of literary history, which suggests that once something has been done, its novelty wears off forever and so ever new aspects of the anaesthetic need to be conquered to move art forward. This is an error, since what people consider to be part of aesthetic writing or art, and what they consider to fall outside this realm, is of course always relative, situated, if not site-specific. Moreover, literature does not necessarily change for the better. It just changes, and quite often by returning to older forms and subjects. Yet once we bracket the assertion of teleology, then the claim that literature in modernity above all changes by bringing in anaesthetic or ugly phenomena starts to make a lot of sense. In the course of the nineteenth century the ugly was approached time and again. What Schlegel's study of (pre)modern poetry did for German romanticism, Victor Hugo's long introduction to his play *Cromwell* (1827) did for French romanticism. Art portrays nature, Hugo argued, and because nature on occasion is also ugly, its seedier aspects too were to be the subject of writing. Like Schlegel before him, Hugo made beauty turn full circle: here too the ugly and the grotesque were in the end to add lustre to, or to expand, the domain of beauty.[11] This tendency to subjugate the ugly to beauty was also character-istic of Charles Baudelaire. (Baudelaire was an avid reader of Karl Rozenkranz's famous 1853 *Ästhetik des Hässlichen*, one of the first studies in aesthetics to take the ugly, as opposed to beauty or the sublime, seriously.) The title of Baudelaire's most famous book of poetry is obviously telling in this respect: *Les Fleurs du mal*. Thematically introducing in poetry aspects of everyday life that before had no place there – extreme poverty, subjects dying, carcasses – Baudelaire further praised Goya's portrayal of ugly, monstrous figures, because of their imaginative power. Goya's monsters did not exist in reality, and Baudelaire thereby seconded Hugo's earlier observation that the introduc-tion of the ugly into the realm of beauty could also considerably expand that realm's imaginative horizon.[12] With Baudelaire the realm of the anaesthetic was thus enlarged to include not only all given aspects of life outside art, but also all potential products of the imagination that artists and writers could censor while producing art. Schlegel's contemporaries Novalis and Tieck, with their glorification of the unconscious and the dreamlike, had ventured there before.

By the turn of the century, just when aestheticism was celebrating the beauty of the ugly in unprecedented ways, some went so far as to bracket the distinction between ugliness and beauty altogether. Perhaps most importantly, in Italy Benedetto Croce's *Estetica come scienzia dell'espressione e linguistica generale* (1902) broke quite radically with previous approaches to the ugly/anaesthetic by stating that in the aesthetic process of expression or creation the ugliness/beauty opposition simply had to be bracketed. Whatever means an artist or writer draws on in the act of creation is (and remains) aesthetic, Croce's expressivist theory implied. However, Croce's idealist, post-Hegelian view of the ugly remained largely marginal in the new avant-garde and modernist aesthetics of writing that asserted themselves around the same time. Indeed, like their modern predecessors, Italian futurists and other European and American avant-gardists continued to work with the opposition between the ugly and the beautiful, trying to domesticate the former within the latter.

Futurism in particular should perhaps be isolated here, because it went as far as to turn to politics as well, as an aspect of the anaesthetic to be conquered for art. Futurists did not simply contemplate this as a possibility – after the Great War they went out and put it into practice when they created the first (and to my knowledge only) political party ever founded by a group of writers.[13] This highlighted how the ugly before futurism had been mainly conceived as a *noumenal* entity – that is, as an idea, motif, or material form for contemplation. Futurism went on to extend the ugly to the *phenomenal* level – that is, to the domain of the concrete and tangible, to things and actions and practices first and foremost. In futurism, as in many later avant-gardes, art and literature were to be action, *art-action*, as the futurist leader Marinetti called it, experimental practices that could directly impact the spectator-reader and engulf him or her in a total experience. The publication of the 1932 *Futurist Cookbook* and the countless shocking avant-garde performances and public readings of texts need only be recalled here. In all of these examples, the divide between art and non-art simply evaporates, eradicating the need for a term like 'non-' or 'anaesthetic'.

There is not the space here to discuss in detail this dynamic, ever-recalibrated relation between what is considered to be aesthetic and what anaesthetic, suffice it to say that if we were to trace this process further into the present, we would come to notice at least three things. First, that certain writers today are still involved in domesticating the ugly/anaesthetic and on occasion still press specific audiences to challenge, expand or alter their notion of literature. Think, for instance, of MoMA Poet Laureate Kenneth Goldsmith's reading in March 2015 from the St Louis County autopsy report for Michael Brown, which he had appropriated and lightly edited for a poem entitled 'The Body of Michael Brown' (Brown, a black teenager, had been shot a few months before by the police in Ferguson, Missouri; his death led to a series of protests throughout the United States). Second, however, we would probably also come to notice that most writers today no longer appear to be extending this modern – if you want, 'avant-garde' – tradition that worked with the opposition beauty/ugliness, aesthetic/anaesthetic. As a result, the dynamic fuelled by this opposition also no longer seems to work as a mechanism explaining what is currently happening in literature. Thirdly and finally, if we turn our gaze away from literature and art in general, and start to look at the world that surrounds them, then we would come to see how successful the modern tradition, now apparently demised, has been. This tradition seems to have spread or spilled over the confines of the realm of art into culture at large. It is indeed probably no exaggeration to say that in most pockets of Western culture most aspects of daily life are now systematically subjected to the same process of 'beautification'. This process has become inherent to commodity production, circulation and consumption. Locating the anaesthetic, as a result, is increasingly difficult. Beauty, then, while never having been a category of evaluation tied to art alone, but also to nature, human features and so on, is now tied to almost everything, to be found nearly everywhere. This third observation not only shows that beauty, understood in this distinctly modern sense, as a synonym of the aesthetic, has never done better, saturating almost every fibre of our everyday lives; it further evinces how it might be misguided to claim, as do some of the movements and critics discussed above, that the aesthetic is imperilled and in need of recovery or that beauty requires rescue – unless we feel that this commodification of beauty has effectively sapped art of its 'most sacred function', of course. As, among others, Sianne Ngai, in *Our Aesthetic Categories: Zany, Cute, Interesting* (2012), argues, these developments show that above all we need to recalibrate and change our terminology. For at the risk of stating the obvious: literature of course continues to be written and to be experienced as an aesthetic form. 'It is therefore', Ngai concludes, 'aesthetic theory that needs resuscitation in our contemporary moment, not the aesthetic as such.'[14]

## BY WAY OF CONCLUSION

Literature now no longer appears to operate exclusively according to the dynamic tension between the aesthetic and the anaesthetic. Meanwhile, libraries of literary aesthetics are filled with books on other categories that have enjoyed wide circulation in art and literary history. These books cover a range of categories from the uncanny, the sublime and the elegant to the disgusting, the boring and the comical. Ngai in her book adds the cute, the zany and the interesting, instantly reminding the European reader how different European and American culture are – very few of us here would call anything 'zany', and 'cute' is an adjective I seldom hear, except among Americanists. Yet that is in part beside the point: discussing the appreciation of a wide range of artefacts and anaesthetic contexts alongside literature and art, Ngai's book shows how a 'minor' or 'weak' category like the zany, derived from a very specific cultural context, is closely related to our current conception of labour and production, even or especially in non-artistic contexts. The life of an academic, for example, can be rather zany – we hop on planes, deliver papers, train students, do promotion and so on. Our confrontation with and experience of clownish characters in zany narratives – and such characters abound in popular culture as well as contemporary writing – not only makes us aware of the fact that literature does play a peculiar, cognitive and affectual role here, awkwardly confronting us with an aspect of life most of us are familiar with. It also suggests that once we move beyond the seemingly all-encompassing category of beauty, there are many other ways of dealing with the aesthetic of literature, some of which may be more attuned to the ways we produce and consume at this point in history, and to the ways we read and write literature now.

## FURTHER READING

Armstrong, Isobel. *The Radical Aesthetic*. Oxford: Blackwell Publishers, 2000.

Danto, Arthur. *The Abuse of Beauty*. Chicago: Open Court, 2003.

Joughin, John J. and Simon Malpas, eds. *The New Aestheticism*. Manchester: Manchester University Press, 2003.

Leighton, Angela. *On Form: Poetry, Aestheticism, and the Legacy of a Word*. Oxford: Oxford University Press, 2007.

Levinson, Marjorie. 'What's New Formalism'. *PMLA*, 122:2 (2007), pp. 558–69.

Ngai, Sianne. *Our Aesthetic Categories: Zany, Cute, Interesting*. Cambridge, MA: Harvard University Press, 2012.

Mukařovský, Jan. *Aesthetic Function, Norm and Value as Social Fact*, trans. Mark E. Suino. Ann Arbor: Department of Slavic Languages and Literatures, University of Michigan, 1979.

Pop, Andrei and Mechtild Widrich, eds. *Ugliness: The Non-Beautiful in Art and Theory*. London: I. B. Tauris, 2014.

Scarry, Elaine. *On Beauty and Being Just*. Princeton: Princeton University Press, 2001.

Scruton, Roger. *Beauty: A Very Short Introduction*. Oxford: Oxford University Press, 2011.

## CHAPTER 16

# Mimesis

## Thomas G. Pavel

Reflection on mimesis examines the way in which objects, individuals, communities, actions, passions, ideals and norms are presented in artistic and literary works. The artists' and writers' attention to various features of the world changed considerably throughout history, from one culture to another, and quite often within the same cultural period as well. Reference to what is out there or deep within us was sometimes imperatively required, sometimes dismissed. It never faded away; it always was and still is today a touchstone of artistic achievement. In what follows I will examine the historical development of this notion, emphasising both its flexible, multiple uses in various cultural contexts and its remarkably stable features.

The old conversation about mimesis has always involved two basic complementary aspects: artistic imitation (representation, re-enactment) and behavioural imitation. Concerning art, mimesis was assumed to guide the expression of attitudes and emotions, the representation of the perceptible side of the world, and the evocation of the ideas, ideals and values that inform it. Concerning individual behaviour, Aristotle's remark in his *Poetics* that human beings learn by imitating is as true now as it ever was. As for social groups, Democritus argued that human crafts imitate animals, weavers doing what spiders do and builders copying the swallow. More recently, historians attributed the rapid spread of technological innovations over vast territories to the impulse of imitating them, while anthropologists and sociologists reflected on the influential power of new belief-systems, new ways of social organisation, new customs and new fashions.

## PLATO'S SUSPICIONS

The oldest uses of the root *mim-* appear to be related to music, as is the case in a fragment from Aeschylus' lost tragedy *Edonians*, where noise-making musical instruments are referred to as 'bull-voiced [...] frightened *mimoi'*,[1] as well as in Democritus' assertion that, just as crafts follow the example of animals, music imitates birdsong. A *Homeric Hymn to Apollo* mentions a choir of maidens who know how to imitate/

represent (*mimeisthai*) men's voices and castanets. In both cases, musical mimesis projects the acoustic image of a sound produced by a different animated being, animal or human, in order to trigger in the public a strong emotional effect.

It is in Plato's dialogues, however, that the notion of mimesis was examined attentively for the first time and in a way that linked its artistic function with its behavioural aspects. Without leading to a unified doctrine, the discussions around this notion point to Plato's recognition of the persuasive power of poetry but also to his worries about its possibly negative influence on human conduct. Wanting to protect young people against the dangerous contagion of stories in which gods and heroes commit crimes, Socrates recommends the rejection of such stories (including their allegorical interpretations) because they provide bad examples. Reflecting on the education of the future guardians of the city, he argues that a good man should refrain from reciting poetry that depicts immoral attitudes.[2] Souls, especially young souls, are malleable, and poetic images and sentiments perceived in actual performance can make a durable impression on them. In epic poetry, Socrates distinguishes between narrative (*diegesis*) as the general aim of the poem and the local imitation (*mimesis*) of the characters' direct speech, considering that the emotions expressed in the latter can be contagious and thus, in some cases, weaken the soul's commitment to virtue. Drama is an equally dangerous form of poetry, since it often represents reprehensible attitudes, for example the tragic characters' lamentations and their sense that misfortune governs this world. Attending such mimetic acts can lead the spectator to internalise the habits and nature of the person's body, voice and mind.[3] Accordingly, the future guardians of the city should avoid the temptations of poetry and only be allowed to sing virtue-praising songs.

Mimesis as invention of bad examples and as poetic impersonation of contagious human beliefs and emotions is supplemented in *Republic* 10 by a different conception of the term, which refers to the exterior appearance of things, in particular in painting. The dialogue here is linked to Plato's theory of forms, which assumes that the objects that surround us are imitations of ideal forms that reside somewhere outside the dark cave in which mortals lead their lives. In a slightly satirical development, Socrates argues that since God created the idea of 'bed' and the real bed built by the joiner imitates that idea, the painting of a bed is nothing but a pointless resemblance, an imitation of an imitation, twice-removed from its true nature and having therefore no actual value. The argument implies that the painter can paint any kind of object, but build none. Because in an ideal city each individual should master one and only one kind of activity, the inferior status of art and literature is due to the artists and poets' claim of competence about a wide variety of occupations and crafts, while in fact they are only able to depict their appearances.

Plato thus gives two kinds of disapproving accounts of mimesis, one related to the spectator, the other to the artist. The first describes the psychological and possibly ethical contagion of the stories and emotions conveyed by poetry, while the second condemns the inferior kind of resemblance produced by the artist's craft. Plato's reservations concerning poetry and art depend on the point of view adopted in each argument. Psychologically, artistic mimesis is dangerous because it may tempt the public into following bad examples or identifying with unworthy human emotions.

As concrete objects, works of art and literature are much less respectable than the products of other crafts, since instead of being genuinely useful – that is, giving an adequate body to one and only one kind of ideal form – they merely reproduce the appearances of whatever things the poet or artist wants to imitate.

## ARISTOTLE'S TRUST

Plato's suspicions of artistic mimesis as a contagious source of unworthy emotions and as a producer of second-tier, useless images of objects, were over centuries embraced and vastly amplified by various movements, religious and political, such as Byzantine iconoclasm, puritanism, and twentieth-century totalitarianism. Yet a rival, positive attitude towards mimesis virtually always prevailed. It was first formulated by Aristotle in his *Poetics* and, since he didn't subscribe to Plato's theory of ideal forms and therefore had no reason to distinguish between crafts that imitate eternal ideas and those which imitate actual objects, he emphasised the natural, this-worldly aspect of mimetic art and poetry.

Poetry, in Aristotle's view, is an art that rises from two natural causes: the general human inclination to imitative behaviour, both for learning and for pleasure, and our inborn faculty for music and rhythm. Initially spontaneous, musicality and imitation were developed into poetry by slow, gradual improvements. The specific features of mimesis, like those of music, depend therefore on its actual artistic uses.

Perhaps answering Socrates' revulsion for bad fables that tell lies about the gods, Aristotle argues in his *Poetics* that poetic imitation, far from being fully bound to the actual world, is valuable precisely in so far as it evokes a variety of things, including things that exist, things that people consider to exist, and things that might exist.[4] The task of letting us know what actually happened belongs to the historian, while the poet speaks about what would happen, poetry being more philosophical, more general, and more valuable than history. The generality of poetic mimesis means that poetry does not necessarily focus on particular objects (although tragedy depicts real people), nor does it fully imitate them, but rather produces images whose kind can be understood and recognised. In other words, poetic works do not simply mirror what is already visible in the actual world but represent fictional worlds imagined by the poet. The links between mimesis and imagination, which later would become crucial, especially for the romantics, are already present.

By focusing next on the manner in which art imitates its objects, Aristotle distinguishes between poetic genres. Sometimes the poet imitates by speaking in his or her own name, giving rise to the lyrical genre; the epic imitates by blending narration with dramatic dialogue; while drama uses actors who pretend that they are themselves living the represented action. Because Aristotle is not worried by the representation of emotions and its possible contagion, he does not pay much attention to the distinction between narration and dramatic dialogue in epic. For him, one should not focus on this or that emotion imitated in an epic or dramatic poem, but rather consider the unity of the poetic work. He therefore defines tragedy as the (worthwhile) imitation of a whole action of some amplitude. Noting that a whole has a beginning, a middle and an end, Aristotle implicitly warns spectators against the temptation of isolating a given episode or speech from the larger ensemble to which it belongs. In order to be beautiful, the tragedy, like pictures and like any composite object, must be well constructed and of an appropriate size. Since what counts in a tragedy is its unity made manifest by its size and structure, one can assume that in Aristotle's view, the spectator's sympathy for this or that emotion expressed in the play is only momentary and depends on the definite moment of the action to which these emotions are linked, but does not affect the sense that the work forms a whole which is more important than its local components.

As for the general emotions inspired by a tragedy, that is, pity and fear, Aristotle considers them to be the very source of pleasure offered by this particular genre. In the best case, they are produced by the imitation of the action, that is, by the way in which the poet handles the incidents of the plot. The actual theatrical production can also generate these feelings, but such effects are less artistic and put the public at the mercy of a technician – a caveat that twenty-first-century stage directors seem to dismiss. In contrast to Plato's insistence on the dangerous contagion of unworthy emotions that may occur during actual poetic performance, Aristotle, in a short passage that has been the subject of innumerable comments, considers that by arousing pity and fear tragedy in fact accomplishes a *catharsis*, a relief from such emotions.[5]

Since poetry imitates human action, Aristotle distinguishes between the representation of good and bad agents, some being above our level of goodness, while others are beneath us or just similar to us.[6] This typology, which will later play a major role in critical thought, leads him to differentiate between authors who represent noble actions and noble personages, and others who represent the actions of the ignoble. In tragedy, the characters should be better than most of us, but not perfect, in order for their fall to inspire pity rather than indignation, while in comedy, they should be worse.

## IMITATION BEYOND THE VISIBLE

The role of poetic imagination in Aristotle's *Poetics*, as well as his view that literary genres that represent action appeal to various kinds of moral beliefs, suggests that beyond imitating the immediately perceptible side of the world, the artist seeks to capture something else. As we saw, in *Republic* 10, Socrates playfully dismissed artistic mimesis in visual arts by arguing that its representations are twice-removed from the ideal forms. Plotinus, by contrast, explicitly claims in his *Enneads*,[7] that when the artist creates the work of art, it imitates not just its visible model, but is inspired by the ideal form on which this model depends. Plotinus asks us to imagine two blocks of stone lying side by side: a rough, untouched one, and one that has been carefully wrought by the craftsman into a statue of god or man. The latter is not beautiful simply by virtue of being a stone, as the comparison with the rough block shows, but in virtue of the form or idea introduced by art. This form is present in the artist's mind before it enters the stone and, at least to some extent, dwells in it. Arts, Plotinus concludes, should not be criticised for imitating natural objects which owe their existence to the ideal forms, given that the arts don't simply aim at reproducing visible things but go back to the ideal forms themselves. When Phidias, for example, wrought the statue of Zeus, he didn't follow an available model, but apprehended the very form Zeus would take if he decided to become visible.

This is how art reaches ideal beauty, and, if we might generalise this insight to poetry, this is how epic and drama capture the norms and ideals followed or transgressed by their characters. Since, indeed, in epic and drama mimesis is the representation of an action, a wide range of 'invisible' elements contribute to the understanding of what goes on: intentions, moral maxims, social habits, and, more than anything else, the implied scale of valuation according to which the poet and the spectator weigh up the characters' worth, for example Oedipus' greatness, Antigone's courage and Phaedra's duplicity. When later Longinus, in his treatise *On the Sublime*, defined sublimity as the echo of a great soul and emphasised the role of fantasy which allows the poet to visualise the emotive side of poetry and elevate feelings to the noblest level, he also required poetic representation to link the immediately perceptible aspects of reality to something that lies beyond them.

Similarly and in an even more exalted manner, Proclus, the last Platonist of the classical world, distinguished between three types of poetry in his commentary on the *Republic* (fifth century): poetry that conveys the divine based on symbols, didactic poetry based on knowledge, and mimetic poetry, based either on empirical reality or on fantasy. Although he aimed at discrediting mirror-like mimesis by separating it from symbols, Proclus acknowledged the representational function of poetry at all levels, thus confirming that a wider, more inclusive conception of mimesis is possible.

By the time Proclus wrote his commentary, this view of mimesis had already been extended beyond literature and the arts by Christian theology, which considered human beings as having been created in the image of God. The actual, fallen, human condition preserves only part of this image, which can be recovered with the help of divine grace. Developed by Augustine, this view would lead to a doctrine that requires Christians to model themselves after the divinity, either in its invisible perfection, or in its temporal incarnation in the person of Jesus. Thomas à Kempis's *Imitatio Christi* (early fifteenth-century) is the best known guide to spiritual life understood as practical, everyday mimesis of the Saviour. Imitation here is a behavioural principle, but instead of being assumed to be natural and spontaneous, as in Aristotle's *Poetics*, it becomes the object of a special spiritual training.

## RULE-GOVERNED IMITATION

On the practical side, Horace's *Ars poetica*, read in late antiquity, throughout the middle ages, and up to the romantic period, offered a detailed, normative view of the poetic craft. Long before twentieth-century narratologists, Horace noticed that plot-structure is different from storytelling, some stories beginning *ab ovo* and others *in medias res*. Concerning mimesis, although the frequently quoted passage, *ut pictura poesis*, asserts the priority of the world's perceptible aspects, Horace was fully aware that poetry, having a noble, elevated mission, needs to go beyond the mere appearance of things, and, in order not to shock its public, must always respect decorum. In *Ars poetica*, accomplished craft guarantees that unity, harmony and proportion make poetry pleasurable (*dulce*), while attention to nobility and decorum makes it useful (*utile*).

The rediscovery of Aristotle's *Poetics*, its translation into Latin in 1498, its commentary in Latin by Francesco Robortello (1548), and its translation into Italian with a commentary by Ludovico Castelvetro (1570), are still tributary to Horace's normative approach, their advice to writers being consistently related to the nature and beliefs of the audience. Thus, Castelvetro, who translated mimesis by *rassomiglianza*, 'resemblance', reflected on Aristotle's remarks on the unity of action in tragedy and insisted on the unity of time and space, requiring playwrights to keep in mind that people who go to the theatre belong to the lower class, having no memory and imagination, and are therefore unable to believe that the action takes place elsewhere than on the stage they see or that the time of the action is longer than that of the actual representation. In England, Sir Philip Sidney's *Apology for Poetry* (posthumously published in 1595), made a respectful reference to Aristotle, but remained dependent on Horace's views (*ut pictura poesis* and *dulce et utile*).

In French seventeenth-century theatre, mimesis was governed by plausibility (*vraisemblance*) – a notion relative to the public's beliefs and moral attitudes – rather than imitation of the actual world. Truth and plausibility were carefully distinguished. In the original story of El Cid, a Spanish historical character, the protagonist marries the daughter of a nobleman whom he killed in a duel. Corneille included this aspect of the story in his tragedy *Le Cid*. His critics argued, however, that it is implausible for a young woman to marry the murderer of her father. Between truth and plausibility the French Academy chose the latter and, accordingly, censored Corneille's play.

Like Horace's *Ars poetica*, Boileau's *Art poétique* (1674) offered advice and detailed rules for the writers whose public belonged to the milieu of the 'court and the city'. Pope's *Essay on Criticism* (1711) went beyond the normative method: in this poem, only the pedant judges by rules, while the true critic is truthful, sensible, friendly and tactful. A 'man of taste', the critic has internalised so well the rules of the art that there is no need to always explicitly refer to them. The main precept, under which one can still sense the presence of mimesis, is to follow Nature:

> *Unerring Nature*, still divinely bright, [...]
> Life, Force, and Beauty, must to all impart,
> At once the *Source*, and *End*, and *Test* of *Art*.[8]

And since the ancient poets were the most faithful to Nature, whose rules they followed, 'To copy *Nature* is to copy *Them*'.[9]

## REFLECTIVE MIMESIS

The most assertive formulation of Horace's *ut pictura poesis* belongs to Charles Batteux, who argued, in his *Les Beaux-Arts réduits à un seul principe* (1747), that imitation is the fundamental principle of all arts. In the second half of the eighteenth century, however, the conviction that *ut pictura poesis*, as well as the requirement for art to be *dulce et utile* were increasingly questioned. As its title shows, Lessing's *Laocoön, or on the Borders between Poetry and Painting* (1766) rejected the assumption according to which verbal and visual arts operate in the same way. In Lessing's view, because painting uses forms and colours in space while poetry is organised in a temporal fashion, the subjects of painting are bodies and their visible properties, while those of poetry are actions that succeed each other in time. For this reason, painting and sculpture imitate durable features of their objects rather than short-lived expressions. Poetry, by contrast, is particularly apt at representing momentary actions and emotions. The statue of Laocoön, for example, refrains from representing pain with the violence and intensity this topic might make us expect, while in poetry, in Sophocles' *Philoctetes* for instance, the excruciating pain of the main character is expressed as fiercely as needed.

No less innovative, Edmund Burke's *A Philosophical Enquiry into the Origin of our Ideas of the Sublime and Beautiful* (1756) questioned the ancient emphasis on artistic beauty and gives the notion of the sublime – first promoted by Longinus – a new, stronger meaning. The sublime excites 'the ideas of pain, and danger, that is to say, whatever is in any sort terrible, or is conversant about terrible objects, or operates in a manner analogous to terror'. As such, 'it is productive of the strongest emotion which the mind is capable of feeling'.[10] Concerning imitation, faithfulness to the imitated object is thus much less important than expressive power. What counts is the light or darkness that falls unto the represented figures and actions rather than the resemblance between them and the actual world.

In 1795, Friedrich Schiller's *On Naïve and Sentimental Poetry* distinguished between old-time 'naïve' poets who simply represent nature and emotions and more recent 'sentimental' poets who *reflect* on the impressions the imitated objects make on them. Because sentimental poets oscillate between reality and their own ideal, they can either emphasise the former or concentrate on the latter, thus producing different kinds of representation, some *satirical*, when the sense of reality is dominant, some *elegiac*, when the aspiration towards the ideal prevails. Developing Schiller's views, August Wilhelm Schlegel argued that literature and art should not be enslaved to a strictly empirical world accessible to our senses, but aim at capturing its inner creative development. For the romantics, who considered that mimesis was subject to the inner orientation of the poet, faithfulness to the exterior aspects of the world ceased to be a permanent requirement of art and literature.

By contrast, nineteenth-century realist writers revived the notion that the most important task of literature consists in being true to external reality. Formulating a new assignment, they required that literature should offer its readers a rigorous understanding of the social, historical and, later, physiological reality. In Alexis de Tocqueville's view, in democratic ages the individuals' mobility and desires lead people from different regions and backgrounds to mix together, thus for the first time making visible in the broadest light the general aspect of mankind. As a consequence, all the details of human existence, its vicissitudes and its future become the object of poetry.[11] In the 'Avant-propos' to his *Comédie humaine* published in 1842,

Balzac, echoing Tocqueville's point, presented his novels as the literary equivalent of the registrar's office, while Stendhal, prefiguring Tocqueville's dynamic message, had earlier stated in his *The Red and the Black* (1830) that a novel is 'a mirror carried along a high road'.[12]

In order to achieve a full correspondence between his novels and contemporary French society taken as a whole, Balzac built a vast fictional universe populated by a large crowd of characters, a universe whose task was to represent life in Paris, the French provinces, French social classes, types of families, professions, moral inclinations, religious and philosophical beliefs, artistic options and sexual preferences. His achievement was founded on a strongly and repeatedly asserted social theory which blended confidence in meritocratic social mobility and suspicion of capitalism, demagogy and corruption. The artistic representation of human actions, passions, aims, motivations and moral ideals – in one word, mimesis – was accompanied, as in Schiller's theory of sentimental poetry, by the author's reflection on the represented objects. But instead of adopting a personal, emotional approach, reflection here targeted – just like history and, later, sociology – the objective factors that shape human existence. It generated a version of mimesis grounded in intelligence, reason and science, a version that converged with several major nineteenth-century philosophical views: Hegel's conviction that art has finally reached its end (and purpose) by coalescing with knowledge, Auguste Comte's sense that the world's progress had brought humanity to the threshold of a radiant future ruled by science, as well as François Guizot and Karl Marx's attention to concrete social evolution and class conflict. In the second half of the century, advances in biology and medicine persuaded Émile Zola to equate novel-writing with experimental science, thus giving a new legitimacy to the patient, attentive depiction of the appearance of things.

At the same time, the growing influence of Arthur Schopenhauer's philosophy persuaded many artists that art plays a quasi-religious role which allows a few elect to withdraw from the struggle and torment of the actual world, offering them a privileged access to the realm of ideas. Echoing the romantics and Schopenhauer's interest in the creative depth of the world, Friedrich Nietzsche distinguished, in his *Birth of Tragedy* (1872), between the imitation (*Nachahmung*) of the world's surface and the mirroring (*Wiederspiegelung*) of its inner truth, thus giving the old notion of the artistic mirror a new meaning: the expression of the inner impulse to create. Realist representation of appearances was dismissed by writers and critics influenced by these views. They instead devoted their works to the symbolic depth of the world, as is the case in Maurice Maeterlinck's *Péléas and Mélisande* (1893); to the labyrinth of inner life, as in Marcel Proust's *In Search of Lost Time* (published from 1913 on); to the funny, cruel absurdity of life, as in Franz Kafka's *The Trial* (written 1914–15); or to a mixture of these elements, as in Luigi Pirandello's *The Late Mattia Pascal* (1904). Since according to this artistic approach mimesis gives priority to what lies beyond the visible, modernist writers and artists would soon feel authorised to cut not only the links between art and the visible world, but also those between art and the realm of ideas. Recognition and intelligibility – easy or difficult – would cease to be counted among the obligatory aspects of art.

## MORE RECENT DEBATES

This doesn't mean that all writers and artists suddenly abandoned the credible representation of the appearance of things and of what lies behind them, be it ideal forms, moral values, or social and historical forces. Thanks to the growing cultural dynamism of the last century, the rejection of plausibility and intelligibility, far from being the only artistic option, was born and grew among other trends. Plausible mimesis (in popular literature as well as in the various trends attentive to the reality of social life and human passions), seductive innovative techniques (in the European, North American and Latin-American novel throughout the century), and full denial of representational art (in futurism, dadaism as well as in abstract art) contradicted each other, yet they all prospered. Theoreticians of mimesis were also divided: while Erich Auerbach and Northrop Frye proposed new, powerful theories of the historical development of mimesis, Clement Greenberg, Roland Barthes and Theodor Adorno raised doubts about the relevance of artistic mimesis, in general terms in Barthes' case and specifically linked to modernism in Greenberg and Adorno's. In a positive, confident manner, Kendall Walton's theory of mimesis considers art to be a game of make-believe that includes both resemblance and vicarious contagion.[13] Finally, imitation as a feature of human behaviour became a central topic in the turn-of-the century sociology of Gabriel Tarde and in René Girard's reflections on human nature, as well as in Michael Taussig's anthropological research.[14]

Erich Auerbach's *Mimesis*, written in exile between 1942 and 1945 and published in 1945, is a sequence of close stylistic readings of short excerpts from the works of various important writers from Homer to Virginia Woolf.[15] Although Auerbach did not rigorously define 'realism' – to the extent that Francesco Orlando was able to identify in *Mimesis* twenty-one different meanings of the term[16] – the book argues that over centuries, literary mimesis gradually advanced towards an unprejudiced, precise, interior and exterior representation of the random moments in the lives of different people. This kind of representation emphasises the elementary things which our lives have in common, thus echoing what Auerbach assumed to be the inevitable historical progress towards a universally shared humanity. The first part of Northrop Frye's *Anatomy of Criticism* (1957) also developed a grand historical theory of literary 'modes' or ways in which literature imagines its characters. The initial mythical mode is followed by a heroic one, by a high mimetic, by a low mimetic, and by an ironic mode. In tragedy, these modes depict, respectively, gods, heroes, noble human beings, ordinary people and, finally, weak, pitiful individuals. A similar evolution takes place in comedy, narratives and poetry. Mimesis here amounts to inventing characters whose level of greatness and exemplarity fits the historical period that gave them birth. By contrast with Auerbach's belief in the progress of humanity, Frye subscribed to a cyclical view of history. Yet, both authors simplified the cultural and historical dimensions of literary mimesis by selecting a single kind of representation as typical for a given period and by neglecting the artistic practices which diverge from it.

As for the adversaries of mimesis, they usually considered that the artistic representation of reality is either arbitrary or obsolete. Roland Barthes' 'L'effet de réel' (1968) claimed that the description of a bourgeois interior in Flaubert's *A Simple Heart*, which includes a barometer on a piano, only appears to evoke the historical moment and the social class of the characters, its main function being in fact a semiotic one: to signal 'reality' in general. It is nonetheless unlikely that the barometer on the piano was arbitrarily included by Flaubert as an element of reality in general, since it, too, represents a concrete, well-known mark of middle-class distinction in the second half of the nineteenth-century. Clement Greenberg, defending avant-garde art, thought that the future of art lies in the glorification of the medium rather than the slavish representation of the world. Theodor Adorno, who developed a complex theory of mimesis and its central place in life and art, argued that modernist art does not pursue the imitation of something real but anticipates 'being-in-itself', that is, utopia, and, therefore, indirectly but surely points towards the goal of history as understood by Marxism. His argument captures well the ethos of avant-garde art, but involves an elitist condescension towards the 'semi-cultivated' which is quite different from the Marxist reliance on the toiling masses, better reflected in Berthold Brecht's defence of the craft of mimesis. At a more general philosophical level Jacques Derrida considered that the concept of mimesis has always been tributary to the Platonic views on the ideal forms and their worldly manifestations. Since in Derrida's view mimesis inherits the Platonic tensions opposing these two levels, it only captures the incessant deferral of any possible resemblance between art and its models.

Due to the development of sociology and psychiatry as independent disciplines, the interest in the role of mimesis in human behaviour, social and individual, grew considerably. In Gabriel Tarde's late nineteenth-century sociology, invention and imitation govern social life. Even the most useful inventions – not to speak of the useless ones – fail to spread if they do not inspire the belief that they are essential and, consequently, the desire to adopt them. As the most elementary kind of psychological interaction between individuals in society, imitation of successful models provides a basic explanation of social cohesion and progress. A century later, René Girard's revival of the psychological approach to social imitation incorporated Freud's views on the unconscious. Girard argued that imitation affects virtually all human desires. In his view, one only falls in love with a person who is already the object of someone else's desire. Desire is triangular, linking the subject of desire to its object through a third individual – the model who nurtures the same desire and is, in fact, the true, unconscious target of the subject's aspirations. After applying his insights to the analyses of a large number of literary texts, Girard built a vast socio-psychological theory of human interactions based on imitation, violence and sacrifice.

The most complete recent theory of mimesis is Kendall Walton's, who describes artistic representations as games of make-believe that involve the viewers, the listeners and the readers in fictional worlds and their fictional truths and emotions.[17] Since the public playfully pretends to participate in these worlds rather than truly becoming part of them, the beliefs and the emotions triggered by the games of make-believe have only a vicarious reality. The old Socratic warnings against vacuous similarity and dangerous contagion are still perceptible – and countered – in Walton's theory, which argues, in the tradition of Aristotle's *Poetics*, that the quasi-beliefs and quasi-emotions made possible by artistic mimesis both resemble and are significantly different from real, actual beliefs and emotions.

Whereas predictions about the future are notoriously difficult to make, I am confident that the issue of mimesis will continue to play a central role in literary debates. On the historical side, it would be useful to revisit the entrenched notion of homogeneous eras or cultures and ask whether indeed within a given period or culture mimesis always operates in the same way. The most obvious counter-example is, in our own time, the difference between the non-figurative bias of avant-garde literature and the required presence of mimesis in 'middlebrow' and popular literature. It would be equally productive to reflect on the multiple needs of the literary public – to have fun, to be moved, to witness other lives, to think of one's own, to travel to far-away surroundings, to rediscover the familiar ones, to enthuse about greatness, to witness pettiness, to imagine impossible things, to be reminded of the actual ones, to measure up one's solitude, to feel close to one's human fellows, to understand society, to face its enigmatic side – and analyse the mimetic practices that answer such needs, encourage them or deter them. An important aspect of literary mimesis concerns the target of imitation, which can be either observable human behaviour or the maxims that govern it. The spectators of Corneille's *Rodogune* and George Lucas's *Star Wars* are far from assuming that the two princesses, Rodogune and Lea, act plausibly, yet these spectators easily understand the two princesses' far-fetched actions by recognising the maxims they follow. Mimesis (in the sense of correct representation) of norms and ideals is as important and worthy of study as the imitation of actual ways of acting. Moreover, both are relevant for linking artistic imitation to behavioural imitation, given that readers and spectators identify not only with represented actors and their actions, but also with the norms and ideals that guide them. Behavioural imitation affects writers as well, since their mimetic desire to join a successful trend influences not only their technical, stylistic choices but also the very core of artistic imitation: the kind of attention artists pay to the world.

## FURTHER READING

Abrams, M. H. *The Mirror and the Lamp: Romantic Theory and the Critical Tradition.* New York: Oxford University Press, 1953.

Auerbach, Erich. *Mimesis: The Representation of Reality in Western Literature*, trans. Willard R. Trask. Princeton: Princeton University Press, 1953.

Gebauer, Gunter and Christoph Wulf. *Mimesis: Culture, Art, Society*, trans. Don Reneau. Berkeley: University of California Press, 1995.

Halliwell, Stephen. *The Aesthetics of Mimesis: Ancient Texts and Modern Problems.* Princeton: Princeton University Press, 2002.

Lamarque, Peter and Stein Haugom Olsen. *Truth, Fiction, and Literature: A Philosophical Perspective.* Oxford: Clarendon Press, 1994.

Potolsky, Matthew. *Mimesis (The New Critical Idiom).* London: Routledge, 2006.

Tatarkiewicz, Wladislaw. 'Mimesis', in *Dictionary of the History of Ideas*, vol. 3, ed. P.P. Wiener. New York: Charles Scribner, 1973, pp. 225–30.

Taussig, Michael. *Mimesis and Alterity: A Particular History of the Senses*. London: Routledge, 1992.

Walton, Kendall. *Mimesis as Make-Believe: On the Foundation of Representational Arts*. Cambridge, MA: Harvard University Press, 1990.

Wimsatt, William K. and Cleanth Brooks. *Literary Criticism: A Short History*. New York: Knopf, 1957.

## CHAPTER 17

# Style

Sarah Posman

The contemporary attack on the humanities is lamentable and misguided, we read in Leo Spitzer's *Linguistics and Literary History*, published in 1948. Spitzer, one of the founders of modern stylistics, situates the study of language at the heart of the humanities and argues that the linguistic method he practises enables us to understand not only literary texts but history at large – 'the whole essence of a poet and his time', according to Erich Auerbach in the book's blurb. Although today Spitzer's ideas concerning the 'web of interrelations between language and the soul of the speaker' or literature's function of documenting 'the soul of a nation' sound outdated, the problems he addressed are still relevant to contemporary literary criticism.[1] What is the relation between literary language and language at large? How to approach the dynamics of literary history in relation to wider historical processes? How to navigate between the individual and the collective? And where, ultimately, to position oneself as a literary critic? For all the pertinence of those questions, however, our challenges aren't Spitzer's. Schooled in the traditions of philology and the history of ideas, Spitzer wanted for the different disciplines in the humanities to team up and help us understand our world. To that end he urged literary criticism to shape up and move beyond the venting of impressions. In the essays collected in *Linguistics and Literary History* he scrutinises the lexical, grammatical, syntactical and morphological choices an author makes, he weighs those against the historical norm, and then draws conclusions about the individual psyche and *Zeitgeist*. Present-day literary criticism, by contrast, can hardly be called an insular, amateurish practice. The issue now is that because literary criticism incorporates insights from such diverse fields as critical theory, psychology, neuroscience, anthropology, environmental studies, legal studies, statistics and computing, it has become too far removed from the common reader. Furthermore, 'our' world has diffracted into many different circles and milieus while at the same time '*Zeitgeist*' has been replaced by a global constellation criss-crossed by the acute ripples of conflict and disaster as well as by deep time inflections; the canon has been exposed as an oppressive power structure; the death of the author has been proclaimed and revoked; and the Internet has altered the way in which we understand, read and write texts. In the midst of these evolutions, the questions of what counts as 'style', and of how and why to focus on style, have changed substantially.

A project that enables us to appreciate how recent literature demands we revamp the traditional concept of style – Spitzer's account of literary language as the gateway to the soul ultimately echoes the old debate concerning the relation between rhetoric and truth stretching back to Plato and Aristotle – is Kenneth Goldsmith's project of 'uncreative writing', both for what it accomplishes and for what it fails to accomplish. For Goldsmith, who appears to call for the absolute deflation of style, the rise of the Internet has made redundant the imperative for writers to respond to the world in their own voice. Inspired by the conceptual artist Douglas Huebler's statement 'The world is full of objects, more or less interesting; I do not wish to add any more', Goldsmith argues that we don't need any more language.[2] Rather, we should learn how to deal with the vast quantities of language that surround us. Instead of romantic creators we should become managers, adept at navigating not our soul but the World Wide Web. In intensifying modernist impersonal writing strategies, working with formal constraints and copying someone else's words, Goldsmith's twenty-first-century uncreative writing revokes Buffon's famous eighteenth-century epigram *'Le style, c'est l'homme meme'*. Far from wanting to quench creativity per se, however, Goldsmith wants to unleash it, unencumbered by authorial intention. If, in Spitzer, style provides access to the 'solar system' that is the author's mind, then Goldsmith makes us look at what Michel Foucault calls the autonomous 'shining' of language. In *The Order of Things* Foucault situates the return of 'the raw being' of language, its materiality, in the nineteenth century, and relates it to the way in which language functioned in the sixteenth century, be it this time no longer in correspondence with a transcendent framework.[3] In such a scheme literature is less a medium by which to convey a worldview, than a system that confronts us with the limitless possibilities for organising and structuring, combining, multiplying and evolving. The style we see at work in writing *à la* Goldsmith's – syntactical repetitions, grammatical oddities and mistranslations, absurd diction in author-less stretches of language – surprises and moves not because it unveils little atoms of truth, but because it makes us realise that we, as individual readers and writers, are part of larger, collective processes. The Web visualises the tendency of the language that we use to exceed our grasp: documents leak, comments go viral, citations morph. If, sticking within the Foucauldian paradigm, this is a disturbing insight because it means we are the products of processes beyond our grasp, it also demands we once again invest in style, as the skill to 'manage' language, and in literature as the domain for reflection on this 'managing'. Selecting, organising, cutting and pasting, rephrasing, twisting and marvelling at the unexpected, that is us, forming, rather than being formed – even if reflection on what, how and who to manage is also where Goldsmith's projects falter.[4]

This chapter sketches the way in which the problem of style has informed thinking about modern literature in order to shed light on what I consider to be the spiralling course of that literature and its quest for a pure style or a style that is pure or free in being impure. If style, as Susan Sontag put it in her essay 'On Style', fulfils a mnemonic function, welding immediate to sedimented experience, then every turn towards a new style, often coated as an escape from style, implies a reconfiguration of past and present.[5] Such a 'latest' stylistic turn is never purely on account of an individual writer's flair for literary innovation. This is also what Roland Barthes makes clear, when he proposed we approach the question of style through the prism of a linguistic memory. In *Writing Degree Zero* (1953) he stresses that '[i]t is not granted to the writer to choose his mode of writing from a kind of non-temporal store of literary forms'. Rather:

> It is under the pressure of History and Tradition that the possible modes of writing for a given writer are established; there is a History of Writing. But this History is dual; at the very moment when general History proposes – or imposes – new problematics of the literary language, writing still remains full of the recollection of previous usage, for language is never innocent: words have a second-order memory which mysteriously persists in the midst of new meanings.[6]

In what follows I concentrate on three instances in literary history: aestheticism via Flaubert, modernism via Joyce, and postmodernist collective energies. At each instance, what is at stake is the reinvention of genuine content over empty form, as the recurring figure of flowers in this discourse helps to underscore.

## AESTHETICISM

The story of how the sense of transparency and harmony governing the relations between world, man and language that we project on Buffon's age became problematic in the nineteenth century has been told numerous times. In Barthes' account, literature in the nineteenth century was 'no longer felt as a socially privileged mode of transaction, but as a language having body and hidden depths, existing both as dream and menace'.[7] Aestheticism's dictum 'art for art's sake' captures the new status of art, severed from its former religious, political and moral functions. Freed from its ancillary role and deeply engaged in the crisis of representation, literature confronted writers with new challenges. The 'menace' of form as something that could develop in and for itself derives from the writer's solitude vis-à-vis language and literature. If language does not mirror nature but *makes* it, with truth, as Nietzsche famously put it in 1873, a 'mobile army of metaphors, metonyms, and anthropomorphisms' rather than reality itself, then where to find the footing from which to write truthfully?[8] How to find a form that can combat the imperialist instrumentalist use of language? Furthermore, with the fine arts system crumbling and literary genres reinventing themselves, how to approach this 'body' of language and for whom to engage with it? 'Whatever [the writer] does', Barthes explains, 'it is a scandal: if it stands resplendent, it appears outmoded; if it is a law unto itself, it is asocial.'[9] The writer's solitude, of course, also constitutes his or her freedom. It is the condition that enables writers to dream of exploring uncharted literary territory.

The dream, among literary explorers, was to coin a style that would fit individual experience better than clichéd literary language and that would replace a moral with an aesthetic framework. Nietzsche, with his theory that truth is to be found in aesthetic experience itself as opposed to what the work is supposed to represent, only started formulating his theories from the 1870s onwards. The *'l'art pour l'art'* idea, however, had been circulating since the 1830s.[10] Walt Whitman, for example, solidifies the link between a radical individuality and a pure style in his preface to *Leaves of Grass*:

> The greatest poet has less a marked style and is more the channel of thoughts
> and things without increase or diminution, and is the free channel of himself.
> He swears to his art, I will not be meddlesome, I will not have in my writing
> any elegance or effect or originality to hang in the way between me and
> the rest like curtains. I will have nothing hang in the way, not the richest
> curtains. What I tell I tell for precisely what it is.[11]

Whitman calls upon the writer to resist the temptation of superfluous ornament, curtains veiling poetic truth. Far from implying a bland, colourless poetry, this sets up the poet to explore his individual relationship to language, to forge a language that is uniquely 'his', yet which he can use to help summon a prosperous community. Whitman uses 'himself' as the creative starting point from which to trumpet a new order: American democracy. The writer is no longer a cog in a given order but a creator. Style, in its guise as non-style, here becomes the testing ground for a utopian politics.

The connection between a new style and a new order is also something that Gustave Flaubert touches on in his famous 1852 letter to Louise Colet.

> What seems beautiful to me, what I should like to write, is a book about
> nothing, a book dependent on nothing external which would be held
> together by the strength of its style, just as the earth, suspended in the void,
> depends on nothing external for its support; a book which would have almost
> no subject, or at least in which the subject would be almost invisible, if such a
> thing is possible. The finest works are those that contain the least matter; the
> closer expression comes to thought, the closer language comes to coinciding
> and merging with it, the finer the result. I believe that the future of Art lies
> in this direction. [...] This progressive shedding of the burden of tradition can
> be observed everywhere: governments have gone through similar evolution,
> from the oriental despotisms to the socialisms of the future.[12]

Flaubert's projected emancipation from matter is paradoxical because it combines radical autonomy (literature 'suspended in the void') with a better collective future ('socialisms of the future'). He doesn't elaborate on how those fields are supposed to develop analogously or better each other, however. Flaubert may well have felt drawn to a Hegelian vision of art and society paralleling each other in their upward course, but his dream of a pure style was severing literature from traditional conceptions of meaning and use, and problematised the sense of progressive development.

Writers seeking to perfect Flaubert's dream of a pure style hardly embraced a literary exploration of the 'socialisms of the future'. Rather, aestheticist literature after Flaubert turned more and more abstract, with its only ground for encounter between writer and audience an inversion of Buffon's 'man himself' into a paradoxical notion of impersonality. Flaubert's quest for le mot juste is, as Walter Pater puts it, no 'mere caprice of the individual'. '[T]he one acceptable word', rather, constitutes the ground for 'others "who have intelligence" in the matter' to grasp the impersonal truth of the author's vision.[13] Such 'others', however, hardly represent the public spirit. The desire for pure style was turning literature into an increasingly elitist practice. Mallarmé, the most notable example, spent his lifetime writing and rewriting a small number of 'true' poems in which the quest for a pure style – for 'the flower absent from all bouquets' – is haunted thematically by the perils of sterility and death. A more fertile afterlife of Flaubert's obsession with style can be found in the iconoclasm of the early twentieth-century modernists. They confronted the menace of style acquiring a body, its existing in and by itself, with energetic audacity. Parallel to developments in thought about language, modernist authors reconsidered the relationship between language and world or history, and that between literary and non-literary language. The autonomy of literary language, they pointed out in many different ways, does not lead away from the world but complicates the ways in which to make sense of it.

## MODERNISM

In 1922 Ezra Pound crowned James Joyce as Flaubert's successor, claiming that 'Joyce has taken up the art of writing where Flaubert left it'.[14] The fifth chapter of A Portrait of the Artist as a Young Man (1916) contains a clear echo of Flaubert's direction that '[t]he artist in his work must be like God in his creation – invisible and all-powerful: he must be everywhere felt, but never seen'.[15] In the penultimate chapter Joyce's protagonist Stephen explains his aesthetic theory according to which art evolves from the personal lyric form over the interpersonal epic to the impersonal dramatic form. On the latter Stephen notes:

> The esthetic image in the dramatic form is life purified in and reprojected from the human imagination. The mystery of esthetic, like that of material creation, is accomplished. The artist, like the God of creation, remains within or behind or beyond or above his handiwork, invisible, refined out of existence, indifferent, paring his fingernails.[16]

The issue with A Portrait of the Artist as a Young Man is, of course, that the book itself problematises impersonality and linear progress, ending as it does, not in a dramatic form with the artist 'refined out of existence', but with Stephen's diary. Although Suzanne Lanser has argued that the diary represents the start of Stephen's artistic career with the lyric form and Joyce's dramatic form,[17] Michael Levenson gives a more compelling reading, arguing that the diary shows Joyce addressing the problem of autonomous and self-referential literary creation.[18] If Joyce is a successor to Flaubert it is not because he has further purified style, away from time and world, but because he has 'stylised' impurity, incorporating world and history, from the most mundane to its grandest sounds and reverberations, into his style. In this respect, Joyce sides with Eliot who, with respect to poetry, declared purity a theoretical goal only, underlining the need for 'some "impurity"'.[19]

The diary in A Portrait records Stephen's intentions to leave Dublin ('Away! Away!') and become an artist unhinged from the (Irish) past.[20] The 6 April entry, for example, shows Stephen musing on how 'the past is consumed in the present' before resolving to break that pattern.[21] Alluding to Yeats's poem he notes: 'Michael Robartes remembers forgotten beauty and, when his arms wrap her round, he presses in his arms the loveliness which has long faded from the world. Not this. Not at all. I desire to press in my arms the loveliness which has not yet come into the world'.[22] Stephen's desire to make it new, however, is undercut by the way in which the diary echoes elements of the five earlier chapters, grounding his projected new life in his old life and his new style in that of the classic Bildungsroman blueprint. As Levenson points out, Joyce has the novel return upon its steps. The final diary entry 'old father, old artificer'[23] echoes the first lines of the book in which the father tells a story; the penultimate entry 'Mother is putting my new secondhand clothes in order'[24] recalls the sentence 'His mother put on the oilsheet'[25] from the first chapter; and a reference to Dante Alighieri refers back to the 'Dante' character from Stephen's childhood. The act of burdening the novel's ending with its beginnings, Levenson argues, thwarts the young artist-rebel's aspirations.[26] His very ambition to forge a new existence is rooted in a familiar, much-repeated pattern: he goes to 'encounter for the millionth time the reality of experience and to forge in the smithy of my soul the uncreated conscience of my race'.[27] Furthermore, the circularity, for Levenson, constitutes an attack on the diary as a genre and the genre's understanding of time as progressive historical development.[28] Stephen, ironically, prepares to leave Dublin for the continent, as a classic literary hero, his procrastination mirroring Hamlet's, his aesthetic ambition echoing Wilhelm Meister's theatrical mission.[29] In his later work Joyce perfected his stylistic mastery of the inescapable echoes of past times, weaving together a variety of historical influences, mythological allusions and references to the past in an intricate structure. Ulysses, notably, led T. S. Eliot to proclaim that Joyce's way of writing was the logical next step in the development of literature:

> In using the myth, in manipulating a continuous parallel between contemporaneity and antiquity, Mr. Joyce is pursuing a method which others must pursue after him. [...] It is simply a way of controlling, of ordering, of giving a shape and a significance to the immense panorama of futility and anarchy which is contemporary history. [...] It is, I seriously believe, a step toward making the modern world possible for art.[30]

Like Eliot's The Waste Land and Pound's Cantos, Joyce's Ulysses packs a myriad of historical facts – mixing literature and myth or folk elements, theory and life, politics and anecdote – into a 'new' form of which the stylistic craftsmanship can't help but resonate with the modern dream of progress and plenitude. The technical brilliance of these writers, their dazzling re-ordering of time, invites you to leave behind the maelstrom of modernity and step into a wild, yet beautifully constructed, new form.

The modernist stress on form not as pure idea but as a system for ordering and organising ties in with developments in literary criticism and the study of language. As a critic Eliot was of great importance to what would come to be known as the New Criticism because he tried to come up with a methodology for literary criticism; he suggested concepts (the 'objective correlative' in 'Hamlet and His Problems') and theories (the doctrine of impersonality in 'Tradition and the Individual Talent'). Under the label New Criticism we group the work of British and American intellectuals, contemporaries of Leo Spitzer, who tried to professionalise literary criticism by incorporating scientific insights and whose work had a lasting impact on the ways in which we think about and teach literature today. The Cambridge professor I. A. Richards, for example, famously studied his students' misreadings of poems, which led him into the domains of psychology and sociology, opening the doors for reader-response theory and the empirical study of literature. But the misreadings also made Richards address the question of how literary texts actually work. All of the New Critics are formalists in that they first and foremost deal with the nuts and bolts of the literary text instead of with larger contextual issues. Furthermore, they tend to set literature apart from ordinary language by foregrounding a central mechanism that creates poetic multiplicity, which clashes with (supposedly) efficient everyday conversation or the (supposedly) crystal-clear logic of scientific language. Richards, for example, focuses on metaphor, William Empson on ambiguity, Cleanth Brooks on paradox, Allen Tate on tension and Robert Penn Warren on irony. That literary language works differently and serves a different function from language used in other contexts was also theorised by the Russian formalist Roman Jakobson, whose work would form the basis of structuralism. The Russian and Central European formalists tend to differ from the New Critics in that their approach was more rigorously analytic and not focused on literary texts per se. Jakobson, building on the seminal work of Ferdinand de Saussure concerning the three-part structure of language (signifier – signified – referent), situates the relation between linguistic particles as determined by broader structures. He makes us see, for example, that words function in larger constellations, both on a horizontal axis in that they combine into sentences, and on a vertical axis in that we always select words from a paradigm. He also, importantly, highlights the importance of context in thinking about language. When he posits his famous model of interaction in which six functions are in tension with each other – the emotive, the referential, the poetic, the phatic, the metalingual and the conative – the question of which function gets highlighted depends on the situation of the speech act.[31]

## COLLECTIVE ENERGIES

The focus on style in aestheticism and modernism implied the by now notorious 'death of the author'. The demands of language left little room for a personal agenda and in their 1960s essays dealing with the problem of the author, Barthes and Foucault urged readers to work with *écriture* and discourse rather than authorial figure in interpreting literary texts. And language, or writing, implicates the reader. Ever since I. A. Richards's *Practical Criticism* (1929), readers and the act of reading have gained in importance in thinking about literary language. Barthes, for example, deals with the process of reading in *S/Z* (1970) in which he tries to distinguish between the reader of the classical novel, who takes in and processes conventions, and the active reader of the 'writerly' text, who co-authors the text. That modernism should have triggered the importance of the reader is ironic. On the one hand we can understand that the death of the author is the birth of the reader. On the other hand it is precisely modernist literature that has shattered the possibility of a shared language, leaving room only for individual readers, not a community. Joyce's individual artist may carry within himself layers of modern artistic aspiration, but he is caught in conventions much more than he uses them for rhetorical purposes. Not surprisingly, 'the reader' in twentieth-century theories tends to be an abstract figure. In a sense, notions such as a super-reader (Riffaterre), an informed reader (Fish), an implied reader (Iser) or a model reader (Eco) shift the central organising principle of the text from crafted paradox or tension to apprehended paradox or tension.

No work makes clearer the incompatibility between the modernist un/making of order and literature's potential to speak for and to a community of readers than Jean Paulhan's *The Flowers of Tarbes or Terror in Literature*. With this book, begun in the 1920s and published in 1941, Paulhan voices his worry about the modernist obsession with originality. In this respect, Paulhan explains, modern literature finds itself at a great distance from rhetoric. Where classical rhetors told us how to respond to certain stylistic features, modern literature leaves us clueless and alone. This is what Paulhan understands by literature as 'Terror'; it is a literature that, in analogy with the French revolution, brings down the old regime and marks an end. Literature does not, however, affirm a new order in which we can all live. And that, Paulhan worries, threatens to take language per se away from us.[32] The good thing about terror would seem to be that it offers an honest perspective, where rhetoric, of course, deals only in clichés. The situation of modern literature, however, has become such that we can never be quite sure what counts as cliché and what as a (less felicitous or worn) attempt at originality. Terrorist writers, Paulhan argues, fail to see that in trying to escape from the hold of everyday language they have enslaved themselves to the demands of linguistic originality, that non-style will invariably turn into a style. The solution proposed by Paulhan is that of a reinvented rhetoric, a Rhetoric. With this Rhetoric we would have a collection of clichés at our disposal about which language users had agreed what they mean and how they should function. Language users would refuse to let language slip and ground meaning in use, they would carry real flowers into the garden of literature instead of hoping, perhaps, to stumble upon a clandestine or exotic specimen. Language, however, refuses to be neutralised like this, as Paulhan fully acknowledged. By way of conclusion he writes that ultimately he may well have said 'nothing' since language will always escape control.[33]

For Michael Syrotinski, Paulhan's emphasis on language use, his appreciation of the excess of meaning, and his wish to safeguard an ethical responsibility for language by trying to get style back into the public sphere, anticipate poststructur-alist accounts of language and writing.[34] Style, in later twentieth-century vanguard theory and criticism, was not returned to a communal garden. Instead, thinkers and writers have taken Paulhan's apparently light-hearted conclusion – 'let's just say that I have said nothing' – to new levels, imbuing it with ethical force. The trope of alienation or not-belonging, and by extension the idea of a style that manifests itself as *not* part of the era in which it was produced, becomes the basis for a progressive political agenda. In Adorno, for example, the idea of a late style, which he applies to the late works of Beethoven, denotes a form of exile.[35] Works composed late in the artist's or author's life, past his or her 'moment' and in anticipation of death, cancel the idea of a next step or a beyond. They show the maker disembarking from the march of history and refusing the idea of synthesis. While, traditionally, such works are read as a retreat from public life into the self, a reading that burdens them with biography, Adorno, for Edward Said, makes it possible to read them as 'art not abdicat[ing] its rights in favor of reality'.[36] In great artists and writers, late style amounts to more than a repetition of the *no* of the modern predicament. As Said points out, '[t]here must be a constructive element above all, which animates the procedure'.[37] For Adorno, in his discussion of Schoenberg after Beethoven, this lies in a further dismantling of the idea that art can affirmatively relate to society: 'Since the work of art, after all, cannot be reality, the elimination of all illusory features accentuates all the more glaringly the illusory character of its existence. This process is inescapable.'[38]

An amplified oppositional aesthetic stance is what characterises such late twentieth-century avant-garde projects as 'Language Writing' and Goldsmith's 'uncreative writing'. Yet in contrast to Adorno, these projects do not insist on the schism between art and reality but enfold one in the other. Central here is, with Fredric Jameson, a refusal of style 'in the sense of the unique and the personal'.[39] This is writing that intensifies the modernist concern with impersonality; it emphatically does not want to affirm a personal identity. Equally, it tries to ward off an existing social identity while at the same time trying to forge a new understanding of the collective. As William Watkin has pointed out, an ostensibly collective project such as 'Language Writer' Lyn Hejinian's *My Life* (1980) shares with recent work in theory the conception of a yet-to-be-formed or negative community.[40] In Hejinian's poetics, everybody is invited to join the creation of 'her life'. The fragments and shreds of found language making up this prose poem flatten individual experience. The opening sentence of *My Life*, 'A pause, a rose, something on paper', asks us to stop doing whatever it is that we are doing and, with Hejinian, co-create the rose in writing.[41] She does not lead us into a literary garden with neatly identified flowerbeds but only gives us 'something on paper', an image yet to materialise. Goldsmith's projects are more radical in their negative stance in that he focuses on 'collecting' language. For *Day*, for example, he retyped the entirety of *The New York Times* edition of 1 September 2000, explaining in 'Uncreativity as a Creative Practice' that

> [t]he object of the project is to be as uncreative in the process as possible. It's one of the hardest constraints an artist can muster, particularly on a project

of this scale; with every keystroke comes the temptation to 'fudge', 'cut-and-paste', and 'skew' the mundane language. But to do so would be to foil the exercise.[42]

The only flowers that Goldsmith is interested in are those you can find on a website like *The Art of Google Books*, which collects 'strange' images of scanned books, among which pages with imprints of pressed flowers.[43] Such pages in a sense represent writing carrying the weight of real flowers. At the same time, these flowers, or their mark, obscure the writing. No one is interested in actually reading these random pages. What matters is the idea of looking at them, archiving them. They show that, though not quite as Paulhan had anticipated, modern literature's obsession with non-style and originality, even when it is presented as unoriginality, makes language metamorphose into something non-linguistic. The idea is that all digital readers, irrespective of the languages they speak, will find that these images speak to them. They show us that old technologies (the pressing of flowers) reverberate in the digital, that virtual reading in surprising ways confronts us with real objects, that systems, in other words, will leak and slip and lead to error. Although, for Goldsmith, this underlines the collective nature of language, the fact that it is only a system and not a language we can speak and sing and turn inside out alienates us from others.

Style, by now, has little to do with Spitzer's linguistic particularities. It rather points to relations between forms. Already in Chatman's *Literary Style: A Symposium* (1971) several contributors sever stylistics from linguistics per se. Among them is Barthes, who compares style to an onion, 'a construction of layers (or levels, or systems) whose body contains, finally, no heart, no kernel, no secret, no irreducible principle, nothing except the infinity of its own envelopes – which envelop nothing other than the unity of its own surfaces'.[44] For Barthes, literature is one system of signification among many and as such not essentially different from fashion, eating or politics. The only difference is that non-literary sign systems tend to obscure their systemic dynamics by 'reconverting the semantic relation into a natural or rational one'.[45] If Barthes' onion appeared to turn stylistics into an abstract super-grid, thinkers after Barthes have used his insights to dive back into the particularities of literature. In tune with recent literature, literature that wants to go beyond postmodernism, stylistics after poststructuralism has returned to the question of how language actually works, and of how we actually use it.[46] In this respect Gilles Philippe and Julien Piat's *La langue littéraire. Une histoire de la prose en France de Gustave Flaubert à Claude Simon* (2009) is interesting to point to. The book historicises the phrase 'literary language' before it covers an extensive terrain of modern French literature, re-establishing the unity between linguistics and literary history, without putting all of its money on either. Readers are asked to ponder the relationship between literary language and spoken language and to approach literature through the ascent of the noun, the decline of the verb or the notion of the phrase. But those vantages are discussed in connection with debates about rhetoric, typography, existentialist 'hatred' towards language and the ongoing twists and turns of the philosophical debate on the relation between language and reality. 'Language' here is much more than what it was for Spitzer, and much less than what it was for Barthes, even if the authors have clearly incorporated Barthes' views.[47] Other more pragmatic or worldly approaches in linguistics include cognitive stylistics, which takes up Richards's fascination with the reading process, and uses insights from neuroscience and psychology to look into what happens when actual readers read texts, both literary and non-literary. Does reading, for example, make us into more empathic human beings, better citizens?

The ambition to approach literature as it actually works is also what informs a book like Rita Felski's *Uses of Literature*, in which she wants to 'engage seriously with ordinary motives for reading – such as the desire for knowledge or the longing for escape – that are either overlooked or undervalued in literary scholarship'.[48] Felski refuses to look for answers in either language or readers and urges us to take into account the manifold entanglements between texts and readers. Literary critics and theorists, she underlines, are readers too, and readers use literature for many purposes. Because we read widely and wildly, because we switch between Flaubert's purity, Goldsmith's debris and the new lyricism, because we feel energised by writing that refuses to make sense and at the same time find comfort in the thrills and losses that life stories feed us, because engaging with the questions of *how* language is given shape and how we respond to those shapes implies that we think about making, relating, living, we know that the contemporary attack on the humanities is a lamentable and misguided rhetoric.

## FURTHER READING

Barthes, Roland. 'Style and Its Image'. In *Literary Style: A Symposium*, ed. Seymour Chatman. Oxford and New York: Oxford University Press, 1971.

Chatman, Seymour, ed. *Literary Style: A Symposium*. Oxford and New York: Oxford University Press, 1971.

Compagnon, Antoine. *Literature, Theory and Common Sense*. Princeton: Princeton University Press, 2004.

Felski, Rita. *Uses of Literature*. Malden, MA: Blackwell, 2008.

Goldsmith, Kenneth. 'Uncreativity as a Creative Practice'. Kenneth Goldsmith's author page on *Electronic Poetry Center*, at <http://epc.buffalo.edu/authors/goldsmith/uncreativity.html> (last accessed 3 February 2015).

Murry, John Middleton. *The Problem of Style*. Oxford: Oxford University Press, 1922.

Paulhan, Jean. *The Flowers of Tarbes*, trans. Michael Syrotinski. Urbana: University of Illinois Press, 2006.

Philipe, Gilles and Julien Piat. *La langue littéraire. Une histoire de la prose en France de Gustave Flaubert à Claude Simon*. Paris: Fayard, 2009.

Riegl, Alois. *Problems of Style* [1893], ed. David Castriota, trans. Evelyn Kain. Princeton: Princeton University Press, 1993.

Spitzer, Leo. *Linguistics and Literary History*. Princeton: Princeton University Press, 1948.

## CHAPTER 18

# Popular

## David Glover

By the early seventeenth century the word 'popular' had generated a complex domain of meanings whose faultlines and shifts of emphasis have continued to impact upon, and even to polarise, contemporary understandings of what remains an indispensable term within modernity's contested lexicon. On the one hand, some historical uses of the expression have followed a kind of universalising logic: in law, for example, a 'popular action' was a statute that permitted *any* member of the public to bring a legal suit before a court; similarly, in politics, the word referred to the will of the people as a whole, irrespective of their class or other social attributes, and pointed to the power that they might exercise, as in the idea of 'popular government' or 'a populacy'. However, side by side with such usages, a slide into invidious comparisons has also seemed inescapable: 'popular' quickly became interchangeable with 'common', 'low', 'vulgar' or 'plebeian', the passions of the crowd or the masses; or with the dubious treatment of controversial issues by translating them into 'a popular style which boys and women could comprehend'.[1]

In the light of this unstable etymology, the pursuit of popular fiction – whether by authors or readers – can often appear as either a lure or a trap, pulled between instant gratification and the possibility of being immured in a downmarket genre, material success offset by a lack of critical recognition. In his memoir *Miracles of Life*, the novelist J. G. Ballard, who sustained a deeply ambivalent relationship towards what he saw as the 'huge vitality' of science fiction throughout his career, pointedly summed up the acute dilemma he had always faced: the trouble was that '[p]opular fiction was too popular, and literary fiction too earnest'.[2] Yet if Ballard's work epitomises the vicissitudes of a life spent in the shadow of a popular genre, his is also a success story: by the late 1990s he had written a highly regarded bestseller, received two prestigious fiction prizes, and 'Ballardian' had joined kindred adjectives like 'Wellsian' and 'Kafkaesque' in major English dictionaries. At his death in 2009 he left an estate valued at just over four million pounds.[3]

The nature of Ballard's achievement will repay closer scrutiny later in this chapter. But for now it is important merely to note the way in which his writings straddled two different yet overlapping perspectives as to what constitutes popular literature and popular culture, reflecting ongoing uncertainties about the theoretical and methodological status of their objects of inquiry. In fact, one can still say that studies of popular fiction tend to be divided between (1) detailed case histories that focus on the making of extraordinary bestsellers, ranging from individual texts like Daphne du Maurier's *Rebecca* to multiples such as Ian Fleming's James Bond novels and J. K. Rowling's Harry Potter books, and (2) investigations into the appeal of modern commercial genres, those long-familiar bookstore staples – thrillers, mysteries, science fiction, Gothic and romance – that are from time to time irreverently supplemented by more ephemeral and questionable labels like 'chicklit' or 'mommy porn'.

## TRACKING THE BESTSELLER

Neither of these approaches, nor the distinctions on which they are based, is at all straightforward. However innovative a novel might be and no matter how strong its appeal to readers, individual bestsellers are closely linked to, and are typically framed by, the signifiers of what would now be regarded as well-established genre categories. So, while Daphne du Maurier's *Rebecca* (1938) 'weaves a special magic that no-one who reads it will ever forget', this 'world-famous bestseller of romantic suspense' marked the interwar renewal of female Gothic writing in a tradition reaching back across the centuries to Ann Radcliffe's *The Mysteries of Udolpho* (1794) and Charlotte Brontë's *Jane Eyre* (1847).[4] And, like Jane Eyre, it belongs among those select titles that have never been out of print since their first publication.

Indeed, bestseller listings are, for the most part, compilations of prominent genre titles. In 2008 American writer Linwood Barclay's thriller *No Time for Goodbye*, premised on a family's sudden overnight disappearance, was Britain's bestselling novel with sales of 643,225 copies, leading both *The Sunday Times* hardback and paperback fiction lists. Of course, Barclay is a hot property. Like du Maurier, his novels are sold around the globe and have been translated into two dozen languages. Yet his success also mirrors the distribution of genre fiction sales as a whole. Here, as a random perusal of almost any paperback bestseller fiction list will confirm, 'crime and thrillers' regularly account for around 60 per cent of all books sold, with the other major genre categories like 'romance and family sagas' (16 per cent) and 'science fiction and fantasy' (12 per cent) coming some way behind. Perhaps surprisingly, 'war fiction', 'Westerns' and 'erotic fiction' each sell less than 1 per cent of the overall total – though, as will soon become clear, these classifications can be somewhat arbitrary.[5] The relatively low percentage for erotic fiction is one, but obviously only one, reason why the roaring success of E. L. James's novel *Fifty Shades of Grey* – a book that also draws on the masochistic scenarios so central to female Gothic – created such a sensation in June 2012 when it reached the half-million sales mark faster than any other paperback since Nielsen BookScan first began collecting data in 1998.

Bestseller lists provide invaluable guides to popular tastes at particular moments in time, but they also need to be read in relation to the national and regional marketing strategies within local branches of an increasingly global publishing industry. When

*The New York Times* prints its weekly rosters of 'Best Sellers' each Sunday, they differ from their British counterparts like *The Guardian* in providing a slightly more elaborate tripartite classification into 'hardcover fiction', 'paperback trade fiction', and 'paperback mass-market fiction', rather than relying on a simple binary division between hardbacks versus paperbacks. In part these seemingly common sense descriptors are the product of specific publishing histories. From the 1940s to the 1980s, US publishing was dominated by the aggressive proliferation of cheap paperbacks (Bantam, Dell, Fawcett, Pocket Books and others) that were sold in airports, bus terminals, drugstores, newsagents and railway stations, thus bypassing the traditional bookshops and creating a business in which the enormous sales of these 'mass-market' books was responsible for the bulk of the industry's profits. But from the early 1960s the nature of bookselling began to change. With the gradual development of large retail book chains, located in major city centres or out-of-town shopping malls or mega-malls, small independent bookstores found themselves becoming marginalised by competitors who could carry more stock and, using sophisticated computerised inventories, sell in bulk at discount prices. This process had two major effects. First, hardcover books became more profitable and commanded sales figures undreamt of in earlier eras. To take just one extreme example: Dan Brown's *The Da Vinci Code* (2003) sold over 18 million hardback copies in the USA in the first three years of publication. And, second, once hardbacks became more profitable, mass-market paperbacks came under pressure because they started to bring in less money. A bifurcation in the design and marketing of paperbacks – and specifically the rise of so-called 'trade' paperbacks – was the result.[6] This split tells us a lot about how variegated the strategies for attracting popular audiences have been.

Trade paperbacks date back to the 1950s when they were introduced as a relatively inexpensive alternative to hardbacks, yet without the low-grade ground wood paper, cramped layout and cellophane-coated covers that characterised their more degradable mass-market rivals. The idea behind this initiative was that trade paperbacks would be affordable books that readers would want and be able to keep. Thus Doubleday's Anchor Books, the imprint that pioneered this innovation, augmented its fiction list with a particularly strong line in nonfiction. Yet it was the 1990s that marked the point at which trade paperbacks really came into their own when an increasing range of titles were offered to more affluent readers in a larger, more aesthetically pleasing format. If we look at *The New York Times's* 'Best Sellers' charts, the differences might at first appear to be slight. On 29 June 2014, for example, Gillian Flynn's crime novel *Gone Girl* was the top-selling title among trade paperbacks in a list that included books by Neil Gaiman, Carl Hiassen, Khaled Hosseini and Chimananda Ngozi. But if we compare the trade paperback rankings with their mass-market equivalents, two features are immediately apparent. On the one hand, different sorts of authors and paperback editions are present among the mass-market paperbacks: among the crime novels we find Lee Child's *Never Go Back* (Dell), Tami Hoag's *The 9th Girl* (Signet) and Diane Mott's *The Whole Enchilada* (Avon), and it seems unlikely that a romance writer like Daniele Steel would ever be classed as trade. Yet, on the other hand, there are some works of fiction that are so enormously successful that they and their publishers seem to transcend any strict demarcation between these two wings of the US paperback charts. Thus in late June 2014 George R. R. Martin's *Game of Thrones* (Bantam) and Dan Brown's *Inferno* (Anchor) figured prominently in both trade and mass-market lists – though they performed much better among the mass-market bestsellers where they occupied the top first and second positions respectively. Yet, despite these highly visible exceptions, American mass-market paperbacks tend to be far more solidly genre-based than their trade competitors.

A publisher's choice of paperback format is partly a decision about how to market a book and consequently the choice of paperback imprint has only a loose relationship to fictional genres. In the USA, for instance, E. L. James's erotic fiction has been published as a trade paperback under the Vintage label, perhaps because her bold, sexually transgressive narratives were felt to be too explicit and potentially too offensive to be sold openly in many American supermarkets and drugstores. In fact, the intrinsic privacy of the e-book download has frequently been cited as one of the key factors that has boosted her readership. But her example also underlines the rather arbitrary way in which texts have been allocated to different paperback formats. As we have already seen, crime fiction is a genre that has a firm presence both in mass-market *and* trade lists with Lee Child, John Sandford and Tami Hoag in the former and Gillian Flynn and Carl Hiassen in the latter. So what does this ambiguous relationship between popular genres and paperback imprints tell us about the ways in which genres themselves are organised?

## TEXT, GENRES, FORMATS

One answer to the question of how individual genres relate to the received wisdom and established practices within commercial publishing is, rather paradoxically, that their position is seldom fixed – and this is true of their status among readers. Consider the recent history of modern crime writing. In the 1980s American male hardboiled crime fiction, which had seemed doomed to repeat the formulae laid down at its inception in the interwar pulp magazines, underwent a remarkable renaissance. This development occurred simultaneously across several fronts. Most dramatically, the masculine monopoly was breached by a new generation of women writers who created a series of credible and demonstrably tough detectives who vied for the same social space as their male alter egos: Katherine V. Forrest, Sue Grafton, Sara Paretsky and Barbara Wilson. At the same time, the still largely masculine thriller started to diversify into more ambitious and more flexible narrative cycles of confrontation and conspiracy as an abundance of previously little-noticed writers, such as James Ellroy, George V. Higgins, Andrew Vachss, Charles Willeford and particularly Elmore Leonard, began to achieve wider popular recognition.

One spin-off from this new vogue for crime fiction was a surge in the demand for reprints which in turn led to a substantial reappraisal of some of the most unashamedly misogynistic authors whose work had been the backbone of the specially commissioned 'paperback originals' in the American mass-market of the 1940s and '50s. Cheap, disposable paperbacks with gaudy erotic covers that had once sold in drugstores for 25 cents acquired several new leases of life and eventually moved towards an unanticipated respectability. Thus, the works of David Goodis or Jim Thompson reappeared in inexpensive editions whose covers and format offered stylised or pastiche versions of their Gold Medal or Lion forerunners. Not only did small low-budget publishing companies like California's Black Lizard Books or No Exit Press in the UK come into existence to mine this specialist niche, but the critical vocabulary around these texts also adopted an increasingly sophisticated tone. Capitalising on the fact that many of these books had been transformed into movies during the first *film noir* wave in the '40s and '50s, Goodis, Thompson et al. were now re-branded as authors of 'noir mysteries' or 'noir fiction' and acquired cult status. Long-undervalued texts like Goodis' *The Moon in the Gutter* (1953) or Thompson's *A Hell of a Woman* (1954) were effectively in transit from one zone of the literary marketplace to another. So, when Vintage Books (a division of Random House) bought up the Black Lizard back catalogue, they began to reissue these titles as larger, glossy trade paperbacks whose covers incorporated black and white photographs stylishly designed to evoke the mise-en-scène of classic *film noir*. The 1990 Vintage Crime edition of Jim Thompson's 1955 *After Dark, My Sweet*, with its distinctive black lizard logo, exemplifies this upscale treatment, carrying ringing endorsements from *The Washington Post* ('casts a dazzling light on the human condition') and *The New York Times*, rather than the markedly less prestigious *San Francisco Call-Bulletin*, and retailing at $7.95 instead of the original Black Lizard price of $3.95. In the thirty-five years since its first publication, Thompson's short, capriciously violent novel had become a radically different kind of cultural commodity.

But what happened to Thompson's original story? Is there not a danger of losing sight of the original text, allowing it to dissolve into an ungovernable excess of signification: cover art, blurbs, advertising copy, popular journalism, all the busy machinery of publicity that is so central to contemporary publishing. For surely, it might be objected, when all is said and done, *After Dark, My Sweet* remains stubbornly unaltered, the identical set of words on the page that had initially appeared in print in 1955. In a literal sense this is perfectly true; nevertheless, in the intervening period not only had Thompson's readership changed, but the conditions under which his work is read have also changed significantly. A paperback that had once been marketed as 'A Novel of Twisted Lives and Tormented Loves' was now an expensive collectible and its author variously identified as a Dostoevskian cartographer of psychological extremes and 'a prairie populist' training his guns on 'the disfigurements of capitalism'.[7] As with its '50s predecessor, this was still primarily a male audience, but one that was better informed, more alert to stylistic nuances. Nevertheless, the ease with which it embraced the discomfiting forms of male address in texts like *After Dark, My Sweet* suggests a somewhat recalcitrant response, a resistance to recent shifts in the terrain of gender. For readers like these the narrator's ambivalent relationship to being diagnosed as psychotic may be savoured as an amusing irony rather than experienced as the suspenseful *frisson* that it was in the 1950s.

This disturbance within the confines of just one sector of the huge market for crime writing and thrillers raises larger questions about the long-term stability of what

John Frow has termed the 'broader economy of genres' or the configuration of genres taken as a whole.[8] Throughout his wide-ranging overview, Frow contrasts the lives of individual genres whose initial appearance is likened to a contingent 'historical event' with genre as a totality or 'system' or, better, 'sets of genre systems organised by domain', such as drama, film, television or literature.[9] The picture he presents is one of constant flux as genres rise to prominence, their authors seeking to secure ever-widening circles of readers, or fall out of favour and are in turn modified and restructured as conditions of reception change and new writers enter the 'domain'. Of necessity, the scope of Frow's generalisations is vast and his illustrations span many centuries, from the elegies of pre-Christian Roman poets like Ovid to Werner Herzog's 1979 film *Nosferatu: Phantom der Nacht*. But do such scattered examples adequately test his claims? One major problem lies in identifying and assembling the kind of evidence needed to allow us to examine the dynamics of genre systems, especially where one is talking about popular genres consisting of thousands of texts. For in principle Frow's *literary* archive alone would be virtually limitless.

## METHODOLOGY AND DISTANCE

In an exceptionally controversial essay Franco Moretti called for a revolution in the methodology by which we track changes in large bodies of literature, one that would directly address this embarrassment of generic riches. Under the banner of 'close reading', modern literary criticism has become renowned for its sustained attention to detail, the precise analysis of the distinctive qualities to be found in each text. But, for Moretti, 'close reading' is of little help when one is trying to find patterns of development in the totality of fiction, or what he was later to call the 'hidden rhythm' rippling across long stretches of time and space. If we are successfully to mount an investigation on this scale, Moretti argues that we will need to build abstract models that highlight some aspects of cultural forms at the expense of others – looking, for example, at specific literary devices such as the increasing importance of clues in the evolution of the European detective story. The work of abstraction entails standing back from the intricacies of individual texts in order to see similarities and differences across large numbers of novels. To see the wood rather than the trees it is necessary to abandon close reading and turn to what Moretti dubs 'distant reading'.[10]

The gains and losses of Moretti's method are vividly displayed in *Graphs, Maps, Trees: Abstract Models for a Literary History* (2005), where he follows the fate of forty-four British 'novelistic' genres between 1700 and 1900. Genres are shown to be 'temporary structures', each with only a limited time-span – yet a time-span that *is* significant. Two-thirds of the genres in his study lasted for around thirty years, fuelled by 'six major bursts of creativity', and there was also a marked tendency for bundles of genres to go out of existence at roughly the same time.[11] For instance, the picaresque, the epistolary novel, the oriental tale, the sentimental novel and the mid-century 'ramble' novel all seem to drop out of sight in the 1790s. On the other hand, there are some striking discrepancies. A minority of the genres that Moretti studied, such as the decadent novel or the evangelical novel, each had only a ten-year life-cycle, while in a few cases there were short unexpected revivals, as with the oriental tale which came back to life at the close of the second decade of the nineteenth century.

Intriguing and suggestive as these findings are, Moretti's data do not yield easily to explanation. Thus when a number of genres fade away more or less instantaneously, Moretti argues that it is unlikely that their decline reflects some sort of cultural inadequacy common to what are, after all, very different kinds of writing. Instead he tentatively proposes that what has happened is not a generic malfunction, but rather a generational shift as new readers come forward with new demands, a process that was undoubtedly accelerated by the steady rise in the number of books produced after 1820 and the beginning of a boom in genres directed towards distinct reading publics such as the male urban working class in the 1840s. As Moretti readily acknowledges, his answer is provisional at best, but it does have the virtue of linking economics, demography and book history. But perhaps a more fundamental and more worrying question concerns the rationale that Moretti invokes to identify the genres or sub-genres in his study. At the start of *Graphs, Maps, Trees*, Moretti stresses the importance of replacing 'concrete, individual works' by 'shapes, relations, structures' or 'models' forged through a rigorous programme of 'reduction and abstraction'.[12] But that is not what we find here. Instead, by relying upon the specialist knowledge of literary scholars, Moretti has drawn up an oddly assorted collection of labels based upon quite disparate criteria. For example, if we compare the two extremes of Moretti's array we find terms that are poles apart. The word 'picaresque', referring to the adventures of rogues or knaves, was an Anglicised equivalent of the name for a well-known sixteenth-century Spanish literary genre and came into use around 1810, just after this English variant is said to have died out. By contrast, some of the genres from the *fin de siècle*, such as 'imperial romance' and 'imperial Gothic', derive their names from postcolonial cultural criticism in the 1970s and are part of a thoroughgoing re-evaluation of Britain's age of empire. Two very different principles of genre classification are in play here.

By extending his study over two hundred years to the very threshold of the twentieth century, Moretti's analysis begs a far larger set of questions. What is the relationship between his findings and the system of popular literary genres that we know today? Do contemporary popular genres go through the same thirty-year cycles as those that make up the majority of his sample? What happens when we try to extrapolate from his picture of a multitude of relatively short-lived genres towards the history of our own times? Do we find underlying continuities? Or is there a sharp break between this long build-up to 1900 and its protracted aftermath?

Moretti's general answer to the thrust of these queries is that literary genres go through a Darwinian process of evolution with some popular forms proving to be extremely resilient while others fall by the wayside and die out. But Moretti does enter some important caveats which trouble the account of genre that he has been so patiently constructing. First of all, he accepts that there are a handful of genres which enjoy an unusual degree of success and significantly outstrip their rivals. This is not because their production cycles last longer than the thirty-year norm, but rather because these genres account for the largest number of books printed within their period. So, between 1760 and 1850 he picks out three 'hegemonic forms': the episto-lary novel, the Gothic and the historical novel. Why these texts are so dominant or why particular generations of readers take to them is unclear, but Moretti insists that theirs is not an unlimited popularity since the demand for any single genre is always kept in check by the scale of competition across the book industry. For example, the epistolary novel accounted for over 50 per cent of all published fiction at its peak, yet as the numbers of new titles dramatically increased between 1800 and 1850 the market became more segmented, making it virtually impossible for the Gothic novel and the historical novel to do nearly as well as their predecessors. Yet this is by no means the only anomaly. There are other puzzling phenomena that Moretti sets aside too quickly. One that has already been touched on is the phenomenon of recurrence. Why is it that the Gothic novel makes a comeback after 1885 and why does the historical novel reappear 'more than once'?[13] Could this be a sign that the notion of cycles needs to be reconsidered? Moretti's brief remarks on later genres suggest that this is indeed the case. How then are we to account for the absence from Moretti's model of two of the most enduring genres in the twentieth century, namely detective fiction and science fiction, especially since, as he explicitly notes, 'both genres achieve their modern form around 1890'?[14] In fact, when Moretti adverts to their exceptional status, he emphasises that it is their massive presence which requires explication. For these genres are not mere niche markets but should really be considered as 'super-niches' that transcend the confines of genre *per se*.[15] Crime fiction, for example, is such a capacious, heterogeneous and highly differentiated body of writing that it cannot easily be reduced to a simple set of formulae. Because in their restless quest for ever wider audiences these genres never stand still, we might even say that they change the meaning of the term 'hegemonic'. Given their extraordinary longevity and their endless capacity to reinvent themselves, Moretti speaks more truly than he perhaps recognises when he asserts that the 'super-niche' phenomenon will require quite 'a different approach'.[16]

## MAPPING THE POPULAR LITERARY FIELD

Instead of focusing upon cycles of production and consumption, a more fruitful line of investigation might be to turn to the question of when and why the main historical shifts in popular culture have occurred. Surveying developments over the course of the twentieth century, Stuart Hall argued that the period between the 1880s and the 1920s was a moment of 'profound transformation' and therefore 'one of the real test cases for the revived interest in popular culture'.[17] Technologically, there was a revolution in the means of communication which went hand in hand with a variety of new cultural practices: the beginnings of popular photography, the early introduction of telephones into affluent homes and businesses, the spread of cable telegraphy, and the diffusion of film as a popular form of entertainment and information, initially as a sideshow and then finally, through the establishment of the cinema, as a major forum for public narrative. But no less important were a series of key changes in the ecology of print culture. Firstly, there was an unprecedented growth in relatively cheap magazines and story papers such as *Tit-Bits* (1881) or *Answers* (1888), miscellanies that brought together practical advice, news snippets, competitions, travellers' tales, curious facts or sensational events, and dramatic accounts of the latest scientific advances – and, later, fiction; secondly, this period saw the creation of the modern popular daily newspaper led by Alfred Harmsworth's halfpenny *Daily Mail* in 1896, followed by Pearson's *Daily Express* (1900) with its front page news and streamer headlines, and Harmsworth's re-launch of the *Daily Mirror* as the first pictorial daily in 1904; and lastly a new kind of low-cost subscription library came into being to capitalise on the growing demand for single-volume novels, whether through bookstall chains like W. H. Smith's or high street stores like Boots (the Chemist's) Booklovers Library or the network of local twopenny libraries in local tobacconists or newsagents.

The aggregate effect of these developments was a restructuring of the whole literary field that multiplied the number of outlets through which reading matter of every kind could be obtained, but particularly popular fiction. This was a time of intense competition for readers and one in which there was a sustained process of consolidation and innovation across a wide range of popular forms. However, while it is now commonplace to date the inception of a recognisably modern genre system from around 1890 when tags like the 'thriller' (or 'shocker'), 'detective story', or 'scientific romance' came into vogue to describe specific sorts of reading experiences, this newish terminology only very gradually hardened into the familiar matrix of genre compartments around which present-day bookshops have been organised for nearly a hundred years. Instead, most of what we would now consider to be distinct genres were loosely grouped under the general rubric of 'romance', as in 'a grotesque romance' or 'a detective romance', the respective subtitles for H. G. Wells's *The Invisible Man* (1897) and R. Austin Freeman's *The Red Thumb Mark* (1907). Sometimes these 'romances' look like genres that we think we know and can easily recognise. A case in point is R. Austin Freeman's 'Dr John Thorndyke' stories which are mysteries in the Sherlock Holmes mould but with a fussier stress upon forensic science than is found in Conan Doyle's writing. Other narratives are somewhat harder to classify. Wells's *The War of the Worlds* (1897) is now a founding text of science fiction, but at the *fin de siècle* its debt to the widely-read invasion scare stories would have been much more apparent.

To what extent can the concept of the 'literary field' help us towards a better understanding of how new genres are formed and why they become so popular? The idea originated in a set of studies of art and culture by the sociologist Pierre Bourdieu in which he argued that the major zones of human activity (politics, art, religion and so on) consist of practices and institutions which adopt different strategies in order to maintain or, better, to improve their positions vis-à-vis the others in their field. These constantly shifting combinations of positions and strategies are what give each field its distinctive structure. However, for Bourdieu, appeals to the notion of the 'popular' were highly suspect, no matter in which field they occurred, since they seemed largely without content. In the literary field, for instance, he believed that popular writing could only be defined negatively – that is, as a lower order of fiction which, when judged by the standards of the elite that dominated the field, was without any redeeming aesthetic value. Bourdieu also underlined the fact that the consumption of books written to attract the largest possible numbers showed hardly any correlation with the 'educational level' of potential buyers – in other words, very little effort or skill was required to read them – and their very accessibility reduced their cultural standing dramatically. From a publisher's perspective, Bourdieu insists, the target audience for these disposable 'bestsellers with no tomorrow' are defined statistically as an ephemeral and undistinguished mass that is carried along on an endless flow of short-term peaks and troughs.[18] This is an astonishingly oversimplified diagram of popular reading and, whether it is empirically accurate or not, one which certainly mirrors Bourdieu's own preferences. In his case studies the further Bourdieu moved away from popular literature, the more convincing his analyses became. His account of the cautious economic logic underpinning the gradual success of Samuel Beckett's modernist play *En Attendant Godot* (1952) for the small French publishing house Minuit casts fresh light on the plight of the avant-garde, whereas his withering dismissal of French regional novelists for their 'more-or-less idealized' portrayal of the 'people' closes down any real discussion before it has begun, not least when he characterises this sub-genre as little more than 'a refuge against failure or exclusion'.[19] To follow Bourdieu and yet to give serious attention to popular fiction is a deeply paradoxical enterprise. So we find Ken Gelder forced into the position of arguing, for *and* against Bourdieu, that popular fiction can be considered as a field, but a field in its own right, distinct from that of 'Literature'.[20]

Between these two extremes Peter D. McDonald's fascinating study of 'the literary field of the 1890s' suggests an alternative line of investigation that avoids Bourdieu's tendency to privilege structure over history and neither disparages the popular nor isolates it from developments elsewhere in the field. McDonald concentrates on one of the major factors that made the 1890s such a transformative moment: the huge growth in newspapers and periodicals aimed at a rapidly expanding reading public and the host of new publishing opportunities this opened up for writers of fiction. More specifically, he looks in depth at practices of serialisation, such as breaking down a single narrative into a set of episodes or bringing out a run of short stories linked by a single set of characters. For determined authors the advantages were considerable, for the serial market allowed them to sell the same text several times over, with separate serial and book rights for Britain and the United States, augmented by the prospect of world translation rights. In 1898 Arnold Bennett was an unknown and largely untried writer who had won a competition in *Tit-Bits*. Yet by 1902, with the help of an astute literary agent, the serial of his romance *The Grand Babylon Hotel* had become an international bestseller and from 1906 to 1912 his annual income of £1,000 rose to £16,000, enabling him to buy a large yacht and a country house.[21] Of course, very few authors could match Bennett's achievement, but these market conditions help to explain why popular literature flourished in this period.

Serialisation could be the making of a writer in more than one sense. When Arthur Conan Doyle began to feature his Sherlock Holmes stories in *The Strand Magazine* in 1891, interest in his detective hero reached a new high and allowed him to abandon a career in medicine. But Sherlock Holmes was also re-made. His language was cleaned up, his use of cocaine diminished appreciably, and although there are severed ears and a brutally amputated thumb, no contorted corpses like that in *The Sign of Four* (1890) are on display – all delicate adjustments in the detective's world at the behest of a publication whose intended readership was the modest suburban middle-class family. As McDonald notes, this editorial censure was never one-sided, for it engendered a battle of wits between author, publisher and readers in which Conan Doyle invoked the sensational tropes of the 'penny dreadful' only to cunningly neutralise them with Holmes's own lofty knowingness. This literary gamesmanship was also a mark of Conan Doyle's divided literary ambitions, as was the fact that his Holmes narratives were hybrids of mystery, Gothic and adventure. That he could mock the conventions of one popular genre by invoking those of another is a reminder that Conan Doyle wished to be known for his historical romances like *The White Company* (1891) rather than his detective stories. The 'death' he famously contrived for Holmes in the Reichenbach Falls was no slip of the pen.

The success of the Holmes stories changed the fortunes of *The Strand* and not only attracted more lower-middle-class readers but also attracted skilled labourers who could just about afford the monthly sixpence. McDonald cites the results of a competition in February 1910 to find the best art by British artisans which included submissions by 'house painters, compositors, weavers, detective officers, railway porters, bakers, miners, French-polishers, shoemakers, and bottle-washers'. Even if these contestants do not provide a wholly accurate guide to the class composition of *The Strand*'s readership, they do suggest that the magazine's audience was more varied than was sometimes thought.[22] And, it might be added, they are not so different from some of the minor characters – cashiers, ship's carpenters, market stallholders and commissionaires – to be found in Holmes's own casebook. If we begin to consider the possibility of a cross-class audience, then posing the question of how a bestseller can bring together a plurality of different readers becomes the basis for a new research agenda.

## NEW CONFIGURATIONS OF READING

One way of approaching this issue is to look again at the way in which a writer's texts are positioned in relation to other texts. Under the imprimatur of *The Strand Magazine* the Sherlock Holmes stories stand in stark contrast to the difficulty of early modernist writing, yet they are also several removes from the brute sensationalism of the 'shocker' or 'thriller', represented by the figure of the man on the run in John Buchan's *The Thirty-Nine Steps* (1916), who desperately struggles to understand why he is being pursued. With hindsight – for the term was only coined in the early 1920s – Conan Doyle's detective fiction might be described as 'middlebrow': respectable, unpretentious and highly entertaining. 'Middlebrow' is sometimes equated with 'middle class', and there is a case to be made for conceiving of middlebrow fiction as falling under the sway or cultural hegemony of the middle class. But it is the potential linkage between different kinds of readers and who those readers are that makes 'middlebrow' a much-disputed notion. For modernists like Virginia Woolf it was synonymous with mediocrity; for avowedly populist writers like J. B. Priestley the real danger was that 'middlebrow' was not inclusive enough, and he coined the term 'broadbrow' to gesture towards a more relaxed, but nevertheless independent-minded culture in the making. Interestingly, his preferred cultural inventory provocatively placed 'grand opera' next to 'film shows' and 'detective stories' alongside 'tragedies in blank verse'.[23]

Priestley's use of the neologism 'broadbrow' was essentially performative: by inventing and promoting a name he was seeking to create a mode of social awareness that would help to consolidate a new kind of audience or perhaps even bring it into being. Similarly, when some crime writers in the 1920s and '30s (Dorothy L. Sayers, R. Austin Freeman, or Ronald A. Knox) started to champion the detective story as a rational, puzzle-solving pastime and rigorously distinguish it from the disorderly excitement associated with the thriller, they were elevating one set of reading practices over another. How writers imagine and address their readership plays a key role in redrawing the boundaries of popular literature and changing its significance. This is one of the factors that make J. G. Ballard such an intriguing figure. From the mid-'50s onwards Ballard published regularly in a wide range of British and American science-fiction magazines – *Science Fantasy*, *Amazing Stories* and *Fantasy and Science Fiction* – but it was the increasingly experimental direction taken by *New Worlds* that solidified his reputation as an author whose exploration of inner landscapes rather than parallel universes showed him to be working at the margins of the genre. Ballard has always been a painterly writer, strongly influenced by the obscurely haunting surrealist panoramas associated with Dali, de Chirico and Tanguy, but also directly linked to the British precursors of Pop Art such as Richard Hamilton and Eduardo Paolozzi in the immediate postwar period – so much so that one can read Ballard's later novel *Crash* (1973) as a perverse narrative variation on Richard Hamilton's erotic stylisations of American automobiles in works like *Hommage à Chrysler Corps* (1957).

Ballard shared with these visual artists a sense that the growth of a consumer society had dramatically enlarged the variety and quality of images, whether through advertising or product design, and that these developments had radically altered the contours of contemporary culture by breaking down the barriers between high art and everyday life. By the late 1960s this intuition had mutated into the belief that the traditional hierarchies of taste were rapidly being eroded and that it was the unmediated impact of the modern environment, its shocks and surprises, which were simultaneously bringing into being new forms of art and a different kind of audience.[24] In a 1970 interview Ballard argued that writers now tended to think of themselves as working with 'responses that are not that much more sophisticated than ordinary people's', a change that he thought 'makes for a more popular kind of writing'. In a world 'already absolutely overloaded with fiction', the role of the writer was like that of the scientist: to investigate 'what the reality is behind this fictional mix', to 'explain what is really going on in this huge novel we are living in'.[25]

But Ballard's work is part of the 'fictional mix' in a double sense. On the one hand his stories and novels allude to a variety of writers and artists whose texts stand in uncanny counterpoint to the narratives which they haunt: Jarry, Conrad, Kafka, and film directors like Hitchcock and Pasolini, to name just a few. On the other hand, Ballard's fictions become implicated in a different, less malleable exterior web of 'inter-textuality', those discourses that create new framings for his work, sometimes setting unexpected or uncongenial agendas.[26] As John Sutherland has noted, Ballard's *Empire of the Sun* (1984) was marketed as a 'radical departure' from his 'previous fiction', not only avoiding any mention of science fiction or speculative fantasy, but inserting the book into a long line of war and anti-war texts such as Erich Maria Remarque's *All Quiet On The Western Front* (1929) and Norman Mailer's *The Naked and the Dead* (1948).[27] Furthermore, by foregrounding Ballard's childhood experiences as a Japanese internee and silently passing over the book's subtitle ('a novel' – words completely omitted from some later paperback editions), *Empire of the Sun* was tendentiously presented as an autobiographical key to the writer's entire oeuvre. All this was three years *before* Steven Spielberg's very freely adapted film version first appeared in American cinemas in December 1987, featuring a cameo appearance by Ballard himself, and added a fresh layer of significations to an already fast-moving literary phenomenon.

This final example again shows how complex the cultural construction of a many-sided composite readership can be. And it is also a reminder of how, in the process of becoming popular, narratives circulate in a variety of forms that are only partly anchored in genres and can be set adrift to flow towards other frames and discourses that will create new configurations of reading. It is perhaps no accident that Ballard's sequence of novels in the decade after *Empire of the Sun*, including *Cocaine Nights* (1996), his most commercially successful book from the 1990s, involved a turn towards the futuristic thriller or crime story as a vehicle for exploring the long-term psychopathologies of the late twentieth century. One might well say that they exist in a no-man's land between the two major 'super-niches' in Franco Moretti's methodology of 'distant reading': detective fiction *and* science fiction. For, notwithstanding the problems that his work raises, Moretti's provisional hypothesis does capture an important truth: that the most dynamic modes of popular writing are best conceived as open-ended zones where, in historical terms, the formulae are never fixed for long and where the looseness of narrative forms and the fluidity of reader affiliations constantly run in search of each other.

## FURTHER READING

Bourdieu, Pierre. *The Rules of Art: Genesis and Structure of the Literary Field*, trans. Susan Emanuel. Stanford: Stanford University Press, 1996.

Bennett, Tony and Janet Woollacott. *Bond and Beyond: The Political Career of a Popular Hero*. Basingstoke: Macmillan, 1987.

Frow, John. *Genre*. New York: Routledge, 2006.

Hall, Stuart. 'Notes on Deconstructing "the Popular"'. In *People's History and Socialist Theory*, ed. Raphael Samuel. London: Routledge and Kegan Paul, 1981.

Haut, Woody. *Pulp Culture: Hardboiled Fiction and the Cold War*. London: Serpent's Tail, 1995.

McDonald, Peter D. *British Literary Culture and Publishing Practice 1880–1914*. Cambridge: Cambridge University Press, 1997.

Moretti, Franco. *Graphs, Maps, Trees: Abstract Models for a Literary History*. London: Verso, 2005.

O'Brien, Geoffrey. *Hardboiled America: Lurid Paperbacks and the Masters of Noir*. Expanded edition. New York: Da Capo Press, 1997.

Sutherland, John. 'Fiction and the Erotic Cover'. *Critical Quarterly* 33 (1991), pp. 3–18.

Thompson, John B. *Merchants of Culture: The Publishing Business in the Twenty-First Century*. Second edition. New York: Plume, 2012.

## CHAPTER 19

# Genre

Jonathan Monroe

Readers interested in a broad view of historical and current thinking about questions of genre within the academy in general, and the ongoing renewal of interest in such questions within the field of literary studies in particular over the past decade, could scarcely do better than consult Ralph Cohen's insightful, provocative article 'History and Genre',[1] the lively, heterogeneous collection of essays edited for a special issue of *PMLA* by Bruce Robbins, *Remapping Genre*,[2] and, most recently, Jonathan Culler's magisterial 'Lyric, History, and Genre'.[3] Situating its approach squarely within a certain *dominant* in the history and field of literary studies, Culler's essay offers what we might call a centripetal, intra-disciplinary synthesis and analysis, a meta-analysis of the 'state of the art' of genre studies, which argues for its importance as not just one concept and area of literary studies among others but rather, in effect, as a synecdoche of what literary studies might involve and *should* involve at its best, in other words what might be said to define the field of literary studies, or the study *of literature as such*. A 'crucial instrument', as Culler rightly observes, 'offering us versions of history that take us beyond the period-by-period agenda of our ordinary studies', notions of genre allow us to avoid, as Culler, Cohen and Robbins all agree, 'various narrower modes of reading and interpretation' in ways that 'enlarge our vision of historical discursive possibilities'. Thus, with respect to the lyric, as to other genres, only a 'broad concept' will do, one with the scope to 'sweep across eras and languages' and so 'activate possibilities occluded by narrower conceptions'. Notions of genre are in this sense comparable, as Culler argues, echoing Robbins's formulation in the 'Afterword' to *Remapping Genres*, to 'the norms in the socioeconomic realm that allow [...] transnational comparison of living standards'. The case of genre is 'in a nutshell' that of 'historical comparison' tout court.[4]

If there are signs of a renaissance of interest in questions of genre among literary theorists and scholars, as Culler has argued, rejuvenating what was for a time an 'unpopular topic', then the first challenge of an auspicious return to such questions for poetry is surely to avoid categorical separations of the genres 'poetry', 'criticism', 'theory' and 'history'. With that goal in mind, rather than rehearse in detail the meticulous steps of Culler's extraordinarily useful analysis and programme for literary studies – including the 'desire to correct' 'erroneous conceptions', in particular about 'lyric forms of address'[5] – I want to offer in what follows a more 'centrifugal', synchronic approach to the question of genre. Understanding the terms 'centripetal' and 'centrifugal' as antipodes of a continuum rather than as a strict binary, I want to do so from the point of view of an increasing sense of the landscape for such questions being shaped by a present and future in which, in the prescient words of Marjorie Perloff's *Radical Artifice: Writing Poetry in the Age of Media* (1991), 'not only [...] the boundary between "verse" and "prose" break[s] down but also the boundary between "creator" and "critic"'. The 'interactive' character Perloff described of '"fiction" being written for the computer' – the then newly developing genre of 'hypertext' fiction – has become over the past twenty-five years an integral part of what we now call 'life on the web'.[6] The pervasiveness and dominance not just of 'media' in general but of *digital* media in particular has come to blur completely, if not entirely to erase, bureaucratically maintained distinctions, both 'within' and 'outside' the academy, not only between 'creator' and 'critic', but also between 'writers' and 'readers', the 'verbal' and the 'visual', 'aesthesis' and 'poiesis'. Such formerly *divisible* binaries now interanimate each other increasingly in ways that promise (risk? threaten?) to bring distinctive genres to the point of being indistinguishable from each other, a point of (anxiety-provoking? fortuitous?) *in*-difference.

In the twenty-first century's digital-media-saturated environment, it has become impossible to think questions of genre centripetally without thinking questions of media, *centrifugally*, impossible to think genre studies apart from media studies and vice-versa. As Friedrich Kittler remarks in *Discourse Networks 1800/1900* (1990), channelling Gertude Stein as Marshall McLuhan a few years before Perloff's *Radical Artifice*: 'A medium is a medium is a medium.'[7] Among contemporary genres, discourses, disciplines and media, the genre-specific act of *poiesis* called 'poetry', at the heart of what has come to be called 'creative writing', the *Gedicht* in *Dichtung*, would seem to occupy, by all accounts and appearances, an especially tenuous position. Yet no other genre has played a more central, foundational, enduring role in rethinking questions of genre – at once 'empirical and theoretical [...] theoretical and historical'[8] – in poetry, poetics, criticism, theory and literary history, in the classification, understanding and practice of forms literary and extra-literary, as in all of these combined.

## CONTEMPORARY POE(TRY)

Perhaps no writer of his time, or of any time, bumped up so hard against the question of genre as Edgar Allan Poe.[9] Certainly no writer of his or any era, even including his 'soul-mate' on the other side of the Atlantic, Charles Baudelaire, stood up to the encounter more consequentially. Widely considered to be the inventor of several modern genres – detective, horror and science fiction – that have remained as 'absolutely modern', in Rimbaud's terms, as current over a century and a half later in the first two decades of the twenty-first century as they were at their inception in the 1830s and 1840s, Poe is of special importance in the history of genre as a representative figure of 'The Great Divide' between 'popular' and 'serious' ('critically acclaimed') literature, between 'popular culture' and 'the literary' tout court. At the crossroads of that moment in literary history that prompted Pierre Bourdieu's now dated Franco-parochial map of genres (*The Field of Cultural Production*),[10] and provocative question '*Did You Say "Popular"?*' (*Language and Symbolic Power*),[11] Poe, that most enduringly popular of American writers in France, remains an exemplary figure for considering what Gertrude Stein called, in her post-Rimbaldian question, the 'contemporary', what questions of genre have come to *now*. While Poe's multi-genre oeuvre includes poems, short stories and one novel, along with several justly celebrated essays of crucial importance in the history of poetry, what remains perhaps most striking in his literary production is the degree to which he keeps these genres *separate*, and the extent to which his poems (*as verse*) represent a constraining past as surely as his prose represents a future of unlimited possibility. A handful of 'greatest hits' notwithstanding – 'To Helen' (1831 and 1848 versions), 'The Raven' (1845), 'Annabel Lee' (1849) or 'The Bells' (1849) – the impact of Poe's undeniably accomplished, yet assiduously conventional poems has been no match, as many would concede, for the more innovative poetics of Whitman and Dickinson, or of Poe's transatlantic soul-mate and translator, Charles Baudelaire. Where Poe's essay, 'The Rationale of Verse' (1846), rehearses and encourages a tortuous apprenticeship to received poetic forms, conceiving of what 'counts' in poetry in the most tediously technical, rhetorical terms, his two companion essays from the same period, 'The Philosophy of Composition' (1846) and 'The Poetic Principle' (1848), create the condition of possibility, and make possible the breakthrough, of the *petits poèmes en prose* of Baudelaire's *Le Spleen de Paris*[12] – through their radical *mise-en-question* of the equation 'poetry = verse'. As Baudelaire understood, it was in Poe's prose, his short fiction – of which the prose poem can be considered a further condensation – that Poe found liberation from the constraints of poetry, at once formal and thematic, in his era, constraints that so manifestly and decisively constrained his output *in verse*. Where Poe's poetic *practice* remained deeply, assiduously, melancholically conventional, the more manifestly *theoretical* opening of his essays onto the *philosophy* of composition and the poetic *principle* laid the foundation for what Barbara Johnson called the 'second Baudelairean' revolution, a revolution of *form*, shifting the terrain of poetry, as I have argued elsewhere,[13] from verse to prose, that succeeded the revolutionary introduction of a 'prosaic' *content* into the conventional, albeit masterful, alexandrines of *Les Fleurs du mal*.[14]

Standing at the threshold of this revolution, preparing the way conceptually without crossing over in practice, the two more consequential of Poe's three essays on poetry share with Baudelaire's prose poems and Poe's short fiction, as also with Poe's undervalued meta-fictional novel, *The Narrative of Arthur Gordon Pym* (1838), an orientation towards uncharted literary territory, an opening of the question of genre onto what remains to this day Poe's most powerful legacy, the exploration of a dynamic interplay – if not necessarily a 'dialectic' – of form and content. Such an emphasis on the sustained development of an awareness of the 'content of the form' and the 'form of the content', the development of 'theory' *at the heart of the work itself*, contains the potential for parody of the *scholarly genre* as well in 'How to Write a Blackwood Article' (1838), the germ that would later yield Borges's 'El Aleph' (1949).

Poe may be said to have abandoned poetry in effect without ever quite leaving it behind, continuing to write poems until the end alongside his burgeoning prose – albeit noticeably, tellingly, less prolifically – retaining a nostalgic attachment to its conventional themes and forms which he would call deeply into question, however ambivalently yet profoundly. In the last two years of his short life, the *crisis of genre* his oeuvre puts on display between the two reigning media of the day, verse and prose – destabilising a certain (suddenly dis-)unified 'identity' of the genre 'poetry' and the 'poetic self' – has much to tell us about how the question of genre continues to play itself out in the twenty-first century, in what is called 'literature' *now*. Commencing always with 'the intention of composing a poem that should suit at once the popular and the critical taste',[15] a goal he clearly thought realistic but which most writers and readers today would agree can no longer be assumed, Poe proceeds to establish, in his famous rejection of the idea (on the example of *Paradise Lost*) that there is any such thing as a long poem, the category of length as essential to his understanding of what constitutes a poem: 'Holding in view these considerations, as well as that degree of excitement which I deemed not above the popular, while not below the critical taste, I reached at once what I conceived the proper *length* for my intended poem – a length of about one hundred lines.'[16] As Baudelaire's prose poems offered a condensation of the Poe short story, so later Pound, in his radical reduction of the iconic imagist poem, 'In a Station of the Metro', would offer a further condensation of the Poe poem, developing from Poe's disruption of the equation 'poetry = verse' the Poe-derived dictum '*Dichtung* = *condensare*'. Understanding that breaking the pentameter was 'the first heave' – in the American tradition through Whitman's free verse, in the French through Baudelaire's prose poems – Pound soon realised, as *The Cantos* make clear, that his radical reduction of Poe's poetic programme to imagism's extreme minimalism risked constraining poetry as much as the nostalgia for conventional forms and theme that so constrained Poe's poetic output and led to his growing embrace of the seemingly infinite possibilities of prose. With 'the poetical', Poe had written in 'The Philosophy of Composition', it 'stands not in the slightest need of demonstration that Beauty is the sole legitimate province of the poem'.[17] The key passage concerning *what makes poetry poetry* – which does not equal verse – continues as follows:

> That pleasure [...] most intense [...] elevating [...] pure [...] not a quality [...] but an effect [...] intense and pure elevation of *soul* – *not* of intellect, or of heart – [...] an obvious rule of Art [...] effects [...] from direct causes [...] objects [...] through means best adapted for their attainment [...] elevation [...] *most readily* attained in the poem. Truth [...] Passion [...] attainable, to a certain extent, in poetry, far more readily attainable in prose.
> [...]
> [...] Beauty [...] my province [...] the tone [...] *sadness*. Beauty [...] excites the sensitive soul to tears. Melancholy [...] most legitimate of all the poetical tones.

> The length, the province, and the tone [...] key-note in the construction
> of the poem [...] upon which the whole structure might turn [...] the usual
> artistic effects [...] *points*, in the theatrical sense [...] universally employed
> [...] the *refrain*.[18]

Presenting Poe's pivotal ('upon which the whole structure might turn') calculations, recalibrations – to use a properly *mechanical* metaphor – in this condensed,
elliptical form highlights the 'key(-note)' terms of his approach to the genre of
poetry, as he defines it, in a way that his exposition, with all its careful, syntactical
suturing, to some extent tends to obscure. The definition is in the end tautological
in the extreme – as perhaps all definitions ultimately are? as perhaps all *genres*
are? – its chain of associations substituting effects for causes and causes for effects,
metonymic displacements masquerading as metaphors ('elevation') channelling
concepts ('Beauty') mixing metaphors ('poetical', 'theatrical') in an endless, yet
finite, series of terminological accommodations and approximations at once affective
and conceptual, where 'thoughts' and 'feelings' become indistinguishable from one
another, precisely in the sense Pound later describes, channelling Poe's emphasis
on brevity, intensity, in his definition of the *image* as 'an intellectual and emotional
complex presented in an instant of time'.[19]

'A definition of poetry can only determine what poetry should be', Friedrich
Schlegel posited some four decades prior in the famous *Athenaüm-Fragment 114*,
'not what it really was and is; otherwise the shortest definition would be that poetry
is whatever has at any time and at any place been called poetry.'[20] Where shall we
look, in considering the question of genre, to consider how best to address the term's
resonance and currency *now*? One of the most enduring, and enduringly *functional*
concepts in literary studies, a nexus of interaction of pivotal importance to literary
criticism, literary theory (and literary history alike that calls into question the very
divisibility of the critical, the theoretical and the historical from one another, as
well as the relative autonomy of the literary and aesthetic spheres), the term 'genre'
resides in close proximity both to the *idea* and to the discursive *fact* of diverse disciplinary formations, to the separation of disciplines, the discursive organisation of
academic curricula, and the distribution of media 'sites', as we say now, both virtual
and actual, within and beyond the university.

## THE GROUNDLESS GROUND OF POETRY

What Derrida figures as the 'groundless ground' of Reason, that *Abgrund* or falling
away into the abyss of 'Unreason', finds its equivalent, in the history of poetry as a
genre, in the prose poem, that 'antigeneric', 'genreless genre', as I have described
it elsewhere, that 'does not want to be itself'.[21] If what meta-theories and meta-
poetics alike reveal, of genre(s) as of all other subjects and objects of inquiry, is not
their universal applicability but a certain *partiality* (*ceci n'est pas un* 'truth claim'),
the groundless abyss beneath all Reason (logic, theory, but also poetry), it follows
that to speak *of* genre is to be *in* genre. Attempting to balance the empirical and

the theoretical – or theory and history – theory, the theoretical, (almost) always wins (or does it?), even if, sometimes, *by a nose*. Not content for examples to be themselves, left to their own devices, genre study – genre theory? – demands that the empirical be lifted up, *aufgehoben*, without a trace, without remainder. In this sense, with or against Hegel, theory (or 'Theory') of whatever kind, as such, by definition, remains fundamentally Hegelian, Platonic, precisely in the sense that prompted Marx to want to turn philosophy on its head, 'not just to interpret the world but to change it', to let 'things', including reified humans-as-things, subjected (*abjected*) to *Verdinglichung*, speak for themselves: with genre, the 'devil is in the details', in 'concrete' 'instantiations'.

In the digital era's all-inclusive discursive environment, what counts as 'genre' or 'discourse' must be understood to include an endless production, circulation and relay of visual, sonic and other non- and more-than verbal as well as verbal material, the whole range of what digital media makes almost effortlessly available. Anticipating such an environment in the mid-nineteenth century with the rise of the 'new media' of their day, the novel and the commercial newspaper, what I have elsewhere called the 'anti-generic' impulses of the prose poems of Baudelaire's *Le Spleen de Paris* (*Paris Spleen*) marked a turning point in the history of poetry's capacity to be, or become, a resolutely 'self-questioning genre'. Surpassing Baudelaire's revolutionary infusion of gritty urban *content* in *Les Fleurs du mal*, within strict adherence to the *monarchical* dominance of the alexandrine that had been French poetry's equivalent of the iambic pentameter in English, Baudelaire's 'second revolution', in Barbara Johnson's apt formulation,[22] offered a revolution of both content *and form*. The second Baudelairean revolution contributed decisively to and set the stage for, even more than tends still to be acknowledged, the as-yet-unimaginable challenges to what Michel Delville has called 'traditional generic boundaries'[23] that have today become widely accepted as normative and, at the same time, deceptively overestimated in their ability to successfully contest the 'policing' of such boundaries which Jacques Rancière has rightly identified as a defining feature of the 'politics of aesthetics'.[24] While the relative autonomy of the aesthetic sphere, as of the category of 'genre' itself, is increasingly open to question, cast ever more seriously in doubt in our age of omnidigitalisation, it is still possible, and indeed necessary, in considering works of both the 'critical' and 'poetic' genre, with stakes at once 'aesthetic' and 'political', to distinguish between more 'centripetal' and more 'centrifugal' orientations to questions of genre. As options for thinking about such questions tend to be divided, as Culler has observed,[25] between the 'theoretical' and the 'historical', terms that need to be thought together rather than separately, we may prefer to think of a continuum, rather than a binary or dichotomy, of 'readers' and 'writers', of 'centripetal' and 'centrifugal' approaches to aesthesis, poiesis and the 'groundless ground' in between, a distinction usefully elaborated by means of Mikhail Bakhtin's inclusively expansive concept of 'speech genres' and Roman Jakobson's anti-essentialising 'six functions' of language.[26]

One of the central conceptual tensions informing the constellation of texts referred to earlier for rethinking questions of genre – Culler's 'Lyric, History and Genre', Robbins's *Remapping Genre*, and Cohen's 'History and Genre' – is the tension

Jakobson left unresolved, a tension perhaps ultimately unresolvable, between the descriptive and the normative, between constative claims and performative utterances. There is, perhaps, no getting around it, no way of eliminating, as Robbins perceptively argues in his 'Afterword' to *Remapping Genre*, the question of judgement, of value, of hierarchies of organisation and comparison, at the heart of discussions of genre, which concerns both 'theory' and 'practice', both the 'what' and the 'how' of texts, their production and reception, their circulation and dissemination, their internal patterning and institutional constraints, their discursive dispositions and (im)mobilities across time.[27] There is nothing to keep 'what is called poetry', as Charles Bernstein understands, from valuing and instantiating meta-theory, however thoroughly ironised, at the 'heart' of its own practice:

> This line is stripped of emotion.
> This line is no more than an
> illustration of a European
> theory. This line is bereft
> of a subject. This line
> has no reference apart
> from its context in
> this line. This line
> is only about itself.
> This line has no meaning:
> its words are imaginary, its
> sounds inaudible. This line
> cares not for itself or for
> anyone else – it is indifferent,
> impersonal, cold, uninviting.
> This line is elitist, requiring,
> to understand it, years of study
> in stultifying libraries, poring
> over esoteric treatises on
> impossible to pronounce topics.
> This line refuses reality.[28]

To be mindful (as we say) – to what purposes? – of our location(s), to 'know our place(s)', where we are, how we're 'situated' (Max Jacob), 'overdetermined' (as 'we' used to say), genre-constrained or liberated, 'in' or 'out of' poetry, included or marginalised, with or without a 'net', from Frost and Walcott to Bernstein and Rankine, from 'natural' print-verse in received metrical forms in New England or Caribbean pastoral landscapes, to the urban-digital interanimation of verse, prose and other media, from centripetal to centrifugal discursive environments and poetic-prosaic economies – the question as it poses itself today is, perhaps, as Bernstein's philosophical, political, stand-up-comic poetic economies suggest, how we can learn to stop worrying and love *anti-* and *a-*, a whole *gaggle* of genres?

## FROM CENTRIPETAL TO CENTRIFUGAL PO(I)EAESTHESIS

'The poet is a poet', according to Mikhail Bakhtin's enduringly provocative formulation, 'insofar as he accepts the idea of a unitary and singular language and a unitary,
monologically sealed-off utterance. These ideas are immanent in the poetic genres
with which he works.'[29] Thus, in a pivotal late-career passage of *The Prodigal*, Walcott
acknowledges without retraction the constraints he recognises in his own poetic
practice, the extent to which a certain mid-nineteenth-century image of poetry has
continued to inform his poetics throughout his career, as if the entire history of
modernism since Baudelaire's prose poems – the *second*, not the first, Baudelairean
revolution – had never occurred, or he wished that it had not:

> In the middle of the nineteenth century,
> somewhere between Balzac and Lautréamont,
> a little farther on than Baudelaire Station
> where bead-eyed Verlaine sat, my train broke down,
> and has been stuck there since. When I got off
> I found that I had missed the Twentieth Century.
> [...]
> It was another country whose time had passed,
> with pastoral willows and a belief in drawing.
> [...]
> ... My joy was stuck.
> ... My craft was stuck.[30]

While acknowledging, as the poem nears its conclusion, that 'approbation had
made me an exile',[31] *The Prodigal* yet sutures together and exemplifies, in blank
verse from beginning to end, the kind of 'unitary, monologically sealed-off utterance', acutely self-aware yet hardly, in the end, self-questioning, which Bakhtin
opposes to the novel's *'auto-criticism of discourse'*,[32] that heteroglossia 'in-itself' and
'for-itself' which demands 'a broadening and deepening of the language horizon, a
sharpening in our perception of socio-linguistic differentiations'.[33] The prose poem's
literary historical significance, its vital role in the history of poetry, may be said to
reside precisely in the extent to which it unleashed poetry's 'auto-critical' potential, inaugurating a far-reaching 'novelisation' of poetry, in Bakhtin's sense, that
would become a defining feature of what has proven to be most innovative, most
'centrifugal', in modern and contemporary poetry ever since.

In sharp contrast to Walcott's traditionalist practice, Aimé Césaire, one of the
great twentieth-century heirs of the second Baudelairean revolution, oscillates in
the *Cahier d'un retour au pays natal*[34] between prose and verse, reorienting poetry
'centrifugally', at once formally and thematically, away from the 'centre' (verse,
Paris) towards the 'periphery' (prose, Martinique) drawing into itself, as poetry's
'proper' subject, the most abject, 'prosaic' materials, including the discourse of colonial oppression, even as it decentres and distances itself from received poetic formal

traditions. Thus, in 'Le verbe marronner / à René Depestre, poète haïtien' (1955), Césaire writes to his politically exiled 'comrade' in poetry, against the backdrop of the Breton-Aragon rift over the politics of poetic form:

> It is true this season that they're polishing up sonnets
> for us to do so would remind me too much of the sugary
> juice drooled over there by the distilleries on the mornes
> [...]
> Bah! Depestre the poem is not a mill for
> grinding sugar cane absolutely not
> [...]
> it is undoubtedly a very serious problem
> the relation between poetry and Revolution
> the content determines the form[35]

In the Caribbean context, perhaps no poet has exemplified the drive towards a centrifugal poetics more manifestly and capaciously than Kamau Brathwaite, whose poetry is as expansively heteroglot in its incorporation of non-literary language as Walcott's poetry is self-consciously, centripetally 'poetic'. Thus Brathwaite's 'I was wash-way in blood', in *Born to Slow Horses*, is as apt to include dialectal, idiomatic language from trial testimony, transcribed in prose taken from *The Barbados Advocate, Thursday, January 19, 1995*, as it is the most 'lyrical' verse.[36] While such centrifugal, heteroglot strategies have become increasingly familiar over the past century and a half in so much of the modern poetry that has mattered most, from the prose poems of *Paris Spleen* to *The Waste Land* (especially in its original version, *He Do the Police in Different Voices*) and Pound's *Cantos* to Brathwaite's 'Sycorax video style' poetry and, in a Latin American context, the genre-defying, anti-generic, intermedial poetry of Nicanor Parra and Cecilia Vicuña, the triumph of the centrifugal in modern and contemporary poetry can yet hardly be assumed, even in the first decades of the twenty-first century. It is Walcott, after all, not Brathwaite (at least not yet), who has received the Nobel Prize committee's 'approbation', and for reasons of aesthetic ideology that require little speculation.

With the publication in 2009 of *American Hybrid*, edited by Cole Swenson and David St John, there is evidence of a desire not so much to correct as to heal what Swenson describes as a 'two-camp model', the first camp 'associated with "conventional" work, such as coherence, linearity, formal clarity, narrative, firm closure, symbolic resonance, and stable voice' (akin to what I am here calling the 'centripetal'), the second (closer to but not necessarily the same as what I am calling the 'centrifugal') associated with such 'experimental' values as 'non-linearity, juxta-position, rupture, fragmentation, immanence, multiple perspective, open form, and resistance to closure'. Noting that many hybrid poets 'also work in other media, while others incorporate images as integral elements of their texts',[37] Swenson nevertheless concludes with a strikingly ahistorical, dehistoricising erasure, if not outright rejection, of the very *historical* arguments she has appeared to be advancing in favour of hybridity:

Poetry is *eternally* marked by – even determined by – difference, but that very difference changes and moves. *At the moment, it is moving inside, into the center* of the writing itself [...] to fight [...] for the integrity of language in the face of commercial and political misuse. [...] a battle that *brings poetry back to its mandate* as articulated by Mallarmé: to give a *purer* sense to the language of the tribe. [...] *something that only poetry can do.*[38]

Against Swenson's astonishingly *centripetal* embrace of the idea of *'purifying* the language of the tribe' (with its misleading allusion to the poet of *Un coup de dés*) at the close of an introduction ostensibly arguing the case for *hybridity* even as it gestures towards saving language, presumably the role of all poets, 'in the face of commercial and political misuse', a book such as Cecilia Vicuña's recently reissued, presciently intermedial *Saborami* (1973/2011) represents the centrifugal stakes for poetry, at once linguistic and socio-political, more clearly:

> The search for structure in society is analogous to the search I undertake for form in my works. The social form is easier to find, it's obviously socialism, self sufficient commun/ities, but is harder to do it. The form I search for is harder to find, but easier to do. / The find of paradise will coincide / with the finding of a language.[39]

Suggesting that questions concerning poetry, genre and the politics of form are as vital in 2011 as they were in 1973, the reissue of *Saborami* affirms that work's prescient anticipation, in its pervasive interanimation of poetry and visual and other media, of so much of what is proving to be most interestingly, in all likelihood irreversibly, centrifugal in twenty-first century poetry. Among the ever-growing number of books of poetry moving in this direction, two in particular merit sustained attention as representative examples of the potential to expand poetry's scope and ambition beyond past and present boundaries. Published in 2004 and 2014, respectively, Claudia Rankine's two companion volumes, *Don't Let Me Be Lonely*[40] and *Citizen*,[41] both of which bear the subtitle *An American Lyric*, move freely not only between prose and verse – both are in fact mostly in prose – but between the verbal and the visual. Eschewing that 'asceticism of the word' which the advent of YouTube, Facebook, Instagram and other social media will undoubtedly continue to make that much less appealing, and even possible, with each passing year, Rankine's 'American lyrics' incorporate into themselves such an inclusive, virtually unlimited and unlimitable range of genres, discourses and media that the centripetal impulse to police and maintain the generic identity and insularity of something called 'lyric', or 'poetry', whether from a 'critical' or 'theoretical', 'aesthetic' or 'poietic' perspective, seems doomed to fail. Incorporating into its (more-than) textual body sources as varied as frozen television images, verses by Paul Celan,[42] a graphically 'internalised' representation of a map of America, recollections of a talk by 'the philosopher Judith Butler' on 'what makes language hurtful',[43] video strips from an infamous 'World Cup final', and 'script(s)' for 'Situation video(s)' in collaboration with her husband, John Lucas,

Rankine's 'American lyrics' make it unmistakably clear that, whether in print or on a screen, the age of digital production, circulation and distribution has made visual, sonic and other 'non-verbal' materials as readily available as words in ways that will make it increasingly difficult, if not impossible, for what has been called 'lyric', what has been called 'poetry', to maintain 'itself' as a separate, distinctive *genre*. What is crucial, as Rankine's work helps us understand, is not just that many poets, in Swenson's words, 'also work in other media, while others incorporate images as integral elements of their texts',[44] but that only six years after *American Hybrid* was published, the ever-deepening 'hybridisation' of 'lyric', of 'poetry', with other genres, other discourses, other media, has become increasingly inevitable, unstoppable.

## THE EVERYDAY LIFE OF POETRY: THE REVENGE OF THE 'EMPIRICAL' ON THE 'THEORETICAL'

> ... *even the very language of the writer (the poet or novelist) can be taken as a professional jargon on a par with professional jargons* ...[45]

As the age of *sustainably singular genres* is coming, if it has not already come, to an end, such bastions of mainstream, literate culture as *The New York Times* and *The New Yorker* continue to offer a severely limited place for, and representation of, 'lyric', of 'poetry', that has less and less to do with where the broader digital culture is heading. As a barometer of what 'counts' in considering what the category of poetry as genre has come to in the context of literature now, one could do worse than consult that annual ritual of *The New York Times Sunday Book Review*, its '100 Notable Books', published each December as the year draws to a close. As in previous years, the 2 December 2014 release includes only two categories, of fifty titles each: 'FICTION AND POETRY' and 'NONFICTION'. Such is the state of the question of genre, according to the United States' 'paper of record', that of the top fifty books that make up the former, which include thirty-three explicitly described as a 'novel', a grand total of three on the list are reserved for 'poetry'. If poets, of whatever genre, and poetry critics, theorists, scholars, historians, of whatever orientation, have any question about the current state of the genre and what 'correct' or 'incorrect' ways there may be to approach and understand it, the '100 Notable Books of 2014' – that revenge of the 'empirical' on the 'theoretical' – tells us all we need to know about what the broader, dominant culture thinks poetry's place is. The first thing to know, judging by the one-sentence descriptions of each book's project, is that books of poetry are not really books – coherent, cogent, unified projects – at all, but 'collections' or 'selections' of 'individual', more or less loosely connected, more or less tightly interwoven 'poems', virtually all of which will be – as if the 'second Baudelairean revolution' had never occurred – in verse. The second thing to know is that they will be on 'time-honoured' subjects for poetry. While former US poet laureate Louise Glück's 'latest collection', *Faithful and Virtuous Night*, will address 'with high art and sparkling presence', as its poetic title strains to reassure us, 'the vantage offered by mortality', the Nobel laureate's 'largehearted and essential selection', *The Poetry of Derek Walcott 1948–2013*, can be counted on to offer 'Stroke by patient stroke [...] the work of a painterly hand'. The third and final slot is reserved for that equally time-honoured genre, 'the scandalous newcomer', in this case Patricia Lockwood, whose *Motherland Fatherland and Homelandsexuals* – 'at once angrier, and more fun, more attuned to our time and more bizarre, than most poetry can ever get' – includes the (in)famous ('gone viral') poem, 'Rape Joke', one of only two prose poems, interestingly and 'shockingly' enough, in the 'collection'. In all three cases, the assumption presented to potential readers about poetry is that it is the genre of autobiographical, 'subjective experience' aligned, no less in 2014 than was the case when Poe challenged the idea in 'The Philosophy of Composition' (1846), with 'verse'. Whatever the content, whether of the *eternal* or the *scandalous* genre, governing assumptions about the normative *form* of what counts as 'poetry' remain – a century and a half after Poe, after Baudelaire, in that centripetal, parochial, inward-looking country on the North American side of the Atlantic, if not in Europe, the Caribbean (Walcott notwithstanding), Latin America – all but unchanged.

Desires to 'correct' notwithstanding, *poetry's image*, which is not separate, after all, from its 'reality', continues to inform what we may call, after Henri Lefebvre, the 'everyday life' of poetry in the most elemental ways possible.[46] But what if what poetry 'should be', and whatever 'has at any time and place been called poetry', are, in fact, all there is?[47] What if that is all we can really say about poetry, as about the question of genre – that a genre is what we have said, say, will say, will have said it is, in all its conjugations? That said, what, then, can we do about poetry's still predominantly *centripetal*, insular, self-isolating direction, even as more centrifugal approaches appear every day? To return to my original question, how should we (and who is this 'we', after all, dear readers?) approach genre? While the wide-ranging, productively diverse essays brought together in *Remapping Genre* serve to remind us of the range of empirical, historical, theoretical, geographical, geopolitical, economic, sociological, discursive, disciplinary, cross-genre, cross-disciplinary, (inter)medial perspectives from which one might go about giving an account of one's genre, or self, or discipline – to borrow the formulation of Butler's staged encounter, in *Giving an Account of Oneself*,[48] between the genres or disciplines of rhetoric and philosophy – the decision to proceed more centripetally or centrifugally with respect to a genre's, or discipline's, or self's preconfigured identity, which always has a complex history, is one for us to make, in Glissant's capacious term, 'in relation'.[49]

Whether to proceed in ways that tend to preserve and protect a genre's boundaries, including poetry's, perhaps in part by declaring their descriptive truths, or rather enlarge and expand them, as through more manifest forms of advocacy criticism, is up to us. Rather than face off as separate genres or discourses within the academy, 'poetry' and 'fiction', criticism and theory, criticism and creative writing, would do well – perhaps at least marginally better than they are doing – if they worked together as allies, not least against the stifling insistence of official verse culture on poetry as self-expression, whether in its individual or collective, tribal, group manifestations. While such a situation may not allow itself to be easily corrected, an aesthetics, poetics, po(i)esthetics that seeks above all to police and maintain boundaries among genres, discourses, disciplines and media, as also of individual and collective identities, approaching such boundaries centripetally rather than centrifugally, seems less likely to include and make visible than to isolate and ignore.

## FURTHER READING

Agamben, Giorgio. *The End of the Poem: Studies in Poetics*, trans. Daniel Heller-Roazen. Stanford: Stanford University Press, 1999.

Bakhtin, M. M. *Speech Genres & Other Late Essays*, ed. Caryl Emerson and Michael Holquist, trans. Vern W. McGee, Austin: University of Texas Press, 1986.

Derrida, Jacques. *Geneses, Genealogies, Genres, and Genius: The Secrets of the Archive*, trans. Beverly Bie Brahic. New York: Columbia University Press, 2006.

Dimock, Wai Chee and Bruce Robbins, eds. *Remapping Genre*. Special issue of *PMLA* 122:5 (2007).

Heath, Stephen. 'The Politics of Genre'. In *Debating World Literature*, ed. Christopher Prendergast. London: Verso, 2004, pp. 163–74.

Kittler, Friedrich. A. *Discourse Networks, 1800/1900*. Stanford: Stanford University Press, 1990.

Manovich, Lev. *The Language of New Media*. Cambridge, MA: MIT Press, 2001.

McGann, Jerome. *Radiant Textuality: Literature after the World Wide Web*. New York: Palgrave, 2001.

Seitel, Peter. 'Theorizing Genres – Interpreting Works'. *New Literary History* 34 (2003), pp. 275–97.

White, Hayden. 'Anomalies of Genre: The Utility of Theory and History for the Study of Literary Genres'. *Theorizing Genres 2*. Special issue of *New Literary History* 34:3 (2003), pp. 597–615.

# Notes

## INTRODUCTION

1. Many people and institutions assisted in the coming about of this book. Of note are Dirk de Geest, Gillis Dorleijn and Jürgen Pieters of the Flemish Research Foundation (FWO)-sponsored OLITH group, whom we thank for their initial input and stimulating support. We owe a big debt of gratitude to the people of the Belgian Science Policy (BELSPO)-funded 'Literature and Media Innovation' network (http://lmi.arts.kuleuven.be); their suggestions have been invaluable. Finally, we wish to thank all members of the Leuven-based MDRN research lab, and particularly those involved in the research project (GOA) 'Literature and Its Multiple "Identities", 1900–1950', graciously sponsored by the Research Council of the University of Leuven (http://www.mdrn.be).
2. Hans Blumenberg, *Paradigms for a Metaphorology*, trans. Robert Savage (Ithaca, NY: Cornell University Press, 2010).
3. Mieke Bal, *Travelling Concepts in the Humanities: A Rough Guide* (Toronto: University of Toronto Press, 2002).
4. Jim Collins, *Bring on the Books for Everybody: How Literary Culture Became Popular Culture* (Durham, NC: Duke University Press, 2010).
5. Mark McGurl, *The Program Era: Post-War Fiction and the Rise of Creative Writing* (Cambridge, MA: Harvard University Press, 2011).

## CHAPTER 1

1. Jacques Derrida, *Archive Fever: A Freudian Impression*, trans. Eric Prenowitz (Chicago: University of Chicago Press, 1996), p. 4.
2. Michel Foucault, 'Des espaces autres' [Of other spaces], 1967 lecture, *Architecture/Mouvement/Continuité* 5 (1984), pp. 46–9. Quoted passage p. 48.
3. Michel Foucault, *The Archaeology of Knowledge* (New York: Pantheon, 1972), p. 129; Foucault, 'The Historical *a Priori* and the Archive', in Charles Merewether, ed., *The Archive* (Cambridge, MA: MIT Press, 2006), pp. 28–9.

4. Carolyn Steedman, *Dust* (Manchester: Manchester University Press, 2001), p. 2.
5. Ibid., p. 9.
6. Ibid., p. 5.
7. Ibid., p. 9.
8. Ibid., p. 68.
9. Ibid., p. 68.
10. Ibid., p. 19.
11. Ibid., p. 68.
12. Ibid., p. 69.
13. Derrida, *Archive Fever*, p. 16.
14. Ibid., p. 17.
15. Ibid., p. 17.
16. Ibid., p. 18.
17. Paula Amad, *Counter-Archive: Film, the Everyday, and Albert Kahn's Archives de la Planète* (New York: Columbia University Press, 2010), p. 306.
18. Wolfgang Ernst, *Digital Memory and the Archive*, ed. Jussi Parikka (Minneapolis: University of Minnesota Press, 2012), title of chapter 6 ('Discontinuities: Does the Archive Become Metaphorical in Multi-Media Space?'), p. 113.
19. Ibid., p. 195.
20. Quoted in Marlene Manoff, 'Theories of the Archive from Across the Disciplines', *portal: Libraries and the Academy* 4:1 (2004), p. 10.
21. Lev Manovich, *The Language of New Media* (Cambridge: MIT Press, 2001), p. 225.
22. Ed Folsom, 'Database as Genre: The Epic Transformation of Archives', *PMLA* 122 (October 2007), pp. 1571–9.
23. See David Greetham, '"Who's In, Who's Out": The Cultural Poetics of Archival Exclusion', *Studies in the Literary Imagination* 32:1 (Spring 1999), pp. 1–28.
24. See Paul Voss and Marta Werner, 'Toward a Poetics of the Archive: Introduction', *Studies in the Literary Imagination* 32:1 (Spring 1999), i–viii.
25. Steedman, *Dust*, p. 18.
26. See Geoffrey Little, 'Managing Technology: We Are All Digital Humanists Now', *Journal of Academic Librarianship* 37:4 (July 2011), p. 352.
27. Francis X. Blouin Jr. and William Rosenberg, *Processing the Past: Contesting Authority in History and the Archives* (New York: Oxford University Press, 2011).
28. Robert B. Townsend, 'Processing the Past: A Conversation with Francis Blouin and William Rosenberg', *Perspectives on History* (November 2011), online at <http://www.historians.org/publications-and-directories/perspectives-on-history/november-2011/processing-the-past> (last accessed 17 June 2015).
29. See Franco Moretti, *Distant Reading* (London and New York: Verso, 2013).
30. Stephanie Blalock, 'Walt Whitman's Early Fiction in Periodicals', *Walt Whitman Quarterly Review* 30 (Spring 2013), pp. 171–80.
31. See Roland Barthes, *The Pleasures of the Text*, trans. Richard Miller (New York: Hill and Wang, 1975).
32. Ed Folsom and Kenneth M. Price, The Walt Whitman Archive, www.whitmanarchive.org (1995–).

33. See Walter Benjamin, 'The Work of Art in the Age of Mechanical Reproduction', in *Illuminations* (New York: Houghton Mifflin Harcourt, 1968).

34. Walt Whitman, Ms. Leaf recto (A New Way & The True Way ...), *New York Public Library Digital Collections*, online at <http://digitalcollections.nypl.org/items/510d47df-75fd-a3d9-e040-e00a18064a99> (last accessed 17 June 2015).

35. Walt Whitman, *Prose Works 1892*, ed. Floyd Stovall (New York: New York University Press, 1963), 1:112.

36. N. Katherine Hayles, 'Narrative and Database: Natural Symbionts', *PMLA* 122 (October 2007), p. 1606.

## CHAPTER 2

1. D. F. McKenzie, 'The Sociology of a Text: Orality, Literacy and Print in Early New Zealand', *The Library*, Sixth Series 4 (1984), p. 334.

2. Matthew Kirschenbaum and Sarah Werner, 'Digital Scholarship and Digital Studies: The State of the Discipline', *Book History* 17 (2014), p. 451.

3. Jerome McGann, *A Critique of Modern Textual Criticism* (Chicago: University of Chicago Press, 1983).

4. D. F. McKenzie, 'Printers of the Mind: Some Notes on Bibliographical Theories and Printing House Practices', *Studies in Bibliography* 22 (1969), pp. 1–75.

5. D. F. McKenzie, *Bibliography and the Sociology of Texts*, [1986] The Panizzi Lectures (Cambridge: Cambridge University Press, 1999), pp. 34–5.

6. Alan Galey, '"The Enkindling Reciter": E-books in the Bibliographic Imagination', *Book History* 15 (2012), p. 213.

7. McGann, 'The Socialization of Texts', in *The Textual Condition* (Princeton: Princeton University Press, 1991), pp. 69–83.

8. Leslie Howsam, *Old Books & New Histories: An Orientation to Studies in Book and Print Culture* (Toronto: University of Toronto Press, 2006).

9. Leah Price, *How to do Things with Books in Victorian Britain* (Princeton: Princeton University Press, 2012).

10. James A. Secord, *Victorian Sensation: The Extraordinary Publication, Reception, and Secret Authorship of 'Vestiges of the Natural History of Creation'* (Chicago: University of Chicago Press, 2000).

11. Elizabeth Le Roux, 'Between Complicity and Resistance. University Presses in South Africa' (PhD diss., University of Pretoria, 2012).

12. Claire Squires and Padmini Ray Murray, 'The Digital Publishing Communications Circuit', *Book 2.0* 3:1 (2013), pp. 3–24.

13. Alison Rukavina, 'Social Networks: Modelling the Transnational Distribution and Production of Books', in *Moveable Type, Mobile Nations: Interactions in Transnational Book History, Angles on the English-Speaking World*, vol. 10, ed. Simon Frost and Robert W. Rix (Copenhagen: Museum Tusculanum Press, 2010), pp. 72–83. See also Rukavina, *The Development of the International Book Trade, 1870–1895: Tangled Networks* (Houndmills and New York: Palgrave Macmillan, 2010).

14. Sydney J. Shep, 'Books in Globalised Perspectives', in *The Cambridge Companion to the History of the Book*, ed. L. Howsam (Cambridge: Cambridge University Press, 2014), pp. 53–70.

15. 'FRBR (Functional Requirements for Bibliographic Records)', *International Federation of Library Associations*, online at <http://www.ifla.org/publications/functional-requirements-for-bibliographic-records> (last accessed 17 June 2015).

16. 'Resource Description Framework', *W3C*, online at <http://www.w3.org/RDF>; 'RDA: Resource Description and Access', *Joint Steering Committee for Development of RDA*, online at <http://www.rda-jsc.org/rda.html> (last accessed 17 June 2015).

17. 'FRBRoo Introduction', *International Council of Museums*, online at <http://www.cidoc-crm.org/frbr_inro.html>; 'CIDOC SIG and FRBR-CIDOC CRM Harmonization', *e-Humanities Group*, online at <http://ehumanities.nl/cidoc-sig-and-frbr-cidoc-crm-harmonization> (last accessed 17 June 2015).

18. Frank Upward, 'Modelling the Continuum as Paradigm Shift in Recordkeeping and Archiving Processes, and Beyond: A Personal Reflection', *Records Management Journal* 10:3 (2000), pp. 115–39.

19. N. Katherine Hayles, 'Translating Media: Why We Should Rethink Textuality', *The Yale Journal of Criticism* 16:2 (Fall 2003), p. 277.

20. Roger Chartier and Guglielmo Cavallo, *A History of Reading in the West* (Amherst: University of Massachusetts Press, 1999), p. 4.

21. Paul Eggert, 'Text-encoding, Theories of the Text, and the Work-Site', *Literary and Linguistic Computing* 20:4 (2005), p. 428.

22. N. Katherine Hayles, *How We Think: Digital Media and Contemporary Technogenesis* (Chicago: University of Chicago Press, 2012).

23. Matthew Kirschenbaum, *Mechanisms: New Media and the Forensic Imagination* (Cambridge, MA: MIT Press, 2008).

24. Ibid., p. 11.

25. Johanna Drucker, 'Performative Materiality and Theoretical Approaches to Interface', *Digital Humanities Quarterly* 7:1 (2013), paras 21, 6, online at <http://digitalhumanities.org/dhq/vol/7/1/000143/000103.html> (last accessed 17 June 2015).

26. Ibid., para. 4.

27. Johanna Drucker, 'Humanities Approaches to Graphical Display', *Digital Humanities Quarterly* 5:1 (2011), online at <http://www.digitalhumanities.org/dhq/vol/5/1/000091/000091.html> (last accessed 17 June 2015).

28. Stephen Ramsay, *Reading Machines: Toward an Algorithmic Criticism* (Urbana, Chicago and Springfield: University of Illinois Press, 2011), p. 84.

29. Ibid., p. 85.

30. Matthew Kirschenbaum and Doug Reside, 'Track Changes: Textual Scholarship and the Challenge of the Born Digital', in *The Cambridge Companion to Textual Studies*, ed. Neil Fraistat and Julia Flanders (Cambridge: Cambridge University Press, 2013), pp. 272–3.

HAPTER 3

1. *Oxford English Dictionary*, A.I. 1.
2. *OED* A.II. 4.a.
3. John Durham Peters, *Speaking into the Air: A History of the Idea of Communication* (Chicago: University of Chicago Press, 1999), p. 37.
4. Francis Bacon, *Advancement of Learning* [1605], Project Gutenberg, online at <http://www.gutenberg.org/dirs/etext04/adlr1oh.htm> (last accessed 17 June 2015).
5. Lisa Gitelman, *Paper Knowledge: Toward a Media History of Documents* (Durham, NC: Duke University Press, 2014).
6. David Wellbery, 'Foreword', in Friedrich A. Kittler, *Discourse Networks 1800/1900*, trans. Michael Meteer (Stanford: Stanford University Press, 1990), p. xxxi.
7. Jacques Rancière, *Future of the Image*, trans. Gregory Elliott (London and New York: Verso, 2008), p. 75.
8. Ibid., p. 75.
9. Kittler, *Discourse Networks*, p. 249.
10. Ibid., p. 250.
11. Clement Greenberg, 'Modern Painting', in *20th Century Theories of Art*, ed. James M. Thompson (Ottawa: Carleton University Press, 1999), p. 95.
12. Rancière, *Future of the Image*, pp. 75–6.
13. Kittler, *Discourse Networks*, p. 273.
14. Marshall McLuhan, *Understanding Media: The Extensions of Man* (London and New York: Routledge, 2001), p. 8.
15. Ibid., p. 19.
16. Jay David Bolter and Richard Grusin, *Remediation: Understanding New Media* (Cambridge, MA: MIT Press, 2000), p. 19.
17. Ibid., p. 55.
18. Virginia Woolf, 'The Cinema', in *The Captain's Death Bed and Other Essays* (London: Hogarth Press, 1950), p. 168.
19. F. Scott Fitzgerald, *The Crack-Up with other Pieces and Stories* (London: Penguin, 1965), p. 49.
20. Valentine Cunningham, *British Writers of the Thirties* (Oxford: Oxford University Press, 1988), p. 281.
21. Winifred Holtby, *South Riding* [1936] (London: Random House, 2011), p. 355.
22. George Orwell, *Keep the Aspidistra Flying* [1936] (New York: Harvest, 1956), p. 72.
23. Theodor W. Adorno, *Aesthetic Theory*, ed. Gretel Adorno and Rolf Tiedemann, trans. Robert Hullot-Kentor (London and New York: Continuum, 2004), p. 43.
24. Theodor W. Adorno, *Philosophy of New Music*, trans. Robert Hullot-Kentor (Minneapolis: University of Minnesota Press, 2006), pp. 88–9.
25. André Bazin, *What is Cinema? Vol. 1*, ed. and trans. Hugh Gray (Berkeley and Los Angeles: University of California Press, 1967), p. 62.

26. Ibid., p. 63.

27. Fredric Jameson, *Postmodernism, or, the Cultural Logic of Late Capitalism* (London: Verso, 1990), p. 68.

28. Marshall McLuhan, *Letters of Marshall McLuhan*, ed. Marie Molinaro, Corrine McLuhan and William Toye (Oxford: Oxford University Press, 1987), p. 193.

29. Ron Bush, *The Genesis of Ezra Pound's Cantos* (Princeton: Princeton University Press, 1989), p. 13.

30. Letters from Louis Zukofsky to Ezra Pound, 12 September and 14 December 1931, in *Pound/Zukofsky: Selected Letters of Ezra Pound and Louis Zukofsky* (New York: New Directions, 1987), p. 121.

31. See N. Katherine Hayles, *How We Became Posthuman: Virtual Bodies in Cybernetics, Literature, and Informatics* (Chicago: University of Chicago Press, 1999) and *My Mother Was a Computer: Digital Subjects and Literary Texts* (Chicago: University of Chicago Press, 2005).

32. I hasten to add that these are subjective judgments; but they accord with some canonical statements by Jameson: 'this is essentially a visual culture, wired for sound – but one where the linguistic element [...] is slack and flabby, and not to be made interesting without ingenuity, daring, and keen motivation'. Jameson, *Postmodernism*, p. 299.

33. Karl Marx, 'Economic and Philosophic Manuscripts of 1844', in Robert C. Tucker, ed., *The Marx-Engels Reader*, second edn (New York and London: W. W. Norton & Company, 1972), p. 89.

34. Walter Benjamin, *Illuminations*, ed. Hannah Arendt, trans. Harry Zohn (New York: Shocken Books, 1969), p. 216.

35. Ibid., p. 175.

36. Wellbery, 'Foreword', to *Discourse Networks*, p. xiv.

37. Sara Danius, *The Senses of Modernism: Technology, Perception, and Aesthetics* (Ithaca: Cornell University Press, 2002).

38. Ezra Pound, *Machine Art and Other Writings: The Lost Thought of the Italian Years*, ed. Maria Luisa Ardizzone (Durham, NC: Duke University Press, 1996), p. 77.

39. Danius, *Senses of Modernism*, pp. 191–2.

40. Fredric Jameson, *The Political Unconscious: Narrative as a Socially Symbolic Act* (Ithaca: Cornell University Press, 1981), p. 229.

41. Friedrich Kittler, *Gramophone, Film, Typewriter*, trans. Geoffrey Winthrop-Young and Michael Wutz (Stanford: Stanford University Press, 1999), pp. 15–16.

42. Benjamin, *Illuminations*, pp. 236–7.

43. Jameson, *Postmodernism*, p. 67.

44. André Schiffrin, *Words and Money* (London and New York: Verso, 2010), p. vii.

45. See Stephen J. Kerr, 'Vertical Integration of the Media Industry', 26 April 2013, online at <http://www.bizmark.net/full-length-articles/vertical-integration-of-the-media-industry> (last accessed 17 June 2015).

CHAPTER 4

1. Johann Wolfgang Goethe, *West-östlicher Divan*, [1819] ed. Karl Richter (Munich: Hanser, 1998).
2. Adolf Stern, *Geschichte der Weltliteratur in übersichtlicher Darstellung* (Stuttgart: Rieger, 1888). The title of Theo D'haen's *Routledge Concise History of World Literature* (London and New York: Routledge, 2012) might lead us to think that we had returned to the encyclopaedism of nineteenth-century efforts, but in fact his book is a history of thinking *about* world literature, including chapters on the name 'world literature', on pedagogy, and on translation (pp. 117–32).
3. Fania Oz-Salzberger, 'Translation', in *Encyclopedia of the Enlightenment*, 4 vols., ed. Alan Charles Kors et al. (Oxford: Oxford University Press, 2003), vol. 4, p. 182.
4. Peter France and Kenneth Haynes, eds, *The Oxford History of Literary Translation in English: Volume 4: 1790–1900* (Oxford: Oxford University Press, 2006).
5. Lawrence Venuti, *The Translator's Invisibility: A History of Translation* (New York: Routledge, 1995), p. 40.
6. Shef Rogers, 'Crusoe Among the Maori: Translation and Colonial Acculturation in Victorian New Zealand', *Book History* 1 (1998), pp. 182–95.
7. B. Venkat Mani, 'Breaking Down the Walls: The European Library Project', in *The German Wall: Fallout in Europe*, ed. Marc Silberman (New York: Palgrave Macmillan, 2011), p. 222.
8. Roger Chartier, *The Author's Hand and the Printer's Mind* (Cambridge: Polity, 2014), p. 19.
9. Reinhard Wittman, *Buchmarkt und Lektüre im 18. und 19. Jahrhundert*, Studien und Texte zur Sozialgeschichte der deutschen Literatur 6 (Tübingen: de Gruyter, 1982), p. 119.
10. Christine Haug, 'Buchserien und Anthologien. Wirkungsmächtige Medien zur Etablierung und Durchsetzung von ausländischen Literaturen in Deutschland im 19. Jahrhundert', IASL, online at <http://iasl.uni-muenchen.de/rezensio/liste/Haug3777201162_1215.html> (last accessed 2 July 2014).
11. Itamar Even-Zohar, 'Polysystem Studies', *Poetics Today* 11:1 (1990), p. 47.
12. Gideon Toury, 'Translation, Literary Translation and Pseudotranslation', *Comparative Criticism* 6 (1984), pp. 73–85.
13. Ibid., p. 83.
14. Gideon Toury, 'Enhancing Cultural Changes by Means of Fictitious Translations', in *Translation and Cultural Change: Studies in History, Norms and Image-Projection*, ed. Eva Hung (Amsterdam and Philadelphia: J. Benjamins, 2005), p. 15.
15. Klaus Kaindl and Karlheinz Spitzl, eds, *Transfiction: Research into the Realities of Translation Fiction* (Amsterdam and Philadelphia: J. Benjamins, 2014).
16. Peter Dronke, *The Medieval Lyric* (Cambridge: Brewer, 1996).
17. Susan Bassnett, 'The Translation Turn in Cultural Studies', in *Constructing Cultures: Essays on Literary Translation*, ed. Susan Bassnett and André Lefevere (Clevedon: Multilingual Matters, 1998), p. 127.

18. Christopher Rundle and Kate Sturge, eds, *Translation Under Fascism* (New York: Palgrave Macmillan, 2010).

19. Kate Sturge, '"Flight from the Programme of National Socialism?" Translation in Nazi Germany', in ibid., p. 51.

20. Thomas O. Beebee, *Transmesis: Inside Translation's Black Box* (New York: Palgrave Macmillan, 2013).

21. Douglas Robinson, *Translation and Empire* (Manchester: St. Jerome Press, 1997), p. 31.

22. Stefanie Stockhorst, introduction to *Cultural Transfer Through Translation: The Circulation of Enlightened Thought in Europe by Means of Translation* (Amsterdam and New York: Rodopi, 2010), p. 19.

23. Maria Tymoczko and Edwin Gentzler, eds, *Translation and Power* (Amherst: University of Massachusetts Press, 2002).

24. Vicente Rafael, *The Promise of the Foreign: Nationalism and the Technics of Translation in the Spanish Philippines* (Durham, NC: Duke University Press, 2005).

25. Ibid., p. 144.

26. Gilles Deleuze and Félix Guattari, *A Thousand Plateaus*, trans. Brian Massumi (Minneapolis: University of Minnesota Press, 1987), pp. 105–6.

27. Sean Cotter, *Literary Translation and the Idea of a Minor Romania* (Rochester, NY: University of Rochester Press, 2014), p. 1.

28. Alexander Beecroft, 'World Literature Without a Hyphen: Towards a Typology of Literary Systems', *New Left Review* 54 (2008), pp. 92–8.

29. Franco Moretti, *Graphs, Maps, Trees: Abstract Models for Literary History* (London: Verso, 2005); Matt Erlin and Lynne Tatlock, *Distant Readings: Topologies of German Culture in the Long Nineteenth Century* (Rochester, NY: Camden House, 2014); and *Mapping the Republic of Letters*, online at <http://republicofletters.stanford.edu> (last accessed 27 June 2014).

30. Dan Edelstein and Glauco Mantegari, 'Voltaire's places of publication (1712–1800)', online at <http://republicofletters.stanford.edu/casestudies/voltairepub.html> (last accessed 27 June 2014).

## CHAPTER 5

1. See Dirk Van Hulle, 'The Stuff of Fiction: Digital Editing, Multiple Drafts and the Extended Mind', *Textual Cultures: Texts, Contexts, Interpretation* 8:1 (2013), pp. 23–37.

2. For a rich reflection on the frictions between subject and citizen, see Etienne Balibar, 'Citizen Subject', in *Who Comes After the Subject?* ed. Eduardo Cadava, Peter Connor and Jean-Luc Nancy (New York: Routledge, 1991).

3. Niklas Luhmann, *Die Gesellschaft der Gesellschaft* (Frankfurt am Main: Suhrkamp, 1997).

4. Louis Althusser, 'Idéologie et appareils idéologiques d'Etat' (1970) in *Positions (1964–1975)* (Paris: Editions Sociales, 1976), pp. 67–125.

5. William Wordsworth, 'Preface to *Lyrical Ballads*, 1800', in *Lyrical Ballads, and other poems*, ed. James Butler and Karen Green (Ithaca: Cornell University Press, 1992), pp. 741, 743, 741, 744, 743, 744.

6. Ibid., p. 743.

7. Samuel Taylor Coleridge, *On the Constitution of the Church and State*, ed. John Colmer, vol. 10 of *The Collected Works of Samuel Taylor Coleridge* (Princeton: Princeton University Press, 1976), p. 54.

8. Benedict Anderson, *Imagined Communities: Reflections on the Origin and Spread of Nationalism*, revised and extended edn (London: Verso, 1991 [1983]).

9. Matthew Arnold, *Culture and Anarchy and Other Writings*, ed. Stefan Collini (Cambridge: Cambridge University Press, 1993), p. 110.

10. Robert Browning, 'Porphyria', line 42, in *Selected Poems*, ed. John Woolford, Daniel Karlin and Joseph Phelan (Harlow: Longman, 2010), pp. 70–3.

11. The classic account of the performative confusion complex of sex and gender is Judith Butler, *Gender Trouble: Feminism and the Subversion of Identity* (New York: Routledge, 1990).

12. Browning, 'My Last Duchess', lines 35–6, in *Selected Poems*, pp. 197–200.

13. Browning, 'Porphyria', line 60.

14. D. H. Lawrence, 'Cruelty and Love', lines 64–8, in *The Poems, Volume I*, ed. Christopher Pollnitz, *The Cambridge Edition of the Letters and Works of D. H. Lawrence* (Cambridge: Cambridge University Press, 2013), pp. 13–14.

15. J. M. Coetzee, *Disgrace* (London: Vintage, 2000), p. 160.

16. Gayatri Chakravorty Spivak, *A Critique of Postcolonial Reason: Toward a History of the Vanishing Present* (Cambridge, MA: Harvard University Press, 1999), p. 274.

17. Ibid., p. 287.

18. For the conceptualisation of unreadability in terms of multiple incompatible interpretations of a text, see Paul de Man, *Allegories of Reading: Figural Language in Nietzsche, Rousseau, Rilke and Proust* (New Haven: Yale University Press, 1979).

19. Chinua Achebe, 'An Image of Africa: Racism in Conrad's *Heart of Darkness*', in *The Norton Anthology of Theory and Criticism*, gen. ed. Vincent B. Leitch (New York: Norton, 2001), pp. 1781–94, 1788, 1789.

20. Joseph Conrad, *Youth, Heart of Darkness, The End of the Tether* (London: Dent, 1961), pp. 135–6.

21. Achebe, 'An Image of Africa', p. 1787.

22. Conrad, *Heart of Darkness*, pp. 136–7.

23. The classic account is Simon Baron-Cohen, *Mindblindness: An Essay on Autism and Theory of Mind* (Cambridge, MA: MIT Press, 1997).

24. See Lisa Zunshine, *Why We Read Fiction: Theory of Mind and the Novel* (Columbus: Ohio State University Press, 2006).

25. Vladimir Propp, *Morphology of the Folktale*, [1928] trans. Laurence Scott, rev. Louis A. Wagner (Austin: University of Texas Press, 1968).

26. Gérard Genette, 'Discours du récit', in *Figures III* (Paris: Seuil, 1972).

27. Ian Hacking, 'How We Have Been Learning to Talk About Autism: A Role for Stories' *Metaphilosophy* 40:3–4 (2009), pp. 499–516.

28. A fine example of such reading is Stuart Murray, 'From Virginia's Sister to Friday's Silence: Presence, Metaphor, and the Persistence of Disability in Contemporary Writing', *Journal of Literary & Cultural Disability Studies* 6:3 (2012), pp. 241–58.

29. David Comer Kidd and Emanuele Castano, 'Reading Literary Fiction Improves Theory of Mind', *Science* 342 (2013), pp. 377–80; Gregory S. Berns, Kristina Blaine, Michael J. Prietula and Brandon E. Pye, 'Short- and Long-Term Effects of a Novel on Connectivity in the Brain', *Brain Connectivity* 3:6 (2013), pp. 590–600.

## CHAPTER 6

1. For a detailed account of Western philosophy's disdain for the lower senses, see Carolyn Kormeyer, *Making Sense of Taste* (Ithaca: Cornell University Press, 1999), pp. 38–67.

2. William Wordsworth, *The Prelude: The 1805 Text* (Oxford: Oxford University Press, 1970), p. 210.

3. Georg Wilhelm Friedrich Hegel, *Introductory Lectures on Aesthetics* (Harmondsworth: Penguin, 1993), p. 43.

4. Constance Classen, *The Colour of Angels: Cosmology, Gender and the Aesthetic Imagination* (London: Routledge, 1998), p. 2.

5. Carolyn Korsmeyer, *Making Sense of Taste: Food and Philosophy* (Ithaca: Cornell University Press, 1999), p. 19.

6. Ignatius of Loyola, *Ignatius of Loyola: The Spiritual Exercises and Selected Works*, ed. and trans. George E. Ganss (Malwah, NJ: Paulist Press, 1991).

7. Gertrude Stein, *Look at Me Now and Here I Am: Writings and Lectures 1909–45* (London: Penguin, 1967), p. 179.

8. Christopher J. Knight, 'Gertrude Stein, Tender Buttons, and the Premises of Classicalism', *Modern Language Studies* 21:3 (1991), pp. 35–47.

9. Ibid., p. 36.

10. Ibid., p. 36.

11. Ibid., p. 35.

12. Ibid., p. 46.

13. Denise Gigante, *Taste: A Literary History* (New Haven: Yale University Press, 2005), p. 21.

14. Emile Zola, *The Belly of Paris* (1873), Project Gutenberg, online at <http://www.gutenberg.org/files/5744/5744-h/5744-h.htm> (last accessed 19 June 2015).

15. Aurel Kolnai, *On Disgust*, trans. Barry Smith and Carolyn Korsmeyer (Chicago: Open Court, 2004), pp. 52–62. See also Susan Miller, *Disgust: The Gatekeeper Emotion* (Hillsdale, NJ: The Analytic Press, 2004).

16. Emile Zola, *The Fat and the Thin*, trans. Ernest Alfred Vizetelly, online at <http://www.gutenberg.org/files/5744/5744-h/5744-h.htm> (last accessed 19 June 2015).

17. Jean-Paul Sartre, *La nausée* (Paris: Gallimard, 1938), p. 180. Author's translation.

18. Joris-Karl Huysmans, *Against the Grain* (1884), Project Gutenberg, trans. John Howard, online at <http://www.gutenberg.org/files/12341/12341-h/12341-h.htm> (last accessed 19 June 2015).

19. Ibid.

20. Francis Ponge, *Ponge: Oeuvres complètes*, vol. 1 (Paris: Gallimard, 1999), p. 807.

21. Mikhail Bakhtin, *Rabelais and his World* (Bloomington: Indiana University Press, 2009), p. 19.

22. Ibid., p. 26.

23. Ibid., p. 26.

24. Alain Corbin, *Le miasme et la jonquille: l'odorat et l'imaginaire social aux XVIIIe et XIXe siècles* (Paris: Flammarion, 1981), p. 58.

25. Peter Stallybrass and Allon White, *The Politics and Poetics of Transgression* (Ithaca: Cornell University Press, 1986), p. 193.

26. Cited in Constance Classen, David Howes and Anthony Synnott, *Aroma: The Cultural History of Smell* (London: Routledge, 1994), p. 176.

27. Ibid., p. 176.

28. William Ian Miller, *The Anatomy of Disgust* (Cambridge, MA: Harvard University Press, 1997), p. 67.

29. Carolyn Korsmeyer, *Making Sense of Taste: Food and Philosophy* (Ithaca: Cornell University Press, 1999), pp. 19, 57.

30. Herman Parret, 'From the *Enquiry* (1757) to the Fourth *Kritisches Wäldchen* (1769), Burke and Herder on the Division of the Senses', in *The Science of Sensibility: Reading Burke's Philosophical Enquiry*, ed. Michael Deckard and Koen Vermeir (Berlin: Springer, 2009), p. 104.

31. Milena Marinkova, *Michael Ondaatje: Haptic Aesthetics and Micropolitical Writing* (London: Continuum, 2011), p. 3.

32. Laura Marks, *The Skin of Film: Intercultural Cinema, Embodiment, and the Senses* (Durham, NC: Duke University Press, 2000), p. xi.

33. William Cohen, *Embodied: Victorian Literature and the Senses* (Minneapolis: University of Minnesota Press, 2008), p. 17.

34. Ibid., p. 13.

35. Ibid., p. 14.

36. Ibid., p. 114.

37. Helen Keller, *The Story of My Life* (New York: Dover, 1996), p. 12.

38. Ibid., p. 12.

39. Winfried Menninghaus, *Disgust: Theory and History of a Strong Sensation*, trans. Howard Eiland and Joel Golb (Albany: SUNY Press, 2003).

40. Eve Sedgwick, *Touching Feeling: Affect, Pedagogy, Performativity* (Durham, NC: Duke University Press, 2003).

## CHAPTER 7

1. Jacques Derrida, *The Animal That Therefore I Am*, ed. Marie-Louise Mallet, trans. David Wills (New York: Fordham University Press, 2008), p. 34.

2. Ibid., p. 34.
3. See Robert McKay's recent discussion of texts like Marion Scholtmeijer's *Animal Victims in Modern Fiction* (1993) and Margot Norris' *Beasts of the Modern Imagination* (1985) that 'helped set the stage for the intellectual vibrancy and ethical scope of later contributions to literary animal studies' (p. 637). Robert McKay, 'What Kind of Literary Animal Studies Do We Want, or Need?', *Modern Fiction Studies. Special Issue: Animal Worlds in Modern Fiction* 60:3 (2014), pp. 636–44.
4. Kari Weil, whose work I discuss in some detail later in this chapter, has an entire chapter in *Thinking Animals* called 'Seeing Animals'. Kari Weil, *Thinking Animals: Why Animal Studies Now?* (New York: Columbia University Press, 2012).
5. See Derrida, *The Animal That Therefore I Am*.
6. Philip Armstrong addresses this tendency in the introduction to his landmark book, *What Animals Mean in the Fiction of Modernity* (London: Routledge, 2008).
7. David Clark makes the claim in his discussion of animals in theory that we must turn towards the 'enormity of all that has yet to be said and done regarding animals, even and especially if we cannot see in advance what those words and deeds will look like, much less the day in which all will be said and done' (p. 3). David Clark, 'Animals … In Theory: Nine Inquiries in Human and Nonhuman Life', *CR: The New Centennial Review* 11:2 (Fall 2012), pp. 1–16.
8. I reiterate this agreement with Wolfe in my essay 'Disciplinary Becomings: Horizons of Knowledge in Animal Studies', *Hypatia: A Journal of Feminist Philosophy. Special Issue: 'Animal Others'* 27:3 (July, 2012), pp. 510–15. For Wolfe's argument see Cary Wolfe, *What is Posthumanism?* (Minneapolis: University of Minnesota Press, 2010).
9. See chapter 1 in Carrie Rohman, *Stalking the Subject: Modernism and the Animal* (New York: Columbia University Press, 2009), and Dawn McCance, *Critical Animal Studies: An Introduction* (Albany: State University of New York Press, 2013).
10. See Boggs' thoughtful discussion of these terms, and her useful suggestion that critics ought to keep in mind the limitations of the term 'animality', which tends to make human concerns and perspectives central. Colleen Glenney Boggs, *Animalia Americana: Animal Representations and Biopolitical Subjectivity* (New York: Columbia University Press, 2013), p. 8.
11. See Cary Wolfe, *Animal Rites: American Culture, the Discourse of Species, and Posthumanist Theory* (Chicago: University of Chicago Press, 2003), especially chapter 1. Matthew Calarco also addresses this fundamental problem with 'rights' discourses in *Zoographies: The Question of the Animal from Heidegger to Derrida* (New York: Columbia University Press, 2008).
12. See Traci Warkentin, 'Must Every Animal Studies Scholar Be Vegan?', *Hypatia: A Journal of Feminist Philosophy. Special Issue: 'Animal Others'* 27:3 (2012), pp. 499–504. The six symposium essays in this issue are dedicated to questions about ethics, feminism, theory and activism in relation to animal studies.
13. See Rohman, 'Disciplinary Becomings', and Clark, 'Animals … in Theory'.

14. Wolfe, *Animal Rites*, p. 5.

15. Clark, 'Animals ... In Theory', p. 2.

16. Ibid., p. 8.

17. Marianne DeKoven, 'Guest Column: Why Animals Now?' *PMLA* 124:2 (2009), p. 363.

18. McKay, 'What Kind of Literary Animal Studies'.

19. Critics' understanding of animal 'rendering' is indebted to the work of Nicole Shukin. See *Animal Capital: Rendering Life in Biopolitical Times* (Minneapolis: University of Minnesota Press, 2009).

20. See Susan McHugh's discussion of animals and signifying chains in the introduction to her book *Animal Stories: Narrating Across Species Lines* (Minnesota: University of Minnesota Press, 2011).

21. In this regard, see McHugh, *Animal Stories*; Rohman, *Stalking the Subject*; Weil, *Thinking Animals*.

22. Weil, *Thinking Animals*, p. 7.

23. Ibid., p. 6.

24. Ibid., p. 6.

25. Ibid., p. 7.

26. Alice Kuzniar, *Melancholia's Dog* (Chicago: University of Chicago Press, 2006), p. 28.

27. Ibid., p. 123.

28. Ibid., p. 122.

29. Derek Ryan, *Virginia Woolf and the Materiality of Theory: Sex, Animal, Life* (Edinburgh: Edinburgh University Press, 2013), p. 141.

30. See also David Herman's recent work on *Flush* that makes use of Uexküll's concept of the *Umwelt*, or a lived phenomenal world that is specific to a given organism. Herman shows that in *Flush*, Woolf refuses a 'hierarchy of kinds of minds, in which modes of human consciousness take precedence over nonhuman modes' and instead 'works in a more horizontal way, suggesting how human experiences unfold in the context of a wider ecology of minds'. David Herman, 'Modernist Life Writing and Nonhuman Lives: Ecologies of Experience in Virginia Woolf's *Flush*', *Modern Fiction Studies* 59:3 (2013), p. 558.

31. Karalyn Kendall-Morwick, 'Mongrel Fiction: Canine *Bildung* and the Feminist Critique of Anthropocentrism in Virginia Woolf's *Flush*', *Modern Fiction Studies. Special Issue: Animal Worlds in Modern Fiction*, 60:3 (2014), p. 523.

32. Many of the texts I examine in *Stalking the Subject* demonstrate how human subjectivity is precarious at best, and how this precariousness is made especially evident through the 'threat' of animality, both from within and without.

33. Wolfe, *What is Posthumanism?*, p. xxv.

34. Clark, 'Animals ... In Theory', p. 8.

35. McHugh, *Animal Stories*, p. 2.

36. Ibid., p. 2. While beyond the scope of this chapter, it should be noted that 'life' itself is increasingly more difficult to define, and moreover, the attentions to non-human 'action' in thinkers such as Latour and Bennett make it all the more necessary to identify the ethical stakes of 'who' or 'what' is acting. For a

useful treatment of these questions see Cary Wolfe, *Before the Law: Humans and Other Animals in a Biopolitical Frame* (Chicago: University of Chicago Press, 2013).

37. McHugh, *Animal Stories*, p. 130.
38. Ibid., p. 130.
39. Lauren Berlant and Michael Warner, 'Sex in Public', *Critical Inquiry* 24:2 (1998), pp. 547–66.
40. McHugh, *Animal Stories*, p. 133.
41. Ibid., p. 133.
42. David Herman, 'Narratology Beyond the Human', *DIEGESIS. Interdisziplinäres E-Journal für Erzählforschung / Interdisciplinary E-Journal for Narrative Research* 3:2 (2014), pp. 131–43.
43. Eduardo Kohn, 'How Dogs Dream: Amazonian Natures and the Politics of Transspecies Engagement', *American Ethnologist* 34:1 (2007), pp. 3–24. Quoted in Herman, 'Modernist Life Writing and Nonhuman Lives', p. 558.
44. Herman, 'Narratology Beyond the Human', p. 133.
45. There is some debate about the usefulness of Agamben's work in recent animal studies. While his notion of the 'anthropological machine' by which we distinguish humans from animals has provided some critical traction, for instance, many find a problematic 'flattening' of the category of the animal in Agamben's work. For a useful summary of this debate, see Wolfe, *Before the Law*, especially section 2.
46. Boggs, *Animalia Americana*, p. 14.
47. Ibid., p. 16.
48. Ibid., p. 19.
49. Laura Brown, *Homeless Dogs and Melancholy Apes: Humans and Other Animals in the Modern Literary Imagination* (Ithaca: Cornell University Press, 2010), p. ix. Quoted in Boggs, *Animalia Americana*, p. 20.
50. Ibid., p. 138.
51. Ibid., p. 141.
52. Ibid., p. 147.
53. Ibid., p. 152.
54. Ibid., p. 151.
55. Ibid., p. 148.
56. Akira Mizuta Lippit, 'Magnetic Animal: Derrida, Wildlife, Animetaphor', *MLN* 113:5 (1998), p. 1113. Quoted in Boggs, *Animalia Americana*, p. 151.
57. Ibid., p. 151.
58. Cary Wolfe, 'Neither Beast nor Sovereign: Wallace Stevens' Birds', in *Animality and Sovereignty: Reading Derrida's Final Seminars*, ed. Ted Toadvine and David Alexander Craig (forthcoming).
59. Wolfe, *Before the Law*, p. 63.
60. See Donna Haraway, *The Companion Species Manifesto: Dogs, People, and Significant Otherness* (Chicago: Prickly Paradigm Press, 2003).
61. McHugh, *Animal Stories*, p. 20.
62. Jason Skeet's compact discussion of becoming usefully emphasises the

'intensity' that 'is the line between', as in Gregor's experience in Kafka's *The Metamorphosis*. See Jason Skeet, 'Becoming', in *Understanding Deleuze, Understanding Modernism*, ed. Paul Ardoin, S. E. Gontarski and Laci Mattison (New York: Bloomsbury, 2014), pp. 253–4.

63. Gilles Deleuze and Félix Guattari, *A Thousand Plateaus: Capitalism and Schizophrenia*, trans. Brian Massumi (Minneapolis: University of Minnesota Press, 1987), p. 279.

64. See Carrie Rohman, 'Dancing with Deleuze: Modernism and the Imperceptible Animal', in *Understanding Deleuze, Understanding Modernism*, ed. Ardoin, Gontarski and Mattison, pp. 169–81.

65. Carolynn Van Dyke, ed., *Rethinking Chaucerian Beasts* (New York: Palgrave MacMillan, 2012), p. 2.

66. Christopher Roman, 'Contemplating Finitude: Animals in *The Book of the Duchess*', in *Rethinking Chaucerian Beasts*, ed. Van Dyke, p. 144.

67. Derrida, *The Animal That Therefore I Am*, quoted in ibid., p. 144.

68. Roman, 'Contemplating Finitude', p. 150.

69. Ibid., p. 152.

70. Ibid., p. 153.

71. Carrie Rohman, 'No Higher Life: Bio-aesthetics in J. M. Coetzee's *Disgrace*', *Modern Fiction Studies. Special Issue: Animal Worlds in Modern Fiction* 60:3 (2014), pp. 562–78.

72. Ibid., p. 577.

73. Ibid., p. 577.

74. See for instance Cary Wolfe's introduction in *Zoontologies: The Question of the Animal* (Minnesota: University of Minnesota Press, 2003).

75. Clark, 'Animals ... In Theory', p. 10.

76. Ibid., p. 5.

## CHAPTER 8

1. Henry Gee, *In Search of Deep Time: Beyond the Fossil Record to a New History of Life* (New York: Free Press, 1999).

2. There are many places to look for arguments in support of this. See for instance Timothy Morton, 'She Stood in Tears Amid the Alien Corn: Thinking Through Agrilogistics', *diacritics* 41:3 (2014), pp. 90–113.

3. Sigmund Freud, *The Ego and the Id*, trans. Joan Riviere, revised and ed. James Strachey, intro. Peter Gay (New York: Norton, 1989), p. 24.

4. Shelley, *A Defence of Poetry* (1840), Project Gutenburg, online at <http://www.gutenberg.org/files/5428/5428-h/5428-h.htm> (last accessed 22 June 2015).

5. Harold Bloom, *The Anxiety of Influence: A Theory of Poetry* (Oxford: Oxford University Press, 1997), p. 70.

6. Jacques Derrida, 'Hostipitality', trans. Barry Stocker with Forbes Matlock, *Angelaki* 5:3 (2000), pp. 3–18.

7. Shelley, *Defence*, unpag.

8. Karl Marx, 'The Eighteenth Brumaire of Louis Bonaparte', in *Selected Writings*, ed. David McLellan (Oxford: Oxford University Press, 1987), pp. 300–25 (p. 302).

9. Andrew Hamilton, 'Falling into the Singularity of a Black Hole', online at <http://casa.colorado.edu/~ajsh/singularity.html> (last accessed 22 June 2015).

10. See Jean-Paul Sartre, *Being and Nothingness: An Essay on Phenomenological Ontology*, trans. and ed. Hazel Barnes (New York: the Philosophical Library, 1984), pp. 61–2.

11. Samuel Beckett, 'Letter to Hans Naumann, February 17, 1954', in *The Letters of Samuel Beckett: Volume 2, 1941–1956*, ed. George Craig, Martha Dow Fehsenfeld and Lois More Overbeck (Cambridge: Cambridge University Press, 2011), p. 462.

## CHAPTER 9

1. These lectures have a complicated publication history. References here are to Georg Friedrich Wilhelm Hegel, *The Philosophy of History*, trans. and intro. J. Sibree, Preface Charles Hegel, intro. C. J. Friedrich (Mineola, NY: Dover, 2014).

2. Ibid., pp. 18–20.

3. Ibid., pp. 38–9.

4. Ibid., p. 33.

5. Ibid., p. 53.

6. Ibid., p. 81.

7. Aristotle, *Politics*, trans. Ernest Barker, rev. with intro. and notes by R. F. Stalley (Oxford and New York: Oxford University Press, 1995).

8. Ibid., 1275a19.

9. Ibid., 1301a25.

10. Ibid., 1301b26.

11. H. N. Brailsford, *The Russian Workers' Republic* (London: George, Allen and Unwin, 1921), pp. 52–3.

12. Leon Trotsky, *Literature and Revolution*, trans. Rose Strunsky (London: George Allen and Unwin, 1925), p. 14.

13. Theodor W. Adorno and Max Horkheimer, *Dialectic of Enlightenment*, trans. John Cummings (London and New York: Verso, 1986), p. 3.

14. Jean-Luc Nancy, *La Communauté désœuvrée* (Paris: Christian Bourgois, 1990), p. 242. All translations in this chapter are mine.

15. Ibid., p. 247.

16. Ibid., p. 240.

17. Ibid., pp. 257–8.

18. Giorgio Agamben, *Homo Sacer: Il potere sovrano e la nuda vita* (Torino: Einaudi, 1995), p. 4.

19. Ibid., p. 15.

20. Ibid., pp. 135, 202.

21. See for example Alain Badiou, *Manifeste pour la philosophie* (Paris: Seuil, 1989), p. 10.

22. Alain Badiou, *L'Hypothèse communiste* (Paris: Lignes, 2009), pp. 189–90.

23. See Badiou's claim to this effect in Alain Badiou, *Abrégé de métapolitique* (Paris: Seuil, 1998), pp. 129–38.

24. 'The Janus-Face of Politicized Art: Jacques Rancière in Interview with Gabriel Rockhill', in Jacques Rancière, *The Politics of Aesthetics: The Distribution of the Sensible*, trans. and intro. Gabriel Rockhill (London and New York: Continuum, 2004), p. 51.

25. Ibid., p. 63.

26. Jacques Rancière, *Politique de la littérature* (Paris: Galiliée, 2007), pp. 11–24.

27. Jacques Rancière, *Malaise dans l'esthétique* (Paris: Galilée, 2004), p. 37.

28. Jacques Rancière, *Le maître ignorant* (Paris: Fayard, 1987), p. 120.

## CHAPTER 10

1. Gotthold Ephraim Lessing, *Laocoön: An Essay on the Limits of Painting and Poetry*, trans. Edward Allen McCormick (Indianapolis and New York: The Library of Liberal Arts, 1962), p. 78.

2. Ibid., p. 79.

3. For a summary of the first part of Kant's *Critique of Pure Reason*, the 'Transcendental Aesthetic', see Immanuel Kant, *Critique of Pure Reason*, ed. Paul Guyer and Allen W. Wood (Cambridge: Cambridge University Press, 1998), pp. 153–85.

4. Martin Heidegger, *Kant and the Problem of Metaphysics*, trans. Richard Taft (Bloomington: Indiana University Press, 1990), p. 134.

5. Ibid., p. 134.

6. Wilhelm Dilthey, *Poetry and Experience*, ed. Rudolf A. Makkreel and Frithjof Rodi (Princeton: Princeton University Press, 1985), p. 36.

7. Ibid., p. 35.

8. Ibid., p. 164.

9. In *Selected Essays of Erich Auerbach: Time, History, and Literature*, ed. James I. Porter, trans. Jane O. Newman (Princeton: Princeton University Press, 2014), pp. 65–113.

10. Ibid., p. 104.

11. Ibid., p. 109.

12. Hayden White, 'Auerbach's Literary History: Figural Causation and Modernist Historicism', in *Figural Realism: Studies in the Mimesis Effect* (Baltimore: Johns Hopkins University Press, 1999), pp. 87–100.

13. Ibid., p. 92.

14. Martin Heidegger, *Being and Time*, trans. John Macquarrie and Edward Robinson (New York: Harper and Row, 1962); Hans-Georg Gadamer, *Truth and Method*, trans. Garrett Barden and John Cumming (New York: Crossroad Publishing, 1975).

15. Gadamer, *Truth and Method*, p. 144.

16. Paul Ricoeur, *Time and Narrative*, vol. 3, trans. Kathleen Blamey and David Pellauer (Chicago: University of Chicago Press, 1988), p. 221.

17. Gadamer, *Truth and Method*, p. 304.

18. Ibid., p. 304.
19. Paul Ricoeur, *Time and Narrative*, vol. 1, trans. Kathleen McLaughlin and David Pellauer (Chicago: University of Chicago Press, 1984), p. 51.
20. Roland Barthes, 'Myth Today', in *Mythologies*, trans. Annette Lavers (New York: Hill and Wang, 1972), p. 112.
21. Gérard Genette, *Narrative Discourse: An Essay in Method*, trans. Jane E. Lewin (Ithaca: Cornell University Press, 1980).
22. Peter Brooks, *Reading for the Plot: Design and Intention in Narrative* (Cambridge, MA: Harvard University Press, 1984).
23. Fredric Jameson, *The Political Unconscious: Narrative as a Socially Symbolic Act* (Ithaca: Cornell University Press, 1982).
24. Walter Benjamin, 'The Storyteller', in *Illuminations*, ed. Hannah Arendt, trans. Harry Zohn (New York: Schocken, 1969), pp. 83–110.
25. M. M. Bakhtin, *The Dialogic Imagination: Four Essays*, ed. Michael Holquist, trans. Caryl Emerson and Michael Holquist (Austin: University of Texas Press, 1981), p. 84.
26. Ibid., p. 84.
27. Ibid., p. 85.
28. Walter Benjamin, *The Arcades Project*, trans. Howard Eiland and Kevin McLaughlin (Cambridge, MA: The Belknap Press of Harvard University Press, 1999), p. 456.
29. Ibid., p. 462.
30. Ibid., p. 463.
31. Walter Benjamin, 'Literary History and the Study of Literature', trans. Rodney Livingstone, in *Selected Writings*, vol. 2, ed. Michael W. Jennings, Howard Eiland and Gary Smith (Cambridge, MA: The Belknap Press of Harvard University Press, 1999), p. 464.
32. Paul De Man, 'Literary History and Literary Modernity', in *Blindness and Insight: Essays in the Rhetoric of Contemporary Criticism*, second revised edn (Minneapolis: University of Minnesota Press, 1983), p. 164.
33. Ibid., p. 164.
34. Ibid., p. 165.
35. Ibid., p. 165.
36. Gilles Deleuze, *Cinema 2: The Time-Image*, trans. Hugh Tomlinson and Robert Galeta (Minneapolis: University of Minnesota Press, 1989).
37. Tyrus Miller, *Time-Images: Alternative Temporalities in Twentieth-Century Theory, Literature, and Art* (Newcastle: Cambridge Scholars, 2009), p. 3.

## CHAPTER 11

1. John Milton, 'Lycidas', in *The Complete Poems of John Milton* (New York: Digireads, 2009), p. 66.
2. Wyndham Lewis, *The Demon of Progress in the Arts* (London: Methuen, 1954), p. 64.

3. Joshua Reynolds, 'Notes on *The Art of Painting*', note xii, verse 109, in *The Literary Works of Sir Joshua Reynolds*, 2 vols (London, 1886), p. 307. Quoted in Katharine Everett Gilbert and Helmut Kuhn, *A History of Esthetics*, rev. edn (Bloomington: Indiana University Press, 1954), p. 218.

4. Stefanie Buchenau, *The Founding of Aesthetics in the German Enlightenment: The Art of Invention and the Invention of Art* (Cambridge: Cambridge University Press, 2013), p. 226.

5. Ibid., p. 227.

6. Wallace Stevens, *The Necessary Angel: Essays on Reality and the Imagination* (New York: Knopf, 1951), p. 175.

7. Wallace Stevens, 'Of Modern Poetry', in *Parts of a World* (New York: Knopf, 1942), p. 105.

8. Arthur Rimbaud, *Complete Works, Selected Letters*, trans. Wallace Fowlie (Chicago: University of Chicago Press, 1966), p. 307.

9. Ibid., p. 309.

10. Ezra Pound, *Make It New, Essays by Ezra Pound* (London: Faber and Faber, 1934).

11. Hugo Ball, *Flight Out of Time: A Dada Diary*, ed. John Elderfield, trans. Ann Raimes (New York: Viking, 1974), p. 56.

12. Victor Shklovsky, 'Art as Technique', in *Russian Formalist Criticism: Four Essays*, trans. Lee T. Lemon and Marion J. Reis (Lincoln: University of Nebraska Press, 1965), p. 22.

13. Ibid., p. 13.

14. Bertolt Brecht, *Brecht on Theatre: The Development of an Aesthetic*, ed. and trans. John Willett (New York: Hill and Wang, 1964), p. 144.

15. Armand Mattelart, *The Invention of Communication*, trans. Susan Emanuel (Minneapolis: University of Minnesota Press, 1996), p. xiv.

16. Hesiod, *The Homeric Hymns and Homerica*, rev. ed., trans. Hugh G. Evelyn-White (Cambridge, MA: Harvard University Press, 1936), p. 81.

17. D. H. Lawrence, *The Complete Poems*, ed. Vivian de Sola Pinto and Warren Roberts (New York: Viking, 1971), p. 250.

18. Tristan Tzara, 'Manifesto on Feeble Love and Bitter Love', trans. Ralph Manheim, in *The Dada Painters and Poets: An Anthology*, ed. Robert Motherwell (New York: Wittenborn, Schultz, 1951), p. 92.

19. Kenneth Goldmith, *Uncreative Writing: Managing Language in the Digital Age* (New York: Columbia University Press, 2011), p. 1.

20. Wassily Kandinsky, *Complete Writings on Art*, ed. Kenneth C. Lindsay and Peter Vergo (New York: Da Capo, 1994), p. 832.

21. Lázló Moholy-Nagy, 'Sharp or Fuzzy?', in *Moholy-Nagy*, ed. Krisztina Passuth (New York: Thames and Hudson, 1985), pp. 308–9.

22. Richard Huelsenbeck, 'En Avant Dada', trans. Ralph Manheim in *The Dada Painters and Poets: An Anthology*, ed. Robert Motherwell (New York: Wittenborn, Schultz, 1951), p. 43.

23. Richard Huelsenbeck, 'Dada Lives', trans. Eugene Jolas, *Transition* 25 (1936), p. 80.

24. Theodor W. Adorno, *Aesthetic Theory*, trans. Robert Hullot-Kentor (Minneapolis: University of Minnesota Press, 1997), p. 2.

25. Karl Wilhelm Friedrich Schlegel, *Literary Notebooks 1797–1801*, ed. Hans Eichner (Toronto: University of Toronto Press, 1957), p. 116.

26. Stéphane Mallarmé, *Le 'Livre' de Mallarmé: Premières Recherches sur des Documents Inédits*, ed. Jacques Scherer (Paris: Gallimard, 1957), p. 286.

27. Umberto Eco, *The Open Work*, trans. Anna Cancogni (Cambridge, MA: Harvard University Press, 1989).

28. Ibid., p. 7.

29. Darren Wershler-Henry, *The Tapeworm Foundry, andor The Dangerous Prevalence of Imagination* (Toronto: Anansi, 2000).

30. Robert Duncan, *Collected Essays and Other Prose*, ed. James Maynard (Berkeley: University of California Press, 2014), p. 99.

31. Michel de Certeau, *The Practice of Everyday Life*, trans. Steven Rendall (Berkeley: University of California Press, 1984), p. 23.

32. Ibid., p. 28.

33. Ibid., p. 30.

34. Ibid., p. 38.

## CHAPTER 12

1. Prosper Lissagaray, *Histoire de la Commune de Paris* (Brussels: Librairie Contemporaine de Henri Kistemaeckers, 1876).

2. For an excellent overview see Martin Jay, 'Historicism and the Event', in *Against the Grain: Jewish Intellectuals in Hard Times*, ed. E. Mendelsohn, S. Hoffman and R. Cohen (New York: Berghahn, 2013), pp. 143–67.

3. Ibid., p. 156.

4. Alain Badiou, *Being and Event*, trans. Oliver Feltham (London: Continuum, 2007), p. 175.

5. Paul Ricoeur, *Time and Narrative*, vol. 1, trans. Kathleen McLaughlin and David Pellauer (Chicago: University of Chicago Press, 1990), p. 96.

6. Ibid., p. 96.

7. Ibid., p. 96.

8. Ibid., pp. 96–7.

9. Ibid., p. 97.

10. Ibid., p. 97.

11. Ibid., p. 97.

12. Terry Eagleton, *The Event of Literature* (New Haven, CT: Yale University Press, 2012), p. 200.

13. Ricoeur, *Time and Narrative*, vol. 1, p. 207.

14. Fernand Braudel, *On History*, trans. Sarah Matthews (Chicago: University of Chicago Press, 1982), pp. 3–4.

15. Fernand Braudel, *The Mediterranean and the Mediterranean World in the Age of Phillip II*, trans. S. Reynolds (London: Collins, 1972).

16. Braudel, *On History*, p. 3.

17. For an interesting discussion of Braudel's work see Fredric Jameson, *Valences of the Dialectic* (London: Verso, 2009), pp. 532–43.

18. Ricoeur, *Time and Narrative*, vol. 1, p. 107.

19. Ibid., p. 217. 'Time becomes human time', Ricoeur suggests, 'to the extent [...] that it is organised after the manner of narrative; narrative, in turn, is meaningful to the extent that it portrays the feature of human experience' (ibid., p. 3).

20. Ibid., p. 224.

21. For a fuller version of this reading see Scott McCracken, 'All Bets Are Off: Woolf, Benjamin, and the Problem of the Future in Jacob's Room', *Le Tour Critique* 2 (2013), pp. 31–43.

22. Virginia Woolf, *Jacob's Room* (Oxford and New York: Oxford University Press, 1999), p. 246.

23. Ibid., p. 247.

24. François Hartog, *Régimes d'historicité: Presentisme et expériences du temps* (Paris: Éditions du Seuil, 2012), p. 57.

25. Ibid., p. 57.

26. Cited in ibid., p. 58.

27. Walter Benjamin, 'On the Concept of History', in *Selected Writings, Volume 4: 1938–40*, ed. Howard Eiland and Michael W. Jennings, trans. Edmund Jephcott et al. (Cambridge, MA and London: The Belknap Press of Harvard University Press, 2003), p. 392.

28. Ernst Bloch, *The Principle of Hope*, 3 vols. (Oxford: Blackwell, 1986).

29. Nigerian independence was won two years after the novel's publication in 1960.

30. The Igbo are one of the three largest ethnic groups in modern Nigeria and live in the south-east of the country, where Achebe was brought up.

31. Chinua Achebe, *Things Fall Apart* (Oxford: Heinemann, 1986), pp. 147–8.

32. Benjamin, 'On the Concept of History', p. 391.

33. Ibid., p. 391.

34. Ibid., p. 395.

35. Ibid., p. 395.

36. Ibid., p. 396.

37. Literally, those without documents.

38. Ibid., p. 390.

39. Originally published in the April 1913 issue of *Poetry Magazine*.

40. 'Un événement est la création de nouvelles possibilités. Il se situe, non pas simplement au niveau des possibles objectifs, mais à celui de la possibilité des possibles.' Alain Badiou, *Circonstances 5: L'Hypothèse Communiste* (Paris: Lignes et Manifeste, 2009), p. 191.

41. Alain Badiou, *The Rebirth of History: Times of Riots and Uprisings*, trans. Gregory Elliot (London: Verso, 2012), p. 53.

42. Eagleton, *The Event of Literature*, p. 136.

43. Ibid., pp. 188–9.

44. A phrase Eagleton borrows from Fredric Jameson, *The Political Unconscious: Narrative as Socially Symbolic Act* (London: Methuen, 1981).

45. Rita Felski, 'Modernist Studies and Cultural Studies: Reflections on Method', *Modernism/modernity* 10:3 (2003), p. 511.
46. Derek Attridge, *The Singularity of Literature* (London: Routledge, 2004), p. 59.
47. Rita Felski, 'Context Stinks', *New Literary History* 42:4 (2011), pp. 573–91.
48. Jameson, *The Political Unconscious*, p. 35.

## CHAPTER 13

1. June Edmunds and Bryan S. Turner, 'Global Generations: Social Change in the Twentieth Century', *British Journal of Sociology* 56:4 (2005), p. 560.
2. Marius Hentea, 'The Problem of Literary Generations: Origins and Limitations', *Comparative Literature Studies* 50:4 (2013), p. 567.
3. David I. Kertzer, 'Generation as a Sociological Problem', *Annual Review of Sociology* 9 (1983), p. 125.
4. See for example Julian Hanna, 'Blasting After *Blast*: Wyndham Lewis' Late Manifestos', *Journal of Modern Literature* 31:1 (2007), pp. 124–35.
5. Wyndham Lewis, *Blasting and Bombardiering* (London: John Calder, 1982), pp. 293–4.
6. Karl Mannheim, 'The Problem of Generations', in *Karl Mannheim: Essays*, ed. Paul Kecskemeti (New York: Routledge, 1972), p. 286.
7. William Strauss and Neil Howe, *Generations: The History of America's Future, 1584–2069* (New York: William Morrow, 1991), p. 32.
8. Mannheim, 'Problem of Generations', p. 287.
9. Jane Pilcher, 'Mannheim's Sociology of Generations: An Undervalued Legacy', *British Journal of Sociology* 45:3 (1994), p. 481.
10. José Ortega y Gassett, *The Modern Theme*, trans. James Cleugh (New York: Harper, 1961).
11. Marius Hentea, *Henry Green at the Limits of Modernism* (Brighton: Sussex Academic Press, 2014), p. 12.
12. Quoted in Oliver Holmes, 'José Ortega y Gasset', *The Stanford Encyclopedia of Philosophy* (Spring 2014 edn), ed. Edward N. Zalta, online at <http://plato.stanford.edu/entries/gasset> (last accessed 25 June 2015).
13. Pew Research Center, *Millennials: A Portrait of Generation Next*, last modified 24 February 2010, online at <http://www.pewresearch.org/millennials> (last accessed 25 June 2015).
14. William Wordsworth, *The Excursion* (London: Edward Moxon, 1853).
15. Mannheim, 'Problem of Generations', p. 278.
16. Ibid., p. 290.
17. Ibid., p. 289.
18. Ibid., p. 310.
19. Umbro Apollonio, ed., *Futurist Manifestos* (Boston: MFA Publications, 2001), p. 22.
20. Virginia Woolf, *Mrs Dalloway* (London: Penguin, 2000), p. 94.
21. Jay Winter, 'Demography', in *A Companion to World War One*, ed. John Horne (Oxford: Blackwell, 2012), p. 260.

22. Robert Wohl, *The Generation of 1914* (Cambridge, MA: Harvard University Press, 1979), p. 5.

23. Mannheim, 'Problem of Generations', p. 309.

24. Ibid., p. 310.

25. Samuel Hynes, *The Auden Generation: Literature and Politics in England in the 1930s* (London: Bodley Head, 1976).

26. John Lowney, *History, Memory, and the Literary Left: Modern American Poetry, 1935–1968* (Iowa City: Iowa University Press, 2006), p. 11.

27. Harold Bloom, *The Anxiety of Influence: A Theory of Poetry*, second edn (Oxford: Oxford University Press, 1997).

28. Pierre Bourdieu, *The Rules of Art* (Cambridge: Polity, 1996), p. 157.

29. Hentea, 'Literary Generations', p. 572.

30. Mannheim, 'Problem of Generations', p. 311.

31. Apollonio, ed., *Futurist Manifestos*, p. 27.

32. Mannheim, 'Problem of Generations', p. 292.

33. Ibid., pp. 293–301.

34. Ibid., p. 293.

35. Henry David Thoreau, *Walden* (New Haven: Yale University Press, 2006), p. 8.

36. Lewis, *Blasting and Bombardiering*, p. 35.

37. Apollonio, ed., *Futurist Manifestos*, p. 23.

38. Ibid., p. 23.

39. Wyndham Lewis, *Creatures of Habit and Creatures of Change*, ed. Paul Edwards (Santa Rosa: Black Sparrow Press, 1989), p. 38. My italics.

40. Vassiliki Kolocotroni, Jane Goldman and Olga Taxidou, eds, *Modernism: An Anthology of Sources and Documents* (Edinburgh: Edinburgh University Press, 1998), p. 263.

41. Peter Nicholls, *Modernisms: A Literary Guide* (Berkeley: University of California Press, 1995), p. 167.

42. Mannheim, 'Problem of Generations', p. 297.

43. Ibid., p. 303.

44. Ibid., p. 303.

45. Ibid., p. 304.

46. Ibid., p. 304.

47. Ibid., p. 306.

48. Malcolm Cowley, *Exile's Return* (New York: Viking, 1951), p. 236.

49. Mannheim, 'Problem of Generations', p. 306.

50. William C. Wees, *Vorticism and the Avant-Garde* (Manchester: Manchester University Press, 1972), p. 53.

51. Malcolm Bradbury and James McFarlane, eds, *Modernism* (Harmondsworth: Penguin, 1976), p. 202.

52. Julius Petersen, *Die literarischen Generationen* [1930], quoted in Hentea, 'Literary Generations', p. 575.

53. Mannheim, 'Problem of Generations', p. 307.

54. Ibid., p. 307.

55. Ibid., p. 308.

56. Ibid., p. 314.
57. Ibid., p. 320.
58. Ibid., p. 298.
59. See for example Hentea, 'Literary Generations', and Edmunds and Turner, 'Global Generations'.
60. Will Self, 'How Has England Changed Since 1994?' *The Guardian*, 17 January 2014, online at <http://www.theguardian.com/books/2014/jan/17/how-has-england-changed-will-self> (last accessed 25 June 2015).
61. Marianne Hirsch, 'The Generation of Postmemory', *Poetics Today* 29:1 (2008), p. 103.
62. Art Spiegelman, *Maus: My Father Bleeds History* (New York: Pantheon, 1987).
63. Bruno Latour, *Reassembling the Social: An Introduction to Actor-Network-Theory* (Oxford: Oxford University Press, 2007).

## CHAPTER 14

1. Srinivas Aravamudan, 'The Return of Anachronism', *MLQ* 62:4 (2001), p. 333.
2. Marshall Brown, 'Periods and Resistances', *MLQ* 62:4 (2001), 313.
3. Fredric Jameson, *The Political Unconscious* [1981] (Abingdon: Routledge, 2002), p. 28.
4. Eric Hayot, 'Against Periodization; or, On Institutional Time', *New Literary History* 42:4 (2011), pp. 739–56.
5. Rita Felski, '"Context Stinks!"', *New Literary History* 42:4 (2011), p. 577.
6. Arthur O. Lovejoy, 'On the Discrimination of Romanticisms', *PMLA* 39:2 (1924), p. 234.
7. Ibid., p. 236.
8. Ibid., p. 252.
9. Ibid., p. 253.
10. Ibid., p. 236.
11. Micah Mattix, 'Periodization and Difference', *New Literary History* 35:4 (2004), pp. 686, 694.
12. Frances Ferguson, 'Planetary Literary History: The Place of the Text', *New Literary History* 39:3 (2008), pp. 661, 662.
13. Katie Trumpener, 'In the Grid: Period and Experience', *PMLA* 127:2 (2012), p. 349.
14. Sandra M. Gilbert and Susan Gubar, '"But Oh! That Deep Romantic Chasm": The Engendering of Periodization', *The Kenyon Review* 13:3 (1991), p. 74.
15. Jonathan Goldberg and Madhavi Menon, 'Queering History', *PMLA* 120:5 (2005), p. 1609.
16. Valerie Traub, 'The New Unhistoricism in Queer Studies', *PMLA* 128:1 (2013), p. 22.
17. Barbara Fuchs, 'Golden Ages and Golden Hinds; or, Periodizing Spain and England', *PMLA* 127:2 (2012), p. 322.
18. Pascale Casanova, 'The Literary Greenwich Meridian. Thoughts on the Temporal Forms of Literary Belief', *Field Day Review* 4 (2008), pp. 7–23.

19. This example is based on Bruno Latour, *Reassembling the Social. An Introduction to Actor-Network Theory* (Oxford: Oxford University Press, 2007), pp. 200–1.

20. Bruno Latour, *We Have Never Been Modern*, trans. Catherine Porter (Cambridge, MA: Harvard University Press, 1993), p. 73.

21. Jonathan Gil Harris, 'Four Exoskeletons and No Funeral', *New Literary History* 42:4 (2011), p. 622.

22. Felski, '"Context Stinks!"', p. 579.

23. Wai Chee Dimock, 'Weak Theory: Henry James, Colm Tóibín, and W. B. Yeats', *Critical Inquiry* 39:4 (2013), pp. 734, 736. For her critical view of Greenblatt, see Dimock, 'A Theory of Resonance', *PMLA* 112:5 (1997), pp. 1060–71.

24. Harris, 'Four Exoskeletons', pp. 615, 620.

25. Jonathan Gil Harris, *Untimely Matter in the Time of Shakespeare* (Philadelphia: University of Pennsylvania Press, 2009), pp. 3, 25.

26. Ibid., p. 10.

27. Ibid., p. 170.

28. Felski, '"Context Stinks!"', p. 578.

29. Wai Chee Dimock, 'Literature for the Planet', *PMLA* 116:1 (2001), p. 175.

30. Evelyn Gajowski, 'Beyond Historicism: Presentism, Subjectivity, Politics', *Literature Compass* 7/8 (2010), p. 678. The phrase originally comes from Margreta de Grazia.

31. Ibid., p. 680.

32. Goldberg and Menon, 'Queering History', pp. 1609, 1616.

33. Traub, 'New Unhistoricism', p. 32.

34. Harris, *Untimely*, p. 20.

35. Elizabeth Outka, 'Dead Men Walking: Actors, Networks, and Actualized Metaphors in *Mrs Dalloway* and *Raymond*', *NOVEL* 46:2 (2013), p. 260.

36. Brown, 'Periods and Resistances', p. 311.

37. René Wellek and Austin Warren, *Theory of Literature* (New York: Harcourt, Brace and Company, 1949), p. 281.

38. Ibid., p. 277.

39. Ibid., p. 278.

40. Ibid., p. 282.

41. Ibid., p. 265.

42. Ibid., p. 263.

43. Ibid., p. 281.

44. Ted Underwood, *Why Literary Periods Mattered: Historical Distance and the Prestige of English Studies* (Stanford: Stanford University Press, 2013), p. 3.

45. Ibid., p. 105.

46. Ibid., p. 96.

47. Ibid., p. 143.

48. Ibid., p. 157.

49. Ibid., p. 165.

50. Ibid., p. 16.

51. Ibid., p. 174.

52. Ibid., p. 41.

53. Richard Grusin, 'The Dark Side of Digital Humanities: Dispatches from Two

Recent MLA Conventions', *differences* 25:1 (2014), pp. 79–92.

54. David James and Urmila Seshagiri, 'Metamodernism: Narratives of Continuity and Revolution', *PMLA* 129:1 (2014), p. 91.

55. Rajeswarai Sunder Rajan, 'Zeitgeist and the Literary Text: India, 1947, in Qurratulain Hyder's *My Temples, Too* and Salman Rushdie's *Midnight's Children'*, *Critical Inquiry* 40:4 (2014), p. 449.

56. Fredric Jameson, 'Periodizing the 60s', *Social Text* 9/10 (1984), p. 178.

57. See Hayot, 'Against Periodization', p. 747.

58. Caroline Levine, *Forms: Whole, Rhythm, Hierarchy, Network* (Princeton: Princeton University Press, 2015), p. 67.

59. Ibid., pp. 27, 45.

60. Carlo Ginzburg, 'Microhistory: Two or Three Things that I Know about It', *Critical Inquiry* 20:1 (1993), p. 22.

61. Fernand Braudel, 'History and the Social Sciences: The *Longue Durée*', *Review (Fernand Braudel Center)*, 32:2 (2009), pp. 181, 174, 179.

62. Franco Moretti, 'Graphs, Maps, Trees: Abstract Models for Literary History 1', *New Left Review* 24 (2003), p. 76.

63. Susan Gillman, 'Oceans of *Longues Durées*', *PMLA* 127:2 (2012), pp. 330, 331.

64. Jo Guldi and David Armitage, *The History Manifesto* (Cambridge: Cambridge University Press, 2014), p. 36.

65. Brian Boyd, 'Literature and Evolution: A Bio-Cultural Approach', *Philosophy and Literature* 29 (2005), p. 3. For an insightful critique of this movement, see Jonathan Kramnick, 'Against Literary Darwinism', *Critical Inquiry* 37:2 (2011), pp. 315–47.

66. Wai Chee Dimock, *Through Other Continents: American Literature Across Deep Time* (Princeton: Princeton University Press, 2006).

67. Ibid., p. 80.

68. Ibid., p. 92.

69. Ibid., p. 87.

70. Ibid., p. 6.

71. Mark McGurl, 'The Posthuman Comedy', *Critical Inquiry* 38:3 (2012), p. 533. Also see the subsequent debate between Dimock and McGurl in *Critical Inquiry*.

72. Dipesh Chakrabarty, 'The Climate of History: Four Theses', *Critical Inquiry* 35:2 (2009), p. 201.

73. Dipesh Chakrabarty, 'Climate and Capital: On Conjoined Histories', *Critical Inquiry* 41:1 (2014), p. 23.

74. Dipesh Chakrabarty, 'Postcolonial Studies and the Challenge of Climate Change', *New Literary History* 43:1 (2012), p. 13.

75. Srinivas Aravamudan, 'The Catachronism of Climate Change', *diacritics* 41:3 (2013), pp. 6–30.

76. Bruno Latour, 'Agency at the Time of the Anthropocene', *New Literary History* 45:1 (2014), p. 3.

77. Nicholas Mirzoeff, 'Visualizing the Anthropocene', *Public Culture* 26:2 (2014), p. 215.

78. See Rosalind Williams, *The Triumph of Human Empire: Verne, Morris, and Stevenson at the End of the World* (Chicago: University of Chicago Press, 2013).

79. Patricia Yaeger, 'Editor's Column: Literature in the Ages of Wood, Tallow, Coal, Whale Oil, Gasoline, Atomic Power, and Other Energy Sources', *PMLA* 126:2 (2011), p. 305.

## CHAPTER 15

1. John J. Joughin and Simon Malpas, 'Introduction', in *The New Aestheticism*, ed. John J. Joughin and Simon Malpas (Manchester and New York: Manchester University Press, 2003), p. 1.
2. See Heather Dubrow, *A Happier Eden: The Politics of Marriage in the Stuart Epithalamium* (Ithaca: Cornell University Press, 1990).
3. For surveys of individual proponents of the New Formalism, see Marjorie Levinson, 'What's New Formalism', *PMLA*, 122:2 (2007), pp. 558–69, and Verena Theile and Linda Tredennick, eds, *New Formalisms and Literary Theory* (New York: Palgrave Macmillan, 2013). In my brief survey of the New Formalism here, I rely heavily on Levinson's excellent discussion.
4. Richard Strier, 'How Formalism Became a Dirty Word, And Why We Can't Do Without It', in *Renaissance Literature and Its Formal Engagements*, ed. Mark David Rasmussen (New York: Palgrave Macmillan, 2001), p. 213.
5. Joughin and Malpas, 'Introduction', p. 3.
6. Isobel Armstrong, *The Radical Aesthetic* (Oxford: Blackwell Publishers, 2000), p. 3.
7. For a quick glance at Scruton's take on beauty, consult his *Beauty: A Very Short Introduction* (Oxford: Oxford University Press, 2011).
8. T. E. Hulme, *Further Speculations*, ed. Samuel Hynes (Minneapolis: University of Minnesota Press, 1955), p. 98.
9. For an extensive discussion of Schlegel in this context, see Günter Oesterle, 'Entwurf einer Monographie des ästhetisch Hässlichen. Die Geschichte einer ästhetischen Kategorie von Friedrich Schlegels *Studium*-Aufsatz bis zu Karl Rosenkranz' *Ästhetik des Hässlichen* als Suche nach dem Ursprung der Moderne', in *Literaturwissenschaft und Sozialwissenschaften 8: Zur Modernität der Romantik*, ed. Dieter Bänch (Stuttgart: Metzler, 1977), pp. 217–97.
10. Hans Robert Jauss, 'Die klassische und christliche Rechtfertigung des Hässlichen in mittelalterischer Literatur', in *Alterität und Modernität der mittelalterlichen Literatur* (Munich: Fink, 1977), pp. 143–68.
11. Victor Hugo, *Préface de Cromwell* (Paris: Larousse, 2006).
12. For a discussion of the ugly in Baudelaire, see Michelle Hannoosh, *Baudelaire and Caricature: From the Comic to an Art of Modernity* (University Park: Penn State University Press, 1992).
13. For a more detailed discussion of this strange patch in modern literary history, see Sascha Bru, 'Politics as the Art of the Impossible: The Heteronomy of Italian Futurist *Art-Action*', in *Aesthetic Revolutions*, ed. Ales Erjavec (Durham, NC: Duke University Press, 2015), pp. 19–41.
14. Sianne Ngai, *Our Aesthetic Categories: Zany, Cute, Interesting* (Cambridge, MA: Harvard University Press, 2012), p. 242.

## CHAPTER 16

1. Full text of 'Aeschylus, with an English translation by Herbert Weir Smith', online at <http://archive.org/stream/aeschyluswithengo2aescuoft/aeschylus-withengo2aescuoft_djvu.txt> (last accessed 25 June 2015).
2. Alain Badiou, ed. and trans. *Plato's Republic* (Cambridge: Polity, 2012), 396 d–e.
3. Ibid., 395 d1–3.
4. Aristotle, *Aristotle's Poetics*, trans. James Hutton (New York: Norton, 1982).
5. Ibid., 1449b.
6. Ibid., 1448a.
7. Plotinus, *Enneads*, trans. A. H. Armstrong, 7 vols (Cambridge, MA: Harvard University Press, 1996).
8. Alexander Pope, *An Essay on Criticism, The Rape of the Lock and Epistles to several persons*, ed. Raymond Southall (London: Collins, 1973), lines 70, 72–3.
9. Ibid., line 140.
10. Edmund Burke, *A Philosophical Enquiry into the Origin of our Ideas of the Sublime and Beautiful* [1756], ed. James T. Boulton (Oxford: Basil Blackwell, 1987), part I, section VII.
11. Alexis de Tocqueville, *Democracy in America*, [1840] trans. Harvey C. Mansfield, Jr. and Delba Winthrop (Chicago: University of Chicago Press, 2000), vol. II, book I, chapter 17.
12. Stendhal, *The Red and the Black*, trans. Stirling Haig (Cambridge: Cambridge University Press, 1989).
13. Kendall Walton, *Mimesis as Make-Believe: On the Foundation of Representational Arts* (Cambridge, MA: Harvard University Press, 1990).
14. Michael Taussig, *Mimesis and Alterity: A Particular History of the Senses* (London: Routledge, 1992).
15. Erich Auerbach, *Mimesis: The Representation of Reality in Western Literature*, trans. Willard R. Trask (Princeton: Princeton University Press, 1953).
16. Francesco Orlando, 'Codes littéraires et référents chez Auerbach', in *Erich Auerbach: la littérature en perspective*, ed. Paolo Tortonese (Paris: Presses Sorbonne Nouvelle, 2009), pp. 211–62.
17. Walton, *Mimesis as Make-Believe*.

## CHAPTER 17

1. Leo Spitzer, *Linguistics and Literary History* (Princeton: Princeton University Press, 1948), p. 10.
2. Kenneth Goldsmith, 'It's Not Plagiarism. In the Digital Age, It's "Repurposing"', *The Chronicle of Higher Education*, 11 September 2011, online at <http://chronicle.com/article/Uncreative-Writing/128908> (last accessed 3 February 2015).

3.  Michel Foucault, *The Order of Things: An Archaeology of the Human Sciences* (London: Routledge, 2002), p. 48.

4.  For an interesting response to Goldsmith, see <http://venepoetics.blogspot. be/2013/09/goldsmith-y-el-imperio-retro-conceptual.html>

5.  Susan Sontag, *Against Interpretation and Other Essays* (London: Penguin, 2009).

6.  Roland Barthes, *Writing Degree Zero and Elements of Semiology* (London: Jonathan Cape, 1984), p. 16.

7.  Ibid., p. 5.

8.  Friedrich Nietzsche, 'On Truth and Lies in an Extra Moral Sense', in *The Portable Nietzsche*, ed. Walter Kaufman (New York: Viking Press, 1954), p. 42.

9.  Barthes, *Degree Zero*, p. 5.

10.  Ben Hutchinson, *Modernism and Style* (Basingstoke: Palgrave Macmillan, 2011), p. 92.

11.  Walt Whitman, *Leaves of Grass: The Original 1855 Edition* (New York: Dover, 2007), p. 10.

12.  Gustave Flaubert, *The Letters of Gustave Flaubert, 1830–1880*, sel., ed. and trans. Francis Steegmuller (London: Picador, 2001), p. 213.

13.  Walter Pater, 'Style', in *The Works of Walter Pater, Vol. 5* (New York: Cambridge University Press, 2011), p. 36.

14.  Ezra Pound, 'Ulysses', published as 'Paris Letter', *The Dial* 72:6 (1922), in *The Literary Essays of Ezra Pound* (Westport, CT: Greenwood Press, 1979), p. 403.

15.  Flaubert, *Letters*, p. 313.

16.  James Joyce, *A Portrait of the Artist as a Young Man*, ed. John Paul Riquelme (New York and London: Norton, 2007), p. 189.

17.  Suzanne Sniader Lanser, 'Stephen's Diary: The Hero Unveiled', *James Joyce Quarterly* 16:4 (1979), pp. 417–23.

18.  Michael Levenson, 'Stephen's Diary in Joyce's *Portrait* – The Shape of Life', *ELH* 52:4 (1985), pp. 1017–35.

19.  T. S. Eliot, 'From Poe to Valéry', in *To Criticize the Critic and Other Writings* (London: Faber and Faber, 1978), p. 39.

20.  Joyce, *Portrait*, p. 223.

21.  Ibid., p. 222.

22.  Ibid., p. 222.

23.  Ibid., p. 224.

24.  Ibid., p. 224.

25.  Ibid., p. 5.

26.  Levenson, 'Stephen's Diary', p. 1029.

27.  Joyce, *Portrait*, p. 224, my emphasis.

28.  Levenson, 'Stephen's Diary', p. 1031.

29.  Gerald Gillespie, *Proust, Mann, Joyce in the Modernist Context* (Washington: Catholic University of America Press, 2003), pp. 137ff.

30.  T. S. Eliot, 'Ulysses, Order and Myth', in *Modernism, An Anthology of Sources and Documents*, ed. Jane Goldman and Olga Taxidou (Edinburgh: Edinburgh University Press,1998), pp. 372–3.

31. Roman Jakobson, 'Closing Statement: Linguistics and Poetics', in *Style and Language*, ed. Thomas Sebeok (Cambridge, MA: MIT Press, 1960).

32. Jean Paulhan, *The Flowers of Tarbes*, trans. Michael Syrotinski (Urbana: University of Illinois Press, 2006).

33. Ibid., p. 94.

34. Michael Syrotinski, translator's introduction to Paulhan, *The Flowers of Tarbes*, pp. ix–xxiii.

35. Theodor W. Adorno, *Philosophy of Modern Music* (New York: Continuum, 2004).

36. Edward W. Said, *On Late Style: Music and Literature Against the Grain* (New York: Pantheon, 2006), p. 9.

37. Ibid., p. 18.

38. Adorno, *Philosophy of Modern Music*, p. 70.

39. Fredric Jameson, *Postmodernism, or, The Cultural Logic of Late Capitalism* (London: Verso, 1992).

40. William Watkin, 'The Poetics of Presentation: Lyn Hejinian's *My Life* Project and the Work of Giorgio Agamben', *Textual Practice* 27:2 (2013), pp. 225–48.

41. Lyn Hejinian, *My Life* (Los Angeles: Sun & Moon Press, 1987), p. 7.

42. Kenneth Goldsmith, 'Uncreativity as a Creative Practice', Kenneth Goldsmith's author page on *Electronic Poetry Center*, at <http://epc.buffalo.edu/authors/goldsmith/uncreativity.html> (last accessed 3 February 2015).

43. Krissy Wilson, 'The Art of Google Books', online at <http://theartofgoogle-books.tumblr.com/page/7>; Kenneth Goldsmith, 'The Artful Accidents of Google Books', *The New Yorker*, 4 December 2013, online at <http://www.newyorker.com/books/page-turner/the-artful-accidents-of-google-books> (last accessed 3 February 2015).

44. Roland Barthes, 'Style and Its Image', in *Literary Style: A Symposium*, ed. Seymour Chatman (Oxford and New York: Oxford University Press, 1971), p. 10.

45. Roland Barthes, *The Fashion System* (Berkeley: University of California Press, 1990), p. 285.

46. Poets like Juliana Spahr, for example, are combining postmodernist conceptual writing (Language Poetry, Goldsmith) with a new lyricism.

47. Gilles Philippe and Julien Piat, *La langue littéraire. Une histoire de la prose en France de Gustave Flaubert à Claude Simon* (Paris: Fayard, 2009).

48. Rita Felski, *Uses of Literature* (Malden: Blackwell, 2008), p. 14.

## CHAPTER 18

1. Thomas B. Macaulay, *The History of England from the Accession of James II*, vol. 2 (London: Longman, Brown, Green, and Longmans, 1849), p. 109. Macaulay was referring to doctrinal attacks upon Roman Catholicism by Church of England clergy in the late seventeenth century.

2. J. G. Ballard, *Miracles of Life: Shanghai to Shepperton. An Autobiography* (London: Fourth Estate, 2008), pp. 161, 167.

3. Will Self, 'Ballard, James Graham (1930–2009)', *Oxford Dictionary of National Biography* (Oxford: Oxford University Press, 2004–15), online at <http://www.oxforddnb.com/view/article/101436?docPos=7> (last accessed 5 May 2014).

4. Blurb from the paperback cover of Daphne du Maurier, *Rebecca* (London: Arrow, 1992).

5. Anna Chambers, 'The Information. Genre Fiction Sales', *Financial Times Weekend Magazine*, 18/19 April 2009, p. 14.

6. John B. Thompson, *Merchants of Culture: The Publishing Business in the Twenty-First Century*, second edn (New York: Plume, 2012), pp. 27–41.

7. Woody Haut, *Pulp Culture: Hardboiled Fiction and the Cold War* (London: Serpent's Tail, 1995), p. 11. The cover of the 1955 Popular Library paperback of *After Dark, My Sweet* is reproduced in Geoffrey O'Brien, *Hardboiled America: Lurid Paperbacks and the Masters of Noir*, expanded edn (New York: Da Capo Press, 1997), p. 148. O'Brien dubs Thompson 'a dimestore Dostoevsky' (p. 150).

8. John Frow, *Genre* (New York: Routledge, 2006), p. 132.

9. Ibid., p. 124, my emphasis.

10. Franco Moretti, 'Conjectures on World Literature', reprinted in *Distant Reading* (London: Verso, 2013), pp. 44–62. This essay was first published in 2000.

11. Franco Moretti, *Graphs, Maps, Trees: Abstract Models for a Literary History* (London: Verso, 2005), p. 18.

12. Ibid., p. 1.

13. Ibid., p. 31.

14. Ibid., p. 31.

15. Ibid., p. 8.

16. Ibid., p. 31.

17. Stuart Hall, 'Notes on Deconstructing "the Popular"', in *People's History and Socialist Theory*, ed. Raphael Samuel (London: Routledge and Kegan Paul, 1981), pp. 229–30.

18. Pierre Bourdieu, *The Rules of Art: Genesis and Structure of the Literary Field*, trans. Susan Emanuel (Stanford: Stanford University Press, 1996), p. 147.

19. Pierre Bourdieu, 'The Uses of the "People"', in *In Other Words: Essays Towards a Reflexive Sociology*, trans. Matthew Adamson (Cambridge: Polity Press, 1990), p. 151.

20. Ken Gelder, *Popular Fiction: The Logics and Practices of a Literary Field* (London: Routledge, 2004).

21. Peter D. McDonald, *British Literary Culture and Publishing Practice 1880–1914* (Cambridge: Cambridge University Press, 1997), pp. 68–88.

22. Ibid., p. 156.

23. J. B. Priestley, 'High, Low, Broad' (1926), quoted in John Baxendale, *Priestley's England: J. B. Priestley and English Culture* (Manchester: Manchester University Press, 2007), pp. 17–18.

24. For a thoroughgoing updating of this argument that focuses on the convergence of digital technologies and literary, visual and consumer cultures in the making of the modern bestseller, see Jim Collins, *Bring On The Books For Everybody:*

*How Literary Culture Became Popular Culture* (Durham, NC: Duke University Press, 2010).

25. Frank Kermode, 'Is an Elite Necessary?' *The Listener*, 29 October 1970, pp. 572, 574.

26. This notion of 'inter-textuality' derives from Tony Bennett and Janet Woollacott, *Bond and Beyond: The Political Career of a Popular Hero* (Basingstoke: Macmillan, 1987), pp. 44–5, 53–9.

27. John Sutherland, 'Fiction and the Erotic Cover', *Critical Quarterly* 33 (1991), p. 4. These quotes are taken from the dust-jacket of the hardback edition, reproduced in his article as an illustration.

## CHAPTER 19

1. Ralph Cohen, 'History and Genre', *NLH* 17:2 (1986).

2. Wai Chee Dimock and Bruce Robbins, eds, *PMLA, Special Topic: Remapping Genre* 122:5 (2007).

3. Jonathan Culler, 'Lyric, History, and Genre', *New Literary History* 40:4 (2009).

4. Ibid., p. 896.

5. Ibid., pp. 882, 883, 889.

6. Marjorie Perloff, *Radical Artifice: Writing Poetry in the Age of Media* (Chicago: University of Chicago Press, 1991), p. 17.

7. Friedrich A. Kittler, *Discourse Networks, 1800/1900* (Stanford: Stanford University Press, 1990), p. 265.

8. Culler, 'Lyric, History, and Genre', p. 880.

9. Edgar Allan Poe, *Complete Tales and Poems* (New York: Vintage, 1975).

10. Pierre Bourdieu, *The Field of Cultural Production: Essays on Art and Literature*, ed. Randal Johnson (New York: Columbia University Press, 1993), p. 49.

11. Pierre Bourdieu, *Language and Symbolic Power*, ed. John B. Thompson, trans. Gino Raymond and Matthew Adamson (Cambridge, MA: Harvard University Press, 1991), p. 90.

12. Charles Baudelaire, *Le Spleen de Paris*, in *Oeuvres Complètes*, 2 vols, ed. Claude Pichois, (Paris: Gallimard, Éditions Pléiade, 1975).

13. Jonathan Monroe, *A Poverty of Objects: The Prose Poem and the Politics of Genre* (Ithaca: Cornell University Press, 1987).

14. Baudelaire, *Oeuvres Complètes*.

15. Edgar Allan Poe, *Poems and Essays on Poetry* (New York: Routledge, 2003), p. 140.

16. Ibid., p. 141.

17. Ibid., p. 141.

18. Ibid., p. 142.

19. Ezra Pound, 'A Retrospect' [1918], reprinted in *Modernism: An Anthology of Sources and Documents*, ed. Vassiliki Kolocotroni, Jane Goldman, Olga Taxidou (Chicago: University of Chicago Press, 1998), p. 374.

20. Friedrich Schlegel, *Athenäum-Fragmente*, in *Charakteristiken und Kritiken I*

(*1796–1801*), Kritische Friedrich-Schlegel-Ausgabe, ed. Ernst Behler; vol. 2, ed. Hans Eichner (Paderborn: Ferdinand Schöningh, 1967), p. 182.

21. Jacques Derrida, 'The Principle of Reason: The University in the Eyes of Its Pupils', *diacritics* 13:3 (1983), pp. 3–20 (p. 28); Jonathan Monroe, 'Poetry, the University, and the Culture of Distraction', in *Poetry, Community, Movement*, ed. Jonathan Monroe, *diacritics* 26:3–4 (1996), p. 334; Jacques Derrida, 'The Law of Genre', trans. Avital Ronell, in *Glyph* 7, and *Critical Inquiry* 7:1 (1980), p. 15.

22. Barbara Johnson, *Défigurations du langage poétique: La seconde révolution baudelairienne* (Paris: Flammarion, 1979).

23. Michel Delville, *The American Prose Poem* (Gainesville: University Press of Florida, 1998), p. 14.

24. Jacques Rancière, *Dissensus: On Politics and Aesthetics*, ed. and trans. Steven Corcoran (New York: Continuum, 2010).

25. Culler, 'Lyric, History, and Genre'.

26. Roman Jakobson, 'Closing Statement: Linguistics and Poetics', in *Style in Language*, ed. T. A. Sebeok (Cambridge, MA: MIT Press, 1960).

27. Bruce Robbins, 'Afterword', *PMLA* 12: 5 (2007).

28. Charles Bernstein, 'This Line', in *All the Whiskey in Heaven: Selected Poems* (New York: Farrar, Straus & Giroux, 2011).

29. Mikhail M. Bakhtin, 'Discourse in the Novel', in *The Dialogic Imagination: Four Essays*, trans. Caryl Emerson and Michael Holquist, ed. Michael Holquist (Austin: University of Texas Press, 1981), pp. 296–7.

30. Derek Walcott, *The Prodigal* (New York: Farrar, Straus & Giroux, 2004), pp. 5–6.

31. Ibid., p. 79.

32. Bakhtin, 'Discourse in the Novel', p. 412.

33. Ibid., p. 366.

34. Aimé Césaire, *Le cahier d'un retour au pays natal* [1939], in *The Collected Poetry*, trans. Clayton Eshleman and Annette Smith (Berkeley: University of California Press, 1983).

35. Aimé Césaire, 'Le verbe maronner / à René Depestre, poète haïtien' [1955], in ibid., pp. 368–71.

36. Kamau Brathwaite, 'I was wash-way in blood', in *Born to Slow Horses* (Middletown, CT: Wesleyan University Press, 2005), p. 58.

37. Cole Swenson, *American Hybrid: A Norton Anthology of New Poetry*, ed. Cole Swenson and David St. John (New York: Norton, 2009), pp. xxi–xxv.

38. Ibid., pp. xxi–xxv. My emphases.

39. Cecilia Vicuña, *SABORAMI* (Oakland and Philadelphia: ChainLinks, 2011 [1973]), p. 71.

40. Claudia Rankine, *Don't Let Me Be Lonely: An American Lyric* (Minneapolis: Graywolf Press, 2004).

41. Claudia Rankine, *Citizen: An American Lyric* (Minneapolis: Graywolf Press, 2014).

42. Rankine, *Don't Let Me Be Lonely*, p. 61.

43. Ibid., p. 90; Rankine, *Citizen*, p. 49.

44. Swenson, *American Hybrid*, introduction.

45. Bakhtin, 'Discourse in the Novel', p. 289.
46. Henri Lefebvre, *The Critique of Everyday Life: The One-Volume Edition* (New York: Verso, 2014).
47. Schlegel, *Athenäums Fragmente*, p. 182.
48. Judith Butler, *Giving an Account of Oneself* (New York: Fordham University Press, 2005).
49. Edouard Glissant, *Poetics of Relation*, trans. Betsy Wing (Ann Arbor: University of Michigan Press, 1997).

# Index

Note: 'n' denotes references to chapter notes. *Italic* numbers indicate an illustration.

distraction, 34–5
Dostoyevsky, Fyodor, 94
drama, 79, 216, 217–18
Dronke, Peter, 65–6
Drucker, Johanna, 43, 44
du Maurier, Daphne, 239
Dubrow, Heather, 206
Duchamp, Marcel, 115, 211
Duncan, Robert, 161
*Dust* (Steedman), 24–5, 26, 27, 35
Dzhabayev, Dzhambul, 65

Eagleton, Terry, 174–5, 177
Early English Books Online, 44
Earth and big history, 199–202
ebook *see* digital form
Eco, Umberto, 160, 163
Edmunds, June, 178, 189
Eggert, Paul, 41
electronic form *see* digital form
Eliot, T. S., 52, 179, 182, 186, 232–3
Ellis, Havelock, 181
Ellison, Ralph, 122
*Embodied: Victorian Literature and the Senses*
    (Cohen), 95–6
Emerson, Ralph Waldo, 33, 185
emplotment, 144–7
Engels, Friedrich, 125–6
Enlightenment, Age of, 44, 47, 48, 49, 76, 96, 211
    and translation, 60, 63, 70
Erlin, Matt, 69–70
Ernst, Wolfgang, 26–7, 35, 41
Esposito, John, 105, 106
*Essay on Criticism, An* (Pope), 220
event, 164–76
    creating literature as, 174–6
    defining, 165–6
    and *Jacob's Room* (Woolf), 169–70
    as a modern invention, 170–2
    narrative, 167–9
    revolution as, 173–4
    and *Things Fall Apart* (Achebe), 172–3
Even-Zohar, Itamar, 64, 66

*Fat and the Thin, The* (Zola), 92–3
Faulkner, William, 56, 66, 85
Felman, Shoshana, 84
Felski, Rita, 175, 177, 192, 195, 198, 237
Ferguson, Frances, 193, 197
fiction
    hunger, 92
    and the mind, 84
    *see also* novel

*Fifty Shades of Grey* (James), 239, 241
*Figura* (Auerbach), 141–2
film *see* cinema
Fitz, Earl E., 71
Fitzgerald, F. Scott, 51–2, 187
Flaubert, Gustave, 132, 224, 229–32
*Florante at Laura* (Balagtas), 68
*Flowers of Tarbes, The* (Paulhan), 234, 237
*Flush* (Woolf), 102, 277n
Flynn, Gillian, 240, 241
Fontane, Theodor, 94
fonts, 41–2
food *see* senses
formalism, 205–8, 233
formats, and the popular, 241–3
*Forms of Time and of the Chronotope in the Novel*
    (Bakhtin), 146–7
*Forms: Whole, Rhythm, Hierarchy, Network*
    (Levine), 198–9, 202
Foucault, Michel, 35, 88, 91, 105, 162–3, 194,
    195, 228, 234
    and archive, 24–5, 26, 32
    and politics, 130, 131, 134
*Founding of Aesthetics in the German Enlightenment,
    The* (Buchenau), 153, 163
France, Peter, 61
FRBR object-oriented community, 40
freedom, 9, 123–4
Freud, Sigmund, 26, 84
Friedlaender, Salomo (Mynona), 94
Frow, John, 243, 250
Frye, Northrop, 223
Fudge, Erica, 109
future *see* time
Futurism, 212–13, 291n
*Futurist Manifestos* (ed. Apollonio), 184, 185

Gadamer, Hans-Georg, 142–4
Garrington, Abbie, 95, 97
Gaskell, Philip, 45
gastroesthetics, 91–2
Gebauer, Gunter, 225
Gee, Henry, 120
gender, 3, 79–81
generation, 178–89
    and the future, 188–9
    'isms' and 'schisms', 187–8
    Mannheim's theory, 179, 180–6, 187–8
    and the new, 184–7
*Generation of 1914, The* (Wohl), 182, 190
*Generations: The History of America's Future,
    1584-2069* (Strauss and Howe), 178, 179
Genette, Gérard, 144–5, 150

longue durée, 199, 200
Lovejoy, Arthur O., 193, 196, 202
Lowe, Elizabeth, 71
Loyola, Saint Ignatius of, 90
Luhmann, Niklas, 4
Lundblad, Michael, 100
lyric, 3, 66, 79

Macaulay, Thomas B., 294n
McBride, Eimear, 85
McCarthy, Cormac, 92
McDonald, Peter D., 38, 248, 250
McFarlane, James, 187
McGann, Jerome, 38, 264
McGurl, Mark, 5, 200, 201, 202
McHugh, Susan, 103–4, 109
McKay, Robert, 101, 108, 276n
McKenzie, D. F., 36, 38, 44, 45
McLuhan, Marshall, 51, 53, 55
Macmillan, Harold, 167, 168
McTige, Trish, 95
Make It New (Pound), 155
Mallarmé, Stéphane, 160, 162, 231
Malpas, Simon, 205–6, 208, 214
Mani, B. Venkat, 62
Mannheim, Karl, 179, 180–6, 187–8
Manoff, Marlene, 35
Manovich, Lev, 27, 33, 264
manuscript, 30–1
   digital analysis, 42–3, 44
Mao, Douglas, 120
Mapping the Republic of Letters (Stanford Literature
   Lab), 43–4
Mapplethorpe, Robert, 210
Marcuse, Herbert, 134
marginalia, 42
Marinetti, F. T., 90, 212
Marinkova, Milena, 95
Marks, Laura, 97
Martin, George R. R., 241
Marx, Karl, 10, 115, 119, 125–6, 222
Marxism, 121–2, 127–8, 224
mass media see medium/media
Mattelart, Armand, 163
Mattix, Micah, 193
Maurice, F. D., 197
Medieval Lyric, The (Dronke), 65–6
medieval studies, and animals, 3, 107–8
medium/media, 26, 27, 46–57
   and cultural production, 56–7
   remediation, 50–2, 55
   senses, history of, 54–6
   transposition, 52–4

and writing, 46–50
   see also digital form; genre
Meier, Carol, 71
Melville, Herman, 92
memory studies, 1, 189
Menninghaus, Winfried, 96–7
Menon, Madhavi, 202
Mentré, François, 179
Merewether, Charles, 35
Merleau-Ponty, Maurice, 95–6
metaphysics see ontology
Millennials: A Portrait of Generation Next (Pew
   Research Center), 180
Miller, John, 109
Milton, John, 152
mimesis, 215–25
   Aristotle's trust, 217–18
   imitation beyond the visible, 218–19
   mimetic order, 49
   Plato's suspicions, 215–17
   recent debates, 223–5
   reflective, 220–2
   rule-governed imitation, 219–20
Mimesis and Alterity: A Particular History of the
   Senses (Taussig), 223, 226
Mimesis as Make-Believe (Walton), 223, 224–5,
   226
Mimesis: The Representation of Reality in Western
   Literature (Auerbach), 223, 225
minor literature, 68–9
Mirzoeff, Nicholas, 201
Mitchell, David, 85
Modern Theme, The (Ortega y Gassett), 179–80,
   181, 187
modernism
   and generation, 185–7, 189
   and invention, 152–3, 154
   and medium/media, 50, 54, 55
   and period, 198–9
   politics of, 132
   stream of consciousness, writing, 85
   and style, 231–3
modernity, and event, 170–2
Moholy-Nagy, László, 159, 163
Montmartre cannon, 164–5, 166, 168
Moretti, Franco, 29, 69, 199, 243–5, 250, 251
Morris, William, 201–2
Morton, Timothy, 91, 100, 120
Mrs Dalloway (Woolf), 154, 182
Mukařovský, Jan, 207, 214
Murphet, Julian, 58
Murry, John Middleton, 237
Mynona, 94